The Clinical Handbook of
DEPRESSION

**GARDNER PRESS SERIES
IN CLINICAL SOCIAL WORK**

Mary Gottesfeld, Editor

**SEPARATION—INDIVIDUATION:
Theory and Practice**
Joyce Edward, Nathene Ruskin and Patsy Turrini

**EXISTENTIAL PSYCHOTHERAPY:
The Process of Caring**
David Edwards

CLINICAL SOCIAL WORKERS AS PSYCHOTHERAPISTS
Florence Lieberman

CLINICAL HANDBOOK OF DEPRESSION
Janice Wood Wetzel

Janice Wood Wetzel

Clinical Handbook of
DEPRESSION

GARDNER PRESS, INC.
New York & London

Copyright © 1984 by Gardner Press, Inc.

All rights reserved. No part of this book
may be reproduced in any form,
by photostat, microform,
retrieval system, or any means now known or later devised,
without prior written permission
of the publisher

Gardner Press, Inc.
19 Union Square West
New York, N.Y. 10003

Library of Congress Cataloging in Publication Data

Wetzel, Janice Wood.
Clinical handbook of depression.

(Gardner Press series in clinical social work)
Bibliography: p.
Includes index.
1. Depression, Mental.   I. Title.   II. Series.
RC537.W4   1984   616.85'27   84-5949
ISBN 0-89876-098-4

Printed in the United States of America

Designed by Raymond Solomon

Production by Publishers Creative Services, Inc.

For my children — Rick, Kathryn, and Rob

In memory of my parents

Faith and doubt both are needed—not as
antagonists but working side by side—
to take us around the unknown curve.

Lillian Smith, *The Following*

Contents

Acknowledgments

How do I thank the people who had no idea that they helped to mold and shape my thinking? Some perhaps never would agree that our mutual experience deserved recognition. Others might not recognize me. Many of them attended workshops on depression, and convinced me of the need for a handbook of this kind. I thank them all, along with those who consciously encouraged me in this work. Each was important to the process. Some dear friends were supportive of the project long before it took shape. Jean Gorham planted the seed, and the early commitment of Sue Ann Wood, Dorriece Pirtle, and Mary Schulte will always mean a great deal to me. Later, Susan Donner provided the personal support that was needed.

I want to pay tribute to Eli Robins, particularly in regard to the development of the Person-Environment model. His encouragement was special because his convictions are in the organic field. I was impressed by his generosity of spirit and openness to a broad spectrum of ideas when I was at Washington University, a fledgling student of semiadvanced age.

Thanks to Derek Gill who reviewed the original prospectus, and to those who assisted in editing the manuscript along the way. Francine Krasno's ideas helped me to get from the first very rough draft to a second. And my particular gratitude to Lois Ahrens who carefully read each original chapter, making insightful suggestions for improvement. Her steady support kept me going when the task loomed large. Thanks, too, to Charles Arthur who believed in the importance of the work, to Gardner Spungin who committed himself to its publication, and to my editor, Bessie Blum, whose professional touch buffed the rough edges.

I couldn't have managed without the skill and good nature of the people who typed the manuscript — Marianne Johnson, Nancy Pohlemus, and Barbara Kirouac — and to Joyce Leamy, who also provided ongoing assistance and expertise, thank you. My thanks, too, to David Fite, Larry Askling and Bev Sweet who computerized the references. Their skills were imvaluable as time became precious.

Aaron Beck, Max Hamilton, Rudolph Moos, and Walter Hudson generously permitted me to reprint their instruments. I thank them.

xv

Acknowledgment is made to the International Transactional Analysis Association for permission to reprint the diagram from Stephen B. Karpman's article entitled, "Fairy Tales and Script Drama Analysis," *Tab 7*, 26 (April 1968).

I also appreciate the permission granted by journals which allowed me to reprint portions of my published articles. They include *Social Casework*, published by the Family Service Association of America, *The Journal of Applied Social Science* at Case Western Reserve, and *Arete* at the University of South Carolina. In addition, acknowledgment is made for permission to reprint portions of "The Work Environment and Depression: Implications for Intervention" by Janice Wood Wetzel in John W. Hanks (editor), *Toward Human Dignity: Social Work in Practice*, National Association of Social Workers, Inc., 1978, excerpt, pp. 239 – 243.

Preface

To see the world in a grain of sand.
William Blake, *Auguries of Innocence*

The Clinical Handbook of Depression is a comprehensive manual designed to create linkages between seemingly disparate personality, environmental, and biochemical theories of depression, and between theory, research, clinical practice, and social services. This interdisciplinary perspective also provides form and reason for the high rates of depression among women and, when relevant, other vulnerable groups. The tendency is for theoreticians, researchers, and clinicians to work within their own disciplines, seldom crossing lines of ideological demarcation. Even when other ideas are valued, pressures of time and lack of ready information make integration most unlikely. Not only is this true of scholars, but the clinical and social application of theory and research also is affected. It is my hope that this effort will help to heal the rifts between disciplines and fields of practice. My intention is to foster mutual respect, while providing useful information for our common purpose — the prevention and treatment of depression. This book may serve as a catalyst for further explorations, hopefully providing a much needed resource along the way. When concepts are similar, though disguised by professional jargon, they are cross-referenced. I have made a point of retaining language indigenous to each discipline, translating it for the professional reader who is outside of a given field and the lay reader who is unnecessarily mystified.

Chapter 1 summarizes the diagnosis of depression and populations at risk (the epidemiology) from a historical perspective. Current facts, issues, and trends are also discussed, bringing the reader up to date on the identification of depression.

Chapters 2 through 8 might be considered the core of the book. Each chapter provides a different conceptual framework, following a consistent format. They begin with an introduction in which the framework's major theoretical precepts and derivatives are summarized. Next, the theory is presented in detail with attention given to underlying assumptions, clarification of the perspective, and a synopsis of the central issues and relevant research.

Each of the core chapters has a Women at Risk section which addresses facts, assumptions, and issues regarding women and their high-risk status in relation to the theory put forth. The Women at Risk section is largely a prevention-oriented critique designed to bring abstract ideas about depression into the realm of reality. The information provided is purposed to educate the reader to the implications of each theory for women — pro and con. While self-help suggestions are made, emphasis is on insight in regard to counseling and therapy. When other populations are identified as at risk (male suicides, for example), the same process is employed. Readers should be aware that those attributes or situations ascribed to one sex, age, race, or class are only meant to reflect general trends. Another person or group may fit the description given regardless of the at risk statistics. Remember, "at risk" only refers to those who are *most likely* to be depressed. That leaves a great many others who are less likely to be, but still equally, distressed.

Because differing viewpoints reflect different assumptions concerning human beings in relation to the world, assumptions that in turn influence what it is important to pay attention to, each concept provides inherently different values and insights critical to the understanding of the whole human being. I have addressed their implications when I felt them to be important, particularly in regard to at-risk populations. To ignore them would be to hide behind a veneer of "scientific objectivity" which is neither scientific nor objective. It would be inherently irresponsible, particularly in regard to implications for prevention. Those who do not agree with my values will at least know my viewpoints and be able to refute my ideas, rather than some vaguely implied messages. The inter-relationship of ideas is referenced across chapters as well as within each one. Each chapter is devoted to traditional preventive and interventive methods of treatment based upon relevant theory and research. Each chapter also applies less conventional interventions that are theoretically and ideologically consistent with the underlying assumptions and focus of the given model. These interventions have been selected for their preventive qualities as well.

Chapter 9, "Analysis plus Synthesis equals Synergy," integrates the core theories, identifying common denominators found in all of them. By synthesizing the essential themes, the paradoxes become clearer, providing possible answers to the depression riddle. I have included in this chapter a "Guide to the Self in Evolution," an admittedly subjective conclusion, though based on an encompassing objectivity.

Chapter 10 integrates appropriate methods of suicide prevention, while Chapter 11 details the criteria for depression based upon the *Diagnostic and Statistical Manuals* (II and III). Instruments for measuring depression in inpatient and outpatient populations are reproduced for clinicians and researchers. Self-help assessment tools are also available, as well as dependence and independence measures and family and work environment scales. A hopelessness scale, useful in assessing suicide risk, also is provided.

While psychosocial and biochemical research is promising, to date the empirical validation of therapeutic models remains elusive. We have no guarantees that preventive efforts are successful and relatively little research that supports most interventions. In the 1960s, Hans J. Eysenck upset the psychoanalytic community by reviewing selected studies on the effects of psychotherapy and finding them to be largely ineffective. Others have followed suit with a variety of treatment modalities. While critics argue that the studies themselves are invalid, few are able to cite sound research supporting their efforts. Learning theories lend themselves to experimental designs, but often are limited to measures of frequency, duration, and intensity, gauges of well-being questioned by more intrapsychic disciplines. Two common denominators that even staunch behaviorists are conceding are the importance of empathic understanding and the relationship between client and therapist, qualities that are difficult to measure. Many believe that a renewed respect for qualitative research may provide substantive insights. Meanwhile, the inclusion of cognitive techniques that enhance positive self-perception has shown significant results. It is important to note that most theories incorporate a cognitive component despite seemingly disparate perspectives.

While a devotee of the subject may read this book cover to cover, it is not intended to be read like a novel. Rather, it is a practical, comprehensive reference book intended for ready consultation, replete with cross-references. All of the suggestions, of course, should not be employed indiscriminantly. They are meant to provide a resource for work with individuals and groups and for program and policy development geared to preventive efforts. The suggested interventions are by no means designed to take the place of empathic understanding and relationship. They are an adjunct to these qualities which are always essential and often sufficient for healing. Still, knowledge and love need not be mutually exclusive.

Those who want more in-depth knowledge in a given discipline will find appropriate references. There are a number of books that specialize in single perspectives. Each discipline and field of practice has its own wisdom, its own "truths" about which many fine minds have devoted concerned thought and effort. It seems to me that we have much to learn from one another. This book represents an attempt to understand their separate insights, combining and correlating them in order to have an even greater impact than they do individually. This is synergism, a doctrine of cooperative action whose time has come. This is only a beginning—

J.W.W.
Iowa City, Iowa

Clinical Handbook of
DEPRESSION

Chapter 1

Diagnosis and Epidemiology

PAST AND PRESENT

My name is Legion: for we are many.
Mark, *V*, 9, New Testament

HISTORICAL OVERVIEW

Depression has been recognized clinically for over two thousand years, and yet no satisfactory explanation of its puzzling and paradoxical features has been discovered. Although it ranks as the leading mental health problem known today, major unresolved issues regarding its nature, classification, and etiology are still prevalent. Our knowledge of depression dates back to 1033 B.C. in the Old Testament where King Saul in the book of Job recounts recurrent symptoms of depression and suicide. The actual recording of melancholia, however, has been credited to Hippocrates, the father of modern medicine. Around 400 B.C. he confronted existing Greek beliefs in the gods' arbitrary ordaining of mental disorders. For the first time, these disorders were attributed to brain pathology which in turn was said to affect thought and action. He also recognized the influence of the environment and emotional stress on both the body and the mind. Unlike his forefathers, Hippocrates rejected earlier tortures devised to exorcise demons. Instead, he prescribed sobriety, tranquility, nutrition, and sexual abstinence as treatment for melancholia. Clearly an improvement over earlier perception, he espoused a humoral pathology wherein melancholia was credited to a preponderance of black bile. He divided mental illness into three categories—melancholia, mania, and phrenitis or brain fever—a division that was to last until the collapse of Greek and Roman civilization toward the end of the fifth century A.D.

1

With it, the Hippocratic view of mental illness as a scientifically treatable phenomenon also collapsed.

The Middle Ages saw the treatment of melancholia largely under the jurisdiction of priests. The inflicted person was viewed as a sinner possessed of the devil. What began as a prayerful lamentation ended in punishment and ostracism. Whether unwillingly possessed by Satan or willfully doing his bidding, the melancholic were usually women perceived as evil witches and heretics. Witch hunting was an integral part of European life through the seventeenth century, extending to the American colonies. Still, there were practitioners and scholars who argued for more humane views.[1]

Robert Burton was a leading English humanist who published a major treatise in 1621 called *The Anatomy of Melancholy*, the most exceptional literary treatment of depression ever devised.[2] He wrote under the name Democritus Junior, publishing five subsequent editions by 1651. The work is an insightful, yet satirical and even romantic compendium of everything from antiquarian lore to the psychology of morals that cause, cure, or compound what is now called depression. Burton was quite concerned with the influence of poverty and oppression on the incidence of melancholia, noting that women were most likely to be afflicted. Even though widely read, his ideas were not to take hold for another three centuries.

Benjamin Rush, considered the father of American psychiatry, believed that mental disorder was caused by an excess of blood in the brain. Practicing medicine in the late 1700s and early 1800s, he treated melancholia, among other ailments, by drawing great quantities of blood. He also contended that "lunatics" could be cured through fright and, to that end, recommended convincing patients of their impending death. The atrocities perpetrated in keeping with this hypothesis are legion. It was Vincenzo Chiarugi, an Italian physician of the same era, who courageously maintained the need for fundamental reform in the treatment of the mentally afflicted. He presented the diagnosis and prognosis of mental diseases, dividing insanity into melancholia, mania, and dementia. Melancholia, he argued, was but a partial insanity. Emil Kraepelin, a German physician, had similar purposes, but his were grounded in somatogenic hypotheses. In 1883, he ushered in modern diagnostic criteria with their insistence, in the medical tradition, on the identification of causal factors, clinical course, and outcome. Manic-depressive insanity and dementia praecox (the early term for schizophrenia) became dominant classification subdivisions. All insanities were divided among acquired and morbid predisposition, with manic-depressive illnesses generally categorized as acquired, though this was disputed even then. To this day, the assessment is unresolved. Kraepelin's classification system became the basis of contemporary schemas. Adolph Meyer was a dominant figure of equivalent stature in American psychiatry between 1900 and World War II. He developed a psychobiologic concept of reaction types rather than disease entities, replacing the term melancholia with the term depression. Meyer prepared the way for social-science and psychoanalytic concepts.

Historically, depression in women often was viewed as hysteria, a disease of the hypothetical "wandering womb" arising ostensibly from disorders of the sexual process. Burton himself referred to the enormous ancient literature on the presumed role of disturbed sexual function in the causation of emotional disorders. Unconscious sexual motivation and the forced continence of women resulting in the denial of their reproductive system were seen as fundamental factors in the genesis of mental illness. Thought to be specifically a female malady to be treated by compression of the ovaries or by uterine surgery, the idea still persists to this day. The current frequency with which hysterectomies are performed when depression is the symptom in menopausal women is cited as evidence. Anton Mesmer is credited with the development of psychotherapy as a distinctive form of psychological treatment as far back as the eighteenth century. Viewing hysterical disorders as caused by a certain distribution of universal magnetic bodily fluids, Mesmer employed a trance technique called "Mesmerism" to correct the imbalance. Though soon discredited, it was a precursor of hypnotism which John Charcot, Pierre Janet, Joseph Breuer, and Sigmund Freud employed in the treatment of hysteria toward the end of the nineteenth century. Freud's work with hypnosis ultimately resulted in his development of a form of psychotherapy called psychoanalysis, based on the detailed exploration of the early life of his patients, with the emotional reliving of those experiences in the treatment setting.

Though many authorities deviate from Freud's classical approach to treatment, American psychotherapeutic literature can be traced back to psychoanalysis in most instances. Most share the psychoanalytic aim of facilitating increased insight into the patient's feelings and behavior, and expressing those insights verbally. Psychic pain is interpreted as symptomatic of general adaptational difficulties, the alleviation of which is not viewed as a primary goal. Rather, evocative therapists try to increase the client's maturity, creativity, and spontaneity. Contrary to popular opinion, patients in actuality are influenced indirectly as much as they are in directive therapies. The contents of dreams, thoughts, and expression may follow the therapist's unconscious leads, and feelings and behavior that reflect maturity, creativity, and spontaneity are interpreted in terms of the therapist's particular ideology.

During Freud's era, the Russian physiologist I.P. Pavlov demonstrated through laboratory experiments that insolvable conflicts could cause neuroses in dogs. These demonstrations led to the "conditioned reflex" theory of mental illness and its treatment. In recent years, American experimental psychologists have developed learning theories based on experiments with both animals and human beings. Most comtemporary theories of mental health problems such as depression, and their treatment, have been derived from combinations and modifications of the ideas of Freud, Pavlov, and social-learning schools. These conceptual schemas are not at all incompatible; they afford a scientific rationale for contemporary modes of psychotherapy.[3]

Even so, we must not ignore the possibility that each of the conceptual schemas put forth may be incorrect. We have no assurance that our views and procedures are any more enlightened than those of yesteryear. Where definitive facts are lacking and definitions of depression are culture-bound, it is inevitable that the subject of depression is prey to all manner of myths, suppositions, stigmatization, and oppression. One fact seems clear: depression, like other mental health labels, is socially defined. Thus it is that depression often is treated as an illness in one society, ignored in a second, punished in a third, and given over to priests in a fourth. The society stipulates the boundaries within which particular behaviors are tolerated and accepted.[4]

CONTEMPORARY TRENDS

Insane Societies

Thomas Szasz, a leading contemporary physician disputing the assumption of mental illness itself, maintains that psychiatrists and their counterparts are not treating mental illness. In reality, he argues, they are dealing with personal, social, and ethical problems of living. People such as Erich Fromm, Thomas Scheff, Robert Laing, and David Cooper, to name a few, also led the way in the 1960s, contending that emotional problems cannot be viewed only in the context of a lack of adjustment on the part of individuals, but the nonadjustment of the culture to the individual as well. This theory of "normative humanism" asserts that societies exist that are not sane. Just because millions share the same behavior does not mean that they are mentally healthy.[5] Thus, it is possible that scores of depressed people today are "saner" than many others, though their behavior does not fit the norms of society. While there is a great deal less discussion at the present time, the same healthy skepticism that was prevalent twenty years ago is still a viable stance. There remains little agreement among so-called experts, despite the fact that great efforts have been made to that end.

Classification Issues

While many authorities regard depression as essentially a single entity, others believe that it is multifaceted. Another division, in an attempt to establish the basic etiology of depression, distinguishes what is caused mainly by internal factors (called *endogenous*), and what is caused by external psychogenic factors (called *exogenous*). Because one may not recognize pervasive environmental influences, misclassification is common within this schema.

Distinction between the degree of reactivity to external events is further divided. Those cases that follow an unrelenting course, regardless of any favorable environmental conditions, are regarded as *autonomous*, while those that respond positively to medication, support, and understanding are called *reactive* cases. The possibility for subjective bias on the part of the clinician is obvious. Not only is one's effectiveness at stake, but one's values concerning favorable conditions may distort perception.

Some contemporary authorities clearly differentiate psychotic and neurotic depressions, although others indicate that the differences are quantitative rather than qualitative. Psychotic episodes usually manifest severe depression together with visual or auditory hallucinations and delusions that something impossible is true. Even in less obvious cases, loss of contact with reality is evident. Neurotic depression is less intense and free of bizarre symptoms, apparently maintaining contact with reality despite depression symptomatology. Caution must be taken in assessing reality for the patient, for what is real to the clinician may not be real to another quite reasonable but distraught person. In addition, psychotic episodes can be temporary and should in no way label the patient permanently. One day may be quite markedly different from another in this regard. Neurosis as a concept also is rife with ambiguity. There is no consensus as to its definition at either end of a continuum from health to pathology. What some view as a descriptive process, others see as a disorder, while a third group might unify the term implying a direct association between them.[6]

In recent years, the concepts of primary and secondary affective disorder have been refined.[7] This definition is concerned with chronology of symptoms. Primary affective disorder (PAD) occurs in people whose histories do not reflect previous episodes of psychiatric disorder other than depression or mania. Secondary affective disorder (SAD) occurs in individuals who have had preexisting psychiatric or medical illness other than affective disorders, depression, or mania. PAD and SAD criteria have been validated empirically, unlike the previous diagnostic labels.[8] While the concept is useful in establishing homogenous groups for research purposes, it has been criticized as somewhat limited since it does not address intensity or the presumed cause of depression. Secondary depression cases may have striking endogenous characteristics,[9] for example, while in others, clear exogenous factors are present. This heterogeneity, however, is behind the motivation for a clear primary/secondary dichotomization. It is one of the few certainties that can be established. This classificatory system ushered in a resurgence of interest in—or at least implications for—a connection between mania and depression, an association that appears to have little credibility except to the degree that all mental disorders are related. This commentary holds true for the unipolar/bipolar dichotomy as well.

"Manic-Depressive Illnesses" (MDI) are further defined as unipolar (UP) and bipolar (BP) types. Unipolar types involve depression only, while affective disorder is defined as bipolar when mania occurs, whether or not depression is present. The dichotomy is now considered by some to represent mood alterations reflected in depression (UP) (which covers a wide range of causal possibilities), or a normal range of euthymic moods that fluctuate to either depression, intense physical and mental excitement and elation, or dysphoric or psychotic states.[10] It should be noted that the evaluation and management of these two subgroups are dissimilar, although both are concerned with patient history and clinical description. Again, intensity and presumed cause of the disorders are not addressed. More important, a clear profile cannot be drawn by labeling people as bipolar whether or not they have ever experienced depression. This same criticism can be made of the manic-depressive illness classification, since the majority (68 – 85 percent) of "manic-depressives" have had episodes of depression without mania, according to epidemiological research.[11] The ambiguity and potential inaccuracy of all of these nosologies continue to foster controversy and debate. Still, they can be helpful tools for understanding the multiple possibilities that must be considered. The depression classification issues are compiled below for easy reference.

Classification Issues

Endogenous/Exogenous Schema
> *Endogenous*: depression caused by internal factors.
> *Exogenous*: depression caused by external factors.

Reactive/Autonomous Schema
> *Reactive*: characterized by positive response to treatment and modification of the environment.
> *Autonomous*: characterized by lack of response to intervention.

Psychotic-Neurotic Schema (separate entities or continuum)
> *Neurotic*: depressive symptoms are from mild to severe intensity without loss of contact with reality.
> *Psychotic*: depressive symptoms are of extremely severe intensity with loss of reality contact.

Primary/Secondary Affective Disorder (a chronological schema)
> *Primary Affective Disorder*: no previous history of psychiatric disorder other than depression or mania.
> *Secondary Affective Disorder*: preexisting history of major mental or physical illness other than depression or mania.

Unipolar/Bipolar Types
> *Unipolar Type*: recurring depression only.
> *Bipolar Type*: recurring mania fluctuating into severe manic (euphoric) or depression (dysphoric) episodes.

Diagnostic Signs and Symptoms

Some authorities still contend that depression is primarily psychogenic in origin. Others maintain just as adamantly that it is an organic disorder. A third group believes that depression has social origins, while still others would accept the reality of all premises. Additional dichotomies to be addressed in subsequent chapters exist within these generalized categories of psychological, physiological, and sociocultural depression. Whatever the causal mechanism, the symptoms of depression can be divided into four major areas of assessment: affective, cognitive, behavioral, and physical.

Affective Feeling State

Depression ranges on a continuum from mild blues common to the human condition to severe despair. Everyone who is depressed suffers some degree of sadness, although some may conceal depressed affect consciously, while others hide behind a mask of denial. Children may appear hyperactive or particularly well behaved rather than depressed when in fact they are seriously despondent. In all cases, gentle probing will reveal a dysphoric mood state, replete with anxiety, guilt, and resentment. Depression and anxiety as separate entities can be confused and, when in question, should be diagnosed as depression for purposes of precaution.

Cognitive Thought Processes

Difficulty with thinking processes is characteristic of almost all depressed people. Problems with concentration and decision making are a direct result. Negative rumination about the world, the self, and the future has been causally linked to depression as well, often encompassing recurrent suicidal thoughts.[12] Hallucinatory ideation, noted in psychotic depressions, is less common.

Behavioral Activity

Social withdrawal is a typical behavior found in depressed people who have lost interest in activity and relationships of all kinds. Nonassertive dependence is also a common attribute credited to causality, as well as a symptom of depression. While many people seem to slow down their motor responses, others become agitated, irritable, and even aggressively hostile.

Physical Functioning

Debate continues as to whether body chemistry influences affective, cognitive, and behavioral symptoms, or if the presence of such symptoms impacts on body chemistry. The chances are that both conditions exist. In either case, physical functioning is affected. The more severe the depression, the more likely it is that physical functioning is problematic. Gastrointestinal disorders, muscle aches, and headaches are common, as are eating and sleep disturbances. The tendency is toward loss of appetite and inability to sleep, but the opposite conditions are not unusual. Sex-drive disturbances range along a similar continuum. Whatever the physical profile, fatigue is sure to be present. Because these physical symptoms may mask depression, patients initially turn to physicians for relief. It is essential that a thorough physical examination be made to rule out alternative organic illness before a psychiatric evaluation is made. It should be noted that about 70 percent of antidepressant prescriptions are written by nonpsychiatrist physicians.[13] For that reason, it is important that these physicians avail themselves of information concerning the subject of depression.

A number of diagnostic measures of depression have been developed, based on combinations of these criteria. They can be found in Chapter 11, together with a discussion of national and international systems of classification, including the most recent criteria for depression based on the *Diagnostic and Statistical Manual* (DSM III). Emerging research reveals that milder symptoms of depression are often present long before more serious episodes occur. Diagnostic signs and symptoms of depression are compiled below for easy reference.

Diagnostic Signs and Symptoms

Affective Feeling State
> Dysphoric mood—sad, blue, dejected
> Fearfulness
> Anxiety—nervousness, worry, apprehension
> Inadequacy
> Anger—resentment, rage
> Guilt
> Confusion
> Tiredness
> Hopelessness
> Irritability

Cognitive Thought Processes
> Negative view of the world, the self, and the future
> Irrational beliefs
> Recurrent thoughts of helplessness, hopelessness, worthlessness
> Recurrent thoughts of death or suicide
> Self-reproach
> Low self-esteem
> Denial
> Indecisiveness
> Slow thinking
> Disinterest in activities, people, and pleasure
> Confused thought
> Poor concentration
> Agitation

Behavioral Activity
> Dependence
> Submissiveness
> Nonassertiveness
> Poor communication skills
> Controlled by others

Crying
Withdrawal
Inactivity
Careless appearance
Slowed (retarded) motor response—poverty of speech, slowed
    body movements
Agitated motor response—pacing, handwringing, pulling at
    hair or clothing
Physical Functioning
Low energy
Weakness
Fatigue
Sleep disturbance—insomnia or hypersomnia
Weight loss or gain
Appetite disturbance
Indigestion
Constipation
Diarrhea
Nausea
Muscle aches and headaches
Tension
Agitated or slowed psychomotor reflexes
Sex-drive disturbance

EPIDEMIOLOGY OF DEPRESSION

Epidemiology is the study of the distribution and major determinants of a particular problem. The concept of "populations at risk" has long served as an epidemiological approach to physical disease. In recent history, the concept has expanded to mental and social ills. Evolving from the study of epidemics, the epidemiological method assesses causal inferences that are derived from the statistical association between individual or group attributes and the condition being studied. By so doing, the prevention and control of social problems leave the realm of ideology and enter the domain of possibility. We are able to explore "at-risk" populations: whom the problem is most likely to affect (the statistical "point prevalence"), and in what population the condition is increasing most rapidly (the statistical "incidence"), generally assessed within a one-year time period. "Period prevalence" is a combined measure that does not distinguish between point prevalence and incidence, but includes cases that fit both categories. Most genetically oriented theorists point out that chronic parental depression, like all other chronic illnesses, increases one's risk for depression.[14]

The epidemiological investigation of depression is a relatively recent undertaking. Myrna M. Weissman and her colleagues at the Yale Depression Research Unit in New Haven, Connecticut, can be credited with a disproportionate amount of ongoing study. They have reported the difficulties encountered owing to misclassification and/or the diversity or nonspecificity of diagnoses and nomenclature. Epidemiological data regarding "Manic-Depressive Illness," for example, rarely have been analyzed to reflect those cases who were depressed in contrast to those who had experienced mania. They have had to develop creative methods of analysis in order to adapt and clarify existing reports. Most recently assessing "non-bipolar" depression, which corresponds roughly to the DSM III diagnosis of Major Depression, they have come to the following conclusions, necessarily tentative, concerning risk factors:[15]

Sex Differences—Grand Statistics

Women—4% to 9% point prevalence
    20% to 26% lifetime risk
    8% annual incidence (single study)
    (6% of females have been hospitalized for major depression).
Men—3% point prevalence
    8% to 12% lifetime risk
    (3% of males have been hospitalized for major depression).

Boyd and Weissman suggest that their methods reduce the variability from one study to another, resulting in greater consistency in rates. The male-female differences in rates previously concluded by Weissman and Klerman continue to be real. The evidence in support of these rates is best established in Western industrialized nations.[16]

Marital Status and Children

Reports are inconclusive in part. Some indicate that single, divorced, and widowed women have lower rates of mental illness, including depression, than men.[17] Others conclude that separated and divorced women between the ages of 25 and 44 have the highest rates, although those recently separated have considerably more depression symptoms. Among married women, those who have low-income, low-status jobs and young children are at high risk. The conflicting reports may represent economic factors as well as children in the home, factors not taken into account in all studies. Studies indicate that married working-class women who do not work outside the home and who have two or three children are at highest risk.[18] Older women whose children have left home have fewer symptoms.[19] One researcher also found that the unhappily married are more depressed than the separated and divorced.[20] What is clear is that never-married women who are heads of households are least likely to experience depression. They are in direct contrast to never-married (or widowed) men who are heads of households who *are* at risk. In both sexes, those who are never married but *not* heads of households (in short, dependent) also are likely to become depressed.[21] According to epidemiological studies, although women experience more stress than men, they are more likely to seek professional help. Those who hold nontraditional sexual attitudes experience less distress despite cultural pressures.[22]

Economics, Occupation, Class, and Ethnicity

Those most likely to be depressed are the poorly educated (particularly if female), the poor, the unemployed, those with low-status occupations, those who are physically ill, the young, and students.[23] With the exception of the last three categories, all are statistically more likely to be true of females. Some research indicates, however, that depressed women who are employed outside the home reduce their risk of depression. It is the low-level job factor plus responsibility for children that leads to high risk.[24] Although Weissman and Myers find that depression is highest in the lower social classes, unlike previous surveys, their data suggest that this relationship holds true for minor affective disorders only, a finding they relate to demoralization. Current rates, rather than lifetime rates of major depression are correlated with social class as well, but the relationship is not consistent across all affective disorders.[25] It has been my experience that ethnic differences are likely to reflect diagnostic bias and differential use of public facilities. Hence, no clear trends can be reported. People of color are often misdiagnosed as schizophrenic, for example, when depression is the more accurate diagnosis. Their more frequent use of public facilities in contrast to private ones skews the data, while their relative nonuse of any facilities results in a general lack of knowledge concerning ethnic differences. We *do* know that both urban and rural communities are equally afflicted, particularly where women are concerned.

Suicide Variables

Suicide is three times more likely to occur in males, although suicide attempts are five times as frequent among females.[26]

The National Institute of Mental Health reports that 12 percent of all suicide attempts in the United States are made by adolescents. Suicide, in fact, is the number two cause of death among teenagers. Ninety percent of these young people are adolescent girls, and single, pregnant teenage girls are ten times more likely to commit suicide than other adolescent females.

The very highest rates of suicide are among white elderly males over 65 with white males over 85 at highest risk.

Among middle-aged and elderly Americans, the white suicide rate is three times the rate for blacks. In 1978, there were 40.8 suicides for every 100,000 white men 65 years and older and 7.9 suicides for white females of the same age and older. Nonwhite rates were 12.1 for men and 3.1 for women.

Young black men have the most rapidly increasing suicide rate.

Rising rates of suicide among Third World groups may reflect poverty and low status or upward mobility. Both are viable possibilities according to theories regarding suicide.

Biorhythms

More people are admitted to mental health facilities in the spring. Although people often talk of "feeling depressed" during the winter holidays, rates of admittance do not reflect a higher incidence. Weather and seasons have long been postulated as causal possibilities, but research has only recently been undertaken. Biological rhythms within twenty- four-hour periods, monthly lunar cycles, and episodic depressions and mania are all of considerable interest.[27]

More defined epidemiological information will become available concerning the prevalence and incidence of affective disorders in the coming decade. Three large-scale studies conducted in New Haven, St. Louis, and Baltimore under the aegis of the National Institute of Mental Health will include 12,000 interviews initiated several times during a one-year period. The study uses a standardized interview schedule that encompasses most of the *Diagnostic and Statistical Manual* (DSM III) diagnoses, so it should prove to be insightful.[28]

Etiological Inference

There are two major foci in regard to the epidemiological investigation of depression. One centers on the demographic distribution of depression, assessing such variables as sex, age, marital status, and so on. The second assesses the distribution of the problem relative to causal factors. Common determinants are sought in apparently unconnected events and evaluated in terms of possible causal association. Since causal inferences are problematic in uncontrolled, nonlaboratory studies, epidemiologists have developed relevant criteria for natural settings. First, time sequence is assessed. The supposed causative variable must precede the supposed effect. Second, the strength of the association is scrutinized. The stronger the association, the more likely the possibility of causality. And third, the factors involved must be consonant with existing knowledge.[29] These are the premises upon which the following chapters are developed. Each theoretical perspective will be examined in light of our present knowledge of at-risk populations, with special emphasis on women because of their high at-risk status.

NOTES

1. Foucault, Michel, *Madness and Civilization: A History of Insanity in the Age of Reason* (New York: Pantheon Books, 1965); see also Gerald C. Davidson and John M. Neale, *Abnormal Psychology* (New York: Wiley, 1978), *Holy Bible*, Book of Job.

2. Burton, Robert (Democritis Junior), *The Anatomy of Melancholy* (Oxford: Printed by John Lichfield and Iames/Short, for Henry Cripps. Anno Dom. 1621); see also "Life Events Models" (Chapter 4, this volume) for further reference to Robert Burton's insights.

3. Frank, Jerome, *Persuasion and Healing* (Baltimore: Johns Hopkins University Press, 1965).

4. Brodhead, Constance, "Mental Illness," Unpublished manuscript (Washington University, St. Louis, MO, 1971); see also Thomas S. Szasz, *The Myth of Mental Illness* (New York: Dell Publishing Co., 1961); George Rosen, *Madness and Society* (London: Routledge and Kegan Paul, 1968); August B. Hollingshead and Frederick C. Redlich, *Social Class and Mental Illness* (New York: Wiley, 1958); Thomas J. Scheff, *Mental Illness and Social Processes* (New York: Harper and Row, 1967); Ronald D. Laing, *The Politics of Experience* (New York: Ballantine Books, 1967); David Cooper, *Psychiatry and Anti-Psychiatry* (London: Tavistock Publications, 1967).

5. Fromm, Erich, *The Sane Society* (Greenwich, CT: Fawcett Publications, 1955).

6. American Psychiatric Association, *Diagnostic and Statistical Manual of Mental Disorders*, 1st ed. (Washington, D.C.: APA, 1952, out of print).

7. Feighner, John P., Eli Robins, Samuel B. Guze, Robert A. Woodruff, Jr., George Wilnokur, and Rodrigo Munoz, "Diagnostic Criteria for Use in Psychiatric Research," *Archives of General Psychiatry 26* (January 1972): 57 – 63.

8. Murphy, George E., Robert A. Woodruff, Jr., and Marijan Herjanic, "Primary Affective Disorder," *Archives of General Psychiatry 31* (August 1974): 181 – 184.

9. Baldessarini, Ross J., "A Summary of Biomedical Aspects of Mood Disorders," *McLean Hospital Journal 6*, 1 (1981): 1 – 34 (Belmont, MA).

10. APA, DSM I (1952).

11. Boyd, Jeffrey H., and Myrna M. Weissman, "Epidemiology of Affective Disorders," *Archives of General Psychiatry 38* (September 1981): 1039 – 1046.

12. Beck, Aaron T., *Depression: Clinical Experimental and Theoretical Aspects* (New York: Harper and Row, 1967); see also Chapter 6, "Cognitive-Behavioral Theories," for a detailed discussion of depression, cognition and behavioral response.

13. Hollister, L. E., "Tricyclic Antidepressants," *New England Journal of Medicine 299* (1978): 1106 – 1109, 1168 – 1172.

14. McMahon, Brian and Thomas F. Pugh, *Epidemiology Principles and Methods* (Boston: Little, Brown, 1970); see also Jeffrey H. Boyd and Myrna M. Weissman, "Epidemiology of Affective Disorders," *Archives of General Psychiatry 38*, (September 1981): 1039 – 1046. See the section on genetic theories in Chapter 8 for a discussion of familial studies regarding depression.

15. Boyd, Jeffrey H. and Myrna M. Weissman, "Epidemiology of Affective Disorders," *Archives of General Psychiatry 38* (September 1981): 1039 – 1046.

16. Weissman, Myrna M., and Gerald L. Klerman, "Sex Differences and the Epidemiology of Depression," *Archives of General Psychiatry 34*, 1 (January 1977): 98 – 111.

17. Gove, Walter R., "The Relationship between Sex Roles, Marital Status and Mental Illness," *Social Forces 51* (1972): 34 – 44; see also Walter R. Gove, "Sex, Marital Status and Mortality," *American Journal of Sociology 79* (1973): 45 – 67; Mrna M. Weissman, and Gerald L. Klerman, "Sex Differences and the Epidemiology of Depression," *Archives of General Psychiatry 34*, 1 (January 1977): 98 – 111.

18. Brown, George W. and Tirril Harris, *Social Origins of Depression* (New York: The Free Press, 1978).

19. Guttentag, Susan Salasin, and Deborah Belle, eds., *The Mental Health of Women* (New York: Academic Press, 1980): pp. 93 – 110; see also Lenore Sawyer Radloff, "Risk Factors for Depression," in Sandor Rado, "Psychodynamics of Depression from the Etiologic Point of View," *Psychosomatic Medicine 13* (1951): 51 – 55.

20. Renne, K. S., "Health and Marital Experience in an Urban Population," *Journal of Marriage and the Family 33* (1971): 338 – 350; see also Lenore Sawyer Radloff, "Sex Difference in Depression: The Effects of Occupation and Marital Status," *Sex Roles 1*, 3 (1975): 249 – 265.

21. Hall, Jacqueline H., "Women's Task Force Position Paper on Women's Service Issues," submitted to the National Council of Community Mental Health Centers, June 1980.

22. Brown, P., and R. Manela, "Changing Family Roles: Women and Divorce," *Journal of Divorce 1*, 4 (1978): 315 – 328; see also Jacqueline H. Hall, "Women's Task Force Position Paper on Women's Service Issues," submitted to the National Council of Community Mental Health Centers, June 1980.

23. Radloff, Lenore Sawyer, "Sex Difference in Depression: The Effects of Occupation and Marital Status," *Sex Roles 1*, 3 (1975): 249 – 265; see also Marcia Guttentag, Susan Salasin, W. W. Legg, and H. Bray, "Sex-Differences in the Utilization of Publicly-Supported Mental Health Facilities: The Puzzle of Depression," Mental Health Services Development Branch, NIMH, 1976.

24. Fisher, Anne E., *Women's Worlds: NIMH Supported Research on Women* (U.S. Department of Health, Education and Welfare, DHEW Pub. No. [ADM], NIMH, (1978): pp. 78 – 660; see also Jacqueline H. Hall, "Women's Task Force Position Paper on Women's Service Issues," submitted to the National Council of Community Mental Health Centers, June 1980.

25. Weissman, Myrna M., and Jerome K. Myers, "Depression and Its Treatment in a U.S. Urban Community: 1975 – 1976," *Archives of General Psychiatry 38* (1981): 417 – 421.

26. See Chapter 10, "Suicide Prevention," for further discussion of at-risk populations.

27. Refer to the work of Norman Rosenthal, NIMH Clinical Psychobiology Branch.

28. National Center for Health Statistics; see also U.S. Dept. of Health and Human Services, *Special Report on Depression Research*, National Institute of Mental Health, DHHS Publ. No. [ADM] 81-1085, 1981).

29. Boyd, Jeffrey H. and Myrna M. Weissman, "Epidemiology of Affective Disorders," *Archives of General Psychiatry 38* (September 1981): 1039 – 1046; see also Janice Wood Wetzel, "An Epidemiological Approach to Social Problems," paper presented at the Council on Social Work Education, APM, New Orleans, February 26 – March 1, 1978.

Chapter 2
Psychoanalytic Theories

> But what am I?
> An infant crying in the night:
> An infant crying for the light:
> And with no language but a cry.
> Alfred, Lord Tennyson, "In Memoriam"

The early work of Freud has been and continues to be in dynamic evolution. Psychoanalytic theory concerning depression has evolved along with the theory in general. Never static, clinically derived thought and observations extend from the classical psychoanalytic theory of Freud and his disciples to contemporary ego-psychology and object-relations theories, among others. This chapter will be limited to these three major conceptual frameworks because they have addressed the problem of depression to a greater degree than others in the psychoanalytic field.

According to classical psychoanalytic theorists, depression results from the imagined or real loss of love "objects," those who are significant in a child's life — usually the parents, most often the mother. The term "love object" has been borrowed from philosophy where one's self is Subject and others are Object. The love object for Freudians is symbolically internalized and retained, thereby masking hostility directed toward the loved one. When the individual is fearful that rage felt in reaction to threatened or real abandonment will insure rejection, anger toward the love object is turned inward, only seemingly against the self. For the orthodox, the conscience or superego is the seat of depression, responding to unacceptable instinctual drives emanating from the id. Dissatisfaction with oneself on moral grounds is by far the most outstanding characteristic according to Freud.

Ego-psychologists shift their theoretical focus to the ego. For them, depression is triggered by an intolerable breach between one's actual ego-state, who one is, and one's ideal ego-state, whom one would like to be, resulting in low self-esteem. Proneness to depression reflects an excessive dependence on others in order to maintain a fragile self-esteem.

Contemporary ego-psychology now embodies the field of object-relations theory, a concept akin to attachment bonding. The object relation, that person who was most significant in the young child's life, remains an enduring influence. Depression is related to early conflicts and stresses with the object relation, generally thought to be within the third year of development but sometimes attributed to experiences in early infancy.

BASIC PSYCHOANALYTIC CONCEPTS[1]

In order to understand the evolution of psychoanalytic theory, one must first be familiar with the concepts of structural theory, psychic energy, and psychosexual drives. All three core constructs provide important information, for they are generally incorporated to some degree even in modified versions of theory.

Structural Theory

The basic structure of the personality assumed by Freud and his followers is composed of the id, the ego, and the superego. The *id*, the inborn component of the personality, is thought to be instinctual and provides the psychic energy for the other components. It operates on the pleasure principle, seeking immediate gratification.

The *ego* is the executive, the primarily conscious mediator between the id and the world. The ego deals with the superego. Operating on the reality principle, the ego assesses and evaluates the reality of situations, delaying gratification when necessary. The importance of the ego expands as theory evolves from Freud's id-psychology to present-day ego-psychology.

The *superego* is the conscience of the personality; it internalizes the values of right and wrong taught by the important people in the life of a child. It also represents the ego-ideal, a learned attribute reflecting values that met with parental approval and reward. While contemporary ego-psychologists agree with Freud that the superego is the last of the structures to be developed, they allude to the existence of early superego components.

Psychic Energy

The concept of psychic energy historically underlies psychoanalytic theory, although it has become an issue of controversy in contemporary psychoanalytic circles. According to classical theory, all energy initially resides in the id, followed by the other two systems, the ego and superego, which derive energy from it. Because the ego needs psychic energy in order to deal with the id and superego and to maintain its defense systems, the more energy that is tied up in this manner, internally, the less there is available to cope with the outside world. Anxiety is a case in point. In contrast to realistic anxiety in reaction to real danger, so-called neurotic anxiety is a common feature of depression, often aroused in connection with the structure of the personality. For example, it is thought that neurotic anxiety results when it is feared that instincts (stemming from the id) will get out of control. Moralistic anxiety, fear of the conscience (emerging from the superego) is reflected by guilt when one's ideas or actions run counter to one's internalized moral beliefs. Thus, conflicts within the personality structure result in anxiety and in depression. Freud believed that depression acts like an open wound, drawing energy to itself from all sides, draining the ego until it is totally depleted.

As psychoanalytic theory evolves, the concept of psychic energy has been criticized and soundly rejected by many psychoanalytic theorists, but their many-faceted judgments lack consensus. Critics consider psychic energy to be a pseudoconcept that confuses it with physical energy and neurophysiology. Others insist on its clinical, metaphorical usefulness, particularly in relation to depression.[2] Besides pointing out the controversy, I have included Freud's original observations because of his uncanny ability to observe basic truths (though often interpreted less than accurately). The concept of psychic energy is supported in a number of disparate disciplines today,[3] and the roots of the concept still run deep in contemporary psychoanalytic theory.

Psychosexual Drive Theory

Freud believed the principal life instinct, *libido*, to be primarily connected with instinctual sexual drive energies. Its source, he said, is located in the erogenous body zones: oral, anal, and genital. This

psychosexual drive theory of personality (or character) development
also is essential to the understanding of the psychoanalytic perspective. How infants negotiate their early experience is said to be reflected
in their future capacity for affection, love and the need for others, the
desire to reproduce, and for creativity. Infancy and childhood are
considered decisive in forming one's basic character, which develops in
response to three chief sources of tension: physiological growth processes, including infantile sexuality, external frustration of innate
drives, and internal or intrapsychic forces. All threaten the ego and
produce tension which the child tries to alleviate, setting the stage for
future coping patterns. When an unusual amount of psychic energy is
required to cope with problems at a given developmental phase, less
energy is available to deal with subsequent developmental tasks. In
such cases, persons may fixate at the level of development attained.
Reference here will be limited to those stages that have been associated
with depression. They are the oral stage (birth to ages 1−2), the anal
stage (ages 1−3), and the phallic stage (ages 3−5).[4]

The *oral stage* is thought to be almost totally narcissistic: sexual
pleasures are autoerotic, and infants regard themselves as the entire
universe. The *anal stage* centers on the beginning experience of ambivalence reflected by the existence of strong concurrent, but oppos-
ing, feelings. In the *phallic stage*, the penis or clitoris becomes the focus
of sexual energies and an attendant concern with power in males and
an absence of power in females. The validity of a physiological basis for
these concepts is highly controversial relative to human development
alone, much less in association with depression. Because the psycho-
sexual-equivalent terms are commonly found in the depression literature, they have been described. The most common reference is to the
"oral character" of depressed persons, although recent evidence suggests that it has little basis in reality.[5] (The same may be said for the
reality of anal or phallic personality characteristics.) That is not to say,
however, that depressed persons may not be overly dependent and in
need of nurturance — characteristics of so-called "orality." Too, their
feelings are often conflictual and power issues like those described in
anal and phallic terminology are commonly observed.

CLASSICAL PSYCHOANALYTIC THEORY OF DEPRESSION

Building on the analytic studies of his student Karl Abraham,[6]
Sigmund Freud[7] laid the groundwork for many of today's theories

concerning depression. Their early observations of depressed people, in fact, led to the structural three-part conceptualization of the psyche outlined above. Freud compared depression with grief in his landmark monograph, "Mourning and Melancholia," focusing on loss as central to the phenomenon. His clinical observations led him to believe that depressed persons reflect symptoms similar to those present when one experiences the death of a loved one, or even the loss of an ideal. But unlike those who are in mourning, depressed people seem to lack self-esteem. Freud suggested that loss in depressed persons has more to do with a vaguely perceived internal loss to the self than with the person lost to them. They may know *whom* they have lost, but not *what* it is that this means to them personally. For the bereaved, the world becomes empty and poor. For the depressed, according to Freud, it is the ego itself that becomes empty and poor.

The Abraham-Freud model observes the ambivalence of the depressed person concerning both the self and the lost love object, the important other. This ambivalence seems to stem from an inaccurate identification with the disappointing love object, an identification that does not include positive characteristics.

The dynamic was later reformulated as a lack of clear differentiation between the self and disappointing object images, wherein "bad" aspects obviate the "good."[8] While self-critical, the depressed person's exhortations are often more appropriate to the abandoning person. Freud also observed, though, that many of the depressed individual's self-accusations do appear to be accurate. They do indeed lack independence, feel hostile (however righteously), and are obsessed with hiding their weaknesses, just as they claim. Freud noted that they are uncommonly correct in their self-knowledge, acknowledged only in "illness." Still, though aware that their self-respect has been lost, they appear to be shameless concerning their many shortcomings. Their attitudes, he suggested, reflect revolt.[9] These are keen observations that are seldom addressed, except perhaps by those who fault Freud for his pessimism. To my mind, it is this wrenching dichotomy that is at the core of depression for many people. Understanding why this is so requires a synthesis of insights from many perspectives, a task undertaken in this book. At this point in the journey, suffice it to say that Freud was among the first to notice that people can diagnose themselves quite accurately if clinicians would only take heed. Unfortunately, Freud himself was unlikely to do so, despite the richness of his observation.

In order to maintain self-esteem, Freud conjectured that depressed people withdraw their libido (their sexual energy) for their lost love object, transferring it to their egos rather than to someone new. Thus, in order to retain the abandoned love object, figuratively, the person

symbolically incorporates the important other, identifying so completely that anger meant for the abandoned person is vented within the
self. This love-hate ambivalence is believed to predispose persons to
depression. While Freud described this anger as masochistic, others
have interpreted it as "safely" directed, an action in direct contrast to
masochism.

Neo-Freudians have further developed Freud's ideas in a variety of
ways. Sandor Rado explains the ambivalence of depressed persons as
being torn between coercive rage at not being given a "fair deal" and
submissive fear of expressing their rage.[10] Thus, unable to respond,
their self-esteem is diminished, a factor thought to be both a precursor
and a symptom of depression. Feelings of worthlessness, hopelessness, inferiority, and dependence go hand in hand with the guilt of
harbored resentment.

Melanie Klein, founder of the "English School" of psychoanalytic
theory, viewed the dynamic as the "depressive position," a combination of sorrow over the loss of the good love object and the longing to
regain the object, together with guilt over hostility and rage, the
aggressive drives that ostensibly precipitated the loss. With the exception of Klein, the early psychoanalytic writers viewed depression as
restitution and reparative punishment. By way of contrast, Klein
viewed depression as a reflection of the quality of the mother-child
relationship in the first year of life. Unless the child's experience
promotes feelings of being good and beloved and secure, she argued,
he or she will never be able to overcome ambivalence toward their love
objects and will be forever subject to depressive breakdowns. Her
insights clearly contributed to the formulation of contemporary object-
relations theories detailed later in this chapter.[11]

EGO-PSYCHOLOGY AND DEPRESSION

Viewing people as actors as well as reactors to life, ego-psychology
reflects a more optimistic view of human beings than does Freud's id-
oriented psychology. It is thought that the ego is indeed influenced by
the id's instinctive drives and the superego which responds to the
environment, but the ego is also an autonomous process, capable of
influencing both the instincts and the environment. The autonomous
ego derives pleasure through experience, learning, and mastery. Ego
development, then, is an evolving, lifelong learning and maturational
process.

For Edward Bibring, all depressions are affective states that stem from conflict or tension within the ego itself, rather than between the ego and superego. A focus on self-esteem and the frustration of aspirations, other than orality, can be credited to Bibring, who extended the conceptualization of loss of self-esteem to depersonalization. He viewed depression as punishment accepted by persons who feel powerless and helpless. Their consequent aggressive tensions lead to loss of self-esteem because they are barred from expression. Bibring believed that they give up the struggle because they are tired and feel helpless, not because they are masochistic as Freud suggested. He also shed light on the concept of narcissism in relation to depression. Generally associated with orality and the intensely strong need for oral-narcissistic gratification, Bibring extended the notion to frustrations other than just the need for love and affection. He outlined other narcissistic aspirations that lead to feelings of lack of control and weakness when not fulfilled.[12] They include "the wish to be good, not to be good, not to be resentful, hostile, defiant, but to be loving, etc." Still others, possibly associated with the phallic phase, are "the wish to be strong, superior, great, secure, and not to be weak and insecure." Frustration of these narcissistic aspirations is characterized by feelings of inadequacy and inferiority. While it is clear that narcissism can reflect pathology and inappropriate response, Bibring makes it equally clear that narcissistic aspirations should be respected as a function of normal human development. When the ego suffers a narcissistic injury and collapse in self-esteem, depression is a natural response.

From an ego-psychology perspective, then, depression is the result of an intolerable "credibility gap" between whom one would like to be (the Ideal ego-state) and whom one is (the Actual ego-state).[13] A lowering of self-esteem occurs which many believe triggers depression. Remember that it is the person who becomes depressed, not the ego. The ego is simply a construct that has been created to illuminate intrapsychic dynamics. A similar ego-state construct is described by Helen DeRosis and Victoria Pellagrino[14] when they suggest a conflict between the Perfect Self (the Ideal Self) and the Despised Self (the Actual Self). In such cases, the perception of nonperfection automatically leads to a perjorative self-assessment and depression. In both of these interpretations, low self-esteem is preeminent, with overriding symptoms of guilt and worthlessness; the destructive energies of the superego abound. Researchers have concluded that dependency conflicts coupled with fragile self-esteem lead to depression vulnerability, a conclusion consistent with cognitive-behavioral theory.[15]

The characteristic dependent helplessness of depressed persons has also been viewed as an adaptive survival mechanism. According to

Willard Gaylin, despairing of helping himself the depressed person regresses to infantile dependence as the final solution to survival. So, though being drawn to the pain of depression may appear to contradict Freud's pleasure principle on which he believed motivation was based, Gaylin argues that, in theory, it is consistent.[16] Also interested in an adaptive formulation, Silvano Arieti and Jules Bemporad postulate that the child who experiences the loss of parental love or attention may embark on a lifelong quest to regain the lost love through pleasing a person they call a "Dominant Other" or by achieving a "Dominant Goal."[17] Like their predecessors, Arieti and Bemporad focus on the depriving mother as the most likely early lost love object. Later, they maintain that the person substitutes another Dominant Other to be pleased, often a spouse. The common need of depressed persons to please, to gain approval, and to be "good" is reflected in this conceptualization.[18]

In the psychoanalytic tradition, ego-psychology's emphasis thus continues to reside in past experience and the development of the depressive personality. This focus is true of most, though certainly not all, psychoanalytic thinkers. One exception was Henry Fox, who conducted an extensive study of World War II soldiers in 1945.[19] Depression was found to be associated with dependence and resentment concerning uncontrollable, undesired conditions. Fox's subjects seemed to be confronted by the loss of ideals and self-esteem. Their resentment included being told what to do and what not to do, being forced to do things viewed as not worthwhile, and being placed in jobs (situations) that were not liked. They, in fact, were dependent on conditions they found distasteful, and they revolted. It may be that depressed people today experience similar reasons for resentment whether or not they are in the armed service. These may be the factors that have personal meaning for depressed people, aptly conceptualized by Freud. He noted that they feel they have lost their selves; their egos have become empty and poor. Dependent on others for self-esteem, they are left without internal resources when others abandon them.[20]

While dependence, hostility, and self-esteem are central themes in the psychoanalytic literature, it is often loss that is focused on as the key to depression. Freud's early comparison of depression with grief and loss has been extended, to some degree, to virtually all other psychosocial theories. Though not necessarily relating loss to a love object, theorists posit loss of self-esteem, of an ego-ideal, of a role, of energy, of a goal, of positive reinforcers, of control, and even of existential meaning, to name a few analogs. The conceptualizations will be discussed in relevant chapters along with the insights intrinsic in each theory. While loss may be a factor, it will become clear that some people may never have had the love object, or the control, or whatever, to lose. They may despair what never was and what they believe will never be, rather than what was lost.

SELF-PSYCHOLOGY

The theoretical formulations of Heinz Kohut and his self-psychology colleagues have been of influence in recent years in the psychoanalytic community. Of note is Kohut and Wolf's conception of a two-dimensional narcissistic line of development between the grandiose self and the idealized parent images (called "imagos").[21] First, childhood's natural grandiosity, they propose, matures into healthy adult self-pride with attendant goals and ambitions, enjoyment and self-esteem. Second, the idealized parent image's standards and values are internalized over time, fostering adult self-reliance. Later in life, depressive emptiness is experienced when there are developmental deficits in either area. Parents again are key catalysts, for children require two major responses from them if they are to negotiate their journey to mature adulthood successfully. The first parental function is to "mirror" their offspring, reflected in the communication of admiration and approval for his or her being. Just being noticed, respected, and taken seriously is essential. The second task includes the parental capacity to be reliable and to fill the role of an "idealizable" adult, one worthy of being looked up to. When these experiences are lacking, according to self-psychologists, the unresponsive parent (the self-object) leaves the child wanting and feeling depleted. What results is either apparent grandiosity (unconscious depression, in fact) or depression (reflecting unresolved grandiose fantasies). In either case, such people deny their actions and feelings, their very selves, presenting a "false self" to the world. Hence, we have still another version of the breach between the ideal and the actual, in this case conceptualized as the self rather than the ego. Again, the significant parent is generally (though not necessarily) thought to be the mother. It is in her face that the child is likely to see him or herself mirrored. The child will continue to seek his own reflection while striving to meet her needs, secretly believing his idol to be as unworthy as he is. Given the theoretical primacy of the mother figure, it follows that there should be considerable attention paid to her emotional growth and well-being, as well as to that of her child.

OBJECT-RELATIONS THEORY

Fundamentals

The evolution of psychoanalytic thought via ego-psychology has culminated in object-relations theory, a perspective with varying nuances depending on the theorist. All proponents focus on the vicissitudes of internalized object relations (generally the significant caretaker). It is believed that "psychic apparatus" originates in the earliest stage of a sequential process of such internalization. The current formulation of object-relations theory proposes that the ego itself is the organizer of that process. The ego, therefore, is defined by its functioning. The better the psychic life, the better the functioning. According to object-relations theorists, development is a continuous process that continues despite affronts to the psyche. An adult pathology, therefore, does not reflect an earlier traumatic experience in mirror fashion. Instead, early trauma is believed to slow development by mutating it, not by fixing it at a particular stage, as once conjectured by classical theorists.

Object-relations theory is presently in dynamic evolution, particularly enriched by the clinical observations of Edith Jacobson,[22] Otto Kernberg,[23] and Margaret Mahler and her colleagues whose child-development research has influenced the field.[24] Because personality is not only formed in early life, but may constantly be modified by the environment and by the individual's interaction with that environment, disturbed behavior is perceived as a form of personality adaptation in response to particular social stresses and life situations. Those stressors are related to object representations, the enduring mental images of the "caretaker," the object relation who was the most significant person in the child's life and to whom he or she relates in an evolving developmental process. This concept of object relations is thought to be closely related to attachment bonding, a universal phenomenon among mammals. Research indicates that mammals inherit complex behavioral systems that facilitate mother-infant attachment and other social bonds. Because of their extended extrauterine dependency, the bonds are of greatest importance to the survival of primates in general, and to human beings in particular. Infants are highly vulnerable to separation from the caretaker because of their extreme helplessness. Strongly developed "internal representations" provide reassurance that the attachment bond with the important caretaker exists, thus reducing separation anxiety. These object representations continue to play an important role throughout the maturational process.[25]

Object-relations theorists conceptualize the developmental process around successive stages, broadly represented by *symbiosis*, the symbolic undifferentiation from a significant other (usually the mother), *separation* (from the mother), and *individuation*, a developmental phase, parallel with separation, that represents the process of forming and specializing the individual personality. The developmental process is described below because it is essential to the understanding of object-relations theory as it relates to depression. The focus is on Mahler's rendition of the theory (paychoanalytic davelopmental psychology) which was influenced by Jacobson's earlier work, and which Kernberg states is basically in harmony with his own present theoretical formulations. Mahlerians, however, do not adhere to psychosexual drive theory.

The Developmental Process[26]

At birth the child is thought to be an undifferentiated mass, living in the body alone. Around the third month of life the infant begins to develop a primitive consciousness of the world and enters into a symbiotic attachment with the caretaker; life is blissful. At approximately six months of age, the child begins to experience frustration, for not all needs are being met adequately and immediately. The child's universe, traditionally but not necessarily residing in the mother as caretaker, takes on some negative connotations along with the giving, positive essence. The parent is perceived to be all-powerful, able to nourish or destroy the child.

In the process, the first intimations of differentiation from the mother occur. With the realization of this profound possibility and the new-found perception of vulnerability, the infant must defend against the knowledge. The ego is simply too fragile at this stage of development to do otherwise. By symbolically splitting the all-good, all-loving component of the caretaker off from the bad, frustrating part, the blissful symbiotic state is perpetuated, and the thwarting mother, the frightening half, becomes the object of rage and aggressive wishes. Concomitantly, the loving self and the raging self are also divided into two entities. Children are no more able to accept the negative in themselves than they are able to accept it in the parent figure.

The task of childhood, then, is the reintegration of the self and of the significant object relation. This process is termed *separation-individuation* and requires the development of the self as a distinct, unique, and separate entity. According to Mahler, the first phase of psychological birth of the child, occurring somewhere around eighteen months and extending into the third year, is termed the rapprochement subphase of separation-individuation. It is a time of ambivalence between attachment and undifferentiation from the caretaker, and the beginning development of self-reliance and individuality on the part of the child. It is in this rapprochement subphase that the predisposition to depression is thought to be established. Since the object as part of the self is lost, some depressive affect is to be expected even when separation-individuation is successfully executed. But an even greater hazard is predicted when the needs of the subphase are not responded to.

A delicate balance between protective nurturance, the development of trust, and gentle frustration is required to propel the child toward healthy autonomy. Still, the caretaker must be available to replenish the venturing child's dependency needs. Otherwise, new-found autonomy will be equated with rejection and abandonment. Overprotection also is dysfunctional to growth, for motivation toward the development of competence and separation will not be valued in the face of a blissfully satisfactory symbiosis. It is balance that is critical, for too much nurturance and protection can easily become suffocation of separation-individuation.

OBJECT-RELATIONS THEORY AND DEPRESSION

Edith Jacobson's study of depression[27] is the most comprehensive of all the studies of psychoanalytic theorists to date. Her work provides the contemporary bridge to object-relations theory, noting that the dynamics inherent in affects, drives, and object relations cannot be separated out. Viewing depression as originating within the ego, she is concerned with the natural oral-dependent needs of the child and the ramifications of their frustration, as well as real and ideal self-representations as described in the previous sections of this chapter. But she also stresses the interaction of real and idealized object representations and relationships with actual people. She states that the investment of affects in self and object representations eventually becomes integrated with the superego as well as ego functions. Through this process, the superego controls the ego by means of mood swings. Focusing on psychotic depression as a separate entity, Jacobson points to narcissistic frustration with object relations, partly real and partly fantasied, as the beginning stage of depression. Fear of abandonment and related fear of aggression against the needed and frustrating object lead to the denial of the object's frustrating and aggressive aspects, while denying their own negative aspects as well. When such denial fails, catastrophic self devaluation takes its place. At best, the devaluation is partial and leads to hostile self-affirmation and increased, albeit premature, autonomy. At worst, the devaluation is total and encompasses an impoverishment of the self. In either case, both the idealized object and the corresponding intrapsychic object representation are lost. The difference between neurotic and psychotic depression emerges from this common ground of experience, according to Jacobson. The former reflects minor tendencies toward denial and idealization, while the latter indicates that defensive mechanisms are developed even further.

Anaclitic and Introjective Depression

Sidney Blatt and his colleagues are presently engaged in research that attempts to differentiate simple "anaclitic" depression from "introjective" depression within an object-relations framework.[28] Blatt's review of psychoanalytically based theory, clinical, and research literature leads him to conclude that impairments at each level of development vis-á-vis object relations has an important role in the potential vulnerability to depression.[29] He suggests that loss is often a major precipitant because developmental impairments in the process of internalization of object representations leave the individual vulnerable to object loss and to depression. Hence, while Blatt's reasoning differs from Freud's, Freud's conclusion that loss is a critical factor prevails.

Anaclitic depression is thought to exist when impairment has occurred at the relatively undifferentiated level of separation-individuation; a depressed adult has fears of being unloved and of being abandoned. Expression of anger is understandably guarded, owing to the symbiotic relationship with the parent. Psychological birth has not yet occurred, and since the person is "nothing" without the other, abandonment and loss of love leave the individual without personal identity, a nonentity. Abandonment is deservedly imminent, for the bad object *is* the self in the eyes of the depressed person. Thus interpreted, anaclitic depression is due to a devastating psychological situation. Love objects can only be valued for their capacity to provide gratification, because survival needs are too intense, and frustration of the need for gratification preoccupies the self. Pleasure is short-lived because there is little internalization of gratification. It must come from others. Anaclitic depression also is characterized by feelings of helplessness, depletion, and weakness, with wishes to be cared for, loved, and protected. Relatively little guilt is experienced, but the fear of abandonment is intense. So, too, is the oral quality of the depression and the need to maintain direct physical contact with the need-gratifying object.

In introjective depression, impairment is considered to be at a higher level of development. While the person also shrinks from expressing anger, the overwhelming fear is of being unlovable rather than unloved. Strivings toward separation-individuation are viewed apprehensively. To be separate, to succeed as an individual, is to be unworthy, disloyal to the object of one's love. The Superego is characteristically harsh, reflecting high ideals, morality, and commitment beyond the norm. Ambivalence between feelings of love and hate is marked, and strong identification with "the oppressor" (a dominant power figure) is a chief defense.[30] The profile is that of a high achiever with keen introspective qualities and a strong need for approval, acceptance, and recognition. Nothing is ever enough, for such people can never live up to such unrealistic expectations and standards, nor can their love relationships. Guilt reigns supreme, though it may reflect compliance to external expectations that one *should* feel guilty, rather than sincerely felt guilt.

To empathize with such people is to recognize how dangerous it is for them "to be their own persons," to separate and individuate. They learned early on that they were different from their caretakers, but their differences were not acceptable. The perjorative implications are traumatic to the emerging ego; the internalized negative opinion lives on in the adult. At the same time, a grandiosity may exist, perhaps due to the internalization of vaulted expectations, or very likely because energy must be used to repress anything viewed as either negative (less than perfect) or reminiscent of the bad object. Any negative trait is interpreted as contamination of the positive. Like when there is a drop of ink in clear water, all of the water is "bad."[31] Introjective depression is distinguished by feelings of worthlessness, guilt, inferiority, and a sense of failing to live up to standards and expectations. A wish for atonement is common in such people, and fears focus on loss of love, need for approval, and recognition from the love object. When attained, satisfaction is fleeting and the need to maintain contact, as in anaclitic cases, is evident.

In summary, depression is divided into two entities:

— *Anaclitic Depression* stems from symbiotic attachment to the mother and the fear of abandonment during infancy.
— *Introjective Depression* stems from a higher level of ego development, evolving from fear of separation-individuation from the object relation in early childhood.

In both cases, the focus is on the mother-child relationship with the acknowledgement that the father or other primary caretaker also may be the significant object relation.

WOMEN AT RISK

Classical Psychoanalytic Theory

Childhood dependence is an important determinant in the development of personality. Anna Freud describes a "developmental line" from dependency to emotional self-reliance and adult relationships.[32] Other neo-Freudians follow suit. As a result of animal and human observation, it has been noted that the degree of natural infantile dependence on others for their needs determines the degree to which dependence is a control factor in their development. The external need for such gratification leads to insecurity and a subjectively experienced lack of freedom.[33] While independence is also viewed as developing out of neonatal helplessness, it has been argued that maturational processes are not sufficient for the acquisition of independence. Those who have developed independence, but who are not allowed their freedom because of social conditions, often become secondarily dependent with submissiveness and hostile-dependence as characteristic behavior. If the ego-ideal contains the ideal of autonomy, the aggressive-drive energies necessary for learning to achieve independence will automatically be expended. That ego-ideal must be nurtured by others if it is to function.[34]

These observations may provide insight into Freud's passing remarks that the "good, capable, conscientious woman" is more likely to become depressed than her counterpart. While Freud viewed women's vulnerability to depression as natural female masochism, it is possible to see that the subservient position of traditional women may have more etiological credibility. The evidence in Freud's writings of his misogyny has been well documented.[35] Speaking out ardently against feminists — female and male — his genius was marred by mundane prejudice. The following quotation is a case in point:[36]

[Women] refuse to accept the fact of being castrated. . . . I cannot escape the notion that for women the level of what is ethically normal is different from what it is in men. . . . We must not allow ourselves to be deflected from such conclusions by the denials of the feminists, who are anxious to force us to regard the two sexes as completely equal in position and worth. (p.261)

Accurately observing that "feminine attitudes" are denigrated by both males and females, he found this disdain of the so-called feminine traits to be a mystery, albeit a "natural" condition. He counseled males to become more aggressive and females to accept their inferiority.[37] Never did he connect imposed female subservience and cultural rejection with their prevailing depressions. Despite the fact that feminist professionals and nonprofessionals alike have taken exception to his position, pointing out the lack of valid evidence of his assumptions, psychoanalytic thinking has had an undeniably enormous impact on Western culture.

Karen Horney, a neo-Freudian psychoanalyst, was one of the first to confront Freud with his sexist ideation, arguing that states such as dependency, passivity, submissiveness, and masochism are destructive whenever they occur.[38] She concludes that any attempt to inflict these traits on anyone precipitates a negative reaction. If the reaction cannot be safely expressed (as in the case of the dependent woman), Horney warns that it will appear in a disguised form that is often destructive to the self as well as to others. Depression is a case in point. Horney notes, too, that women have incorporated the idea that their own growth and self-development will be destructive to others. The notion stems from societal values whereby independent attitudes associated with mature men are regarded as unfeminine and anti-male. The classical psychoanalytic model tends to describe the process of women's development as that of overcoming active forces within them, assuming a passive, dependent, masochistic role. Achievement of a worthwhile identity is difficult at best for anyone, but women are given little preparation or experience to develop a healthy sense of self. While reports are mixed, an extensive review of empirical studies concerning psychoanalytic theory and the psychology of women suggests that females from age six on are more dependent, passive, and comforming than males.[39] Traditionally feminine, passive-dependent women are more likely to have difficulty in their roles as wives, mothers, and sexual partners — findings commensurate with Freud's observations of the typical depressed woman.[40]

Depression related to women's dependence can be appropriately assessed in relation to the battered woman, the abused child, the displaced homemaker, the unemployed or low-wage female worker, as well as to the aging woman who is restricted in her activity owing to physical, economic, or emotional dependence.

Third World women are also likely candidates for secondary dependency. In each case, societally induced failure and guilt can be reduced with supportive understanding. It can be expected that anger and resentment will emerge concerning their lost time, imposed restrictions, the stifling of development, financial deprivation, injustices, and misguided counsel. Therapists must help such women to break through cultural restrictions against acceptance of their negative feelings. The denial, discounting, and powerlessness of their anger may be at the core of their depressions. Self-hate at allowing oneself to be part of the exploitation can be expected, together with hostility directed at significant others and society at large. Love-hate ambivalence will come to the fore. With help, as rage subsides and risk becomes feasible, the intellect and the emotions coalesce in spite of fear, with renewed strength and purpose. No longer do dependence, resentment, lack of self-esteem, and depression feed on each other.

Ego-Psychology

It is not difficult to find analogies between lack of self-esteem, as described by Bibring, and women. The wish to be good and loving, and not to be resentful, hostile, or defiant mirrors the attitudes and behavior required of women. To wish to be strong and in control when one's traditional place is the polar opposite can be a devastating secret. That an ego-state conflict exists is clear. What is less clear is which state is Actual and which is Ideal. Society's confusion on the issue is reflected in the depressed woman herself. Is she really an inferior being, vainly wishing to be equal? Is this the reason for her guilty secret? Or is she really stronger and more capable than those around her? Are these the seeds of her repressed resentment? The hidden conflicts must be aired and interpreted in the light of dysfunctional cultural restrictions and interpretations. The egos of women must be developed and nurtured so that self-representations are not distorted to suit societal norms. When the ego-ideal, however reasonable in terms of mature adulthood, is out of reach because society says one must not aspire to personal growth, then it is important to support clients in their struggle to change the environment as well as themselves. The superego fears of women all too often reflect guilt over perfectly healthy developmental needs.

The subject of distorted female self-representations also deserves attention in regard to body image. The culture is so inundated with the "perfect female form" and how to create a desirable physical image, that women cannot escape internalizing these norms, or at least setting them up as criteria. Since no one is likely to live up to the ego-ideal, discussions surrounding their unrealistic nature can be helpful. This is as true for the developing teenager as it is for the aging woman. Therapists find that the female experience in regard to her body image is often devastating. Focusing on the beauty of the human body in all of its different manifestations can be an ego-enhancing experience. To learn to prize one's body for its own sake, not as others may evaluate it, can be a therapeutic undertaking.

Conflicts between the actual and the ideal ego-states, regardless of the model, are common in females. They have often been socialized to conforming and banal scripts regardless of individual differences. Having been denied their potential and ability to act spontaneously in their own behalf, they exhibit predictably low self-esteem. Their ideas regarding the reality of who they "should" be are often irrational, based on restrictive cultural mores, rather than principles of con-structive human development. When referring to women's ideals and reality, then, the therapist ought to guard against fostering social adjustment to the status quo, and remember that social reality is created by human beings and is relative to time and place, not to natural law.[41]

To illustrate: the ideal, all-giving, selfless altruism required of wives and mothers is an unrealistic expectation for any human being over an extended period of time. To couple that expectation with the require-ment to function equally well in the marketplace is delusory; yet, that is the situation in contemporary society. With a rising 50 percent of all married women working, research tells us that the majority have almost full responsibility for housekeeping, care of children, and social life.[42] The burden is inordinate, yet the traditional self-expectations of many women prevail. Jean Curtis conducted extensive interviews with 200 American working women of diverse backgrounds, as well as with their husbands and children. She found that the women per-ceived their husbands to be supportive if they permitted their wives to work, as long as the women kept up with their other responsibilities — "the kids, the cooking, the house, and some sort of social life."[43] These findings were corroborated in the writer's initial person-environment study of 100 white women, half of whom were depressed. The depen-dent depressed women spoke (without probing) about they heavy dual responsibilities, unshared by their husbands. While they were resentful, they regarded their partners as supportive and described their home environment as allowing, even encouraging, autonomy.[44]

From an ego-psychology perspective, one might conclude that their unrealistic ideal ego-states (uncomplaining supermother, super-wife, and superworker) and their actual ego-states (reflected in the realistic assessment of their situations and, hence, their less than "super" identities) were in conflict. Remedying the disparity requires increasing self-awareness, as well as family cooperation. Because any new action on the part of women will result in reaction, the family must also be educated to the dysfunctional nature of their expectations. In addition to the impact on today's women, the example they perpetuate for daughters and sons must be reevaluated if the mental health of future generations of women is to be different. While it might be expected that the women's movement will have an automatic impact on them, recent research indicates otherwise. In 1981 it was reported that while many young women hope that their future husbands will be of some help in the home, they have no thoughts of equally shared home maintenance or parenting responsibility. They also expect to be able to choose to stay at home during the child-rearing years, an expectation that economists do not project as feasible.[45] Unless they learn to face the reality of their roles and to assert themselves as sharing adults, the destructive trend will continue. Therapists can be of help in educating their male as well as female clients to the reality of inequitable ideals.

Adaptation and the Dominant Other

Arieti and Bemporad's conceptual framework regarding the "Dominant Other" which the depressed person symbolically carries with her internally, provides insights that are relevant to women.[46] Ever seeking the approval of this internalized Dominant Other, the theorists believe that the dynamic usually stems from the infant's mother and is then transferred to the spouse. I suggest that the "Dominant Other" is likely to refer to the father in traditional childhood, accurately reflecting the dominant figure in the home and in society at large. Even when the father is not dominant, cultural attitudes prevail in the minds of children. To transfer the need for approval, so typical of dependent persons, to the male spouse is a logical adaptational eventuality. The need for approval must be addressed and analyzed in relation to men and to significant others who encourage traditional relationships if depression is to be prevented. The little girl who learns to ignore or reject her own wishes, pleasing her father and other men as society has taught her to do, enters into what Arieti and Bemporad call a "bargain relationship." Gratification and acceptance will be forthcoming if willingness for self-sacrifice is properly demonstrated. An unhealthy dependency ensues, reflecting a pathological retention of the Dominant Other. The theorists view the process as an unconscious cognitive construct, an ideology that must be unearthed if depression is to be mastered.[47] Further analogy to women's upbringing need not be labored; it is obvious.

Object-Relations Theory

Object-relations theorists also need to be circumspect about making interpretations based on theory without assessing the female experience. The ability to anticipate, judge, and delay gratification, for example, are thought to be among the first signs that the ego is beginning to operate as a mediator. Because many segments of society have been conditioned to delay gratification, careful assessment is advised. To illustrate: most women are taught to put their own desires aside, to wait until the needs of their children and husbands are fulfilled before their own are taken into consideration. Feminists and other theorists note the correlation between depression and their propensity to delay gratification.[48] Yet the practice is perpetuated by the family, the church, educators, and even by mental health practitioners themselves. The practice, of course, is not limited to women. The poor and people of color, for example, are even enjoined to wait until the hereafter for their gratification. The comment is not meant to be facetious; it is a fact. Again, successfully carrying out societal directives is not necessarily equated with high-level ego functioning.

The presence of humor, too, is thought to be an indicator of relatively advanced development. Again, we must be cautious. Apparent good humor also can be a ploy of the person who needs to please. The ever-smiling depressed woman is a case in point (as was the smiling "Negro" of yesteryear). A good-natured mask may reflect a desire or need for approval, typical of the depressed, dependent person. The internalized Dominant Other hypothesized by Arieti and Bemporad[49] may be at the core of the friendly facade. What could be more compelling than parental messages to be good, sweet-tempered, pleasant females?

The superego is another construct that is thought to represent a feature of a high degree of ego organization. Identification with the parents (and with parental training) reflects such superego formation. Contrary to psychoanalytic theory, the female superego is often overzealous because of early restrictive rules and controls. This is not an accurate reflection of a high degree of ego organization. It is a fair indicator, though, of depression vulnerability.

Parental identification is further complicated when it represents the pathological merging of self and object representations.[50] Narcissism, a personal quality often associated with females, is a case in point. Dread and hatred of dependency go hand in hand with the narcissistic personality, bringing unavoidable conflict when dependency is forced upon them. Depression can be expected as women with narcissistic tendencies get older and increasingly recognize their cultural dependency. They may be reacting to their own compliance with an environment that has encouraged them to feign goodness and feminine perfection, and to cherish their youthful beauty as fundamentally important in order to win approval. Having devalued all else, they come face to face with their painful loneliness and superficiality. Efforts should be made to replace their narcissistic raison d'être with a mature, realistic purpose. A healthy narcissism can emerge side by side with wholesome self-esteem. Such women can be taught to accept their limitations by embracing their strengths and developing their unique possibilities. Only those who believe they are inferior and unloved need to be pathologically narcissistic. Narcissus, after all, represents the alienated ego that cannot love — that is to say, cannot give interest and libido to life because it is not yet related to itself. The solution of the problem of Narcissus, then, is the fulfillment of self-love rather than its renunciation.[51] And so it is with the narcissistic depressed woman.

Anaclitic and Introjective Depression

Taking a cultural view of Blatt's concepts and assessing overriding symtomology may also provide insight into the high depression statistics in the female population. For example, the stereotype of the insecure "helpless" female, crying for love and fearing abandonment, is typical of the anaclitic depressive. It is difficult not to make the analogy between Blatt's anaclitic profile and the classic female "clinging vine."[52] Might it be that the anaclitic depressive represents the girl-child, the person socialized to dependence, the one who must not be differentiated from a mother who reflects the same traditional characteristics? Nancy Chodorow's reinterpretation of ego development locates gender differences as early as the first few weeks of life.[53] She notes that girls see themselves as less separate than boys, having more permeable ego boundaries because they view themselves as extensions

of their mothers. Their object representations, therefore, differ markedly from those of boys. While girls' diffuse identification and perception of sexual sameness with the nurturing figure enhances the
development of their relational qualities, they are less likely to become
their own persons. Nancy Chodorow's studies indicate that separation
means danger to women, while intimacy is viewed positively. Men see
separation as an easy task, while intimacy is assessed as dangerous.
Since the discrepant development of girls and boys impact both sexes
noticeably, they are both affected by each other's experience. Females
perhaps emerge as at risk for depression in part because they have not
developed autonomy and environmental mastery, and partially because they are relational beings who are frustrated by their emotional
and instrumental involvement with nonrelational males.

Clinical evidence also suggests that the content and the conceptual
level of parental representations are central to depression, according to
Blatt and his colleagues. Changes in the representation are paralleled
by changes in the clinical situation. What is more, depression has been
found to be related to the perception that parents were lacking in
affection, nurturance, and support. Depressed persons reported that
their parents were insensitive and unavailable, or overly intrusive and
unable to tolerate their autonomy and independence when they were
children. Depressed people who were rated as highly dependent and
self-critical had the lowest conceptual scores. They described their
parents primarily by their activities relative to personal gratification or
frustration. The data indicate, therefore, that the content and cognitive
level of parental representation may be a central dimension in depression.[54] Blatt also reports that the persons most likely to be dependent
and self-critical are women,[55] whether daughters or mothers. It follows
that when mothers of symbiotic daughters are inculcated with societal
expectations that the good mother is dependent, with stringent standards obviating interests in the world at large, the daughter is likely to
internalize the object representation. One might speculate, then, that
the depriving parent might have been equally deprived. Anaclitic
depression, thus, may be perpetuated from generation to generation.

Finally, another cultural scenario might be conjectured. Part of the
task of differentiation supposedly requires the giving up of the libidinal, all-nurturing mother. Two heterosexual, sex-related realities need
to be considered. First, unlike females, when a male gives up his
mother, she is in time replaced by other women who are socialized to
nurture him; there is no final giving up of the mother for males.
Second, the developing child is to relinquish symbiotic omnipotence
for differentiation. The male replaces the mother-son symbiosis with

an eventually superior adult-male status. The female child replaces her symbiotic omnipotence with the recognition of a culturally inferior adult-female status, whatever else her identity may entail. It might be reasonable, on all counts, to predict adaptive resistance to separation based upon such cultural realities. Anaclitic depression may be the developmental price representing a fear of nothingness in separation. This might even be conceptualized as a fear of death, or nonexistence.[56]

As for the introjective profile, fear of life, of separation-individuation, may be the underlying dynamic. If females and males are genetically and psychologically different, the experience of girls born into a male world may be traumatic over and above their individual experience. They may, as children, recognize at a deep and primitive level how alien that world is to their female orientation and propensities. Their differences are disallowed, universally, and more likely to be interpreted as deficits. Retreating into undifferentiation so as not to be alienated, separation-individuation (life) is blocked, signified by depression. Those who feel this deeply should probably be introduced to an existential perspective to develop a more positive view of universal female differentiation and individuation.[57]

PEOPLE AT RISK

Male and Female Idiosyncrasies

Little boys are often encouraged to separate from their mothers long before they are ready. Because premature separation is alienating rather than growth producing, they should be encouraged to attach themselves in the early phases of development. Only then can they develop the feminine aspects of themselves, the traits of the good mother, emotions such as warmth, tenderness, and relationship, too often negated and derided in themselves and other males. Research by Eve Chevron, Donald Quinlan, and Sidney Blatt[58] indicates that warmth and expressiveness are correlated with high dependency and vulnerability to depression in males, unlike females. The researchers conclude that warmth and expressiveness are stereotyped as female traits and are therefore negatively assessed by males when attributed to them. Freud himself noted the cultural negation of feminine traits on the part of females and males alike. While he was confused by it, we need not be, for society has perpetuated the message throughout history. We can begin to reassess masculine aggression in light of new knowledge. While males may have a propensity for more aggressive behavior, culturally induced reinforcement of that tendency, in the absence of the encouragement of nurturing behavior, is destructive to them and to women. Like depression, it may be that rape, battering, and male violence of all kinds can be traced back, at least in part, through object-relations theory.

Studies indicate that girls as young as four years of age are prosocial and boys are less friendly, cooperative, empathic, and self-controlled. Diana Baumrind suggests that the diffuse identification and prolonged contact with a same-sex nurturing figure enhances the possibility of girls' relational development.[59] The masculine personality becomes defined by a denial of feminine, relational merging and interdependence. Whereas girls relinquish their capacity for independence in response to promises of love and approval, boys are bribed, by the promise of power and domination, into prematurely relinquishing their dependence. Male role enactment may be more a posturing than a genuine introjection of sex-related characteristics. As a result, males may suffer persistent performance anxiety, requiring sustained reassurance from maternal surrogates to uphold their pseudo-independent stance. It may not be that boys must overcome an initial feminine identification, as Freud and his followers have purported. Rather, male gender role is a differentiation from the female matrix, in the same way that male sexual development is a differentiation at successive gateways from female physiology. Some believe that male-shared child rearing will reverse the destructive development of boys that results in their alienation and hostile aggression. In object-relations terms, boy children who are reared by nurturing fathers will have a female-equivalent experience of merging with their caretaker, advancing their human-relational potentialities. To be relational is to love and to nurture love—qualities to be desired in both sexes and necessary to healthy human functioning.

The permeability of girls' ego boundaries results in their tendency to define themselves more in relation to others. This propensity may lead to dependence, a need for approval, and stunted development. Yet, as we have seen, their relational qualities also stand them and society in good stead. Only recently have theorists and researchers begun to examine the positive aspects of female relationship and socialization. They are calling for a new paradigm—a renewed vision of a world that could be constructive for both women and men.

A number of feminist writers and researchers are presently focusing on the dynamics of female development and mother-daughter relationships, a long overdue exploration.[60] Their interests are varied but usually focus on the dichotomy between nurturance and autonomy in the relationship, which sets the stage for the developing female's relational qualities. Jane Flax suggests that young girls are not rewarded and, indeed, are punished by their mothers for their moves toward autonomy.[61] In order to be nurtured at all, they must abandon their autonomous wishes. Conversely, if they choose self-fulfillment in the external world, they must reject their mothers and the hope of being nurtured. From an object-relations perspective, as girls move from the symbiotic period toward ego autonomy, they are unable to identify with the more powerful, independent father. They are thrown back on the very person from whom they have not been able to undifferentiate completely, the devalued mother. Because they may not have had an adequate symbiotic experience, they have a need for a sense of fusion with a reliable, caring person. Hence, their double bind, for that person negates their need for autonomy.

While this interpretation of female development may hold a great deal of truth, there is something missing. That something is the father in relation to the daughter. I suggest that his values and principles concerning the behavior of the girl-child may be of critical importance for it may be the father who rejects female autonomy. That is not to say that the mother is providing encouragement, support, and nurturance (nor is it to say that she is not). But one can be more certain that the father is not, given cultural norms. In short, Flax's description is a more valid picture of father-daughter dynamics than of mother-daughter interactions in my opinion. The question, of course, is subject to research. It may behoove therapists, in the meantime, to be aware of both possibilities.

Regarding Androgyny—A Perspective

Many feminist theorists and clinicians in recent years have focused on androgny, a concept that may be defined as an already existing combination of masculine and feminine attributes at the core of all individuals. Because society has perverted the natural qualities of males and females, much must be unlearned in order to "let ourselves be ourselves."[62] While few would argue with that point, some feminists have taken exception to the value of androgyny as a healing principle.

They believe that androgyny implies that women accept what men have been as part of the wholeness they seek. Focusing on the resilience and creative energy of women, they argue that the infusion of masculine qualities with the feminine only incorporates the violence and insensitivity of patriarchal society.[63] The warning should be heeded for there is no doubt that masculine aggression takes cultural precedence, hurting and alienating people rather than bringing them together. Feminine, nurturing qualities in both sexes can be supported and encouraged, as well as autonomous growth and environmental mastery. Still, we must not overlook the reality of human attributes that exist despite their unacceptability in all people.

Regardless of one's sex, a denial of personal characteristics that also are denied expression will be projected onto another unconsciously. Generally this is looked upon as the dark side of one's personality, that which is thought to be inferior (the bad self-representation). The more women insist on being all-good, relational, and nurturing, the more likely they are to deny the existence of anger and to find it in others. This one-sided feminist focus on maternal love may be susceptible to just such a dynamic. It appears to me to be a modern version of Freudian insistence on biological destiny and the glorification of motherhood, which has had less than optimal repercussions. Unless women accept the possibility of both strengths and frailties within themselves, any whisper of imperfection may result in depressive affect. This is not an incorporation of patriarchy, it is an acceptance of humanness.[64]

Resocialization of Males and Females

Therapists must be aware of the possibility of cultural influences and their effects upon human development and emotional dysfunction. In order to correct for them in the treatment situation, one of the goals is to facilitate a full range of feeling and possibility in both females and males. Because people differ in emotional capacity as well as emotional development, they must be freed to become themselves on their own terms. To reject feelings and relationship because of fear is to reject the life process itself. So, too, is rejecting the normal development of autonomy and competence. Maturation is only possible in the presence of acceptance and respect for both positive and negative feelings, together with the push-pull of dependence and independence in both sexes. Object-relations theory provides credibility for the resocialization of males and females to this end. Tenderness and anger, and the desire for relationship and support at one end of the spectrum, and autonomy and achievement needs at the other, all must be respected as normal human requirements for growth and well-being. The pleasantness of an emotion or need, or congruence with gender do not determine its character. Rather, "goodness" or "badness" is assessed by the extent to which it is accepted as part of oneself. Denying negative or unacceptable feelings lessens the ability to think and act positively. Still, note the object-relation therapist's warning that ventilation of aggression is undesirable until the "good" self and "good" object representation have been developed. One might conjecture, for instance, that the violent male is one who annihilates himself as he destroys others, unable to control his impulses, having introjected a bad self-representation, split off prematurely from the good love object. His socialization had denied him his more tender humanness, just as the woman's cultural negation of angry feelings has inhibited her wholeness. Depression, once believed to be caused by repressed anger, is not that simplistically explained. It is possible that woman's unrealistic representation of a self without anger comes face to face with the reality of her unaccepted and unacceptable emotions. Depression is the price she pays for the subterfuge. Or it is equally possible that powerless anger triggers depression or at least exacerbates it. Whatever the dynamic, anger is not used constructively by women or by men.

A positive relationship with a therapist, including the acceptance and understanding of differences, releases the depressed person to use the therapist simultaneously as an identical self and as a glorified object, permitting a unique sense of union. A "safety zone" is thus established in which hostile feelings can be safely released without fear of destruction.

A female therapist who is comfortable with the so-called feminine and masculine aspects of her being may enhance treatment, for differences and sameness may be explored and experienced together. A new respect for the stereotypical feminine or masculine traits in others and in the self can emerge. A male therapist can do this, too, if he is aware and respectful of his own fears of femininity and masculinity and open to development and change.[65]

CLASSICAL PSYCHOANALYTIC PREVENTION AND INTERVENTION

According to classical psychoanalytic theory, depression is the result of anger turned inward due to the real or imagined loss of a love "object," the significant caretaker in infancy (usually considered to be the mother). Because anger clearly directed outward at the object of rage would "insure" rejection, the significant figure is internalized and anger "appears" then to be turned toward the self. Freudians link depression with the conscience, the superego, which punishes the guilty party.

Grief Work

The similarities between mourning and depression have been observed for centuries. In modern times, Karl Abraham and Sigmund Freud both made the analogy, noting possible differences as well as commonalities. Whether or not grief and depression are one and the same continues to provoke controversy.[66] Some social scientists believe that depression is an integral component of the grief experience, while others argue that grief is a separate entity that happens to share some common symptoms. In any case, the historical coupling of loss and depression has vastly influenced the direction of scientific thought and clinical insight for generations. Whether loss is real or imagined or anticipated, many similar symptoms are shared and grief work must be done.

According to Freud, when the work of mourning is completed, depression is relieved. Classical analysts continue to apply this perspective, though they may update Freud's insights with the work of Erich Lindemann whose early research has culminated in an understanding of the successive stages of recovery from loss.[67] He defined grief work as emancipation from bondage to the deceased, readjustment to the environment in which the deceased is missing, and formation of new relationships.[68] Whether the loss is real or symbolic, an understanding of the process provides profound insights for the practitioner and client alike. The four stages central to recovery are considered sequentially.

Stage 1. *Denial*: refusal to see what is clearly true because the recognition of reality would be too painful to the ego; attempts to recover the lost person persist.

Stage 2. *Anger*: protestation against the idea or fact of loss and its unfairness; rage and resentment take over, directed toward the self, the lost person, and the world — including the therapist.

Stage 3. *Depression*: despair that life cannot be lived without the love of the lost person; feelings of hopelessness pervade the bereaved person (often, this is the stage at which the clinician is sought out because of the depth of despair and disorganization).

Stage 4. *Acceptance*: understanding and tolerance of the reality of loss and recognition that one can survive and flourish in spite of loss; reorganization of the personality.

Sometimes the grieving person identifies so closely with the lost love object that values, mannerisms, even symptoms of illnesses are adopted, if only for a brief time. Gradually, through the mourning process, the mourner is freed from bondage to the lost loved one. The time span and intensity of grief reactions manifested by depression vary with the individual and the type and duration of the relationship. Both positive and negative feelings toward the abandoning one should be explored and accepted, for extreme ambivalence and denial can be destructive. Previous losses and how they were coped with, preparation for the loss, and the sufferer's belief that the world is not a safe place to be without the lost person all have impact on the grief reaction.

Freudian-oriented theorists point out that special attention should be paid to termination, a loss with which therapist and client must contend. Termination should be dealt with gently and openly by the therapist so that the feelings of loss already experienced so devastatingly are not compounded. The following discussion of hostility is relevant here.

Hostility

Special attention also may be given to the exploration of the causes of hostile feelings when angry emotions are conscious, and is even more critical when hostility is repressed. Defenses should be eased so that rage and hostility can be consciously experienced in the safety of the transference situation. Transference is an otherwise unconscious process wherein the characteristics of significant persons from the past (generally parents) are displaced or projected onto the therapist. Thus, a person will react to the therapist as if he or she were at times the mother and at other times the father, regardless of the therapist's sex. The aggression, called drive discharge, must be interpreted and worked through its many layers and points of fixation. According to psychoanalytic theory, fixation can occur at any phase of development where there has been a great deal of conflict or difficulty. An inordinate amount of psychic energy is needed to cope with that phase, leaving less available for subsequent development. While this book does not presume to teach the reader all about psychodynamic therapy, it is important to be aware of transference reactions.

Emotional insight is a basic principle, considered to be of more importance than either the expression of emotions or intellectual understanding. Because insight must be emotional as well as intellectual if it is to be effective, it may be threatening to the client. When trust is established, the free-association method can become an appropriate tool. Described by Freud as "releasing the armies of the day," free association is a process whereby the client talks in a stream of consciousness, unmonitored by censorship. Whatever comes to mind is voiced, however inappropriate, foolish, or shocking it may seem. The expression of hostility will eventually emerge in the safety of the therapeutic relationship.

Today we know that while the expression of hostility may have therapeutic value, emotional catharsis is not sufficient to alleviate depression. Research indicates that depression and expressed hostility may even coexist. While aggressive expression does not necessarily eliminate depression (though it may lessen depressive symptoms somewhat), anger and resentment are still quite visible in most depressed people and are masked by denial in many of the rest. Some studies, for example, report that depressed women are often openly hostile toward their husbands and adolescent children.[69] Their anger is as obvious as their depression. Such anger may be thought of as powerless rage, whether overt or covert. When nothing is changed, regardless of the expression of anger, hopelessness and resentment follow close behind.[70] Prevention and treatment of depression should, of course, incorporate awareness and constructive expression of anger, but it is essential to include the possibility of change though personal development as well as a sense of control over one's present situation.[71]

EGO-PSYCHOLOGY PREVENTION AND INTERVENTION

Ego-psychologists are concerned more with the ego than with the id or superego. Depression is considered to be the result of a painful breach between who one is, one's actual ego-state, and whom one wishes to be, the ideal ego-state. While there are variations on this theme, vulnerability to depression always reflects a fragile ego and excessive dependence on others in order to maintain self-esteem.

Characteristics of the Ego

The phrase "ego strengths" has become synonymous for the conglomerate of personality traits that contribute to mental health, in contrast to "ego deficits" or weaknesses of the ego. The components of these categories, however, have not been adequately formulated. For that reason, the insights of Solomon and Patch are especially welcome.[72] The following characteristics are suggested as contributory to ego strength:

Tolerance — "the ability to tolerate the pain of loss, failure, disappointment, frustration, insult, shame and guilt."

Forgiveness — "the ability to forgive and feel mercy for those who have caused one injury."

Acceptance of substitutes — "the willingness to forego what is not currently possible or expedient and seek something else in its stead."

Persistence — "the ability to continue efforts with determination (where there is some degree of hope) despite meager or no early success."

Ability to learn — "ingenuity, creativity, and the ability to be resourceful and innovative."

Vitality — "power, energy or a driving force for generating and sustaining effort and activity."

Note that the last three traits have implications for the first three. While tolerance, forgiveness, and acceptance of substitutes are honorable qualities, they are very subjective. I would caution against their appropriateness until the individual's persistence, learning, and vitality are strengthened. Only then can one be free to interpret the first three traits wisely. While forgiving those who have caused injury, for example, a person may decide to accept a substitute relationship rather than tolerate a painful one. The toleration that characterizes ego strength then is viewed as the ability to tolerate the loss of the disappointing relationship. Without this insight, the qualities put forth might be applied to one's disadvantage. There is no such thing as value-free therapy.

Solomon and Patch note that these mental characteristics of the ego are fundamentally determined at birth, but are subject to the experiences and vicissitudes of life. Physical health, stimulating activity, and joyous feelings increase their potential, while physical distress, impoverished environments, and depression decrease them. I would add that adverse situations, particularly when pervasive over an extended period of time, can lead to depression which will impact markedly on all of the ego strengths, however strong they may be. Still, if we assume that all human beings in varying degrees have these potentials, we can intervene, whether or not we are clinicians, as a preventive measure, or after the onset of depression, to strengthen these essential prophylactic traits.

Descriptive Analysis of Self-Esteem[73]

Edith Jacobson considered self-esteem in relation to depression, developing a comprehensive descriptive analysis that can be helpful if interpreted broadly. She analyzed the ego-related components of depression as follows (the comments in parentheses are relevant points that I believe should be incorporated in the analysis):

1. *Superego Fear* expressed by guilt, influences feelings, thoughts, and actions. Aggression results when they are not congruent with the ego-ideal. (Anger may result when potential is stifled — potential reflecting the ego ideal.)

2. *Self-Critical Ego Functions* are found as the ego matures. The more immature the ego, the less realistic are ideals, expectations, and goals. The more unattainable, the more vulnerable is self-esteem. (The more critical the ego, the less *realizable* are ideals, expectations, and goals.)

3. *The Ego Ideal* that is within reach stimulates ego activity to live up to it, thus enhancing self-esteem. When the ego-ideal is grandiose, depression is likely. When combined with inadequate talents and insufficient ego strength, feelings of insufficiency may be intolerable. (What others consider grandiose may be stifled possibility. Inadequate talents may be limited opportunity.)

4. *The Ego Function* refers to the degree of success in measuring up to the demands of the ego-ideal, influencing self-esteem. A poorly functioning ego is one that does not meet the requisites of the ego ideal. (It also may reflect realistic frustration.)

5. *The Self-Representation* refers to images of the self. When pathologically developed and distorted, one's self-esteem is lowered accordingly. A distorted body image is put forth as an example of a problematic self-representation. (But distorted body images are common in a youth-oriented culture which glorifies sex symbols. Distortion may be inaccurate and self-defeating without being pathological.)

The Resolution of Ego-State Conflicts[74]

Addressing the restitution of the ego from a "mechanism of depression" perspective, Bibring observes that depression will be alleviated as follows:

1. When narcissistically important goals and objects appear to be again within reach.

2. When the ego recovers from the narcissistic shock by regaining its self-esteem with the help of various recovery mechanisms.

3. When defenses are directed against the affect of depression itself.

4. When narcissistically important goals are altogether relinquished.

5. When narcissistically important goals become sufficiently modified or reduced so as to become realizable.

Bibring also provides the following insight:

> In general, one may say that everything that lowers or paralyzes the ego's self-esteem without changing the narcissistically important aims represents a condition of depression. . . .It is exactly [from] the tension between these highly charged narcissistic aspirations on the one hand, and the ego's acute awareness of its (real and imaginary) helplessness and incapacity to live up to them on the other, that depression results.

The exploration of the ego-ideal is central to this perspective. It may take a good deal of gentle probing, for depressed people may not be aware of their uncommonly strict superegos or of the self-destructiveness of their values. Ego-psychologists suggest bringing the object of loss or the desired goal within reach of the depressed person when possible. Ways of helping people to fulfill their wishes should be explored; when not feasible, their desires may be modified. When goals are totally unrealistic, they may be encouraged to relinquish their impossible dreams. These suggestions are well intentioned and certainly sensible, but the less obvious pitfalls also should be addressed, for the intervention may be as destructive as the underlying cause. If it is the helper who decides what should be pursued, modified, or relinquished, the powerless, discounting conditions that may have presaged the call for help may be replicated. To insist that nondirective therapy precludes such a possibility is not valid. Conversely, constructive suggestions that appear to modify standards, too early on, may diminish the helper's credibility in the eyes of those who take pride in their "high standards" (if aware of them at all), having been praised for them in the past, or at the least enjoined to seek their fruition. As the therapeutic relationship develops, more permissive, humanistic values can be a positive influence in the corrective therapeutic experience.

Gestalt Role Play

The ambivalence of depressed people is likely to be unconscious since denial is their common mechanism of defense. Awareness of the polarities between conflicting ego-states can be created through gestalt role-play techniques. With this method, the past is neither analyzed nor interpreted verbally. The person is encouraged instead to reexperience the past in the present therapeutic situation, an attitude that is in keeping with psychoanalytic practice. This facilitates the disparity between what one says and what one does. The process is accomplished through role plays in which each conflicting idea or action is played out by the individual. When the dialogue progresses without conflict resolution, people eventually reach an impasse. They are then enjoined to stay "stuck" in this "empty space," an uncomfortable, creative zero-point of conflict. The process continues through the stalemate, until sudden insights are revealed or an explosive emotion is expressed; creative solutions emerge that can unite both polarities. They will begin to move toward self-awareness and integration, and they will have done it themselves. No longer dependent, they experience themselves as responsible; the ideal self and the actual self are congruent.

Rational Emotive Therapy

It may at first appear to be improper to adapt interventions from other disciplines to ego-psychology. However, when one considers that the proponents of the newer therapies were all Freudians to begin with, the practice is less suspect. The underlying assumptions have been retained, in part, by these Freudian renegades, and it is the intact component that I am adapting in each case. Their interest in the pragmatic application of insights to treatment fills a void in the more traditional psychoanalytic field. Rational Emotive Therapy (RET) is an appropriate example of such a model of intervention. Concerned with self-perception, RET focuses on irrational cognitions. A confrontative, educational, often facetious tack is taken to help clients gain insight into their unrealistic beliefs. Albert Ellis, the founder of RET, graphically describes depression as a combination of "should-hood" plus "s — thood": not only does the vulnerable person become depressed because she has failed, she is not doing what she *should* be doing, nor is she getting what she *should* be getting from others—love and approval. She is also depressed because she thinks she is weak, unworthy, and despicable for being depressed about it. She *should* be strong and honorable enough to rise above her disappointment, or so she tells herself. Voilà, a full-blown depression based on "shoulds"—all of which are irrational. This irrationality does not reflect pathology; it is simply the conventional norm of thought often supported by the culture itself, upholding impossible ideals and expectations to unsuspecting believers. Depressed people are more likely to try to fit into these cultural norms, however unrealistic the norms may be. From an ego-psychology perspective, they must close the gap between their actual and their ideal ego-states. This is accomplished through RET by lowering unrealistic aspirations and illogical expectations of perfection and need to correspond with social reality and worthy self-representation.[75]

Self-Actualization

Efforts can also be made to actualize the ideal ego-state when feasible, by applying self-actualization principles. Hanna Zack's overview of self-actualization concepts conclude that the personal ideal-of-self consists of three main components: the fulfillment of social needs, psychological needs, and the realization of an ideal existence as conceived by the individual.[76] While the content varies with the person, the structure remains static. Therefore, social needs are universal, but the affiliations that fulfill them will differ. Activities that reflect one's inherent talents and inclinations sustain psychological needs, and valued ideas about ideal ways of living can be actualized within reason. Again, intervention may have to begin with awareness. The destructive direction the depressed person's life has taken must be clarified first, along with their incongruent existence vis-à-vis their ideal-of-self.

Transactional Analysis of Ego-States[77]

The concepts of Transactional Analysis (TA) provide a tool that is readily applicable to an ego-psychology perspective. While Eric Berne, the originator of TA, denied a direct analogy between his Parent-Adult-Child ego-state schema and Freud's structural theory, it is difficult to negate the similarity altogether. Well grounded in theory, TA is both faulted for its semantic gimmickry, and praised because it is so easily understood by people of all ages and backgrounds. It is included as an intervention for the latter reason. Components of the transactional model will be included throughout the book where it is appropriate to the theory being discussed.

Transactional analysis posits three observable ego-states in all human beings; the Parent, the Adult, and the Child (P-A-C). The Parent ego-state is modeled after parental figures and is both critical and nurturant. The Child ego-state retains the free, uninhibited feelings of the two- to five-year-old. This is the natural child. The adaptive child, however, is also present — the child who is fearful, who pleases the internal parent. The Adult ego-state is the objective state, the "computer" that processes the Parent and Child messages, ideally making rational decisions. All three ego-states are important, but the Child is probably the most important. It is the Parent's task to treat the Child with respect and love. The Adult's task is to help meet the Child's needs without getting into trouble (called contamination).

The Parent or Child component can interfere with the Adult and contaminate whatever the person is doing or feeling. For example, a man may think he is acting out of his Adult state, but parental injunctions or childhood insecurities that are still functioning confuse his adult thinking. Trouble looms when any or all of the ego-states become "contaminated" by any other. A major goal, therefore, is to get all three components working well together. One way that ego-states become contaminated is through the individual's basic life position. This is reflected in how one thinks, feels, acts, and relates to others. There are four possibilities: The "I'm OK — You're OK" position is the one we are born with, the uncontaminated position. Life experience unfortunately leads to the depressive positions, "I'm OK — You're Not OK," and more commonly, "I'm Not OK — You're OK." According to TA theorists, this last position is the result of an internal dialogue between the critical Parent and the adaptive Child ego-states, wherein the parental injunction "Don't be OK" is obeyed. The dialogue is called an "old memory tape" from childhood, when the real child felt powerless and was discounted. Depression is perceived as a "cover feeling," a facade masking one's disallowed true feelings which, according to TA theorists, can only be mad, sad, glad, or scared. Hence, it is a "racket" that represents early adaptive behavior that is no longer functional. It is called "blue stamp collecting." TA differentiates depression, which is perceived as a racket (a defensive posture), from existential despair. The latter is considered an Adult ego-state based on the reality of human finiteness, and the authentic adult response to the fact that one will not be rescued from ultimate death. Such despair is perceived to be part of the human condition, an experience shared by all people.

Interventions include structural analysis — the analysis of the observable Parent-Adult-Child ego functions from three information sources: the behavior of the client, the emotional reaction of the therapist, and the opinion of the client. Just as the ego-state is the unit of ego-structural analysis, so the transaction, the exchange between people, is the unit of transactional analysis. Therefore, how one relates to others is assessed relative to uncrossed and crossed transactions between P-A-C states. Development of the ability to choose appropriate, complementary transactions is important to full functioning. Figures 2-1a and 2-1b illustrate uncrossed (simple) and crossed transactions.

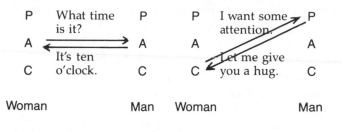

Figure 2-1a. Uncrossed (simple) transactions.

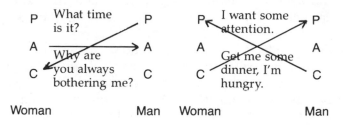

Figure 2-1b. Crossed transactions.

Note that uncrossed transactions are viable even when they are not Adult-to-Adult exchanges. Conscious executive functioning by the Adult ego-state is the key. When the Adult *chooses* to act out of Parent or Child ego-state, such action is valid. Activation of the Parent or Child ego-states when they are inappropriate is a contamination of the Adult. The analysis and practice regarding improved interactions is particularly relevant to depressed clients whose communication skills are lacking, a not-uncommon occurrence.[78]

Redecision Therapy

Depression therapy also involves the redecision to take an I'm OK — You're OK life position. A young man's recognition that he can choose to manage his life and responsibly care for others (two basic tasks of maturity) is inherent in this decision. So, too, is the reevaluation of his "life script" — his life plan. TA therapists, like ego-psychologists, believe that one's life script is decided in the early years, setting the stage for future roles. By examining Parent messages and Child feelings, a script can be assessed. Karpman's Drama Triangle, described in detail in the Life Events Models chapter (Chapter 4) in relation to role theory, is a helpful diagnostic tool. The drama triangle is a script in which one may take the persecutor role, move to the rescuer, and then to the victim role. As a rule, one role is favored, and for the depressed person, the victim role wins out. Our young man can get out of the triangle by focusing on his Adult ego-state, thus neutralizing his anger, and consciously deciding against either of the role positions. If any one role is played out, you can be sure that the remaining two will eventually be chosen. The client can choose an I'm OK — You're OK position in their stead, and depression games will no longer be necessary. The Parent ego-state will be free of demanding "shoulds," becoming primarily nurturant, the Child ego-state will be playful and also free of the critical parent, and the Adult will be rational, factual, and clear as to its ideals. Such "decontamination" will restore the individual to healthy maturity.[79] Those who would like a more in-depth understanding of transactional analysis can refer to the notes for additional reading on the subject. Patricia Palmer, for instance, has developed excellent materials for children and adolescents.[80] Because the language of TA is so easily understandable, it is particularly recommended for work with these populations.

Building the Depressed (Normal or Impaired) Child's Ego

Historically, there has been a general (though not unanimous) agreement in the psychoanalytic literature that depression does not occur in children. Arguments against its existence, while often scholarly and persuasive, do not reflect the abundance of clinical reports to the contrary.[81] Many ego-psychologists solve the dilemma by giving different labels to symptoms in children, or by expanding the label "depression" to cover a broader range of "illness." By so doing, stringent opinions can be bypassed regarding, for example, the possibility or impossibility of childhood mourning or guilt and their necessary presence for accurate diagnosis of depression. Others are coming to the conclusion that clinical observations must be respected and theory appropriately revised when so clearly discordant. Taking the position that depression does exist in children, I recommend ego-related intervention for those who may be concerned with the problem of depression in normal children or in those whose problems are compounded by impairment.

Helping severely depressed children may require a long-term and in-depth ego-building approach to treatment. Adolph Christ developed a method of working with brain-damaged children that can be readily adapted to "neurophysiologically normal" depressed youth.[82] Depression in children is often masked as hyperactivity or delinquency, and those who are diagnosed as learning-disabled or mentally retarded also are likely candidates. Therapy includes providing direct, concrete information, supportiveness, and reality interpretation. Insight will vary, of course, according to the stage of cognitive development. Treatment is divided into four phases: (1) the development of rapport; (2) the development of workable defense mechanisms; (3) exploration; and (4) clarification of defects and termination.

First, the problems for which the child has been referred are spelled out so that he knows what the therapist knows. Next, the child's strengths and skills are explored with interest and respect. He should not be confronted when defensively grandiose and disdainful of those who lose (as opposed to winning) or who are not as knowledgeable as himself. As rapport is established, these defenses will tend to give way. The strengthening and development of workable defenses are essential for all chidren, and especially for those who are impaired. Denial usually predominates in these children and its failure may exacerbate depression. In any case, it is painful and provokes anxiety.

Defenses such as displacement, rationalization, and intellectualization are built into the therapeutic situation. For example, Christ notes that displacement is encouraged by referring to similar feelings in others, such as "Lots of people feel angry when that happens." Rationalization might be enhanced by suggesting, "Maybe your teacher just had her own problems and wasn't really angry with you that day." Intellectualization may be furthered by explaining: "Racing around like that is called hyperactivity." The process — whatever the defense — is gradual and repetitious. The goal is to build defenses that are more workable than denial or projection.[83]

After weeks or even months of ego-building via defenses, the emphasis should turn to control of the child's own reactions. Reality assessment becomes the ego-building focus. Gradual clarification and acceptance of his "normal" problems precede the acceptance of any special impairments he may have. Christ points out that the process is particularly painful for physically handicapped children because their identities may be closely tied to their defects. With the help of the therapist and other significant people, misperceptions are reinterpreted and self-perceptions are markedly improved.

Children should be allowed to return to counseling as new developmental tasks arise. Termination, of necessity, is considered to be indefinite. Cognitive defects, emotional ability, and fragile defenses remain for those who are severely impaired, however successful the therapy relative to depression may be.

OBJECT-RELATIONS THEORY PREVENTION AND INTERVENTION

For object-relations theorists, the most contemporary of the psychoanalytic models, depression is usually related to conflicts between the child and the significant caretaker during the third year of development, although early infancy may be a critical period as well.

Transference Considerations

Transference problems in depressed clients are considered to be especially critical. Difficulties range from resistance and spurious success to premature termination of treatment and more severe depression. The problems are serious enough to alarm therapists, even to a point where they may prefer to avoid depressed patients. Object-relations theory has provided some insight that may demystify the process and alleviate tension. Typically, depressed persons are depleted by the continuous denial of their own and the world's values. They defensively turn to the real object world in order to resolve their inner conflicts. The love of another (the ideal object image) is used as a stimulant for their failing ability to love. In the treatment situation, all available libido is poured into the therapist as love object. Their appeal is desperate, made in order to receive convincing evidence of love, power, and value so as to evoke a libidinal response, enabling them to feel worthwhile. The dynamic is played out in the treatment situation, where the depressed person exhausts him or herself by masochistic submission to the therapist, expecting omnipotent love in return. How this transference situation is handled is crucial, for the therapist cannot live up to such impossible expectations, and the client may become increasingly hostile in response to growing disappointment.

At the same time, the client is less able, as the therapeutic relationship unfolds, to tolerate the therapist's human warmth and sympathy. Only uninvolved distance on the client's part can protect him from deflating the love object. He must insure that the therapist stay unattainable at the same time that every effort is made to win over the object of love. The double-bind conflict intensifies as the client denies his own value in order not to derogate the therapist. This is an imperative position for the client whose self-representation is an infantile, helpless self who draws strength from a powerful, ideal love object. Any indication that this is an illusory estimation of either party can result in depression in this no-win, zero-sum game. The client's existence depends on an all-powerful love object that provides life. Yet, the client's fraudulent self-esteem is contingent on disparaging the glorified object. An immediate and intense need to regress to a worthless position causes the client to be overperceptive of his own flaws and weaknesses, while reinstating the value and strength of the love object. Humility and the therapist's glorification thus see-saw precariously with self-pretention and denigration of the therapist.[84] While this dynamic is usually attributed to manic-depressives, I have taken the opportunity to detail the phenomenon because it also can reflect the severely depressed person's pattern of relating. When engaged in the process, both client and therapist can be nonplussed in the absence of theoretical insights. Interpretation is important to both depression resolution and prevention, for ego strengths increase as primitive defensives are confronted effectively.

A supportive stance must be taken while the possibility of sexual encouragement, a particular vulnerability when transference is in full swing, must be guarded against. Certainly, the goal of treatment is not just to acquire understanding of the destructive nature of one's relationships; one must also practice giving and receiving warmth in an unthreatening atmosphere where the limitations of both client and therapist can coexist without danger. The process can be frightening to a person who has never experienced healthy separation-individuation in tandem with a warm, supportive relationship.

Catalyzing Ego Organization

According to Gertrude Blanck and Rubin Blanck, experts on Mahler's work, it is theoretically incorrect to speak of the treatment of depression, since depression is an affective state.[85] The ego that is experiencing the depressive affect is treated instead. Others argue that such personification of the ego is an example of reification of theoretical terms. With such reservations in mind, techniques that are conceptualized as enhancing ego-building are appropriate interventions. The principle role of the object-relations therapist is that of catalyst of ego-organization. As in psychodynamic therapy, the uniqueness of the therapist's personality is minimized, and the atmosphere is optimally benign and reliably consistent. In this model, though, the therapist is not a parent figure; the therapeutic situations must not replicate the stereotyped, programmed expectations of the client in the interest of a new positive growth experience. The adult client has internalized and retained early malformations of the ego, continuing growth in a necessarily distorted direction. To take on the parental role would only promote this dysfunction. Instead, the client's reorganizing capacity has to be facilitated. In order to correct the malformation without destroying the fragile organizational structure that exists, the therapist must avoid responding to provocation, thereby correcting distorted expectations. Blanck and Blanck detail a number of interventive strategies. Those considered relevant to depression are included here.[86]

Differentiation of Affect

An appropriate ego-building technique is the differentiation of affect, for depressed people often are not aware of the differences between their feelings of anger, sadness, anxiety, and fear. Practicing such awareness can lead to increased self-esteem. As clarified feelings are recognized and accepted as understandable human reactions, self-acceptance follows.

Repair of Splitting

The repair of splitting is essential. Clients must be helped to understand how they have split the "good" and the "bad," the positive and negative aspects of both self and other. In exploring this phenomenon, the therapist should focus on the organizational malformations (such as the splitting process) rather than on the client's behavioral responses, thus avoiding defensive confrontation. This is especially important in relation to the depressed person's anger, a problem that is dealt with in a unique way by object-relations theorists. They insist that the ventilation of aggression is undersirable until "good" self and "good" object representations have been developed. Only then, when the ego is strengthened, can it tolerate the reality of "badness" as well.

Only then is the anger sufficiently neutralized to be constructively available to the ego. This is a crucial point in the treatment of borderline clients who are most likely to have permeable ego-boundaries, unable to differentiate between themselves and others. (Anger is discussed further in the sections of this chapter on Classical Psychoanalytic Prevention and Intervention and on Women at Risk.) If Blatt's conceptualization of depression is correct, the problem of anger is especially critical for the depressed client, despite the fact that the expression of hostility in itself does not necessarily lessen symptoms.[87] Object-relations theory provides another explanation for the phenomenon.

The therapist must assess the degree to which the client is separated and individuated since those who are relatively undifferentiated are in the greatest danger when expressing anger. The "bad" object *is* the self, so both could be destroyed by overt rage. The therapist-client relationship, by analogy, can also be destroyed. Hence, aggression, however righteous, must be neutralized before its full expression can be allowed in the treatment situation. This is facilitated by creating over time a "cushion" of positive experiences between client and therapist. When the going is rough, there will be something to fall back on.

Assessment of Separateness[88]

The degree of separateness can be evaluated within the therapeutic relationship by assessing the client's availability, distance, mutuality, and extreme closeness in relation to the therapist, who must also evaluate whether the client seems to take for granted that the therapist's opinions are identical to his or her own, indicating a degree of undifferentiation. The therapist may also address the dysfunctional need for approval by asking him or herself what it is that the client is doing to keep the therapist "interested." This reflects the general pattern used to please others, translated by the life message, "I can be given to only if I... "[89] Once rapport is established, discussion can focus on the observation. Clients can be encouraged to take an active role in their therapy by inviting recognition of those things that satisfy their needs. This aids in the development of a "self-soothing" capacity that is often lacking in depressed clients. They can ask themselves how close or how separate they wish to be in order to be most comfortable with the therapist, and by having their wishes fulfilled within ethical reason, they learn to soothe themselves, rather than looking to others to meet their needs. These therapeutic methods are designed to advance and strengthen ego-development.

Because growth is a lifelong spiralling process in which no development era is ever totally relinquished, everyone is psychologically pulled toward earlier phases. No matter what their stage of development, therefore, all people may show indications of separation-individuation ambivalence. Blatt's conceptualization should be kept in mind in order to evaluate the degree to which the process is problematic for depressed clients. While relevant research is limited, it is promising. The therapist can help the client accept therapy as a time-limited separation experience, coming together and separating at each session, and finally at termination. As the therapeutic process evolves, separation-individuation becomes the central theme.[90]

In truth, relatively little has been written concerning depression intervention based on psychoanalytic theory in general, or in regard to object-relations theory in particular. Consequently, it is not unusual to find that psychotherapists often apply definitive techniques from outside the psychoanalytic field when conceptually appropriate,[91] along with insight therapy. To illustrate: the transformation of negative self-concepts lends itself to Beck's cognitive therapy. Should the object-relations practitioner wish to apply the model, it is important to avoid doing so superficially. Cognitive-behavioral principles must be incorporated into the treatment plan in order to increase the possibility of successful behavior change. Insight alone will not suffice, as Freud himself discovered. Chapter 6, on Cognitive-Behavioral Theories, provides direction.

COMMENTARY ON PSYCHOANALYTIC TREATMENT

Psychoanalytic treatment is based upon the principle of psychic determinism whereby each psychic event is determined by preceding events, and upon the theory of the unconscious which stipulates that unconscious mental processes cause confused and unobjective reactions to life. These underlying assumptions are congruent with the concept of nondirective therapy. Although some orthodox psychoanalytic clinicians support such a concept, most do not, and it should be remembered that the attitudes of all therapists, whether spoken or unspoken, influence the client. Biases, for example, can stem from countertransference, the feelings that the therapist may develop toward the client because that client represents a significant person from the therapist's own past. For this reason, practitioners are encouraged to explore their own values, assumptions, and beliefs.

There are times when such values are inherent in the theoretical framework itself. For example, critics of psychoanalytic theorists fault them for concentrating on intrapsychic conflicts. Freudians maintain that their focus is psychological because desires and prohibitions are internalized in maturity. Regardless of their origin in the external world, they argue, they become part of one's psychic structure. While the reasoning is clear, the problems perpetuated by ignoring social causality and the extrabiological world may offset the rationale. If psychoanalysts are correct in their belief in the overwhelming parental influence on the child (especially that of the mother), then the forces impacting on her well-being have far-reaching implications. In fact, the more problematic the mother's psyche the less likely it is that she can withstand external stresses without having a negative impact on her child. Psychoanalytic theory can encompass attention to larger environmental influences when warranted, at least in terms of the prevention or exacerbation of destructive conditions. The influence of significant others, in fact, is included in the theory. Delineation of whom significant others may encompass is the point of contention.

Freud was an observer of human behavior par excellence. While he and his followers are often criticized for adhering primarily to uncontrolled clinical observations, as more contemporary, well-researched models are explicated, their consistency with Freudian ideas often becomes clear. Freud's keen observations in regard to depression have been narrowly interpreted, even by himself, because of his emphasis on loss and his lack of attention to the larger social environment. It is helpful to focus on these observations that he did not pursue because he simply could not give equal attention to everything, or because of his blatant misogynist values. For example, note that he includes "lacking in independence" as a prime characteristic of depressed persons (usually women even in Freud's day). Subsequent psychoanalytic theorists have focused their attention on just such a lack, positing helplessness, hopelessness, and resentment as correlates of dependence. Might it be that depressed persons' accurate awareness of their inadequacies leads them to ambivalent anger? As ego-psychologists point out, they are torn between coercive rage and submissive fear of others, but their rage and fear are also directed at their own dependence. Self-esteem can never flourish under such conditions and, as Freud observed, there will be an attitude of revolt. It may be that their ambivalence stems from the healthy part of their psyches which insists upon revolt against unhealthy subservience. The therapist can support clients in this constructive revolt. This may be an appropriate focus for many clients who are dysfunctionally dependent. They can be helped to decide for themselves what changes they will make, what situations they will accept, and how they will choose to develop themselves more fully. Their revolution may be nature's evolution in action. It must be remembered that Freud's view of women as inferior beings has never been substantiated. Indeed, their strengths have proven to be notable.[92]

Cross-Cultural Implications

To date, most of the work of psychoanalytic theorists has focused on the white, middle-class child and the subphases of undifferentiation and separation in relation to the mother as primary object. Third World children generally have been excluded from study and fathers have been largely ignored. Mahler's extensive observational research, for example, included interviews with fathers only once or twice a year, while mother-child observations were a daily occurrence. The questions asked and answers arrived at, therefore, must be assessed in the light of these limitations. Individuation, conceptualized as a quality of differentiation from the object relation, generally considered to be the mother, may profit from a broader interpretation. It may be, for example, that a reintegration of Carl Jung's definition of individuation as differentiation from the general, collective psychology could enrich object-relations theory. This concept speaks to the uniqueness of the individual personality vis-à-vis the universe, not just in relation to the significant caretaker. In order to explore this notion within object-relations theory, the ongoing development of adults as well as of children will have to be investigated across cultures and across sex dimensions.[93]

As a start, Dorcas Bowles' object-relations conceptualization of the development of ethnic self-representations provides ripe possibilities.[94] She suggests that the black child's ethnic sense of self is an additional developmental step negotiated directly following rapprochement. Negative parental and societal responses to the child's blackness can lead to the internalization of a negative ethnic self-representation. Bowles warns that the seeds of future pathology are sown in the process. I suggest that the experience is often played out in depression, sometimes in childhood, more often in adolescence and adulthood. While Bowles refers only to blacks, her concepts can be generalized to other ethnic groups. Parents, she suggests, must continue to serve as auxilliary egos for their children, incorporating positive images about their heritage through adolescence. Issues that have been dormant will be reawakened at that time, requiring and affording another opportunity for working through. Therapists can provide the same function. Whenever possible, the clinician should be of the same race as the developing client to ensure congruent ethnic representation.

NOTES

1. Freud, Sigmund, *Complete Psychological Works*, standard edition, trans. James Strachey, 24 vols. (New York: Hogarth Press, 1953–1966).

2. Mendelson, Meyer, *Psychoanalytic Concepts of Depression*, 2nd ed. (New York: Spectrum Publications, Inc., 1974).

3. See Chapter 3, "Energy Theories," for conceptual frameworks that extend Freud's ideas regarding energy and depression.

4. Solomon, Phillip, and Vernon D. Patch, *Handbook of Psychiatry* (Los Altos, CA: Lange Medical Publications, 1974).

5. Chodoff, Paul, "The Core Problem of Depression: Interpersonal Aspects," in *Science and Psychoanalysis*, Vol. 27 (New York: Grune and Stratton, 1970).

6. Abraham, Karl, "Notes on the Psychoanalytic Investigation and Treatment of Manic-Depressive Insanity and Allied Conditions" (1911), in *Selected Papers on Psychoanalysis* (New York: Basic Books, 1960), pp. 137–156.

7. Freud, Sigmund, "Mourning and Melancholia" (1917) in *Collected Papers*, Vol. 4 (London: Hogarth Press, 1956).

8. Fenichel, Otto, "The Ego and the Affects," in *The Collected Papers of Otto Fenichel*, Vol. 2 (New York: W. W. Norton, 1954), pp. 215–227.

9. Freud, Sigmund, "Mourning and Melancholia" (1917) in *Collected Papers*, Vol. 4 (London: Hogarth Press, 1956).

10. Rado, Sandor, "Psychodynamics of Depression from the Etiologic Point of View," *Psychosomatic Medicine* 13(1951): 51–55.

11. Mendelson, Meyer, *Psychoanalytic Concepts of Depression*, 2nd ed. (New York: Spectrum Publications, 1974).

12. Bibring, Edward, "Mechanisms of Depression," in *Affective Disorders*, ed. Phyllis Greenacre (New York: International Universities Press, 1953).

13. Lindemann, Eugene, "Psychosocial Factors as Stressor Agents," in *Stress and Psychiatric Disorders*, ed. J. Tanner (Oxford: Blackwell, 1960), pp. 13–16.

14. DeRosis, Helen, and Victoria Pellagrino, *The Book of Hope* (New York: Bantam Books, 1977).

15. Hirschfeld, Robert, et al., "Dependency — Self-Esteem — Clinical Depression," *Journal of the American Academy of Psychoanalysis* 4 3 (1976): 373–388.

16. Gaylin, Willard, *The Meaning of Despair* (New York: Science House, 1968).

17. Arieti, Silvano, and Jules Bemporad, *Severe and Mild Depression: The Psychotherapeutic Approach* (New York: Basic Books, 1978).

18. See the section on social roles in Chapter 4, and Chapter 5 for discussions regarding the need for approval.

19. Fox, Henry, "Neurotic Resentment and Dependence Overseas," *Psychiatry 8*, 2 (1945): 131–138.

20. See also Chapter 5, "The Person-Environment Model," for a psychosocial interpretation of these ideas, and Chapter 6, "Cognitive-Behavioral Theories," for discussions of negative cognitions.

21. Kohut, Heinz, and Eugene Wolf, "The Disorders of the Self and Their Treatment: An Outline," *International Journal of Psychoanalysis*, 59, 1978, 413 – 424.

22. Jacobson, Edith, *Depression: Comparative Studies of Normal, Neurotic, and Psychotic Conditions* (New York: International Universities Press, 1971).

23. Kernberg, Otto, *Internal World and External Reality* (New York: Jason Aronson, 1980).

24. Mahler, Margaret S., Fred Pine, and Anni Bergman, *The Psychological Birth of the Human Infant* (New York: Basic Books, 1975).

25. Hirschfeld, Robert, Gerald L. Klerman, Paul Chodoff, Sheldon Korchin, and James Barrett, "Dependency—Self-Esteem—Clinical Depression," *Journal of the American Academy of Psychoanalysis* 4,3 (1976): 373 – 388.

26. Mahler, Margaret S., Fred Pine, and Anni Bergman, *The Psychological Birth of the Human Infant* (New York: Basic Books, 1975).

27. Jacobson, Edith, *Depression: Comparative Studies of Normal, Neurotic, and Psychotic Conditions* (New York: International Universities Press, 1971).

28. Spitz, Rene, "Anaclitic Depression," *Psychoanalytic Study of the Child 2* (1946): 313 – 341.

29. Blatt, Sidney J., "Levels of Object Representation in Anaclitic and Introjective Depression," *The Psycholanalytic Study of the Child 29* (1974): 107 – 157.

30. Note the similarity with Arieti and Bemporad's (1976) interpretation of depression.

31. Frank, Margaret Galdston, Workshop on "Psychoanalytic Developmental Psychology: Application to Social Work Practice," Dallas, TX, March 1 – 2, 1980.

32. Freud, Anna, "The Concept of Developmental Lines," in *The Psychoanalytic Study of the Child*, Vol. 18 (New York: International Universities Press, 1963), pp. 245 – 265.

33. Parens, Henri, and Leon Saul, Jr., *Dependence in Man* (New York: International Universities Press, 1971).

34. See also Chapter 5, "The Person-Environment Model," for further elaboration on dependence, independence, and the environment.

35. Freud, Sigmund, "Female Sexuality" (1931), in *Collected Papers*, Vol. 5 (London: Hogarth Press, 1956), pp. 252 – 272.

36. Freud, Sigmund, "Some Psychological Consequences of the Anatomical Distinction Between the Sexes" (1925), in *Collected Papers*, Vol. 5 (London: Hogarth Press, 1956), pp. 186 – 197.

37. Freud, Sigmund, "Analysis Terminable and Interminable" (1927), in *Collected Papers*, Vol. 5 (London: Hogarth Press, 1956), pp. 355 – 357.

38. Horney, Karen, *Feminine Psychology* (New York: Norton, 1973).

39. Sherman, Julia, *On the Psychology of Women: A Survey of Empirical Studies* (Springfield, IL: C. C. Thomas, 1971): See also the "Social Role" section of Chapter 4, and Chapter 5 for discussion of dependence.

40. Freud, Sigmund, "Mourning and Melancholia"(1917) in *Collected Papers*, Vol. 4 (London: Hogarth Press, 1956).

41. Berger, Peter L., and Thomas Luckmann, *The Social Construction of Reality* (Garden City, NY: Doubleday, 1967).

42. Berk, Richard, Sara Berk, and Catherine Berheide, "The Non-Division of Household Labor," *Science Monographs* (NIMH, DHEW Pub. No. [ADM], 1978), pp. 78 – 660.

43. Curtis, Jean, *Working Mothers* (New York: Doubleday, 1976), p. 75.

44. Wetzel, Janice Wood, "Depression and Dependence Upon Unsustaining Environments," *Clinical Social Work Journal 6*,2 (Summer 1978): 75 – 89; see also Wetzel, Janice Wood, "The Work Environment and Depression: Implications for Intervention," in *Toward Human Dignity: Social Work in Practice*, ed. John W. Hanks (National Association of Social Workers, 1978), pp. 236 – 245.

45. See also Chapter 5 for further discussion of women, work, and the family.

46. Arieti, Silvano, and Jules Bemporad, *Severe and Mild Depression: The Psychotherapeutic Approach* (New York: Basic Books, 1978).

47. See Chapter 6 for further discussion of cognitive constructs.

48. See Pauline Bart's interpretation of Role Theory in Chapter 4, and Alexander Lowen's Bioenergetics in Chapter 3.

49. Arieti, Silvano, and Jules Bemporad, *Severe and Mild Depression: The Psychotherapeutic Approach* (New York: Basic Books, 1978).

50. Freud, Sigmund, "Mourning and Melancholia," (1917) in *Collected Papers*, Vol. 4 (London: Hogarth Press, 1956), p. 153; see also Gertrude Blanck, and Rubin Blanck, *Ego Psychology II: Psychoanalytic Developmental Psychology* (New York: Columbia University Press, 1979).

51. Edinger, Edward F., "Being an Individual," in *Ego and the Archetype* (New York: G. P. Putnam's Sons, 1972), pp. 157 – 178.

52. Blatt, Sidney J., "Levels of Object Representation in Anaclitic and Introjective Depression," *The Psycholanalytic Study of the Child 29* (1974): 107 – 157.

53. Chodorow, Nancy, *The Reproduction of Mothering: Psychoanalysis and the Sociology of Gender* (Berkeley: University of California Press, 1978).

54. Blatt, Sidney J., Steven Wein, Eve Chevron, and Donald Quinlan, "Parental Representations and Depression in Normal Young Adults," *Journal of Abnormal Psychology 88*,4 (1979): 388 – 397.

55. See also Chapter 5 for a discussion of dependence and women.

56. See also Chapter 7 for a discussion of nothingness and women from a positive perspective.

57. See also Chapter 7 for further discussion of women's qualities in relation to the world.

58. Chevron, Eve, Donald Quinlan, and Sidney J. Blatt, "Sex Roles and Gender Differences in the Experience of Depression," *Journal of Abnormal Psychology 87*,6 (1978): 680 – 683.

59. Baumrind, Diana, "New Directions in Socialization Research," *American Psychologist 35*,7 (July 1980): 639 – 652.

60. Miller, Jean Baker, *Toward a New Psychology of Women* (Boston: Beacon Press, 1976), p. 71; see also Dorothy Dinnerstein, *The Mermaid and the Minotaur* (New York: Harper and Row, 1976); Adrienne Rich, *Of Woman Born: Motherhood as Experience and Institution* (New York: Bantam Books, 1977); "Toward a Feminist Theory of Motherhood," *Feminist Studies 4*, 2 (Special Issue) (June 1978); Sara Ruddick, "Maternal Thinking," *Feminist Studies 6*,2 (Summer 1980): 342 – 367; Nancy Chodorow, *The Reproduction of Mothering: Psychoanalysis and the Sociology of Gender* (Berkeley: University of California Press, 1978); Carol Gilligan, *In a Different Voice: Psychological Theory and Women's Development* (Cambridge: Harvard University Press, 1982).

61. Flax, Jane, "The Conflict Between Nurturance and Autonomy in Mother-Daughter Relationships and Within Feminism," *Feminist Studies* 4 (June 1978): 171 – 189.

62. Singer, June, *Androgeny: Toward a New Theory of Sexuality* (New York: Anchor Books, 1977).

63. Rich, Adrienne, *Diving into the Wreck* (New York: W. W. Norton, 1973); see also Carol P. Christ, *Diving Deep and Surfacing* (Boston: Beacon Press, 1980).

64. See also the discussion of the "Shadow," according to Jung, in Chapter 7.

65. See the discussion regarding masculinity and femininity found in the "Social Role" section of Chapter 4; also refer to Chapter 9 for further discussion of the mother-child relationship.

66. Clayton, Paula J., James A. Holikas, and William L. Maurice, "The Depression of Widowhood," *American Journal of Psychiatry* 20 (1972): 71 – 78.

67. Lindemann, Erich, and Elizabeth Lindemann, *Beyond Grief: Studies in Crisis Intervention* (New York: Aronson, 1979), see also Chapter 4 for further discussion of loss and loneliness.

68. Golan, Naomi, *Passing Through Transitions*, (New York: Free Press, 1981).

69. Weissman, Myrna M., and Eugene Paykel, *The Depressed Woman* (Chicago: University of Chicago Press, 1974).

70. See Chapter 6 for a discussion of Learned Helplessness.

71. Refer to Catalyzing Ego Organization in the section on Object Relations Theory in this chapter for a unique perspective that cautions against the early expression of hostility in disturbed clients.

72. Solomon, Phillip, and Vernon D. Patch, *Handbook of Psychiatry* (Los Altos, CA: Lange Medical Publications, 1974).

73. Jacobson, Edith, *Depression: Comparative Studies of Normal, Neurotic, and Psychotic Conditions (New York: International Universities Press, 1971).*

74. Bibring, Edward, "Mechanisms of Depressions," in *Affective Disorders*, ed. Phyllis Greenacre (New York: International Universities Press, 1953).

75. Ellis, Albert, and Robert A. Harper, *A New Guide to Rational Living* (North Hollywood, CA: Wilshire Book Co., 1975); see the section on Rational Emotive Therapy in Chapter 6.

76. Zacks, Hanna, "Self-Actualization: A Midlife Problem," *Social Casework* 61,4 (April 1980): 223 – 233.

77. Berne, Eric, *Games People Play: The Psychology of Human Relationships* (New York: Grove Press, 1964).

78. See Chapter 6 for further discussion of communication skills.

79. See the "Social Role" section of Chapter 4 for a Karpman Drama Triangle diagram and further discussion concerning roles and depression.

80. Palmer, Patricia, *The Mouse, The Monster and Me* (San Luis Obispo, CA: Impact Publications, 1977).

81. Welner, Zila, "Childhood Depression: An Overview," *Journal of Nervous and Mental Disease* 166,8 (August 1978): 588 – 593; also refer to Meyer Mendelson, *Psychoanalytic Concepts of Depression*, 2nd ed. (New York: Spectrum, 1974), for detailed discussion of the issue concerning depression in children; also see Chapter 1 for the demographics of depression.

82. Christ, Adolph, "Psychotherapy of the Child with True Brain Damage," *American Journal of Orthopsychiatry* 48,3 (July 1978): 505 – 515.

83. See Solomon and Patch, *Handbook of Psychiatry*, for a comprehensive and concise discussion of defense mechanisms.

84. Jacobson, Edith. *Depression: Comparative Studies of Normal, Neurotic, and Psychotic Conditions.* New York: International Universities Press, 1971; see also Robert R. Holt, ed., "Motives and Thought: Psychoanalytic Essays in Honor of David Rapaport," *Psychological Issues,* Vols. 18/19 (New York: International Universities Press, 1967).

85. Blanck, Gertrude, and Rubin Blanck, *Ego Psychology: Theory and Practice* (New York: Columbia University Press, 1974).

86. Blanck, Gertrude, and Rubin Blanck, *Ego Psychology II: Psychoanalytic Developmental Psychology* (New York: Columbia University Press, 1979).

87. Refer to "Anaclitic and Introjective Depression" in the section on Object Relations Theory and Depression in this chapter.

88. Frank, Margaret Galdston, Workshop on "Psychoanalytic Developmental Psychology: Application to Social Work Practice," Dallas, TX, March 1–2, 1980.

89. Note the similarity to the concept of Life Scripts and Transactional Analysis in the section on Ego-Psychology Prevention and Intervention in this chapter.

90. Taft, Jesse, "A Conception of the Growth Process Underlying Social Casework Practice," *Social Casework* (October 1950), pp. 1–11; see also Chapter 6.

91. See Meyer Mendelson, *Psychoanalytic Concepts of Depression (New York; Spectrum, 1974)* for further discussion of Cognitive Therapy from a psychoanalytic perspective.

92. Wetzel, Janice Wood, "Female Elders—America's Invisible Strength," Presidential Theme Paper presented at the Mid-America Congress on Aging, St. Louis, Missouri, April 14–16, 1982.

93. Developmental research on aging is in process, 1984); Also see Chapter 9 for further discussion of Jung's ideas on the subject of individuation.

94. Bowles, Dorcas D., *The Development of the Ethnic Self-Representation Unit within the Self-Representation,* Unpublished manuscript, Smith College School for Social Work, Northampton, MA, March 26, 1981.

Chapter 3
Energy Theories

I celebrate myself, and sing myself,
and what I assume you shall assume,
For every atom belonging to me
as good belongs to you.
　　　Walt Whitman, "Song of Myself"

The amount of energy available in the universe has been fixed since time began and always shall remain so.[1] Both ancient Eastern philosophers and contemporary physical and social scientists in the Western world agree that energy is the basis of life and of human culture. Easterners believe that major organs are interconnected by energy pathways, or meridians, that run up and down both sides of the body. Depression is caused by disharmony created by the disruption of this energy flow. The equation of life and energy in oriental cultures, and those influenced by them, encompass many seemingly disparate Western philosophies. For example, Sigmund Freud described libido as the sexually pleasurable and vital energy force that motivates human beings[2] in contrast to Carl Jung's broader interpretation of libido as life energy.[3] Wilhelm Reich also deviated from Freud's position while retaining his sexual focus, concluding that emotional health is maintained through the prevention of accumulated tension.[4] Reich claimed that this is accomplished through the release of excess energy in sexual orgasm. Alexander Lowen synthesized the viewpoints of these renowned social scientists, thereby creating bioenergetics, the study of personality in terms of the energetic processes of the body.[5] It is ironic that the bulk of relevant interest today remains with energy theorists, while many more closely allied followers of Freud have discarded the notion of psychic energy.

This chapter will begin by addressing the phenomena from the perspective of thermodynamics,[6] adopting the principles to the problem of depression. Here, the depressed person is viewed as one whose energy is diffused and dissipated. The Conservation-Withdrawal Reaction Model focuses on depression as a basic organismic reaction pattern. It is established in childhood at a time when it is adaptive to withdraw energy when the child is unable to cope with overwhelming feelings. As a defense against anxiety later in life, the response becomes depressive.[7,8] Bioenergetics, the most comprehensive of the energy theories, focuses on the redirection of energies. Depressed people are believed to channel their energies outward, living vicariously through others. Taking responsibility for their own destiny means redirecting misguided energies, since such individuals have sacrificed their independence for the promise of fulfillment by others. A general depletion of energy is not only common to these theoretical perspectives, it is an experiential reality for all depressed people.

THE LAWS OF THERMODYNAMICS[9]

Everything is made of energy, yet energy cannot be created or destroyed. One can only transform it from one state to another. This is the first law of the physicist's concept of thermodynamics. The second law states that a penalty is exacted every time energy is transformed from one state to another. The penalty is called entropy, and it is a measure of the amount of energy that is no longer capable of being converted into work. Work can only occur when energy moves from a higher to a lower level of concentration. Every time this process takes place, it means that there is less available or free energy; a portion of the energy becomes unavailable, or bound. When there is no longer free energy available to perform work, entropy has reached a maximum, the state of equilibrium which is death. The entropy law further explains that all energy in a closed system (like the earth) moves from an ordered to a disordered state. In the maximum entropy state, available energy has been totally dissipated and diffused. While the law remains fixed in the universe, human beings can exercise free will in the determination of the speed by which the entropy process moves toward death. To prevent dissipating to an equilibrium state, a constant flow of free energy from the larger environment is required. For people, free energy flow is the primary concern, for they are part of an open system rather than a closed one. Since the equilibrium state means death, living things feed off the available energy around them to maintain and prolong life.

While thermodynamics does not govern social phenomena, it does set the stage.[10] It is not too far afield to hypothesize a connection between thermodynamic principles and depression. It may be that depressed persons are those who do not have, or are not allowed to have, a high concentration of available energy for their own functioning. Their energy is diffused and dissipated; they are not ordered or focused in their own development.

The notion of equilibrium may also offer some clues. The concept of homeostasis, a kind of systemic organismic equilibrium, has often been regarded as an adaptive state in the health and mental health fields.[11] Failure of homeostasis is viewed as an antecedent of disease. Might it be that homeostasis is too often translated as equilibrium? Homeostasis may be a state dangerously analogous to the energyless equilibrium of nonliving. Homeostatic balance that is achieved at the cost of compromising one's life may result in depression. It is a warning that a person's energies are being dissipated. Indeed, we are hard put to find a depressed person who does not complain of an overwhelming absence of energy. Motivation to change oneself or situation only comes for some with the disruptive unhappiness of depression. Personal history is much like social history; happiness marks the blank periods and crises mark the inventive ones.[12]

Thermodynamics may provide the broad-based scientific foundation for understanding the dynamics of depression. It may also offer insight into the phenomenon of burnout so common in high-stress helping professions. Burnout is defined as the depletion of positive energy, personal resources, and flexibility to the point where one is psychologically drained. Burnout victims are not only *like* depressed people in that they have no energy left to give,[13] but I believe that they are depressed themselves.

CONSERVATION-WITHDRAWAL REACTION[14]

This model is a comprehensive energy theory of depression based on an extensive body of psychosomatic research and detailed observations of depressed individuals. The work has been developed primarily by George Engel and Arthur Schmale. Conservation-withdrawal reaction is thought to be a psychobiologic state, a basic organismic reaction pattern. It is defined as an automatic adaptive response to anxiety caused by prolonged somatic deprivation and excessive sensory stimulation. Engel and Schmale hypothesize that the central nervous system is organized to respond to a mounting need in one of two ways. First, one overcomes the need or defends against it through active participation, by working hard and directly confronting the stressful situation. The second process represents the conservation-withdrawal reaction wherein one responds typically in an inhibited, inactive manner. It is as though an attempt were being made to conserve resources in the face of a persistent state of need. This reaction is a predisposing factor of depression, a response to feelings of helplessness and hopelessness considered to be a maladaptive outcome of an initially adaptive behavior. According to the model, depression occurs in people who have had difficulty coping with these feelings in childhood. In adult life, when confronted with the same previously overwhelming feelings, they develop a "symptom compromise" that allows some recognition of the affect of depression and some defense against it.[15]

Engel views depressive symptoms as a form of communication reflecting clients' dependence needs. The energy withdrawal of depression is analogous to a hibernating animal that reduces activity in order to conserve energy. Withdrawal of energy sets up barriers to feelings of anxiety, a pattern of response, albeit a passive pattern. The active pattern, the gratification of needs from need-fulfilling external objects, can represent autonomous modes of communication, or it can also reflect dependent functioning if the person is still unable to participate actively in the resolution of stress.[16] Such people may still be vulnerable to depression, even though they are conserving energy.

BIOENERGETICS[17]

Alexander Lowen, the founder of bioenergetics, reasons that life is an excitatory phenomenon. Human beings are charged with energy that rises when they become excited and falls when they become depressed. While his conclusions are primarily subjective, he notes that there are objective, visible data that an energy field surrounds the human body.[18] When individuals are depressed, their "depressed" energy fields reflect that reality.

Energy discharge is as central to the model as energy charge, for living organisms can only function if there is a balance of both. The amount of energy that can be taken in is in direct proportion to the amount that can be discharged in activity. Such activity is an expression of one's being, experienced in discharge as pleasure and satisfaction. These feelings in turn stimulate metabolic activity reflected in deeper, fuller breathing. Limits to self-expression, then, limit the capacity for life. Energy intake is unconsciously reduced in order to maintain an energy balance, thus perpetuating a dysfunctional body state. Bio-energetics must work with both sides of the charge-discharge function, simultaneously, in order to raise energy levels and promote well-being.

Bioenergetics also includes the concept of character structures that are divided into five types, corresponding to syndromes in clinical psychiatry. Each type reflects a particular defense pattern on the psychological as well as muscular level. Outside the realm of this discussion, those interested in bioenergetics as a specialization may wish to pursue their study.

Clinical observations have led Lowen to believe that depressed people, having grown up too fast in order to relieve their parents of the burden of child care, have lost their childhood. They become doers, but never learn "to be." Remaining submissive, they will get depressed when their efforts fail to produce sought-for rewards. In order to overcome depressive tendencies, they must learn to be inner-directed. The development of independence is a natural human thrust that is not forfeited without a future "payoff."[19] The promise of love is the quid pro quo bargain—a bargain bound for disappointment. Disillusionment in the outcome of their misdirected energy is signified by the suppression of emotion, an emotional and physical "dying" which is depression, according to the model.

Clinicians are sometimes nonplused by the apparent contradiction between success and depression. Rather than experiencing disappointment, some people seem to become depressed when they have reached a desired goal—a new job, a raise, a degree, or a coveted prize. If these achievements were not goals in themselves, but were unconsciously conceived as a means of obtaining love, then the dynamics make more sense. Usually out of touch with their disappointment in failing to evoke love, they are unable to express any emotion, and depression ensues.

Lowen also cites examples of people who get depressed because their energies are bound up in denial of negative emotion. While he focuses on rebels as an example, the category might better describe the uncomplaining "saint" whose self-esteem rests on perilous foundations, destined to collapse when hostility is recognized. Surely, submissive persons who deny reaction to domination are vulnerable candidates. They recover from depression as they learn to take responsibility for their own well-being. When they are no longer looking to others to provide them with a sense of self and a feeling of aliveness, their energies can be constructively redirected.

Bioenergetics is a therapeutic technique to put people back in touch with their bodies. In tandem with insight, it is considered essential to human growth and development. According to Lowen, the life of an individual *is* the life of the body. Those who do not breathe deeply, move their bodies freely, and feel fully, reduce and restrict the life of their bodies. Constricted self-expression limits them even further. These restrictions on living are admittedly imposed by the home environment and the larger culture. But to accept them by failing to question them is to betray the body and consequently limit energy, feeling, and growth. The goal of bioenergetics, then, is to help people regain their natural state of freedom, grace, and beauty. Freedom is manifested by the absence of inner restraint to the flow of feeling; grace by the expression of movement; and beauty by inner harmony.

Personality can be evaluated by assessing the amount of available energy that one has and how it is used. In the depressed person, the relationship between energy and personality is quite clear. Typically, breathing, appetites, and sexual drives are depressed. Depressed persons simply do not have the energy to develop interests or relate to others; this absence of energy in turn retards growth. Lowen observes that people come to therapy because they sense that their development has been arrested. "Happiness," he concludes, "is the consciousness of growth."

WOMEN AT RISK

Energy Flow, Direction, and Expenditure

The concept of thermodynamics may have strong implications for women's high depression vulnerability. Since organisms survive by their ability to capture available energy, power belongs to those who can control the process. Rifkin notes that class divisions, exploitation, poverty, and privilege all determine how a society's "energy flow line" is set up.[20] These characteristics determine how work is divided up and how economic rewards are allocated. The division of labor has long exploited the energy of women through their caretaking role. They provide nurturance and daily maintenance without pay or status resulting in a diffusion and dissipation of their energy. Others, using the energy of women, accumulate free, unfragmented energy that can be expressly focused. Given this thermodynamic insight, it is not surprising that many women end up drained of energy and depressed. It may be that the conservation-withdrawal reaction may occur as an adaptive reaction to energy exploitation. As early as 1898, Charlotte Perkins Gilman spoke of still another perversion of energies: the repression of the natural output of creative female energy, an observation which she contrasted with the ferocity of excessive male energy "struggling in the marketplace as in a battlefield."[21]

Growth takes inner-directed energy, a quality that women often are socialized to give up. In relinquishing their own development to live vicariously through others, the successes of husbands and children often are regarded as their own. In the bargain, the failures of family members are also vicariously felt. "How could he do this to me?" is a familiar response to something experienced by the depressed woman's husband or child, not by the woman herself. Independence has been forfeited for the promise of love, the final payoff. Lowen believes that no one gives up the natural propensity for growth and independence without the desire for a payoff. The child thinks, "If I am a good girl, they will love me," and the message replays itself in adulthood as, "If I am a perfect wife and a good mother, I will surely be loved." Those who have sacrificed their independence for the promise of future fulfillment are likely to become depressed when the delayed "payoff" is found wanting. As the at-risk population, depressed women's socialized dependence and vicarious gratification place them squarely in Lowen's scenario. Taught to give of themselves by giving up themselves, they become experts at delaying gratification, but novices in attaining it. Thus, their energies are misspent.

An "energy expenditure profile" (Figure 3-1) for women can be developed to provide insight into how and where life energies have been invested. They should rate themselves on a continuum from 1 to 10 with 1 indicating a very low energy level expenditure and 10 a very high level. By filling in the squares, a bar graph is created. Assessment may center on the distribution of energy output and ways in which energy might be redistributed more satisfyingly. It is also helpful to think about the direction of energy relative to personal fulfillment and development. The areas of consideration can be amended to suit each individual's situation.

An interesting conceptual dichotomy rests in the sphere of "being" and "doing." Lowen notes that depressed people become doers, never learning "to be"—that is, to be inner-directed, an observation congruent with the lives of women. Yet, Nancy Chodorow speaks of males' socialization "to do" as needing to prove themselves through achievement.[23] Females are not given the same mandate, for to be female (that is, feminine) is enough. Women must just "be"; they are not encouraged to develop themselves more fully. The semantic puzzle does not require an either/or solution. The answer lies in the concept of

Expended Energy Area	1	2	3	4	5	6	7	8	9	10	Indicate personal fulfillment

Home Maintenance

Cleaning											
Cooking											
Clothing											
Other											

Caretaking

Children											
Spouse/partner											
Relatives											
Friends											
Acquaintances											
Other											

Work

Career (long-term goals)											
Job (no long-term goals)											
Volunteer job (over 1 day/wk)											
Community service											
Politics											
School											
Other											

	1	2	3	4	5	6	7	8	9	10	Indicate personal fulfillment

Activities

Active sports (participant)											
Passive sports (observer)											
Interests/hobbies											
Sex											
Other											

Emotions

Joy											
Love											
Pleasure											
Anxiety											
Guilt											
Boredom											
Sadness											
Anger											
Pain											
Other											

Figure 3-1. Energy expenditure profile.

life energy itself. Women, first and foremost, must be perceived as human, a mandate too often considered to be radical. The fundamental need of all individuals is more "life," to make ever more accessible the underlying energy, to go with the life process instead of blocking that energy, and to discover and use one's innate capacity for both relationship and creativity.[24] Both "being" and "doing" are needed to allow life-giving energy to flow, regardless of one's sex.

Fathers, according to Lowen's theory, must give women permission to succeed. The blocking of life-giving energy revealed by shallow breathing exposes the absence of that permission earlier in life. Anger may be the natural consequence of the restrictive messages. The suppression of anger, in turn, exacerbates vulnerability to depression for life-giving energy can be blocked along with the expression of anger. This is an area that is particularly appropriate for attention because the right to express anger has been culturally denied to women. They are likely to feel guilty about their secret rage which is often hidden even from themselves. Because suppressed rage and superficiality will culminate in depression, awareness is essential. Viewed as potentially creative energy, anger can be an expressive form of communication, rather than internally destructive to oneself or externally to others. Because the concept of denying the reality of anger feeds into the depressed woman's defense system, facing it squarely in the following constructive manner, for a short time, is recommended.

The Expression of Anger[25]

Women should:

— "Feel" their anger physically.

— Ask themselves how their body feels (eyes, jaw, neck, stomach, etc.).

— Breathe with the feelings and be aware of the energy involved.

— Question their anger; ask *what* the external cause is, then ask *where* the internal cause is (for example, is the cause their values, ego, or defenses?).

— Express their anger fully in a safe situation, away from the external cause; express it *verbally* (by shouting at a chair that represents a person or idea, for example); express it *physically* (by pounding, kicking, running, chopping, and yelling "no" repeatedly).

— Center themselves quietly and channel their anger; ask themselves what they are going to do about it; deal directly with the person, the situation, and so on.

— Express their feelings using sentences that begin with: "I feel _____ when you _____ .[26] Stay specific to one or two occasions; describe what they specifically need changed, for that is their purpose.

— Let their anger go; don't dwell on it or rehash it; get on with living.

— Create bridges back; reconnect positively with the object of their anger — the person or situation, reaffirming acceptance and love.

Behind the depressed woman's anger is an energetic movement, an impulse that represents the desire to stop another from causing her pain. It is also associated with thoughts relating to the situation that provoked the anger.[27] In order to act, there must be energy coming from within, a force that is not present in an undercharged body.[28] For this reason, the reaction time of participants will vary. In all cases, negative energy will be discharged through the process, freeing up energy for positive action.

PREVENTION AND INTERVENTION

Energy is viewed as a life force that must be directed constructively and focused for optimal functioning. Depression results in a depletion of energy when it has been misdirected and dissipated.

Nutrition

It is natural that an after the fact discussion of the prevention of depression or intervention based upon energy concepts should begin with nutrition. Food is the fuel that provides us with the energy to sustain life. This energy is stored in the body in a chemical form, but is measured in terms of the calorie. A unit of thermal energy, the calorie is assessed by the heat it can produce. People are aware that they will die if their caloric intake is too low, and that they will become fat when calories are in excess of energy requirements; but they are often uninformed about the selection of nutritious calories. Because depressed people commonly lose their appetites or indulge in overeating to assuage their pain, it is essential to encourage proper diet and to monitor their food habits. While not within the purview of this book, the growing incidence and prevalence of the anorexia-bulimia food disorder spectrum is a case in point. It is not surprising that the profiles and experiences of this largely young, female population resembles that of depressed women. Clinicians must be aware of the possibility of food disorders in their depressed clients, as well as more basic information regarding proper nutrition. Depression intervention and prevention may be analogous for both populations. (Keep in mind, however, the addictive nature of food disorders, paralleled by substance abuse. Treatment must take these realities into consideration as well.)[29]

Because there are many excellent texts that can provide the fundamentals of nutrition, this discussion will be limited to implications for depression, a subject about which less information is available. While there are claims that depression is a metabolic disorder that can be treated with megavitamin therapy, more research is needed to corroborate the theory.[30] In the meantime, it behooves us to be alert to possible nutritional deficiencies and the signs and symptoms that may also reflect symptoms of depression. The following deficiencies have been selected for that purpose.[31]

DEFICIENCY	SIGNS AND SYMPTOMS
B complex	Inability to concentrate (decrease in metabolic rate of brain).
Vitamin C	Listlessness, irritability (Vitamin C must be replaced daily).
Niacin	Depression (especially psychosis).
B6 (severe deficiency)	Headache, irritability, dizziness, extreme nervousness, inability to concentrate.
Pantothenic acid	Body is unable to cope with stress.
Thiamine	Lack of energy, constant fatigue, loss of appetite, irritability.
Phosphorus-Calcium ratio (1:2)	Entire nervous system is affected.
Iron	Loss of energy, fatigue.
Calcium	Tension, insomnia, fatigue.
Vitamin E	Lack of energy (Vitamin E allows more efficient use of oxygen in the blood).
Thyroxin (iodine-carrying hormone)	Unbalanced blood sugar and hypothyroidism; slowdown of physical and mental activity, forgetfulness, irritability.
Magnesium	Uncooperativeness, withdrawal, apathy, belligerence.

It is important to monitor intake of beverages and medications for their effect on water-soluble nutrients, as well as for their intrinsic properties. Alcohol, coffee, tea, and medication stimulate urine production and, consequently, all but five of forty vitamins are readily lost in urine. (Those five are Vitamins A, D, E, K, and linoteic acid.[32]) Coffee, nonherbal teas, and colas can overstimulate, resulting in irritability, nervous agitation, anxiety, and insomnia — all depression-related symptoms.[33] The same thing can be said for alcohol use, even though alcohol is a depressant. Alcohol adversely affects cognitive skills and impairs memory, symptoms that are familiar to depressed people. Nutritionist Nan Bronfen observes that people often feel like drinking alcohol when they are hungry.[34] Were they to eat something instead, the craving would dissipate.[35] Because alcohol is an effective drug, otherwise moderate drinkers who become depressed may have a tendency to "self-medicate," exacerbating their symptoms rather than alleviating them.

Physical Exercise

Physical exercise has long been thought to be helpful to depressed people, relieving pent-up stress and tension, and channeling hostility constructively. We now know that exercise also prevents the excessive production of hormones by the adrenal glands. Defective adrenal functioning is highly correlated with depression. The physical sciences are finding empirical support for exercise as a preventive activity as well as a therapeutic intervention. Pre-post-test research indicates that depression is reduced in people who exercise because the exercise stimulates biochemical changes. This is particularly true of joggers. Some people suggest that the repetitive rhythm of jogging may have the same therapeutic effect as chanting a mantra in meditation.[36]

While energy comes from the combustion of food, the rate of combustion is directly related to the amount of available oxygen. It follows that the most important effect of exercise is related to the amount of oxygen taken into the cells. Regular exercise strengthens the muscles of the rib cage, which allows more carbon dioxide (deoxygenated, stale air) to be expelled, enabling the lungs to take in more oxygen. Thus, exercise increases one's vital capacity, the usable portion of the lungs. This portion can be determined by measuring the amount of air that can be exhaled after taking a deep breath. Exercise also causes an extra demand for oxygen, causing the body to adapt by producing more hemoglobin and red cells. In short, the oxygen-carrying power of the blood is increased through exercise. Exercise also helps combat fatigue, which is simply an absence of energy caused by a lack of oxygen, and an accumulation of carbon dioxide.[37] Bronfen recommends aerobic exercise as the most beneficial type. This includes brisk, rhythmic, and repetitive activities involving the large muscles, sustained for at least one-half hour. There must be a great enough demand for oxygen over a long period of time in order for the body to adapt and increase the oxygen supply to the cells.

While exercise also has a beneficial effect on the heart, experts caution those who are out of condition to increase the degree of exertion very gradually. People should exert themselves to the point that they can feel their hearts beating harder and breathing becomes heavy, but not to the point of shortness of breath. People should be sure to warm up and cool down before and after exercising. Those who are over thirty-five should consult their physicians before embarking on a new exercise program.

Equally appropriate for walking exercise, the National Jogging Association provides the following method to determine one's proper heart rate.[38] Called a Target Heart Rate Zone, the final figure represents the number of heart beats that should be counted when interrupting exercise to take one's pulse for ten seconds. By way of example, the formula has been applied below to a forty-year-old who is not a jogger, but is normally active.

1. Subtract age from 220:
      220 − 40 yrs. = 180 mhr (maximal heart rate).
2. Multiply by .60
      180 mhr × .60 = 108 (beats per minute).
   Multiply by .75 if a jogger.
   Multiply by .70 if inactive.
   Multiply by .65 if one smokes over six cigarettes daily.
   Multiply by .65 if overweight (don't count 20 pounds overweight
   if pregnant).
3. Divide by 6:
      108 ÷ 6 = 18 (beats per 10 seconds).

The target heart rate zone is between 108 and 135 beats per minute or between 18 and 23 beats per 10 seconds. To get the most out of an exercise program, people should stay within their target heart rate zone. There is no need to exceed it.

Reparenting: The Transformation of Energy Systems[39]

Interventions designed to address the conservation-withdrawal premise require long-term, in-depth therapy to counteract the response of the central nervous system to prolonged deprivation and anxiety. "Reparenting" may provide the necessary means. It is a method of transforming nonproductive energy systems into productive ones, a method proven successful in reversing passivity and psychotic behavior. When a person's needs have not been met at the proper time in life, a contamination of the growth process can be assumed. Reparenting provides a second opportunity to meet the needs of the depressed person at the appropriate time in their unfolding development. Though treatment can occur in a group setting, it is maintained on a one-to-one basis. For purposes of illustration, we present as our client a depressed man, age 30, whom we will call Mr. B. His therapy evolves through the following six stages:

Stage I. Infant Stage: Energy comes from the therapist "stroking" the client.

Encourage regression and childlike behavior, such as crying, as a healthy behavior. Mr. B. learns to make the decision, "I can get what I want," probably for the first time in his life. Work to overcome anxiety stemming from a deeply felt belief that he has no "core" of identity. This will be reflected in his message, "If people get to know me, they'll find out I'm not there."

Stage II. Exploration: Clients learn to explore and move toward energy (life) themselves.

Meet Mr. B.'s withdrawal and dependence needs by making the environment totally responsible for his safety. At the same time, provide sensory stimulation, working to overcome the parental injunctions, "Don't grow up"; "be emotionally disturbed"; or "be depressed." In so doing, Mr. B. explores and moves from negative to positive energy — life itself.

Stage III. Cognitive Phase: Clients learn to move toward positive energy; the focus is on reality and reason.

Concentrate on helping Mr. B. differentiate what he is thinking from environmental reality. When he stubbornly clings to his fantasies, focus on reality and reason. There is a new insistence upon reasonable behavior. This phase is critical for psychotic individuals, and a key stage for those who are less disturbed. Most depressed people are filled with negative ideas that do not reflect the reality of their personalities and the world.[40] Movement toward positive energy is in order.

Stage IV. Empathy and feeling are encouraged, representing shared energies.

Focus on helping Mr. B. to develop empathy through linking awareness of his own feelings with the experiences of others. This is an especially difficult task for men who have not been socialized to be aware of their own and others' feelings. It is important to help them to evolve in this critical area, so often denied to them.

Stage V. Responsibility: Clients begin to learn to use energy constructively; the focus is on separating what one is responsible for from what one is not responsible for. Depressed persons typically use their energy destructively, taking full responsibility for troubles in their families and at work, indeed in the world. It has been found that depressed people also tend to believe, often incorrectly, that they are in control of their environments.[41] Unfortunately, this perception of responsibility does not generalize to their own happiness; for this they look to others. This is, therefore, a critical stage of treatment.

Stage VI. Termination and Autonomy: Energy is contained in the client, to be used constructively in his life.

Meet Mr. B.'s progression of needs all over again. During this final stage, clients normally regress, requiring the strokes and care of the early stages. As observed in the psychoanalytic therapies, clients "work through" all phases of treatment when terminating, though within a shortened time frame. Mr. B. can be expected to test his separateness with rebellion. Still, he is viewed as an autonomous adult as he progresses, finally emerging as a mature human being. Growth is freed of inhibition following this reparenting experience, for his unblocked energy is positive and productive.[42] There is no longer a need for a conservation-withdrawal reaction.

Bioenergetics Therapy[43]

With its simultaneous focus on energy charge and discharge, bioenergetics raises energy levels to restore the flow of feeling to the body and to increase self-expression. Lowen points out that bioenergetics cannot resolve all conflict, remove all chronic tension, or totally restore the full and free flow of feeling. It is meant to be a catalyst for growth that leads in that direction. The emphasis is always on breathing, feeling, and movement. Movement refers to voluntary action, but it is particularly concerned with motility — biologically inherent, spontaneous motion. Since the body is essentially made up of energetically charged fluids, sensations and feelings are pictured as currents or waves, most evident when observing an infant in constant play of involuntary motion, like the waves on a lake. As people age, their motility steadily decreases until, finally, in death all motion ceases. Though depressed persons may be young, their body's motility is similarly rigidified. Emotional life depends on motility to channel the excitation flow throughout the body. Disturbances of this flow occur as blocks in areas where the body's motility is reduced. Lowen notes that the terms "block, deadness and chronic muscular tension" refer to the same phenomenon. Hence, he focuses attention on those parts that clients describe accordingly.

The mind and body are not perceived as separate substances, each independent of the other, as they often are regarded in Western cultures.[44] Instead, the mind is conceived as the inner manifestation of the body, while the body is the outer reflection of the mind. Bioenergetics is based on the principle that persons *are* their bodies. Treatment may be conducted in groups, but when it is, the aim of therapy differs somewhat from other therapeutic groups. Participants are not there to learn about each other. The aim of the therapy is to bring each person in touch with him or herself on a body level. Since all people have the human body in common, they understand others by experiencing their own.

The Concepts of Hara and Grounding

The Japanese concept of hara is central to bioenergetics. To have hara is to be centered in the belly "feeling-wise." The belly is called the "seat of life"; it is the vital center from which individual life emerges. The exact location is thought to be two inches below the navel.[45] When centered, the split is reconciled between the conscious and the unconscious, between the ego and the body, the self and the world. One is inner-directed and balanced physically and psychologically.

There is a paradox that is noted by both philosophers and mental health clinicians. When people try to deny or to overcome — to transcend — their painful feelings, they hang on to them. To surrender to them is to surmount them.[46] This metaphysical phenomenon has been described allegorically by Richard Bach. In order to make a plane airborne, he reminds us, we cannot do what appears easiest — just let the wind blow from behind. Instead, we must "face into the wind" to create a dynamic momentum.[47] In the same way, people must face their deep sadness head on if they are to transcend it. Lowen points out that depressed people resist getting in touch with that pain, committing their energies to the struggle to overcome despair and, thus, wasting them. An analysis of the process of breathing, according to Lowen, reflects the energetic connection to the father, revealing the person's early relationship. Breathing fully and deeply demonstrates parental permission to succeed in life.

Anxiety also accompanies "standing on one's own feet" because it represents helpless aloneness. Yet, people who are not alone in that they are dependent, are those who are most lonely in the world.

Grounding is a process of helping them to complete their delayed emotional maturation — to "stand on their own feet," to become more independent and, paradoxically, less alone.[48] To get fully in touch with feelings in the belly and legs, persons must be grounded, in touch with reality. This is a bioenergetic concept that is not just a psychological metaphor. When electrical circuits are grounded, an outlet is provided for the discharge of energy. In human beings, grounding also serves to release or discharge tension, the excitation of the body. The following grounding exercises are suggested by Alexander Lowen and Leslie Lowen to be implemented for their qualities alone, and to precede all bioenergetic exercises.

Bioenergetic Grounding Exercises[49]

During all exercises, the mouth should be slightly open so that breathing can develop easily and fully. Breathing should extend to the abdomen, and the belly should not be held in. One should be comfortable and not force anything. Breathing must release muscular tension. This is accomplished by becoming aware of:

a.   Which impulses or actions are unconsciously restrained by tension.
b.   How tension acts to limit feeling and excitation.
c.   What effect tension has on behavior and attitudes.

Note that exercises are necessary, but not sufficient, as therapeutic interventions. Insight into one's life history and present environment is also absolutely essential. Therefore, for optimal results, all exercises are to be combined with insight-oriented therapies.

The regular practice of Exercises I and II should be encouraged as preparatory steps to all exercises:

Exercise I:
1. Breathe continuously through the mouth from the abdomen.
2. Stand with knees slightly flexed (preferably barefoot).
3. Place feet parallel, about six inches apart.
4. Balance the weight of the body evenly between the heels and balls of the feet.
5. Make the rest of the body erect with arms hanging loosely at the sides.
6. Focus attention onto the feet.
7. Hold for two minutes.

Result: Involuntary tremors will flow into the body and legs; they are an expression of flow of feeling. Allow the tremors to develop to the extent that they are comfortable, and then stop.

Exercise II:

1. Continue to breathe through the mouth from the abdomen.
2. Stand with knees slightly flexed (preferably barefoot).
3. Place feet about eight inches apart with toes turned slightly inward.
4. Put all weight on the feet.
5. Bend down until fingertips touch the ground, letting the head drop.
6. Keep fingertips on the ground, gradually straightening the knees until vibrations develop in the legs. Do not attempt to stiffen the legs by extending the knees fully.
7. Hold for two minutes.
8. Stop when tired or painful.

Result: Increases breathing and circulation to the hands and feet.

Exercise III:

This exercise is practiced in order to help the client and therapist understand resistance caused by fear of failure or of falling. First, place a folded blanket or padding six inches from the participant's feet and provide two chairs on either side of him. Then instruct him to:

1. Do Exercises I and II.
2. Breathe continuously through the mouth from the abdomen.
3. Stand on one leg and feel the weight of the body on the foot.
4. Bend the knee as far as possible without any part of the foot being raised off the ground.
5. Extend the other leg backward off the ground.
6. Extend arms and rest hands lightly (for balance, not support) on a chair placed on both the right and left sides of the participant.
7. When balance can no longer be maintained, direct the person to fall onto both knees onto the blanket.
8. Repeat the exercise four times. As he falls for the last time, suggest that he stay down, saying, "I give up."

Result: The act of falling creates feelings of aloneness, while falling without being hurt relieves anxiety. The therapist should discuss the participant's tone of voice and the implications of surrender that accompanies saying "I give up" while falling. Is it genuine or false? The depressed person who has given up his childhood has often made a conscious or unconscious pact never again to need anyone. The physical helplessness of his position is symbolic and evokes deep-seated feelings of deep sadness and despair, which must be worked through with the therapist as he yields to his long-denied emotions.

Exercise IV:

1. Do Exercises I, II, and III. Ask the participant to remain down on the floor on both knees.

2. Continue mouth breathing from the abdomen.

3. Hands are clasped together, flat on the floor, elbows are bent, and the forehead rests on the hands (this is the Moslem prayer position).

4. Allow the belly to hang loosely.

5. Push the posterior back as far as possible.

6. Hold for two minutes.

Result: Breathing develops deep in the belly, resulting in feelings of relaxation in the vital center of one's being. As abdominal feelings develop, they often change to sexual sensations because sexuality is a function of the entire body. The client is taught to understand his natural sexuality and to "go with" such feelings.

Exercise V (alternate exercise):

1. Do Exercises I and II.

2. Continue mouth breathing from the abdomen.

3. Bend knees all the way.

4. Hold hands straight out in front, arms extended, just above the floor.

5. Direct the weight of the body forward, while the heels remain on the ground.

6. Hold as long as possible, but not to excess.

7. Drop back to Exercise IV for final relaxation and surrender.

Result: By "letting down" naturally, one learns to surrender to life. According to Lowen, those who do not do so will be "cast down" sooner or later into depression.

Fundamental Stress Position[50]

This exercise is a grounding aid, also called the Bion or Taoist Arch. When done correctly, it helps to release tensions in the belly. Instruct the participant to:

1. Continue mouth breathing from the abdomen.
2. Place feet about eighteen inches apart with toes slightly turned inward.
3. Place both fists with knuckles facing upward into the small of the back.
4. Bend both knees as much as possible without lifting heels.
5. Arch backward over the fists, making certain that weight remains forward on the balls of the feet.

Result: Involuntary tremors will flow into the body and legs. Strain should be felt only in the ankles and feet where one's body weight is supported. Strain in the lower back indicates considerable tension. Any "break" in the bow owing to imperfect arching results in a blocking of the energy flow to the feet.

Selected Bioenergetic Exercises

Alexander Lowen and Leslie Lowen have detailed further exercises that increase the production of energy and discharge through movement. While grounding is essential to the prevention and treatment of depression, the following practices are also appropriate.

Basic Orienting Position

1. Place feet parallel, about eight inches apart.
2. Stand with knees slightly flexed, the upper trunk straight and relaxed.
3. Keep belly relaxed and "out," pelvis tilted back.
4. Lean forward with weight on the balls of the feet.
5. Take four or five deep breaths from the abdomen.
6. Drop the pelvis and "let go."
7. "Let down" into the feet.
8. Continue breathing deeply and easily from the abdomen.

"Joy of Being Alive" Stretch: A Reorientation to Life

1. Begin with the basic orienting position described above.
2. Keeping palms turned away from the body, slowly stretch arms forward, then to the sides and down.

3. Coordinate breathing with the arm movements (breathe out audibly when stretching the arms forward, when they are upright, sideways and downward).

4. Repeat several times.

Exercises to Relieve Tension (for Dyads)

Both partners are as relaxed as possible, breathing easily. The following exercises detailed in Lowen and Lowen are recommended.

Back and Shoulder Massage

1. The person to be massaged sits cross-legged on the floor.

2. The person who is doing the massage kneels behind and lightly places both hands on the shoulders of the partner, moving the fingers over the shoulders and back.

3. Feel for tension "knots," using thumbs to knead them. If too painful, be more gentle.

4. Press down on shoulders firmly and steadily until they drop, being sure partner continues breathing easily.

5. With the sides of the hands, drum with moderate pressure around tense areas.

6. Continue to work in the areas of the upper arm and around the shoulder blades.

Neck Massage

1. Precede with the back and shoulder massage.

2. The person to be massaged continues to sit cross-legged on the floor.

3. The person who is doing the massage kneels on the partner's left side.

4. Place the left hand firmly on the partner's forehead for support and the right hand on the neck (reverse if left-handed).

5. With right-hand fingers, feel the neck muscles at the base of the skull down to the base of the neck.

6. Using the fingers, knead the tense muscles.

7. Check for partner's easy breathing and absence of pain.

Relieving Tension Headache

1. Begin with the preceding exercises in the same position as the neck massage.

2. Continue the massage from the base of the head, working upward over the top of the skull.

3. Keeping the left hand on the forehead, feel for tension behind the ears with the right hand (reverse if left-handed).

4. Massage the muscles firmly, slowly moving upward over the scalp until the right and left hands meet.

5. With the hands encircling the whole scalp, loosen it up by moving it back and forth. When it moves easily, the headache has disappeared.

6. Repeat if relief is only partial. *Note*: Do not persist if it is not successful. It may be migraine and will not yield to this procedure, according to Lowen and Lowen.

Venting Anger Constructively

Saying "No"
1. Breathe deeply.
2. Keep knees slightly flexed, arms hanging loosely at each side.
3. Make fists and bending elbows, bring fists down with force on each side alternately.
4. Say "no!" in rhythm with arm movements.
5. Let voice get increasingly louder as arm movements become increasingly forceful.

"Get Off My Back"
1. Following the "Saying No" exercise, look over one shoulder and make fists.
2. Say "get off my back" while directing both elbows ever more forcefully toward the back.

Remember that exercises release energy carthartically, but must be done in tandem with conscious awareness of the psychosocial forces impacting if they are to be optimally beneficial. Hence, bioenergetics is inextricably linked with insight therapies.

NOTES

1. Rifkin, Jeremy, *Entropy* (New York: Viking Press, 1980).
2. Freud, Sigmund, in Ernest Jones, ed., *The Life and Work of Sigmund Freud*, Vol. I (New York: Basic Books, 1953); for a discussion of Freud's theory of psychic energy, refer to Chapter 2 where it is included because it is so integral to Freud's thinking.
3. Jung, Carl, in R. F. C. Hull (trans.), *The Collected Works of C. G. Jung*. (Princeton, NJ: Princeton University Press, 1971).

4. Reich, Wilhelm, *The Function of Orgasm* (New York: Orgone Institute Press, 1944).

5. Lowen, Alexander, *Bioenergetics* (New York: Penguin Books, 1975).

6. Rifkin, Jeremy, *Entropy* (New York: Viking Press, 1980).

7. Engel, George L., "Anxiety and Depression Withdrawal: The Primary Effects of Unpleasure," *International Journal of Psychoanalysis 43* (1962): 89 – 97.

8. Schmale, Arthur H., "Depression as Affect, Character, Style, and Symptom Formation," in *Psychoanalysis and Contemporary Science*, Vol. 1 (New York: Macmillan, 1971).

9. Rifkin, Jeremy, *Entropy* (New York: Viking Press, 1980).

10. Georgescu-Roegen, Nicholas, "Afterword," in Jeremy Rifkin, *Entropy* (New York: Viking Press, 1980), pp. 261 – 269.

11. Klerman, Gerald L., "Clinical Phenomenology of Depression: Implications for Research Strategy in the Psychobiology of the Affective Disorders," in *Recent Advances in the Psychobiology of Depressive Illness*, T. A. Williams and M. M. Katz (Washington, DC: U.S. Government Printing Office, 1972).

12. See Chapter 10 for further discussion of crises and depression.

13. See Chapter 5 for further discussion of burnout.

14. Engel, George L., "Anxiety and Depression Withdrawal: The Primary Effects of Unpleasure," *International Journal of Psychoanalysis 43* (1962): 89 – 97; see also Arthur H. Schmale, "Depression as Affect, Character, Style, and Symptom Formation," in *Psychoanalysis and Contemporary Science*, Vol. 1 (New York: Macmillan, 1971).

15. Note the similarity of the focus of Conservation-Withdrawal, and Learned Helplessness, which is detailed in Chapter 6.

16. See Willard Gaylin (1968) in Chapter 2 for further discussion of depression as communication.

17. Lowen, Alexander, *Depression and the Body* (New York: Coward, McCann and Geoghegan, 1974); see also Alexander Lowen, *Bioenergetics* (New York: Penguin Books, 1975).

18. Pierkakos, John C., "The Energy Field of Man, Energy and Character,"*The Journal of Bioenergetic Research 1,2* (Abbotsbury, England, May 1970).

19. The wish for a payoff for having lived vicariously through others is also addressed in the section on Role Theory in Chapter 4.

20. Rifkin, Jeremy, *Entropy* (New York: Viking Press, 1980).

21. Gilman, Charlotte Perkins, *Women and Economics* (Boston: Maynard and Company, 1898, reprinted and edited by Carl N. Degler, New York: Harper and Row, 1966).

22. Jongeward, Dorothy, and Dru Scott, *Women as Winners* (Reading, MA: Addison-Wesley, 1976).

23. Chodorow, Nancy, "Being and Doing," in *Woman in Sexist Society*, ed. Vivian Gornick and Barbara K. Moran (New York: Basic Books, 1971), 173 – 197.

24. Taft, Jesse, "A Conception of the Growth Process Underlying Social Casework Practice," *Social Casework* (October 1950), pp. 1 – 11.

25. Christoph, Rosemary, "Anger, The Creative Fire," unpublished paper presented at the Berkeley Anger Workshop, Berkeley, CA, 1978, reprinted in Shanti Shapiro's *Violence between Women* (Northampton, MA: 1980).

26. Gordon, Thomas, *Parent Effectiveness Training*(Reading, MA: David McKay, 1970).

27. See Chapter 6 for further discussion of the impact of thoughts and the expression of anger.

28. Lowen, Alexander, *Depression and the Body* (New York: Coward, McCann and Geohegan, 1974).

29. Bruch, Hilda, *The Golden Cage: The Enigma of Anorexia-Nervosa* (Cambridge, MA: Harvard University Press, 1978); see also C. P. Wilson and I. Mintz, "Abstaining and Bulemia Anorexics: Two Sides of the Same Coin," *Primary Care 9* 3: 1982, 517–530; Steven Levenkron, *Treating and Overcoming Anorexia Nervosa* (New York: Scribner's, 1982); Janice M. Cauwells, *Bulemia: The Binge-Purge Compulsion* (Garden City, NY: Doubleday, 1983).

30. Bronfen, Nan, *Nutrition for a Better Life: A Source Book for the Eighties* (Santa Barbara, CA: Capra Press, 1980).

31. Kirschman, John, *Nutrition Almanac* (New York: McGraw-Hill, 1975).

32. Cheraskin, E., *Psychodietetics* (New York: Bantam Books, 1976); see also Adele Davis, *Let's Get Well* (New York: New American Library, 1972).

33. See Chapter 9 for further discussion of alcohol use and abuse.

34. Bronfen, Nan, *Nutrition for a Better Life: A Source Book for the Eighties* (Santa Barbara, CA: Capra Press, 1980).

35. See Chapter 1 for a detailed discussion of depression symptoms.

36. See Chapter 7 and Chapter 8.

37. Schiff, Jacqui, "Reparenting Schizophrenics," *Transactional Analysis Bulletin 8* (1969): 47–62.

38. Bronfen, Nan, *Nutrition for a Better Life: A Source Book for the Eighties* (Santa Barbara, CA: Capra Press, 1980).

39. National Jogging Association pamphlet on the *Target Heart Rate Zone*, (Washington, D.C. 1981).

40. Note the analogy in this phase with Reality Therapy and Rational Emotive Therapy, both described in Chapter 6.

41. Rotter, Julian, "Some Problems and Misconceptions Related to the Construct of Internal versus External Control of Reinforcement," *Journal of Consulting and Clinical Psychology 43*, 1 (1975): 56–67.

42. See Chapters 6 and 7 for discussions of negativity and depression.

43. Lowen, Alexander, and Leslie Lowen, *The Way to Vibrant Health: A Manual of Bioenergetic Exercises* (New York: Harper Colophon Books, 1977).

44. Descartes, Rene, "Meditations of First Philosophy," in *The Philosophical Works of Descartes*, ed. Haldane and Ross, (New York: Dover Publications, 1955).

45. Durckheim, Karlfried, *The Vital Center of Man* (London: Allen and Unwin, 1962).

46. See Chapter 7 for further discussion of "letting go."

47. Bach, Richard, *Illusions* (New York: Delacorte Press, 1978).

48. See Chapters 2 and 5 for further discussions of independence.

49. Lowen, Alexander, and Leslie Lowen, *The Way to Vibrant Health: A Manual of Bioenergetic Exercises* (New York: Harper Colophon Books, 1977).

50. See Chapter 7 for a discussion of relaxation based on visual imagery and meditation.

Chapter 4
Life Events Models

> The long day wanes: the slow moon
>   climbs: the deep
> Moans round with many voices. Come,
>   my friends,
> 'Tis not too late to seek a newer world.
>   Alfred, Lord Tennyson, "Ulysses"

Life events theorists consider depression to be a psychological response to environmental stress. What those stressors may be is investigated and debated, along with individual variations in depressive response to similar stressors. Findings are beginning to emerge that provide insights into the influence of life events and the coping skills that distinguish people who become depressed from those who do not.

I have separated life events models into three major categories for purposes of discussion. The first alludes to social conditions and their relationship to depression. Stressors range from characteristics of transitional eras to perspectives that assess the quality of events, how often they occur, and when they take place in relation to the onset of depression. Life events theories concerned with the subject of loss are discussed in relation to childhood bereavement and the inability to cope, in addition to loneliness and to difficulties of being alone in later life. Finally, role theory is addressed, with a focus on social roles that impinge on well-being.

The notion that stressful life events cause depression makes intuitive sense to most people. When approached with complaints of depression, it's natural to inquire about events preceding the onset of symptoms. Who hasn't asked a depressed person, or at least wondered, "What happened to make you depressed?" Nor is it unusual for professionals to separate depressions diagnostically into different entities relative to the presence or absence of stressors. A psychiatric diagnosis of exogenous or reactive depression refers to those people who can identify a precipitating stressful life event. When none is obvious, endogenous depression is diagnosed, indicating that the problem is internal.[1] Those who pursue the assessment of life events and depression analyses are becoming increasingly aware that one opinion concerning the existence of a stressful event may be quite different from a second evaluation. Both may be equally correct or incorrect. The range of possibilities lies between discrete major events that predate the onset of symptoms and a pervasive life experience that may increase a vulnerability to depression for individuals and even for whole segments of populations. These different possibilities for stress also will be discussed as they impact on women and men.

SOCIAL CONDITIONS: TRANSITIONAL ERAS

A historical perspective provides credibility for an encompassing interpretation of life events and depression. In the middle and late 1600s, like the present middle and late 1900s, the problem of depression (then known as melancholy) was called epidemic. Both are transitional epochs, a time of intellectual and emotional turmoil. In the 1600s the absolute world of the theologians and divine right of kings was crumbling. The new world of science was not yet clearly delineated and hope was elusive. What had been accepted for thousands of years as true unalterable reality was revealed as an interpretation of the human mind.[2] The same cultural disequilibrium holds true today. Mores and ethics long thought to be absolute have been exposed and rejected as inadequate, out of date, and unrealistic. It appears that entire cultures can produce pervasive climates that result in more likelihood that depression will occur. In 1632 Robert Burton's extensive analysis of depression noted that exploitation of weaker members of society also increased their vulnerability; women were observed to be most vulnerable.[3] Contemporary literature echoes his observations. Even today depression is more prevalent in exploited groups such as women, people of color, the elderly, and the poor.[4] Since over half of people of color, as well as the majority of the elderly and poor in the United States are women, the presence of women as the at-risk population becomes understandable in twentieth-century America. Life events, roles, and social conditions, therefore, will be addressed throughout this chapter, with specific reference to women's experience.

SOCIAL CONDITIONS: QUALITY, QUANTITY, AND TIMING

Because a stressful situation is as much a function of the individual as it is of the environment, how to rate an event has been a continuing dilemma. Thomas Holmes and R.H. Raye pioneered life events research by addressing the problem.[5] Their scales for measuring social adjustment to recent experiences assess life change and psychological stress. Too many life-change "units" in a single year were thought to lead to vulnerability to depression and illness. While the items included in their measures are faulted for not representing the lives of at-risk populations, their work laid the foundation for life events research that has had and continues to have far-reaching influence. Researchers who have pursued this line of thinking conclude that the same events are more stressful when they are recent, although early life events can add to one's future vulnerability. It generally is agreed that it is negative events that cause stress, rather than positive ones or a combination of both. Eugene Paykel conceptualized stressful events in terms of entrances (new people entering one's life) and exits (departures of others).[6] He found that negatively evaluated events, rather than change itself, are correlated with depression. The additive nature of stressful events is particularly detrimental. Depressed people in Paykel's study reported three times as many events as the control group, and the occurrence of the events also was more frequent. Life change itself was not really critical, nor were single negative events in one's life, even when the loss of a loved person was a factor. As a rule, most events were not of a catastrophic nature. They were everyday occurrences, clustered over time. So it appears that it is not necessarily the event prior to the onset of symptoms that causes depression, but a number of events clustered over the same period of time. When a single event appears to antecede depression, it is wise to inquire about other possible events impacting during the same period, for life events researchers have continued to support these findings.[7]

LOSS, LONELINESS, AND DEPRESSION

Loss has been assumed to be an important cause of depression since the days of Karl Abraham and Sigmund Freud. Recent research is delimiting the concept to a less encompassing analysis. For example, a major study found discernible loss or separation only in about 25 percent of clinically depressed patients.[8] Still, the control group had an incidence of even fewer losses (5 to 10 percent). The concept of loss also presupposes that one had something to begin with, an increasingly unrealistic perception. Far too often the depressed person never had "it" to lose, whatever "it" may represent — love, self-esteem, or hope. In fact, positive previous experiences can modify the negative impact of loss.

Though these realities must be considered, it is still important to understand that significant personal loss may be a major contributing susceptibility factor in depression, as well as fostering a general propensity for illness.[9] Observable stages of grief appear to evolve in a somewhat universal process of recovery, regardless of the nature of the loss.[10] Studies of the survivors of the Coconut Grove fire in the 1940s provided the first relevant empirical evidence.[11] Briefly, the stages are initial shock and denial, followed by anger and depression, finally culminating in understanding and acceptance. (This "work of mourning" is discussed in some detail in Chapter 2.) Only the length of time and the intensity of each stage differ with the severity of the loss. Elisabeth Kubler-Ross[12] also has applied the principles to the terminally ill, for dying clients may experience depression preparatory to their many impending losses and the final loss of life itself.[13]

Loss experienced in infancy and childhood has been conjectured, investigated, and debated for years. John Bowlby can be credited with much of the important work in this area.[14] He has concluded that the abrupt severing of an attachment with the caretaking person in infancy can retard the natural growth of independence and self-reliance. Brown and Harris's observations are similar; their research concludes that a woman's sense of mastery and self-esteem may be permanently lowered as a result of the loss of a mother before age eleven. Neurotic, less severe depression and past loss by separation were highly correlated, as was psychotic depression and past loss by death. These "symptom-formation factors" may be similar to object-relations investigator Sidney Blatt's differential assessment of simple anaclitic and introjective depressions, in which he hypothesizes a correlation between age of infant separation and variant depression symptoms.[15] Further, the finding that past loss has a built-in vulnerability factor may be analogous to Martin Seligman's Learned Helplessness model of depression. Depressed persons are those who have "learned" that coping does not help. If they have experienced early loss without effectively working through it, it may be that they will be vulnerable to depression due to later loss or stress of some other kind.[16]

There is recent evidence indicating that past experiences of intimacy lead to an absence of loneliness, even for those who are presently alone. Loss may be a serious problem only when an intimate relationship has never been experienced. The fact that most clients show evidence of profound loneliness, then, has serious implications that must be addressed. It is such a pervasive problem that it has been suggested that social workers should make the understanding and treatment of loneliness the major focus of their field.[17] A large body of research during the past twenty years shows a high correlation between depression and loneliness, yet recent findings indicate that the two emotions are relatively distinct and do not seem to be causally related.[18] The connection between the two appears to be additive, rather than intermediate or interactional. That is to say that one does not cause the other. Rather, loneliness is a vulnerability factor that may "add up" to depression. In my own person-environment studies, I also conclude that depressed people feel alone and uncared for by both their families and their peers at work.[19] Again, the impact seems to be largely additive, rather than interactional.

The loneliness factor may be culturally imposed, for many groups of people fit into the category. They include a diverse spectrum, such as alienated children and adolescents; solitary housewives; displaced homemakers (separated, divorced, and widowed women who have no marketable skills); socially isolated men who are numb to their emotions; homosexuals who must live under cover; hidden victims of battering, rape, and incest; pregnant teenage girls; the physically and mentally impaired; and people of color who are rejected by the majority culture. All may be vulnerable to depression for all experience separation, loneliness, and unsupportive environments. Insight into causal factors may be grounded in pervasive life experience rather than distinct situational events.[20] In each of these cases, people may be misdiagnosed as endogenously depressed by those who are either not sensitive to the issues or aware of their possibility.

SOCIAL-ROLE THEORY AND DEPRESSION

Within social-role theory, depression is believed to be a response to impending or real role loss when identity is closely entwined with one's role. Roles are socially prescribed at birth according to factors such as sex, class, and ethnicity; behavior is thenceforth determined by them. Largely as a result of socialization, people learn to be whom society wishes them to be in order to belong and to be loved. Every role acquires an evaluation relative to status and desirability that includes the perceived usefulness of the role, its inherent power, and the association of the role with others of value. Role expectations change with age, so individuals must be flexible enough to take on new roles and sometimes to shed those that are no longer appropriate. Role discontinuity and role loss can be as devastating to self-esteem as other significant losses and have been attributed to depression. So, too, are roles that restrict development and status, and conflicting roles that result in role strain. Transitional sex roles reflect a major sensitive area relevant to males and females today. The same swiftly moving society that affects such roles also affects other areas of modern life. Role change is required with every move and each new job, with new relationships, as one chooses lovers or marries, as one has children, grows older and takes on new responsibilities, and as children grow older themselves and change their role expectations. Stress accompanies each role adjustment, no matter how welcome the change. Those that are negatively perceived are even more likely to be associated with feelings of depression. Fred Ilfeld's study of approximately three thousand people in the Chicago area looked at daily circumstances or social conditions that are generally considered undesirable.[21] He found that stress related to marital and parental roles are more closely associated with depression than any others. It should not surprise us, for people in recent decades have been telling us that their familial roles are unfulfilling, reflected in staggering divorce rates. Divorce often follows on the heels of depression-related conditions in the home.

WOMEN AT RISK

Pervasive Social Conditions

Most studies regarding stressful life events have concerned men or neglected to mention sex differences.[22] While there is some evidence that women and men may respond differently to the same social stressors, findings are inconsistent and instruments appear to be biased. Life events measures have been faulted for being more appropriate to men than to women. One example is related to a "contagion of stress" concept which some studies indicate is relevant to women, but is not included on life events scales. Many events reported by women as stressful concern other significant people in their lives. These are events they did not control at all, such as work or money problems impacting on a loved one. Perhaps their relational roles as nurturers and caretakers make them more sensitive to the lives of others. Also, their vulnerability may reflect their lack of control, or it might be argued that these events *are* directly related to their well-being, particularly when they are in a dependent position. Life events studies also have excluded major stresses such as personal violence, child and adult sexual abuse and harassment, unwanted pregnancy, abortion, and child-care responsibilities, to name a few not uncommon events in the lives of millions of women.

Further, those events that have been addressed have not been interpreted relative to women's varied experience. For example, moving has been found to be more stressful to women than to men and is correlated with depression.[23] Were their situations closely analyzed, it might be found that it is homemakers, women in low-level jobs, or career women who are moving for their husbands' advancement who are the at-risk population. Not only is the move not related to their own advancement, but their social supports are eroded along with their identities. Women whose reputations are solely grounded in voluntarism and the home must begin afresh in each new environment. They do not carry resumes to provide them introduction to new environments in terms of their expertise and personal reputation. Moving, therefore, is a superficially simplistic vulnerability factor that hides a complex reality for many women. When they move for the same reasons as their husbands do, they also may be free of depression.

George Brown and Tirril Harris developed a social origins of depression model after investigating a sample of British working-class women.[24] The researchers assessed their environments in terms of "vulnerability factors" and "provoking agents." They found that both conditions must be present to precipitate depression. Significant vulnerability factors include the absence of a confidant (particularly a husband or boyfriend), loss of a mother before age eleven,[25] and having three or more children under age fourteen living at home. When these conditions were present, employment halved the risk.

The researchers emphasize the importance of evaluating the meaningful implications of life events to the person herself. A severe or major difficulty does not result in depression unless some other provoking factor increases the subjective perception of trauma. So, for example, pregnancy and birth were found to be associated with a greater risk of depression, but depression only became a reality when in context with a difficulty such as bad housing or a poor marriage. The thoughts and feelings held before, during, and after the occurrence of an event are of particular importance. Indeed, the finding that a male confidant may be more essential than a female intimate may be directly related to cultural perceptions. The British, like Americans, have socialized their women to assess themselves in accordance with their ability to attract men, distrusting other women as competitors in the bargain. The women's movement may not have reached the women in Brown and Harris's study. Otherwise, female support groups may have reduced vulnerability. Conitions, emotional responses to events, and depressive symptoms themselves may even merge together, increasing the severity of depression.[26] For example, loss of self-esteem or dependence may predispose a person to depression and also become a prominent symptom.

The Person-Environment model may provide some highly relevant insight to the growing body of life events knowledge. The model takes into consideration both personality predisposition and pervasive life events relative to the home and workplace. Cross-cultural studies indicate that dependence as a personality factor and lack of supportiveness and control both in the home and at work have an additive negative effect. The more these conditions reflect one's life situation, the more likely one is to be depressed, and vice versa.[27]

Living "Alone" as a Risk Factor

Of the 17.8 million people living alone in the United States, 10,738,000 are women age fourteen and over, according to the 1980 census.[28] Within their numbers are over eight million single mothers and their eleven million children. One million of these mothers are children themselves. There are, of course, many women of all ages who are not mothers, who also are struggling to survive emotionally and physically, alone in the world. There are between two and three million middle-aged, displaced homemakers who have lived in the roles of mothers and wives, roles that are no longer available to them. As for thirteen million elderly women, two-thirds were living alone when they died, often for over fourteen years.

It is generally assumed that these women are dependent and need to learn to become autonomous, to function independently. The assumptions are often correct. Research indicates that women have been socialized to emotional dependence and that cultural realities insure their physical and financial dependence.[29] The innate human propensity of living things to develop competence and environmental mastery appears to be stunted in many women. Not only do they seem unable to cope, but they lose their desire to do so. This is a natural outcome of inhibited autonomy,[30] or so it seems. I suggest we take another look at the realities of women's lives, for their culturally sub-scribed dependence does not reflect the actuality of their daily exis-tence. They are neither weak, unable to cope or function, inadequate, inept, unskillful, nor ineffectual. They are often courageous, flexible, and able to handle a multiplicity of responsibilities and problems, not only of their own, but of their families and friends. Many are, or long have been, the supportive caretakers of children, husbands, elderly parents, and others in need. They are the people who are feeding, clothing, and sheltering their kin, despite their long hours, low wages, and poverty. They are the ones who retain the burden of home care and maintenance, even when they take on full marketplace respon-sibilities. They are the teenagers who bravely keep their babies, however foolishly, alone and unnurtured themselves. These are the women "alone," dependent to be sure, in need of autonomy, yes, but strong and capable too. The problems that they cope with daily are often monumental. It is not the personhood of many women that needs to be changed, but their self-perception. They are already self-reliant and they do not recognize themselves.[31] Interventions that address cognition and self-esteem are in order.[32]

There are indications that people who are content when alone are free of depression and tend to be well adjusted individuals. Singleness as a viable way of living represents a shift in American values that has evolved of necessity, since one out of every five households now consists of a single person. Because that person is usually a woman, learning to live alone contentedly is especially relevant to them. De-pression is a common experience for those who are recently single, though it may be a temporary experience. Women typically feel bereft, unable to cope with the worldly demands placed on them. Their fiscal problems are realistic, for single elderly women are much more likely to live in poverty than any other senior group. As for coping with their environments, the outlook is more hopeful. Tasks relegated in tradi-tional households to their husbands can be learned and often are. In so doing, depression is alleviated through mastery of the environment, despite financial stress. Provided they have their physical health and *some* means of support, the initial trauma following divorce or widow-hood need not be long endured.

As women grow older, despite double standards of aging and their likelihood to be single, research is beginning to indicate that they tend to become happier.[33] In fact, the presence of a nonsupportive husband who requires care and attention has been found to exacerbate the problems of elderly women in contrast to those who live alone.[34] While empirical data are not conclusive, women's increasing contentedness may be correlated with their growing independence, their abilities to care for themselves, and their often superior relational qualities.[35] Whether or not they live alone does not appear to be critical. Rather, it is the presence or absence of an intimate, supportive person in their lives that is the key. Indeed, there are a growing number of heterosexual and homosexual women who choose never to marry and live alone contentedly. Since never-married women have the lowest rates of mental illness, there is little cause for alarm based on their aloneness itself. Remaining alone need not mean loneliness; it can mean solitude. The difference between the two conditions is vast.[36]

The plight of the single male is not as encouraging. They appear to have more difficulty adjusting to divorce and widowhood. Some believe that, apart from their larger field of choice, their propensity to rush into remarriage is a reaction to their inability to be alone. Their ex- or deceased wives often have been their only intimate friends. Generally credited with having "instrumental" qualities that reflect being able "to do" things, their instrumental shortcomings are emerging along with relational deficits as central factors related to their profound discomfort when faced with the reality of living alone. The inability to maintain their homes, to care for their clothing, to shop for food and cook their meals looms large in the lives of recently single men. The household is as frightening for them as the larger world is to women who are alone for the first time.[37] They need to know that learning how to master daily household tasks is as important and appropriate to them as it is to women.

The ability to forge a nurturing environment should not be related to gender. Both women and men can overcome their discomfort with being alone by creating their own nutritive surroundings through learning to care for themselves. This caring encompasses household caretaking activities and transcends them, for it refers to caring in the deepest sense of the word. People must learn to care for themselves by being responsive to their own needs for nurturance, taking responsibility for their own well-being. While we are often aware that women neglect such self-responsibility, we overlook the fact that men are dependent on the continual support provided by women. They, too, are at risk in this area. Most of the characteristics of caring — devotion, trust, patience, humility, and honesty — apply directly to caring for oneself. It is not self-idolatry but self-nurturance that leads to personal growth. Self-caring also enhances relationship, for people relate to others in the same general way that they relate to themselves.[38] Both women and men can be encouraged to treat themselves as they would treat someone whom they wish to entertain or make especially comfortable and happy. By exploring what such activities might be, they will simultaneously get in touch with what pleases themselves. Learning to live alone contentedly can be one of the most difficult, but also the most enjoyable, of therapeutic tasks for both sexes. Laura Primakoff includes in her formula for alone-contentedness, self-nurturing behavior such as cleaning and cooking for oneself, self-loving behaviors reflecting sensuality and sexuality, and self-guiding behaviors, such as journal writing.[39]

Sexual Desirability as a Risk Factor

If any event can be singled out as detrimental in and of itself, it may be threats to sexual desirability. The most frequently mentioned stressors in the longitudinal study by Melitta Leff and her colleagues of events occurring prior to the onset of depression were personal experiences that led to a questioning of one's sexual desirability.[40] Depression usually developed slowly over weeks or months following such an event. Whether or not vulnerability stemming from feelings of rejection was compounded by fear of abandonment is not clear, but feelings of diminished self-worth were evident. In these times of changing sexual mores, role redefinition, and ambiguity, clinicians must be aware of the possibility of increased susceptibility to depression. Neither women nor men can be certain of what sexual desirability entails. To illustrate, some women are still attracted to traditionally dominant males, while many others are repelled by them. And there are men who are attracted to the home-oriented woman, while others find her less than interesting, and find the career woman more appealing. Not only do people vary, but their ideals and their sexual responses may be in conflict. It is not unusual to find that women and men who voice a preference for one type of person react emotionally and sexually to the exact opposite. Cultural mores do not change overnight, nor do the people who practice them. It is more important to explore the subject with clients, to instill a positive perception of their particular sexual identity despite external exigencies. People must learn that sexuality, like personality, is an individual matter where being true to oneself is the essential. When one is open to relationship, there will be others that will be attracted to genuineness, whatever one's propensity. This holds true for homosexuals as well as heterosexuals.[41]

Social Roles as a Risk Factor

Role theory, as a theoretical frame of reference, can be effective in understanding the roots of depression in women. Roles are directly related to the life conditions that pervade the environment in which events occur. The roles to which women are socialized reflect a pervasive life condition that may result in their greater vulnerability to depression. They are taught to concentrate primarily on marriage, the home, and children. But statistics indicate that the average woman who marries and has children lives forty-five years after her last child begins school, thirty years after her last child leaves home and/or marries, and fourteen years after her husband dies.[42] Yet, women continue to be taught to rely on a male provider for sustenance and status. More and more they desire to work or must work outside the home, but their jobs are often at low levels and are dead-ended. They are likely also to live alone without male providers, to take on the burdens of home, motherhood, and bread-winning. These women, incidentally, represented the highest poverty risk in the nation even before the onslaught of budget cuts at the national and local levels in the early 1980s.

Women rather than men are expected to be nurturant, to suppress anger, and to be nonassertive. Yet these are the attributes that research reveals as vulnerability factors relative to depression.[43] They are taught that only youthful beauty is attractive. But since women are more likely to outlive men, this limited standard of beauty often leaves them feeling rejected as they age, by the relatively few available men. Sociologist Pauline Bart's study of middle-aged depressed women revealed that women who live out their lives in the traditional feminine wife-mother role are at risk.[44] The subjects of her study had histories of self-sacrifice and perfectionism, living vicariously through their husbands and children. One cannot help noticing the similarity between Bart's "good women" and Freud's description in 1917 of the "good, capable, conscientious woman" whom he was perplexed to find "more likely to fall ill of the disease" than her less traditional, less altruistic counterpart.[45] Bart interpreted her findings, on the basis of role theory, as reflecting an "empty nest syndrome." These women felt betrayed by their children's adult independence and their husband's lack of attention. They became depressed when they realized that they had given up their personal lives without any reward. The conformist who represents society's approved norms found her value to the world obsolete as her children grew up. She lost hope of future fulfillment as her mother role declined. A major symptom of depression, her sense of hopelessness, was very real. She really had little hope of regaining her outlived role in the future. An early insight of Freud's is applicable here. "For all we know," he observed, "it may be that she has come very near to self-knowledge. We only wonder why a woman must become ill before she can discover truth of this kind."[46] Depression in women, according to social-role theory, is the result of societal demands and restrictions. Symptoms may reflect the inevitable stress born of trying to fit into a preconceived niche—a sex-role stereotype that demands conformity.

The female role in today's society is fraught with ambiguity. Expectations are often unclear, or more importantly, conflicting. Role conflicts may occur within a single role, wherein a wife is expected to fill two disparate roles such as *femme fatale* and family laundress. Or conflicts may occur between two different roles, such as homemaker and work-role expectations. Today's women are often expected to be all things to all people, within the family structure, in the marketplace, and in relation to the community at large. Expectations are so diverse and so polarized that there is often little connection between women's many role positions. Committed through cultural pressures to narrow and often false images of femininity, their roles tend to be discontinuous. Their development is further stifled by the limited variety of role models in their personal lives or in the media after which they might pattern themselves.

Role restriction is also attributed to the higher rate of depression in women. Most men occupy two roles and therefore have two possibilities for gratification, while housewives occupy only one role and that one is low in prestige. Those women who do work outside the home are likely to be in less favorable jobs. They are also likely to carry the burden of home and caretaking responsibilities regardless of their extrafamilial work. Dual-role strain is a commonplace reality.[47]

Female sex-role conceptions and expectations for the highly educated woman are even more contradictory. These women receive conflicting messages from family, culture, and educational institutions regarding success and future positions in society. Excellence in student roles is often negated later should they prove serious enough to carry the behavior over into adult life. And even today, intelligence itself must be concealed in the search for a man, according to the role expectations of large segments of society. Although this viewpoint has been modified in recent years, it is still common. Adult women with desires for a more autonomous self-concept are often victims of depression. Their expectations are not compatible with those held by others, and their quest for identity may be perceived as a search for meaningful roles. Depression represents the symptoms of this search. The depressed woman can be viewed as a rolemaker in a search for and an attempt to maintain a stable social identity, a basic human need.[48]

Women can be introduced to new possibilities, such as the enrichment of the female sex-role position. This can be accomplished in part through role sharing and the breakdown of role polarization in the home. Work with family members is needed in order to implement these directives. Husbands, male companions, and children of all cultures need to know that existing conditions are depressive for women; adherence to the status quo can be destructive. There is a tendency for stabilized roles to become "legitimate expectations" — a feeling that one should continue in the same role and role behavior. Education to the contrary may be an excellent depression-prevention measure.

Children as a Risk Factor

While Pauline Bart noted that depressed women were resentful of their grown children,[49] Myrna Weissman and Eugene Paykel were impressed by the stressful relationship between adolescents and their depressed mothers.[50] They analyzed the content of 774 interviews with depressed females and found that the vast majority of problems concerned the management of day-to-day problems. One of their central concerns was their adolescent children. The women were angry not only with their husbands, but also with their adolescent children.

More recent research indicates that younger children in the home add to the risk of depression in their mothers to an even greater extent. Recall that George Brown and Tirril Harris found that women who have three or more children under age fourteen were most likely to be depressed.[51] Leonard Pearlin and James Johnson report that female depression is a greater probability the younger the children in the home.[52] Women who are poor and have responsibility for children are at high risk for depression whether married, divorced, or separated, according to a national survey conducted by Lenore Radloff.[53] These criteria cover most women who have children since most of the nation's poor are women,[54] and the majority of married, divorced, and separated women have sole responsibility for their children. While theorists seldom conjecture why female depression and children are linked, the obvious reason that comes to mind is the burden and restrictiveness of the role itself. But there may be more to the picture. It might be that children reflect societal attitudes in regard to their low opinion of women and motherhood. Regardless of claims to the contrary, the roles of mothers in the United States hold little status and no economic reward. In fact, the American government and society fiscally penalize women who are mothers. Those who recall World War II add to their memories the diatribe of Philip Wylie's "momism" popular in the early 1940s.[55] While the term is no longer a household word, the denigration of mothers continues. (Indeed, the word "mother" has even become a profanity.) Given that women are led to believe that motherhood is their most fulfilling role, the discrepancy with the reality of life experience may be devastating. Women experience not only resentment at having been given false information, but guilt that the outcome is due to their poor role performance as mothers. The younger the children in the home, the more likely is their sole identification with the role of mother and the higher the risk of depression.

Despite the American myth, researchers report that children do not make up emotional support systems for their mothers, regardless of their age. Throughout the lifespan, they are in an evolving state of development and change, making the provision of support to a parent as unlikely as it is unreasonable to expect. The mother must constantly adapt to changes in her children;[56] to link a substantial amount of self-esteem to the task is unwise. This reality is no less viable in old age, though a middle-aged daughter (often a mother herself) generally cares for her elderly mother's needs. (Such a daughter is also at risk, for demands converge on her from two generations as well as from her spouse, compounding the stresses in her life.) Still, for the elderly woman, like her middle-aged daughter, research findings indicate that friends are her nurturers, rather than her children.[57] It is friends, after all, who are likely to have shared interests and mutual understanding. The finding makes better sense than the myth.

Facing these facts may help individual women to know that their situation is not due to failure as a parent. It may also provide motivation to develop supports elsewhere, based on reality rather than what I call "The Walton Fantasy," contemporary America's family fairy tale. Research is needed to investigate the disappointment of children regarding their mothers. It may be a developmental phenomena to be accepted,[58] or it may be that the cultural myth of motherhood, so impossible to fulfill, has led to dysfunctional expectations incorporated by children. When children believe that their mothers, unlike others, have let them down, hostility and alienation quite naturally develop. Interventions, therefore, should occur at both the individual and the institutional level. There is no need to perpetuate impossible expectations in the office with one's client. It is equally dysfunctional to extend the fantasy to the classroom, the practicum, and other training forums. Mothers can be viewed, at least by older children and adults, as human beings with attributes both positive and negative. It is to be hoped that the former characteristics will outweigh the latter, but in any case, women should not be competing with a myth of perfection. The inevitable fall from the pedestal is as painful to offspring as it is to the fallen.

Regarding Nontraditional Relationships[59]

While the people least likely to be depressed appear to be never married-women who live independently,[60] they too may be vulnerable to depression when the loss of a relationship is a factor. This is especially true if the relationship is nontraditional, one that may be unacceptable to mainstream society. It is also true for women who have been married but are no longer. Our social mores are changing; marriage can no longer be assumed for a lifetime, nor can the possibility of remarriage be taken for granted. Parenthood is optional, and those who choose to have children are marrying and having them later in life. Yet, throughout the lifespan people continue to form short- and long-term attachments. The family is geographically fragmented, with siblings, parents, and children scattered across the nation. Unmarried women do not necessarily live wtih their relatives, and when they do, they are at risk for depression according to recent data. There are also more couples who live together without marrying. They may be heterosexual couples (spouses, lovers, and friends) or same-sex relationships between people living together as friends or as lovers.

New social structures are fragile and gain cultural acceptance gradually. Consequently, such relationships themselves can be easily shattered. Marjorie Moskol suggests that because there are fewer sexual, social, and economic restraints, intimacy develops quickly and intensely. With few social supports for nontraditional relationships, when separation occurs people often feel bereft and become depressed. Despite recent changes, most women are still brought up to feel they cannot "go it alone." Some of their constraints are real, for they are economically dependent, the targets of violence, and subject to employment discrimination and poverty. Statistics indicate that half of all women who live alone earn less than $3,000 a year.[61] Clinicians find that they are not likely to have learned decision-making skills. Having been taught to avoid conflict, they fearfully accept their fate and more than their share of responsibility and guilt. Women who do not conform to traditional roles because they remain unmarried, are divorced, are lesbians, or are involved in extramarital affairs are often isolated; for them the loss of a relationship can be especially traumatic. Unlike more traditional women, they may not find public solace for their grief. Depression is often the outcome.

Moskol applies appropriate strategies to these women to reduce depression and anxiety that result in renewed energy. To begin, she suggests that the nontraditional woman coming for help be given the opportunity to ventilate her feelings — to express fully the details of the relationship and its termination. It is helpful to probe for past as well as current losses. When connections are made between the past and the present, the woman can understand how feelings from the past reemerge and combine with present emotions. Their resulting distress might otherwise be considered excessive, particularly difficult to comprehend when the end of the relationship is voluntary.

The therapist's acceptance helps reduce any guilt that may be prevalent in a nontraditional relationship. Women often perceive the ending of their unsanctioned partnerships as punishment for their transgressions. They feel they have no right to experience grief, or to seek help. Such women may feel "crazy" because their emotional distress is so contradictory and confusing. Clarification and assurance by the therapist that their feelings are to be expected validate the legitimacy of their pain about the loss.

Feelings of failure are also common, particularly when a heterosexual relationship ends. Women are often taught that they have chief, if not sole, responsibility for their success. They can be educated to the fact that relationships are mutual responsibilities, and that needs and goals change over time, which undermines the equilibrium of the partnership and creates an imbalance that may not be restored. The end of a relationship may be viewed as a part of change, a growth process, rather than a failure. When possible, sessions with both partners are recommended for optimal reduction of guilt and failure. Anger will emerge—at the "wasted time," the spent love and energy, the injustices and unkindnesses, the financial deprivation, and so on. Resentment fades when clients come to realize that nothing is "wasted," that all experience can be educational and worthwhile, and can lead to a healthful future. The energy consumed by anger, causing anxiety, becomes available for building confidence and enhancing feelings of autonomy.[62] Managing one's own affairs, making decisions, training for new work, traveling, learning to live alone comfortably, all help to rebuild confidence.

New friendships are made, old ones renewed, and the need for intimacy returns. Reluctant to risk the pain of another possible ending, such women may need encouragement to begin again. They can be supported in the process of forming close relationships in whatever ways are appropriate to them. Intimacy is to be encouraged on many grounds, and some believe it is especially important to women. Recall that Brown and Harris found intimacy to be a protective factor in their lives. Women who are at high risk may be less likely to experience it.[63] While intimacy is also important to men, women generally fill their need. In the absence of nurturance, men, too, are at risk.

A Political Analysis of Women and Therapy

When women go into therapy, many therapists persist in encouraging them to take the blame for their unhappiness. In fact, there is evidence that women are encouraged to adjust to their roles, that they are implicitly guided toward culturally established feminine norms. "Femininity" is clearly delineated as dependent, passive, submissive behavior, otherwise viewed as childlike. Sexual stereotypes are thus reinforced.[64] The therapeutic encounter is for many women just one more instance of an unequal relationship. They are submissive to the dominant authority figure, usually a male, just as they have been in their relationships with their fathers as children and with their husbands as adults. The fact that they relive this pattern in the therapeutic situation can in no way be dismissed as transference or projection, contrary to traditional professional opinion. Neither can their continued depression or overt anger be considered resistance or manipulation. Female clients often are experiencing, in actuality, a frustrating reality, though they may be told otherwise and further confused.

In a society that values identity through occupational achievement, women are largely excluded from the system. When they work outside the home, too often their work is perceived as a job, not as something to be taken seriously. Their female identities are not assigned on the basis of individual achievement, as the dominant American value would prescribe, but on the basis of physical characteristics, kinship, and marriage ties. Paradoxically, if they insist on their individuality and resist conformity, female clients run the risk of being diagnosed as neurotically immature. The law of self-fulfilling prophesy may ensure the therapist's negative prognosis.

Deviant or culturally labeled "unfeminine" traits are perceived as symptoms of illness for many therapists whose views of women reflect the cultural consensus. A woman has an identity if she is attractive enough to "get a man" and establish a home, and if she is able to find fulfillment in an altruistic role. Marcia Millman and Rosabeth Kanter suggest that the professional view of the psychological needs of women all too often seems to be suspiciously formulated on the assumption of male superiority.[65] Even therapists who have abandoned other orthodox concepts often retain deep-seated attitudinal vestiges. Their teachings continue to provide a rationale for keeping women in subservient positions. Masculine domination, for example, has been viewed as necessary to the fulfillment of the "passive masochistic" needs of women, so events in the lives of women are assessed differentially. Women often experience a denial of their innate feelings and perceptions, the very lifelong conditions that initially led to their psychic pain, confusion, and depression. The expectation that their distress will be relieved motivates them toward compliance with the therapist, whatever his or her theoretical bias.

The practice of repudiating the reality of women's perceptions is therapeutically destructive. In order for growth to be experienced, previous uncomfortable realities must be accepted, not invalidated. While clients often are accused of such denial, therapists also may be guilty of this behavior.[66] The nonacceptance of female sex roles is not a sick rejection of feminine identity; instead, the role rejection may represent a giant step toward a mature self-concept and mental health.

The term "female sex role" too often is analogous to social powerlessness. It is not "what women do, but whatever women do, that is negatively sanctioned."[67] Therefore, it is not role alone, but gender that produces inequity.[68] Gender identity, rather than sex-role identity, is the critical concept. It represents pride, security, and confidence in one's sexual membership, which are all too often denied women. When socialized according to the patriarchal ideals of womanhood, they develop "femininity complexes," which block them from all paths that are incompatible with the introjected feminine identity.[69] Finding that this path leads to nowhere, such women succumb in their disillusionment to depression as their only route to personhood.

A woman who is in treatment with an aware therapist can gain the insight and strength to change. Interpretations should focus on social factors that mitigate against independent womanhood, encouraging dependency, isolation, and helplessness. Dependency in the therapeutic relationship should be discouraged consistently because of its association with depression and low self-esteem.[70] The therapist should be cognizant of her (or his) own feelings of dependency and defenses against them when acting as a therapeutic agent. It is also important to guard against client-therapist relationships that reflect superior over subordinate roles that tend to reinforce feelings of incompetence and inadequacy.

Feminist Therapy[71]

The reevaluation of the client-therapist relationship is at the core of feminist therapy. The therapist, acting as a role model, may be appropriately self-disclosing and is always egalitarian. Because it is believed that sexual, socioeconomic, and professional status barriers reinforce the subordinate position of the woman client and stifle cooperative effort, issues of power and competition are openly addressed. Keen awareness of cultural mores imposed on and adopted by women is essential for understanding how their functioning has been limited. Indeed, inhibited functioning may well include the female therapist herself. (The terms client and therapist are considered objectionable to many feminists. I have used them for convenience in differentiating two people, rather than as role labels.)

While there is no single definition of feminist therapy, there is general agreement that it is based upon the assumption that all human beings are naturally growing and developing, and that they are shaped by social structures (economics and institutions) and by cultural patterns. Those patterns refer to sex-role training, which channels cultural values and practices. Feminist therapy recognizes that society imposes restrictive roles on both women and men that block them in their development. Both the inherent uniqueness and the commonalities they share must be nurtured and allowed to develop if they are to become truly "whole," responsible human beings. The development and advancement of women is affirmed, as are the same opportunities for men. Underlying feminist theory is a single standard system whereby all human beings have personal power: the power to be and to become. Yet no *one* sex (or race) has the power *over* another. The present dualistic system has placed women at the lower end of win-lose continuums, whether they be dominant-submissive, independent-dependent, leader-follower, active-passive, powerful-powerless, or strong-weak. If women of color, they fall at the end point of the political scale. The data regarding women as a population at risk clearly indicate that such dualism is dysfunctional to women, whether we are referring to women as depression candidates, poverty risks, or victims of violence.[72]

Women themselves, having internalized the norms of society, are often unaware of their situation. They are in a unique position in that identification with their reference group is stymied because they generally live with the dominant male group and their self-esteem and acceptance are based largely on male opinion and approval. Research shows that it is not unusual to find the most unhappy housewife deny her misery[73] and the woman who is clearly overburdened by her dual family and work roles insisting on her husband's supportiveness.[74] While a study by Leonard Pearlin did not find women more likely than men to exhibit denial, he did find the attribute correlated with depression. It has been my experience that women's depression is often strongly linked with denial that is being threatened. Depression may be the defense of last resort. The whisper of truth is at the periphery of the formerly well-defended woman's consciousness. Those women who indicate that they are not disenchanted with their lot and are not depressed despite oppressive situations may be manifesting strong denial that has not yet been fractured.[75] That does not mean that they are invulnerable to depression.

Women who were invested equally in both work and family roles were found in Pearlin's study[76] to be in conflict and depressed. A feminist therapist would not counsel such a person to divest herself of her work interest (or her family investment, for that matter). Instead, she would focus initially on consciousness raising to break through the barrier of denial. Resolution cannot come about until she becomes aware of the conflict between her social-role position and its attendant cultural expectations and norms, and her own emerging need for individuation.[77]

With the client's new recognition of dysfunctional cultural influences that are inhibiting her development, she can explore her lifestyle and the choices available to her, as well as those she will have to make a special effort to open up. She can gauge where she wishes to focus her energies by reflecting on her values — those she wishes to retain and those she seeks to revise.[78] Whatever her decisions, the assumption of her inherent right to personal power — the power to be and to become — is inherent in the model.

While consciousness raising is possible in a one-to-one situation, groups are generally considered to be most effective. It is important that women be provided the opportunity to identify with other women and to recognize the similarity of their experience. Their feelings are thus legitimized, their anxieties reduced, and their energies liberated. Newton and Walton's study of women in consciousness-raising groups identify five major changes in the persons involved: altered world views; identity changes; changes in reference groups; changes in job/career orientation; and enhanced self-acceptance and worth, concomitant with decreased feelings of guilt and self-doubt.[79]

The consciousness-raising process has direct implications for the alleviation of depression caused by disequilibrium and conflict between personal growth and social roles. Feminist therapy, as detailed, is a major source of resolution, but many of the insights and methods discussed elsewhere in this handbook can be incorporated into a feminist therapy model. The underlying theory and assumptions are what make the qualitative difference.

PREVENTION AND INTERVENTION

Life events theorists agree that depression is a psychological response to environmental stress, although they differ when it comes to assessing the stressors. Some focus on events preceding onset while others are more concerned with social roles or pervasive societal conditions that may impact on a person.

Loneliness and Friendship

Reality therapy is appropriate to life events models, for relationship and loneliness are explicitly taken into consideration. William Glasser developed the model, observing that people who come for therapeutic help lack the most critical factor for need fulfillment: a person whom they genuinely care about and who they feel genuinely cares about them.[80] In short, they are lonely and need a friend. In Glasser's opinion, the therapist must become that friend. Throughout the therapeutic process, involvement and commitment on the part of the therapist is open, sincere, and unflagging. Thus, the basic needs of depressed persons — to love and be loved, and to feel worthwhile to oneself and to another significant person — are enhanced. While the therapeutic relationship provides a new beginning, a safe place to risk involvement, it is, of course, limited. Attachment is necessarily one-sided and transitional. Therefore, people must be encouraged to make friends outside of the treatment situation, a principle that is not left to chance by reality therapists. The therapist can act as a catalyst, as well as a model, by encouraging their clients to be real, to be without facade whenever possible. If therapists are willing to risk unveiling their imperfection and humanness, then their clients are more likely to follow suit. They can be taught that people who are not truly themselves attract others to their disguised image. It follows that such people become fearful of being known, for the same acquaintances may not be attracted to the real self. It is much more realistic to be oneself in the first place and attract compatible friends.[81]

The second task centers on personal responsibility. In order for persons to feel that they can tolerate the multiple events impinging on their lives, they must learn to take the responsibility for fulfilling their own needs without depriving others of the ability to fulfill theirs. One learns responsibility through involvement with other human beings who themselves are responsible. Those who lack that experience must learn it later in life. Hence, reality therapists confront the client with the direct suggestion that the client is "doing" the depressing, an irresponsible behavior that must be eliminated. Still, clinicians who wish to adapt this model should not focus on depression, according to Glasser. Rather, discussion centers on the client's interests in order to develop self-worth and to establish a relationship with a responsible person — the therapist. As treatment progresses, clients are encouraged to set goals based upon what they want. The reality therapist simply asks clients who behave counterproductively (by being depressed) if they are doing something helpful relative to their avowed goal. Clients are encouraged to make more realistic plans, and to commit themselves to these plans. Deviations are not punished, nor are reasonable consequences interfered with. The therapist simply acknowledges what has happened in a matter-of-fact manner, and reformulates the goal-setting plan with the client. While reality therapy may appear to be concerned with the ordinary, it is one of the few interventions that directly addresses the reality of loneliness from a pragmatic perspective.

Interest Development and Values Clarification

The inability to make friends, a lack of interest in the world, and an absence of mastery in any area of life are all conditions associated with depression. That they may be intertwined causally makes common sense. People are less inhibited, more easy going, more open to sharing and relationship, and more interested in the community when they are self-assured about at least one thing.[82] The encouragement and development of a major interest should be included in a treatment plan. It makes no difference what the interest is, as long as an individual learns to do something well that he or she regards highly. One is never too old to develop interests or expertise.[83] Because depressed people often have no idea what is pleasing to them, interest development may be more problematic than it would appear. Values clarification, then, is essential in order to identify and freely choose an area of special interest. People can be helped to assess how they spend their lives, and to make plans for desired changes in roles, activities, and relationships — the significant events in their lives. Changes may be partial, temporal, or total, depending on the values and the realities of their situations. The values-clarification and life-planning process is detailed further in Chapter 6, so it will not be discussed here.[84] Suffice it to say that it is fundamental to the prevention and treatment of depression from a life events perspective.

Role Interventions

Karpman's Drama Triangle

The application of Karpman's Drama Triangle, (Figure 4-1) an interpretation generally applied by transactional analysts, is conceptually consistent with life events theory and dysfunctional roles.[85] Analysis of the Karpman Drama Triangle describes how the depressed person usually takes the role of the Victim, relating to another person who plays the Persecutor and treats the Victim badly. The Persecutor then feels guilty and comes to the rescue because the Victim is depressed. The depressed Victim quickly switches to the Persecutor role, telling the ex-Persecutor to "forget it." Thus, the Rescuer becomes the Victim and the Victim switches to the Rescuer role — remorseful, guilty, and subservient. And so goes the game. The goal of treatment is to get out of the triangle by refusing to play the game at all. People learn that the roles are reversible, and that anyone who is capable of playing one role is likely to switch to the other two, given the opportunity. The vivid description of the triangular process facilitates their understanding and commitment to change.

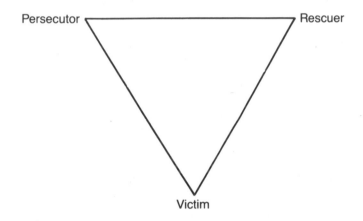

Figure 4-1.   Karpman's Drama Triangle.
Copyright 1968, The International Transaction
Analysis Association, Inc. Reprinted by
permission.

Role-Stripping Exercise[86]

People are often so inculcated with the playing of roles that it is difficult for them to get in touch with who they really are. Many roles have been taken on unwillingly because of societal pressures, while others are important to personal happiness. Given the opportunity, people can be taught to assess their roles and to reorder their time, commitment, and activities appropriately. A role-stripping exercise can help them explore these questions, guiding them in future decisions. The following is an illustration of such an exercise.

Begin by instructing group participants to write down five different roles, each of which is an important aspect of their lives, on five cards (one role per card). The five roles may be conceived as attributes (thin, black, tall), relationships (brother, mother), strengths (courageous, accountable, loving), and/or perceived weakness (selfish, impatient, unhealthy). Whether positive or negative, the roles should reflect the uniqueness of the individual. After the five roles are identified, the group members are instructed to arrange the cards in order of importance, from 1 (most important) to 5 (least important). Their assessment of "importance" is a personal decision and may include quantity of time spent in a role, quality of time, and values and ethics, among other criteria. Prioritizing is often ambiguous and will provide material for discussion.

Beginning with the least important role (number 5), participants are allowed to take a few minutes to think about themselves in that particular role. They are then asked to close their eyes and visualize themselves in the role. Instruct them to put the card face down in front of them, stripping themselves of the role. As the facilitator, the therapist should take time to allow them to express their loss or occasionally experienced relief, and then open up discussion of their feelings — are they happy, sad, lonely, relieved? The exercise is repeated until all five roles have been visualized and stripped. Participants are allowed to fantasize about who they are without their roles. It may be an emotionally vulnerable time, but it will help them to come to terms with their identities. The facilitator must be sensitive to feelings as reactions are explored. (The exercise is not advised for psychotic clients who have difficulty staying in touch with reality, whose depression is severe or who are really experiencing profound loss.)

Finally, participants are asked to assess which roles they can live without and which would be most difficult to give up. They should also assess whether they have taken on a role for someone else and if so, whether or not the benefits are worth the costs. The roles can be reassumed and reordered at this time, or eliminated where truly possible. When one role is discarded, it may be replaced with a more desirable one. A role that cannot realistically be rejected may be altered. For example, a shy woman may commit herself to becoming more assertive, while retaining her quiet identity. Or a man who sees himself in the role of breadwinner may decide to try to share that responsibility with his wife. Accordingly, a homemaker who enters the marketplace needs to reevaluate her housekeeping responsibilities, sharing maintenance tasks to provide for her new role.

The exercise will evoke a good deal of thought, emotion, and discussion of responsibilities, values, social constraints, and expectations. Conflicting expectations such as work versus family roles will emerge, as will the realization that it may be impossible to fill all the roles willed by society. Those who have actually experienced role loss will also become aware of the incongruity between their priorities and the realities of their lives. Such role loss is relevant to the displaced homemaker, the woman with grown children, the noncustodial divorced parent, and the elderly widow and widower alike. The reality of loss also impacts the woman who is no longer young in a youth-revered society, the middle-aged man who has lost his hair and muscle tone, and the recently impaired person. All are vulnerable candidates for depression. While the role-stripping exercise can be effective for individuals, sharing the process in a group as described above is even more powerful. The group members find that they are not alone in their experience. Discussion is usually lively and the interactions can be very supportive. Finding that validation in persons other than the therapist provides the opportunity for generalizing the experience to nontherapeutic situations.

Life Planning: The Past[87]

The idea of charting the lives of clients was introduced by Adolph Meyer in the 1930s.[88] Life-planning exercises have become useful tools in recent years, advanced by business and industrial management-training programs, as well as by specialists who work with women in transition. Depressed clients who are in the process of renewing their lives and planning their futures first need a clear understanding of their past and how they evolved to the present. The Personal Lifeline facilitates self-understanding and increases mastery over the direction of their lives, an experience that few depressed clients have had. The facilitator directs people in the lifeline exercise as follows:

Ask them to draw their lifelines, using crayons on a large sheet of paper. The left side of the page represents their birth and the right side represents the present. Life events are placed at appropriate intervals along the lifeline, creatively depicted in picture form, the use of color, with stick figures, graphs, or in the abstract. There are no stringent rules. The creativity of the participants encompasses all possibilities. They are to include both positive and negative major events, pervasive moods of each life phase, and turning points in their lives. As the facilitator, discuss the lifelines in detail together with the participants. When working in a group, participants can share the information with one another. Many similarities again emerge in the process, reassuring them that their lives are not radically different from everyone else's.

People can be encouraged to explore the ramifications of the events in their lives, as well as their personal decisions in regard to the events. For example, having a baby or moving to a new part of the country may have influenced their lives considerably. Whether or not they went through an event voluntarily makes a difference in their perception of the event as negative or positive. It is important to avoid stereotyped ideas concerning events, for it is common to find that people feel guilty about not fitting stereotypes. The woman who did not want her child and the man who did not want to take on a more prestigious job will be relieved to find that their true feelings are not as strange as they have been led to believe. Akin to the Life Review, relating one's life history has been found to be a therapeutic validation of one's life.[89] This is especially important for those who are in the process of change, for there is a human tendency to denigrate the past when moving toward mature functioning. The personal lifeline honors and integrates the past, paving a solid foundation upon which to proceed.

Life Planning: The Future

Following discussion of the lifeline exercise, which can take anywhere from minutes to hours in workshop sessions, participants are directed to imagine themselves at a point toward the far right-hand side of another sheet of paper, which represents a point in the future (from one week to perhaps five years hence, depending on the planned goals of the group or individual). The left-hand side now represents the present. Participants are instructed to imagine that they are looking back in time, drawing their autobiographical lifeline beginning with this day from a future perspective. Then, discuss the attributes, events, experiences, and achievements that might stand out as especially important during that period of time. As in the lifeline exercise, the events are depicted freely in representational form. The future lifeline is designed as a catalyst for goal setting and action. Therefore, the final life-planning phase is the goal-setting process, for as long as ideas remain abstract, they have limited life-change possibilities. When people learn to set goals and implement them, they become assured of their abilities to direct and take control of many of the events in their lives. This is as important to preventing depression as it is to alleviating symptoms.

The Goal-Setting Process[90]

Instruct each person to:

1. Choose a desirable goal that it is possible to obtain, however abstract or general.

2. Formulate the goal in a less abstract fashion, thus limiting its scope and pinpointing the goal.

3. Make the goal behavioral, and therefore observable, by asking:
   a. What specific things will I be doing or saying if I reach my goal?
   b. To whom or with whom will I be saying or acting what my goal entails?
   c. In what situation or circumstances will I be accomplishing my goal?

4. Establish a base rate of progress on this goal by asking how well the goal is presently accomplished. Ask:
   a. What do I do and say right now, specifically, in regards to my goal?
   b. To whom or with whom do I say it or act it?
   c. In what situations or circumstances do I carry out my present level of accomplishment with the goal?

5. Establish criteria of failure for the goal by asking how I will be behaving if I don't reach my objectives. Include:
   a. Words and/or actions.
   b. Persons involved.
   c. Situations and/or circumstances.
   d. My feelings inside as I fail.

6. Assess the reality dimension of accomplishing the goal by asking how likely it is that I can accomplish this goal in terms of:
   a. My present behavior regarding the goal.
   b. My motivation to change.
   c. My capacity to change.
   d. Whether external circumstances in my social environment will help or hinder my trying.

7. Plan for action translation of the conceived goal. Plans include detailed actions not specifically described in the goal formulation, but required in order to reach goal attainment.

Since the idea of setting goals is new to most people, they may have difficulty formulating them realistically.[91] Self-defeating goals can be avoided by identifying the steps necessary to alter previous behavior, as well as deciding on a realistic pace at which such a change can be achieved. For example, the student's goal, "I will go home and study tonight and I will keep studying for the rest of the semester," is self-defeating, whether or not the student is depressed. It might be broken down as follows, making allowances for concentration difficulties experienced in depression:

1. I will make a schedule for the week and allot specific time for study.
2. I will attempt to seriously follow my schedule for one week.
3. I will record on my daily schedule if I studied or the reasons why I did not study.
4. I will sign up for a study-skills group.
5. At the end of the week I will critically evaluate my progress and design a new schedule based on the evaluation.

Although many people are initially repelled by the idea of structured goal setting because of its apparent rigidity, in fact, the most functional goals are highly flexible. Multiple options should be left open whenever possible, for the success of the plan is increased along with options that aid in reaching the goal. More often, we find that structure is something that is lacking in depressed persons' lives. The very act of structured goals can help to create a safely contained world for such people.

THE DESPAIR OF NUCLEAR DESTRUCTION

The concept of a safe world provides an opportunity to acknowledge the pervasive despair created by the contemporary threat of worldwide nuclear destruction.[92] Joanna Macy suggests that, "as a society, we are caught between an impending sense of apocalypse and an inability to acknowledge it." We become anesthetized to the reality of our despair because it is so overwhelming to us. The suppression of our pain denies what has become possible — the annihilation of our species, an anathema to a culture committed to the American dream. The only hope is to be open to our despair, to face the darkness of the most devastating life event of our era together. Letting go of defenses opens us to true community and the power to turn the tides. Every day clinicians are finding that their clients, be they children or adults, are consumed by the psychological effects of the nuclear threat. While one might assess their despair as a kind of projective depression, a defense against whatever is *really* troubling them, it is just as likely that their depression is linked to the very real fear of a holocaust.

NOTES

1. See Chapter 1 for further discussion of classification issues.

2. Evans, Bergen, *The Psychiatry of Robert Burton* (New York: Octagon Books, 1972).

3. Burton, Robert (Democritis Junior), *The Anatomy of Melancholy* (Oxford: Printed by John Lichfield and Iames/Short, for Henry Cripps, Anno Dom. 1621).

4. Schwab, John, "A Rising Incidence of Depression," *Attitude 1*, 2 (January/February 1970): 2.

5. Holmes, Thomas, and R. H. Raye, "The Social Readjustment Rating Scale," *Journal of Psychosomatic Research 11* (1967): 213.

6. Paykel, Eugene, "Life Events and Acute Depression," in *Separation and Depression*, ed. J. P. Scott and E. C. Senay (Washington, DC: American Association for the Advancement of Science, 1973).

7. Note that the observation of symptoms clustered over time is also reflected diagnostically in primary affective disorder and DSM III; see Chapters 1 and 11. Also see "The Despair of Nuclear Destruction" discussed at the end of this chapter.

8. Weissman, Myrna M., and Eugene Paykel, *The Depressed Woman* (Chicago: University of Chicago Press, 1974).

9. Klerman, Gerald L., and J. E. Izen, "The Effects of Bereavement and Grief on Physical Health and General Well-Being," *Advances in Psychosomatic Medicine 9* (1977).

10. Lindemann, Erich, and Elizabeth Lindemann, *Beyond Grief: Studies in Crisis Intervention* (New York: Aronson, 1979).

11. Colgrove, Melba, Harold H. Bloomfield, and Peter McWilliams, *How to Survive the Loss of a Love* (New York: Bantam Books, 1976).

12. Kubler-Ross, Elisabeth, *On Death and Dying* (New York: Macmillan, 1979).

13. See Chapter 10.

14. Bowlby, John, *Attachment and Loss* (series), Vol. 1, *Attachment*, (1969); Vol. 2, *Separation: Anxiety and Anger* (1973); Vol. 3 *Loss, Sadness and Depression* (1980) (New York: Basic Books).

15. See the discussion of object-relations theory in Chapter 2 for further discussion of separation and depression.

16. See the section on learned helplessness in Chapter 6.

17. Polansky, Norman, "On Loneliness: A Program for Social Work," *Smith College Studies in Social Work 50* 2 (March 1980): 85 – 113.

18. Weeks, D., J. Nichela, L. A. Peplov, and M. Bragg, *Loneliness and Depression* Unpublished manuscript, University of California, Los Angeles, April 1979.

19. Wetzel, Janice Wood, "Depression and Dependence upon Unsustaining Environments," *Clinical Social Work Journal 6*, 2 (Summer 1978): 75 – 89; see also Janice Wood Wetzel and Franklin C. Redmond, "A Person-Environment Study of Depression," *Social Service Review 54*, 3 (September 1980): 363 – 375; see also Chapter 5.

20. Primakoff, Laura, "Patterns of Living Alone and Loneliness: A Cognitive-Behavioral Analysis," Unpublished Doctoral dissertation, University of Texas at Austin, August 1981.

21. Ilfield, Frederick W., Jr., "Characteristics of Current Social Stressors," *Psychological Reports 39* (1976): 1231–1247; "Current Social Stressors and Symptoms of Depression," *American Journal of Psychiatry 134* (1977): 161–166.

22. Dowrenwend, B. S., and B. P. Dowrenwend, eds. *Stressful Life Events* (New York: Wiley, 1974).

23. Makosky, Vivian P., "Stress and the Mental Health of Women: A Discussion of Research and Issues," in *The Mental Health of Women*, ed. Marcia Guttentag, Susan Solosin, and Deborah Belle, (New York: Academic Press, 1980).

24. Brown, George W., and Tirril Harris, *Social Origins of Depression* (New York: Free Press, 1978).

25. See Chapter 2 for theories of possible causation.

26. See Chapter 6 regarding cognitions, and Chapter 7.

27. Wetzel, Janice Wood, "Depression and Dependence Upon Unsustaining Environments," *Clinical Social Work Journal 6*, 2 (Summer 1978): 75–89; see also Janice Wood Wetzel and Franklin C. Redmond, "A Person-Environment Study of Depression," *Social Service Review 54* 3 (September 1980): 363–375; see also Chapter 5.

28. U.S. Bureau of Census, 1980.

29. Wetzel, Janice Wood, "Mental Health, Working Class Women and Their Work," *Journal of Applied Social Sciences 5*, 1 (Fall/Winter 1980–1981): 1–13.

30. White, Robert, "Motivation Reconsidered: The Concept of Competence," *Psychological Review 66* (1959): 297–333.

31. Wetzel, Janice Wood, "Women Alone: Facilitating Autonomy," paper presented at the Third Annual Conference on Women in Crisis, New York, New York, June 1981.

32. See Chapters 5 and 6.

33. Sheehy, Gail, "The Happiness Report," *Redbook*, July 1979, pp. 29, 54–60.

34. Block, Marilyn R., Janice L. Davidson, Jean D. Grambs, and Kathryn E. Serock, *Uncharted Territory: Issues and Concerns of Women over 40* (Center on Aging, College Park: University of Maryland, 1978.

35. See the discussion regarding Male and Female idiosyncrasies in the People at Risk section of Chapter 2.

36. See Chapter 7 for further insights regarding solitude.

37. Bikson, Tora Kay, and Jacqueline K. Goodchilds, *Old People and New Ideas: Receptivity and Rigidity* (Santa Monica, CA: Rand Corporation, August 1979).

38. See Chapter 5 for a discussion of the depressed elderly. These insights, applied to alone-contentedness, have been adapted from Milton Myeroff, *On Caring* (New York: Harper and Row, 1977).

39. Primakoff, Laura, "Patterns of Living Alone and Loneliness: A Cognitive-Behavioral Analysis," Unpublished Doctoral dissertation, University of Texas at Austin, August 1981; also see Chapter 7 for detailed information regarding journal writing.

40. Leff, Melitta J., John F. Roatch, and William E. Bunney, Jr., "Environmental Factors Preceding the Onset of Severe Depressions," *Psychiatry 33* (1970): 293–311.

41. See Chapter 7 for further discussion regarding authenticity.

42. Neugarten, Berniece, "Education and the Life Cycle," *School Review 80* (1972): 209–216.

43. See Chapters 2 and 5 for further discussion of women's socialization.

44. Bart, Pauline, "Depression in Middle-Aged Women," in *Women in Sexist Society*, ed. V. Gornick and B. Moran (New York: Basic Books, 1971), pp. 99 – 117.

45. Freud, Sigmund, "Mourning and Melancholia,"(1917) in *Collected Papers*, Vol. 4 (London: Hogarth Press, 1956).

46. Ibid.

47. Wetzel, Janice Wood, "Mental Health, Working Class Women and Their Work," *Journal of Applied Social Sciences 5*, 1 (Fall/Winter 1980 – 1981): 1 – 13.

48. Spitzer, Stephen P., Robert M. Swanson, and Robert K. Lehr, "Audience Reactions and Careers of Psychiatric Patients," *Family Process 8*, 2 (September 1969): 159 – 181.

49. Bart, Pauline, "Depression in Middle-Aged Women" in *Women in Sexist Society*, ed. V. Gornick and B. Moran (New York: Basic Books, 1971), pp. 99 – 117.

50. Weissman, Myrna M., and Eugene Paykel, *The Depressed Woman* (Chicago: University of Chicago Press, 1974).

51. Brown, George W., and Tirril Harris, *Social Origins of Depression* (New York: Free Press, 1978).

52. Pearlin, Leonard, and James Johnson, *Marital Status, Life Strains and Depression*, Unpublished manuscript, 1975.

53. Radloff, Lenore A., "Sex Difference in Depression: The Effects of Occupation and Marital Status," *Sex Roles 1*, 3 (1975): 249 – 265.

54. U. S. Bureau of Census, *Statistical Portrait of Women in the United States* (Special Studies, Series P-23, 1978).

55. Wylie, Philip, *Generation of Vipers* (New York: Farrar and Rinehart, 1942).

56. Wechsler, Beth, "Depression and the Female Role," Unpublished master's thesis, Smith College School for Social Work, Northampton, MA, 1972.

57. Block, Marilyn R., Janice L Davidson, Jean D. Grambs, and Kathryn E Serock, *Uncharted Territory: Issues and Concerns of Women over 40* (Center on Aging, College Park: University of Maryland, 1978).

58. See discussion of The Developmental Process in the section on Object-Relations Theory in Chapter 2.

59. Moskol, Marjorie D., "Using Relationship Loss as a Catalyst for Growth in Social Work with Women," Paper presented at the Sixth National Association of Social Work Biennial Professional Symposium, San Antonio, TX, November 15, 1978.

60. Radloff, Lenore A., "Sex Difference in Depression: The Effects of Occupation and Marital Status," *Sex Roles 1*, 3 (1975): 249 – 265.

61. U.S. Department of Labor Statistics, *Handbook of Labor Statistics*, Bulletin 2070, December 1980.

62. See Chapter 3 for further reference to the concept of energy.

63. See Chapter 5 for a discussion of women as "nurturers in search of nurturance."

64. Broverman, Inge K., D. M. Broverman, F. E. Clarkson, P. S. Rosenbrantz, and S. Vogel, "Sex Role Stereotypes and Clinical Judgements of Mental Health," *Journal of Consulting and Clinical Psychology 34*, 1 (1970): 1 – 7.

65. Millman, Marcia, and Rosabeth M. Kanter, *Another Voice: Feminist Perspectives on Social Life and Social Science* (New York: Octagon Books, 1978).

66. Laing, Ronald D., *The Politics of the Family* (New York: Vintage Books, 1972).

67. Mead, Margaret, *New Lives for Old: Cultural Transformation* (New York: Greenwood, 1980).

68. Bem, Donald, *Beliefs, Attitudes, and Human Affairs* (Belmont, CA: Brooks/Cole, 1970).

69. Krause, C., "The Femininity Complex and Women Therapists," *Journal of Marriage and the Family 33* (August 1971): 476 – 482.

70. Hirschfeld, Robert, Gerald L. Klerman, Paul Chodoff, Sheldon Korchin, and James Barrett, "Dependency — Self-Esteem — Clinical Depression," *Journal of the American Academy of Psychoanalysis 4, 3* (1976): 373 – 388; also see Chapter 5 for a discussion of dysfunctional dependence.

71. This section was largely influenced by Christine Dougher, "Therapeutic Intervention with Women: The Necessity for a Feminist Orientation" Unpublished manuscript, Washington University, St. Louis, Mo., 1975.

72. Pirtle, Dorriece, Christine Dougher, and Janice Wood Wetzel, "The Consequences of Being Female: Feminist Theory and Social Work Practice," presented at the 50th Anniversary Conference of the George Warren Brown School of Social Work, Washington University, May 14, 1976.

73. Goode, William J., *Women in Divorce* (New York: Free Press, 1969).

74. Wetzel, Janice Wood, "Depression and Dependence Upon Unsustaining Environments," *Clinical Social Work Journal 6, 2* (Summer 1978): 75 – 89; "The Work Environment and Depression: Implications for Intervention," in *Toward Human Dignity: Social Work in Practice*, ed. John W. Hanks (National Association of Social Workers, 1978: 236 – 245).

75. See Chapter 2 for further discussion of defenses.

76. Pearlin, Leonard, "Sex Roles and Depression," *Life-Span Developmental Psychology Conference*, 4th, ed. Nancy Datan and Leon Ginsberg, West Virginia University, 1974 (New York: Academic Press, 1975).

77. Datan, Nancy, and Leon Ginsberg, eds., *Life-Span Developmental Psychology Conference*, 4th, West Virginia University, 1974 (New York: Academic Press, 1975) pp. 191 – 207.

78. See Chapter 5 for a detailed discussion of dependence-independence and family and work environments.

79. Newton, E., and S. Walton, "The Personal is the Political: Consciousness-Raising and Personal Change in the Women's Liberation Movement," paper presented at the American Anthropological Association, 1971.

80. Glasser, William, *Reality Therapy: a New Approach to Psychiatry* (New York: Harper and Row, 1975).

81. See Chapter 7 for further discussion of authenticity.

82. Beck, Aaron T., *Depression: Clinical Experimental and Theoretical Aspects* (New York: Harper and Row, 1967).

83. See Chapter 5 for a discussion of interventions in institutions for the elderly.

84. See Chapter 6 for further discussion of values clarification exercises and life planning within a workshop format.

85. Karpman, Stephen B., "Fairy Tales and Script Drama Analysis," *Transactional Analysis Bulletin 7, 26* (April 1968): 40.

86. Teague, Mary, Material incorporated in Janice Wood Wetzel's workshop on *Depression: Theory and Treatment*, Texas Department of Human Resources, April 1978 through July 1980.

87. Ibid.

88. Meyer, Adolph, in E. E. Winters, ed., *The Collected Papers of Adolph Meyer*, Vol. 3, *Medical Teaching* (Baltimore: John Hopkins University Press, 1951).

89. Butler, Robert N., and Myrna S. Lewis, *Aging and Mental Health: Positive*

Psychosocial Approaches (St. Louis: C. V. Mosby, 1973); also see the discussion of Life Review and the elderly in Chapter 5.

90. Teague, Mary, Material incorporated in Janice Wood Wetzel's workshop on *Depression: Theory and Treatment*, Texas Department of Human Resources, April 1978 through July 1980.

91. Ibid.

92. Lifton, Robert J., "Beyond Psychic Healing: A Call to Awareness," *American Journal of Orthospsychiatry 52*, 4 (1982): 519 – 629; see also Joanna Rogers Macy, "How to Deal with Despair," *New Age* (1979), pp. 1 – 6; Frederick L. Ahearn, "Psychological Effects of the Nuclear Threat: An Issue for Clinicians," paper presented at the First NASW Clinical Conference, Washington, DC, November 18, 1982.

Chapter 5
The Person-Environment Model[1]

> This we were, this is
> how we tried to
> love,
> and these are the
> forces they had
> ranged against us,
> and these are the forces
> we had ranged within
> us,
> within us and against us,
> against us and within
> us.
> Adrienne Rich, *Diving into the Wreck*

T he search for a psychosocial psychology of depression has crossed many disciplines, usually concentrating on personality factors. This focus has led to the observation and investigation of personality variables, their interrelationship, and how traits function relative to the environment. In regard to depression, dependency is one of the most frequent psychological themes. Traditional psychoanalytic theory, ego-psychology, energy theories, and cognitive models of depression all identify dependence as an attribute common to depressed people. Though the language of each discipline may be different and the context may vary, psychological dependence remains a common thread.[2]

There is growing evidence that substantial proportions of behavioral differences are due to situational factors, regardless of personality predisposition. In environmental models of depression, the external situation is usually examined in relation to stress affecting the individual.[3] Though findings are mixed, most behavioral and life events researchers agree that single events, however traumatic, are seldom highly correlated with clinical depression. Instead, clusters of negative events appear to be more likely to influence well-being. This finding has led some researchers to an awareness of pervasive life experience as a possible causal factor.[4] Still, a new problem is appearing. Walter Mischel warns us about an emerging "situationism" — an evolving overemphasis on environments, similar to previous "traitism."[5] Either focus is a one-dimensional distortion. The interaction of the individual and the environment and the additive impact of both factors have not been systematically investigated until very recently, despite the accumulation of evidence. The charge certainly includes depression studies.[6]

The person-environment model of depression provides an encompassing conceptual framework combining dependence as a personality characteristic and as a socially prescribed trait with pervasive life experience. Depression is viewed as a joint function of the two sides of this person-environment equation. Dependence alone is not considered to be causal as long as there are "reliable others" in the environment to sustain dependency needs. Because dependent people have fewer alternatives and may become depressed if they lose their supports, they are more likely to be vulnerable. Depression occurs when "reliable others" are unreliable or missing altogether. Still, independence is not a certain deterrent. When independent people are not allowed to act autonomously, they become "secondarily dependent" and may also become depressed.[7] There are fewer such cases because independent people are more likely to have alternatives and are less likely to stay in restrictive, dysfunctional environments. Even so, the exigencies of economics, religion, and cultural values or responsibilities do not obviate the common possibility of secondary dependence.

On the environmental side of the ledger are the concepts of emotional supportiveness and control in the family and at work. While dependent people require more support than independent people, all human beings need emotional nurturance. Such supportiveness is generally recognized as essential within the family, but its importance at work is often ignored. While the support of employers is desirable, the support of peers has been found to be even more critical to well-being. As for controlling work situations: no one desires control and everyone finds it to be a dysfunctional environmental quality, regardless of dependence or independence orientation.

Because family and work environments (among others) both may impact on well-being, both should be included in any person-environment assessment. The number of hours spent in a given milieu and one's commitment or involuntary presence are all factors that can be taken into consideration. Since traits are not always similar across diverse situations,[8] more than one environment should be explored. Though individuals are generally consistent, they do not necessarily exhibit the same personality traits in different situations. A person, for example, may be dependent at home and independent at work, depending on the environmental circumstances and their socialization to behave differently and to have differing needs for approval and worth in varying situations. Imagine the businessman who enjoys working autonomously, but who is helpless at home, dependent upon his wife for self-esteem. As long as he is allowed to be independent at work, and as long as his wife provides approval, he will be free of depression. Should either situation change for an extended period of time, depression can be predicted. Further, if both realities change, depression is virtually assured.

We often don't stop to realize that environments are made up of people. We *are* one another's environment. Therefore, our personality traits affect ourselves and also impact on others. Instead of thinking in person-environment terms, it might be more accurate to conceptualize a relational person-to-person model.[9] Because of the possible confusion inherent in such identical terminology, the person-environment labels have been retained for the sake of subject-object clarity.

PERSON-ENVIRONMENT DEPRESSION RESEARCH

Both persons and environments are made up of multiple characteristics, rather than single entities. A person's predisposition to be dependent, therefore, reflects a number of subtraits, and a person may be dependent in one situation and not in another. Environments are similarly complex. Social environments are created by its members and defined by overall characteristics that produce a general atmosphere. They are distinguished by the demands and expectations made, the kinds of activities and behaviors encouraged or discouraged, and the style of life valued in a given environment from the perspective of each participant.[10] While we may question one's perceptions, it is the individual, after all, who reacts to the environment from the perspective of his or her particular social reality.[11] It should be remembered as well that environments may be characterized in physical terms — geographically, temporally, and structurally, to name a few possibilities. For example, where one makes one's home or goes to work, the time of day, the season, or even the era in which one lives makes a difference. The structural dimensions of a building can also impact dramatically on the opportunity for interaction on the positive side, or imposition of others on the negative.

It has become increasingly evident that neither the person nor the environment can be accurately assessed in isolation. Yet, despite the fact that theorists have included person-environment interactions as etiological models of human behavior for over forty years,[12] the concept did not become an empirical reality until the 1960s and 1970s.[13] Given that awareness of the interdependence between human beings and their environments is not at all new, one might wonder why so little is known. No doubt the inherent perplexities have deflected us from addressing the issues. The intricacies of conceptualization, design, and measurement are often overwhelming. How do we know what personality or environmental dimensions are relevant to human functioning? If these dimensions can be isolated, can they be generalized to all persons and all behavior, or are they only applicable to specific persons' situations? Are all person and environment variables of equal importance to human functioning? How are they to be measured and assessed relatively? The person-environment model applied to the problem of depression is a beginning effort to answer some of these questions.

Two investigations have provided empirical support for the model. The first was a study of fifty depressed white women between eighteen and seventy-five years of age, and fifty nondepressed women who were matched for sex, race, age, and occupation.[14] The second was a cross-cultural study of 300 white, black, and Mexican-American women and men, half of whom were not depressed and were matched with the depressed group accordingly.[15] There were three highly significant findings that were shared by all three cultures and both sexes of every age. Family support was the most discriminating variable separating the depressed from the nondepressed groups. Those who perceived themselves as living in nonsupportive families were likely to be depressed. Feeling psychologically dependent at home and controlled at work were also highly influential factors that differentiated the two samples, especially when compounded by nonsupportive situations. Peer support, like family support, emerged as an important function. Those who did not have supportive peers in their work situations were likely to be depressed. Conversely, independent people in supportive, noncontrolling family and work situations were usually free of depression. It is clear that personality predispositions and environmental conditions both in the family and at work have an additive effect. The greater the number of vulnerability factors, the greater the risk of depression and vice versa.[16] Though we have a great deal more to learn, we can act on what we already know in order to prevent depression as well as to alleviate it.

PERSON-ENVIRONMENT CONCEPTUAL BASE

Regarding Dependence

The human infant is born utterly dependent on others for its needs. Most developmental theorists contend that childhood dependence is an important determinant in the development of personality, ranging on a continuum described by Anna Freud as a developmental line from dependency to emotional self-reliance and adult object relationships.[17] Studies based on both animal and human observation conclude that the degree of natural infantile dependence on others for their needs determines the degree to which dependence is a central factor in the development of the organism. Conversely, the degree to which individuals are incapable of bringing about gratification of their own needs determines the degree to which they are dependent on the object. Such dependence often leads to insecurity and a subjectively experienced lack of freedom. Clinical observations have led researchers to conclude that emotional well-being is determined largely by inner sustainment. Age-appropriate competence, which results in self-confidence, is a contributing factor.[18]

Social scientists theorize that the direction of the human infant's development is socially determined by the internalization of society's reality through the roles and attitudes of others. The desires of the powerful are internalized by the dependent, resulting in submissive loss of freedom and lowered level of aspiration.[19] Such characteristics have been called the "mark of oppression,"[20] also interpreted as identification with the oppresser, a defense mechanism that reduces the pain occurring in meeting the demands of the powerful other.

The Social-Exchange Theory of John Thibaut and Harold Kelley further describes the relationship between dependence and power.[21]

These authors define power as control over another, derived from the other's dependence. Dependence is viewed as a state of helplessness due to the inequities of the social environment. Thibaut and Kelley call it "fate control." They note that one of the common disadvantages of dependence is the care one must exercise in interactions with those upon whom one is dependent. The possession of superior power relieves people from paying close attention to their own or their partner's action. It also makes it possible for the person in power to determine the course and pace of the relationship and to receive the most rewards more frequently ("the better of the outcomes potentially available in the relationship"). While these theorists assert that "dependency is no problem with a perfectly reliable giver of the rewards," the person in the dependent position clearly has the greatest need for maintaining the relationship. While other values may take precedence, from this point of view there appears to be little incentive for the one in the power position to contemplate giving rewards to another. In any event, the costs are increased when one is dependent upon an unreliable person or persons, a theoretical position that is incorporated in the person-environment framework. Social-Exchange Theory is founded primarily upon observation. It may have been the forerunner of Julian Rotter's Internal-External (I-E) dimension, about which a great deal more is known.[22]

Hundreds of studies concerning the I-E construct have been undertaken over the past twenty years. The construct is based on Social-Learning theory, which stresses the notion that behavior is learned in social situations and is generalized to similar situations. Rotter was one of the first to bridge learning theory and cognitive theory by including an internal dimension to the reinforcement of behavior, previously only considered to be external to the individual.[23] Internal control represents the degree to which valued reinforcements are perceived as due to one's own efforts. External control exists when valued reinforcements are perceived as determined by factors beyond one's control.[24]

The internal-external paradigm is a powerful-powerless continuum that refers to one's self-evaluation of the ability to get what one wants. The construct also provides cement to the foundation upon which the person-environment model is built. However, it is not an inclusive concept although externality has been associated empirically with females, blacks, and lower socioeconomic groups. Depressed and alcoholic women and men have scored as internals, for internality also can be interpreted as self-blame. It is important, therefore, to know if a person is internally controlled in the sense that he or she is not dependent on others for approval. Hence, Rotter's paradigm has been integrated into a dependence-independence construct that assesses outer versus inner sustainment on a continuum. An examination of the concept of independence will clarify this rationale even further.

The Need for Independence, Mastery, and Control

According to clinical observations, independence develops over time out of neonatal dependence, but the maturational processes are not sufficient to complete the task successfully. Those who are never allowed to develop independence become submissive or hostile-dependent, and those who have lost freedom because of social conditions may become secondarily dependent.[25] Further, those who are socialized to dependence may *never* learn to be independent for the ego-ideal must contain the ideal of independence in order to release the energies necessary for its development.[26] Freedom to be independent depends upon the possession of multiple possibilities for behavior choice. Those who have limited skills or solutions have equally limited degrees of freedom. Being able to facilitate or retard environmental experiences influences the development of personal power, for if people perceive themselves to be masters of their fate, they will be active toward the environment and vice versa.[27] Numerous social scientists have observed that human beings are direct and persistent in efforts to attain competence, perhaps reflecting a universal need for environmental mastery. While empirical evidence is limited, the theories are in universal agreement that independence reflects psychological maturity and well-being.[28]

The Need for Supportiveness

Although the development of independence is fundamental to human growth, it does not negate the reality of interdependence and the need for mutual supportiveness. To be connected to others, to belong, and to give and receive social support are also essential to well-being.[29] It is becoming increasingly clear that "natural helping networks" can be a deterrent to mental illness.[30] Whether this is a direct effect due to their role in modifying the negative effects of stress, or if support systems are effective because coping efforts are strengthened, is not yet clear. The chances are, given the complexity of reality, that all three conditions may hold true. The fact is that both informal supports and linkages with more formal social services in the community can be effective in improving the quality of life. It is not surprising that supportiveness was the most significant finding in the person-environment depression research in regard to both the home and the workplace.

Support and the Family Environment

Family supportiveness has a highly significant nondepressing effect. The family environment proved to be of even greater importance than personality factors in the person-environment studies.[31] This finding is consistent with Frederick Ilfield's investigation of almost 2,300 adults which reported that marital and parental stressors had the highest correlation with depressive symptoms.[32] These facts indicate that family relationships should be assessed whenever possible. While mutual support between husbands and wives has long been endorsed, the reality of such support within the nuclear family may leave much to be desired. Neither can support be assumed for those who are members of an extended family; mere numbers do not constitute supportiveness. Family systems may be superficial at best and even blatantly destructive.

While the pre-industrial, pre-urban extended family has survived only in selected rural settings and ethnic groups, in recent years a new family structure called the "new extended" family, has developed. Though we tend to continue to think in nuclear-family terms, the reality of American households is quite different. The new extended family is made up of a social network created by divorce and remarriage. It is predicted that 40 percent of all marriages in the 1980s will end in divorce. While four out of five people remarry within three to five years, second marriages have an even higher divorce rate than first unions.[33] When we include family of origin, reconstituted families, and close friends who consider one another to be family, in our definition of family, it is clear that the family is not dead; it has been reincarnated to provide needed support.

Support and the Work Environment

Contrary to general opinion, the work environment is as crucial as the family to the mental health of both women and men, regardless of class and ethnicity. It should not be surprising, for philosophers and social scientists have long agreed on satisfaction in work as a central attribute of mentally healthy, emotionally mature human beings. They have spoken in a variety of metaphors. To name a few: Sigmund

Freud[34] refers to work as necessary to self-esteem; Abraham Maslow[35] talks of work as self-actualizing; Martin Buber[36] attests to work as a prerequisite of authenticity; and Robert White[37] speaks of competence, effectance, and environmental mastery associated with the world of work, as values needed for survival.[38] While the importance of work outside the home has always been recognized in regard to men, its value to women has been overlooked. When we compare the quantity of time spent at work outside the home with time at home, the quality of the work activities compared with many household tasks, and the possible rewards of extradomestic work (economic opportunity for advancement, recognition, status, friendship, knowledge, and so on), perhaps we can begin to understand why the work environment is influential to the well-being of all people.

Just as men and women share the need for work, so, too, do they suffer from its negative aspects. Though the needs of individuals regarding their work environments may differ, it has been found that gender is not a relevant variable.[39] Research from the late 1960s to the 1980s indicates that workers in low-skilled and unskilled jobs, whether male or female, have poorer mental and physical health than those in more skilled situations. To illustrate, conclusions reached in Arthur Kornhauser's well-documented twenty-year study of more than a decade ago still hold true:

Poorer mental health occurs whenever conditions of work and life lead to continuing frustration by failing to offer means for perceived progress toward attainment of strongly desired goals which have indispensable elements of the individual's self-identity as a worthwhile person. Persistent failure and frustration bring lowered self-esteem and dissatisfaction with life, often accompanied by anxieties, social alienation and withdrawal, a narrowing of goals and curtailing of aspirations — in short . . . poor mental health.[40]

Regarding Controlling Work Environments

The "climate of opinion" among social scientists is that optimal work environments are high on autonomy, individual satisfaction, and consideration, and low on imposed structure.[41] They also can be described as noncontrolling. There is evidence that an open, participative form of organization is both economically and socially rewarding.[42] Feminists, too, insist that autonomous, nonhierarchical, egalitarian work environments are vitally linked to the enhancement of personal development.[43] The fact that such structures are more conducive to mental health, to productivity, and to community involvement attests to the stability of the feminist premise.[44]

Control has been the essential characteristic of management throughout history.[45] The hierarchical, pyramidal structure of organization reflects such a value system, instigated primarily to centralize information and thus, power, at the top. The lower one ranks, the less control and the fewer personal abilities one can use. Leadership is more directive and the workers are dependent. Chris Argyris' personality and organization theory concludes that such an organization requires individuals to be dependent, to act as infants, rather than adults. To the extent that an incongruence exists between the individual's needs and the organization, workers will experience frustration, psychological failure, short time perspective, and conflict. The end result is often depression.

The single most important trend in the public and private sectors mirrors such discontent. Internal deterioration and lack of effectiveness in producing services or products is an increasing reality in the world of work. A worldwide Quality of Work-Life Movement is demanding an expansion of worker participation in job decisions. Participatory workplace projects, being piloted internationally, range from autonomous work teams to labor-management panels and profit sharing.[46] Running counter to traditional production and "scientific" management practices, studies indicate that a majority of workers believe they are entitled to self-determining work roles. "Irresistible pressures" are battering hierarchical structures, shifting from a top-down to a sideways decision-making process.[47]

The majority of employers, however, have shied away from innovation, despite the obvious success of pilot programs. Some evidently hesitate because they don't know how to proceed. Others are skeptical, believing that their work situations are not similar enough to those in the successful projects. Many, contrary to the repeated findings that costs remain the same or improve, are reluctant to make changes because of transitional costs and fear of capital risks.[48]

The labor side of the coin appears at first glance to be more encouraging. Unions are becoming increasingly supportive of worker's "mental illness" claims resulting from work-related stress. Indeed, a growing number of workman's compensation cases have been won, costing management concern as well as dollars. The effects of outside stresses are secondary in such cases. Industry need only be shown to precipitate mental injury. That injury is often severe depression.[49]

It is a paradox, therefore, that unions are no more supportive than management of the Quality of Work-Life Movement. Reasons given for union distrust are centered in the argument that their efforts should be focused on the unemployed, rather than the unhappily employed. Their emphasis has traditionally been on extrinsic rather than intrinsic reward. Unions, in fact, have been even slower than management to come to grips with the discontent of their workers. The outcome is an increasing frustration and rebellion of workers concerning the unresponsiveness and irrelevance of union leadership, as well as of management. Humanization of work is an ever-growing demand that must be considered in these trying economic times, whether productivity or mental health is one's chief concern. The two improve simultaneously when work environments are supportive and noncontrolling. When the product is a service rather than a commodity, the dynamic still holds true.

WOMEN AT RISK

Women as Persons: Dependence and Independence

In order to gain deeper understanding of women's high risk for depression, the concepts of dependence and independence in relation to their socialization must be subjected to scrutiny. Historical research indicates that power has been in the hands of men since the earliest days of patriarchy. Women have been kept in a state of dependence while men have determined what women's lot should be with regard to men's own interests, needs, and fears. Throughout history the majority of women have resigned themselves to their place without attempting to take action. They recognize the world as male oriented for the most part — fashioned, ruled, and dominated by men.

In 1953, Simone de Beauvoir elaborated on the socialization of women in her classic, *The Second Sex*. She explained that young girls learn to see themselves as the inessential (while males are the essential) which gives rise to their feelings of female insufficiency.[50] Girls become convinced of their relative inferiority at an early age, viewing men as masters of the world, economically and socially superior. Women have been taught to believe that it is unfeminine, contrary to nature, and offensive to be independent. Elizabeth Janeway points out that it has been necessary for women to be carefully instructed to do what is alleged to come naturally, that is, to be "femininely dependent." They are socialized to play a subordinate role, representing who society thinks they ought to be.[51]

Research concerning the learning of gender roles suggests that the early learning of sex-specific roles is only one mechanism for the maintenance of sex differentiation. Sanctions such as social ridicule, institutional and law enforcement, and sex-typed models reinforced by mass-media presentations are all highly persuasive factors. Studies also indicate that gender roles and identities are clearly correlated with variation in social stereotypes. The implication is that gender is indeed quite different from sex. If gender has a biological source, culture makes its detection impossible. Hence, the dependent role of women sanctioned by society may be the choice of those in power positions rather than any "normal" aptitude or condition of woman.[52] It even has been argued that the study of sexual differentiation should distinguish between biological gender, sexual orientation, sex roles, and masculinity and femininity as individual characteristics.[53] There is much to learn.

Social roles are evaluated relative to status and desirability. Included in this evaluation is the perceived usefulness of the role, its inherent power, and the association of the role with others of value.[54] Females are socialized into an inferior role, often without the conscious motivation of those around them.[55] Data indicate that a woman's status is lowered and her powerlessness and dependent position are reinforced as she fulfills her traditional sex role. It is understandable that adult women with unfulfilled desires for a more autonomous self-concept are often victims of depression.[56]

Despite changing sex roles, women today are still expected to develop attributes that are linked with immaturity, such as helplessness and dependency. Even today, many people believe that it is unfeminine for women to grow toward independent attitudes, often associated with mature men. There is, in fact, no model of growth for women. Rather, the classic psychoanalytic model tends to provide the best description of the process of women's development — that of overcoming active forces within them, so as to assume a passive, dependent, masochistic role. Jean Baker Miller notes that achievement of a worthwhile identity is at best difficult. Women, however, are given little preparation or experience to develop that sense of self.[57]

Some observers believe that women have exchanged private power in the home for public submission. Historically, when this bargain is fulfilling, as when their activities are viewed as socially and economically valued, women have accepted their position graciously. In these transitional times, many women would like to gain the self-respect that they once enjoyed when they possessed genuinely useful and sophisticated skills. More and more women are no longer willing to live vicariously; they want "control over their own lives and authority or influence commensurate with their abilities in the external world."[58]

The desire is seldom commensurate with reality. Lack of control of their own lives continues to be socially sanctioned. Depression all too often is the price paid.

Conformity and persuadability are not the traits of only one sex.[59] Still, powerful societal demands associated with sex typing and female sex-role differentiation cause many girls and women to be more susceptible to external influence. Low self-esteem and general passivity, indicators of high persuadability, are reflected in a lack of self-worth and insecurity regarding one's knowledge and reasoning powers. Such people are more likely to submit to others who claim higher status and authority, a profile most likely to be female.[60] Socialized to be dependent, they have tended to allow others to direct and control them. Karen Horney long ago concluded that dependence, passivity, and submissiveness are destructive wherever they occur,[61] precipitating reactions in both the person and her environment. Depression and resentment are common reactions.

In the American culture, independence through achievement and competence is rewarded in men and not in women. Research tells us that females who display these attributes are ignored, not listened to and interrupted, or worse, punished by means of social rejection or criticism.[62] It is not surprising that they show signs of conflict and ambivalence as they develop independence and competence.[63] Depression may be a reality for such women. To be dependent may seem, initially, to be less painful and more conducive to love. The larger life screen tells us otherwise as the characters play out their stories; the tragedies generally reflect dependence roles.

Depression founded in dependence appears to be more pervasive and less easily alleviated than that associated with independence. The independent woman may become deeply depressed, but she is less vulnerable because she has more external options and internal strengths to put to good use.

Women and the Family Environment

The Supportiveness Factor

While the development of independence in women seems to lessen the probability of serious depression, lack of family supportiveness leaves them vulnerable. Their high-risk status may be connected with the fact that women are socialized to nurture men, while men are not encouraged to be supportive of women.[64] The absence of male nurturing behavior has also been noted in mental health studies concerning female depression[65] and female alcoholism,[66] a condition not alien to depression symptomatology.

Jean Baker Miller's analysis of sex roles concludes that men are taught that serving others is a feminine characteristic — to be nurturant is to be less than masculine and a disdainful condition. Their fear of femininity is so great that they are socialized against it intensely. Indeed, even Freud noted the amazing degree of hostility directed toward women[67] (while he unfortunately perpetuated its presence). Miller argues that male conditioning closes their senses and responsiveness; they are often simply not aware of another's needs. Men have no idea "what women are talking about," a fact that marriage therapists corroborate, and an observation not far afield from Thibaut and Kelley's concepts of power and dependence.[68] It is not unusual to find that a wife is considered to be her husband's "best friend" though the friendship is not reciprocated. This reality suggests underlying reasons for the observation by researchers that depressed women are often hostile toward their husbands.[69] Another rationale may be found in Peter Lewinsohn's home observations which indicate that depressed people often provide positive reinforcement for family members, receiving little or none themselves.[70] His subjects were primarily depressed women.

The initial person-environment depression study supported the hypothesis that dependent, easily influenced women who were in autonomous home environments would be depressed. Conversely, as predicted, independent women in nonautonomous environments were also found to be depressed.[71] This person-environment interaction explains the necessity for attention to a woman's dependence-independence predisposition within the family. The autonomous environment dimension reflects the extent to which family members are encouraged to make their own decisions, to be assertive, to be self-sufficient, and to think things out for themselves.[72] Dependent women wanted to be relieved of these pressures, while independent women viewed them as desirable environmental conditions. This is not to say that dependent women wanted to be controlled, because they gave permission to others to care for them; those who were conscious of having been forced into submission were depressed.

An interesting difference emerged in relation to Mexican-American women who were independent and clinically depressed during the larger cross-cultural person-environment study. They, like "Anglo" and black women, felt that their husbands were not supportive of their independence. But they also experienced a great deal of pressure from their mothers who they felt restricted their freedom and development. The finding has been informally corroborated by clinicians serving the Chicano community in the southwest. As Mexican-American daughters become acculturated in contemporary American society, they come to question time-honored mores. When parental norms are rejected, the family feels threatened. This is especially true of the traditional mothers who believe that their daughter's independence is immoral, which in turn reflects on the mother as a failure in the daughter's upbringing. Clearly, the daughters are in need of counseling, but their mothers, too, must not be neglected. Groups have been found to be very effective in helping such women to come to terms with their disparate ideologies.

Informal interviews with independent, depressed women indicated, without probing, that they were consciously resentful of the fact that their husbands did not share in family (housekeeping, child-care, and social) responsibilities. The women wanted egalitarian, sharing relationships; yet, despite such conscious complaints, when interviewed, they often regarded their husbands as "supportive" and their home environments as "uncontrolling." It appears that such women are consciously grateful for their freedom to work and consciously resent their unequal responsibilities, but have no consciousness of the inconsistency of their experience with the perception of supportiveness. This finding, while informal, is important because of the dual roles of 50 percent of all married women.[73] Their reality is a contemporary version of the "superwife, supermom syndrome" so typical of yesteryear's traditional dependent depressed homemakers.[74]

It may be that women who are now emerging as independent must correct their cultural myopia if they are to function optimally. The extensive studies of Rotter and his colleagues concerning internal and external control conclude that those people who do not know they are controlled, but indeed are, are subject to depression.[75] Whether one is dependent or independent, perception obviously has a profound influence, as has denial.

The socialization of women to financial dependence has also been dysfunctional to them, for they are the leading poverty risk in the nation. The separation of roles and limitation of monetary rewards has not constituted a support system. Though the times may be changing, much is left unchanged. For example, while 49 percent of women over sixteen are now employed outside the home, 80 percent of these women are concentrated in the same lower job levels held for decades by their predecessors. Women earn an average of 59 cents for every dollar earned by men, and the wage gap widens each year.[76] Given these hard facts, any perception of a supportive egalitarian work environment is a myth.

Physical dependence due to size is a natural attribute of most women, though there is evidence that physical strength can be increased along with assertive attitudes. The dysfunctional aspect is more likely to be in the socialization of women to submissiveness and of men to physical aggression. Such polarities have resulted in an inordinate amount of violence on the part of men in terms of battering and rape alone. The statistics, however incomplete, are staggering. According to FBI figures, the number of reported wife beatings is three times the number of reported rapes, with rapes amounting to one in every nine minutes. It is estimated that these figures represent less than 10 percent of the actual number that occur.[77] Thus, it would be a conservative estimate to say that at least one woman is beaten by her husband every eighteen seconds,[78] an occurrence in 50 percent of all marriages. There are few who can argue coherently for the destructive socialization of men relative to physical aggression. Any reference to a support system for women in these millions of homes is a fantasy. If the family is to provide support for its members, we must face the disagreeable fact that the traditional family itself has emerged statistically as emotionally, physically, and economically destructive to many women and children. While the figures are new, the dynamics are not. Depression is only one of the outcomes.

Interventions with women are not meant to obviate or in any way detract from the responsibility of men to change their own damaging behaviors toward women, indeed toward themselves. They must stop encouraging female dependence — denying girls and women their personhood by punishing them for independent attitudes and actions. Such punishment takes psychological and physical forms, as well as financial. It is no coincidence that women are at high risk, the major population of victims, whether one refers to mental illness, family violence, or poverty.

It has long been implied that the "battle of the sexes" is a reflection of the natural order. The fact is that hostility between women and men is a learned phenomenon. Only by changing patterns of relating can the warfare subside, along with the rising incidence of female depression. To begin, men must learn to nurture women in the same way that women have nurtured them. There is an irony here. Since women are socialized to dependence, research tells us that they need more nurturing than do people who are independent. Yet, it is women who are taught to nurture others. The inability of men to provide emotional support for women has been found to be related to the high incidence of mental illness in women. While men learn to develop personal competence and to support themselves and their families economically, anything viewed as feminine is demeaned and denied in themselves and others. The expression of emotion and their nurturing qualities are therefore left undeveloped. This lack is often as painful to men as it is to women, for the expression of human emotion is a basic human quality. A classic syndrome is emerging in our culture, long familiar to marital counselors. The theme has become so common that books, television, and movies are capitalizing on it, usually inaccurately interpreting the phenomenon:[79] Men are shocked and bewildered by their wives' complaints of frustration regarding their husband's lack of introspection, exploration, expression of feelings, and absence of mutual emotional sharing. These men insist that they have successful marriages even while their wives are leaving them.[80] Complementary attributes obviously do not reflect a support system for either women or men.

Contrary to conventional wisdom, it is not only women who have developed their identities vicariously. Men are taught from childhood to compare themselves to women in a superior way. Thus, if there is any awareness or indication that they are not superior, that they are merely human, they tend to devalue themselves. They must pretend superiority and feign mastery and self-sufficiency even when they feel inadequate. Any advancement of women is a personal affront to an already fragile male ego, fragile only because of the unrealistic expectations of traditional masculinity. Evidence of female competence is translated as diminished male competence, of impotence and failure. The principle of scarcity is at work. It is as if competence were a rationed commodity, too scarce to be shared.[81]

Teenage Pregnancy

A discussion of the socialization of girls and boys would be remiss without mention of sexuality and our changing mores. There is reason to believe that despite the so-called sexual revolution, vestigial good-girl/bad-girl labels subsist. The duplicity remains in the double standard that encourages boys to "score" and girls to be sexual only for love. Boys are sanctioned by society to tell girls that they love them in order to have sex. The custom undermines mutual relationship and caring through authorized deceit and exploitation. While boys are systematically taught to demean their human counterparts, girls are taught to accept such deception from boys without anger. The girl's responsibility for abstaining from sexual activity is emphasized, and an unwanted pregnancy is regarded as her responsibility alone. Of course, there are exceptions on both sides, but the cultural reality endures. One need not experience the dynamic personally to be tainted by it. Adult confidantes should be aware of the practice and engage in relevant discussions with young women. Contraception and abortion counseling is essential but never sufficient. Discussion will enhance their perceptions and uncover resentment stemming from sexual norms prevalent in most, if not all, cultures, classes, and ethnic groups. These are not caretaking behaviors that nourish growth and foster human attachment; they are alienating, depression-provoking norms.

Supportiveness of women includes respect for their evolving sense of identity, a mutually satisfying sexual life, and the creation of intimate friendship, as well as shared work and family responsibilities. This will require reeducating men and women in regard to traditional roles, not an uncomplicated undertaking. The processes involved in role change have been compared with the deprogramming of cult members.[82] Even the most consciously receptive people find it stressful. A lifetime of familial, cultural, and even worldwide messages concerning appropriate behaviors and attitudes cannot be reversed easily. An initial clear understanding of the need for revamping gender ideologies and nurturance practices is essential. As in all therapy, the counselor can be an effective change agent. The outcome, mutual supportiveness without subservience, can influence the reversal of our soaring depression statistics.

If prevention of depression is a sincere goal, these principles and customs should be instilled at a very early age. People who work with children, families, and educators can be instrumental in creating a nurturant society for both women and men. Teaching boys and girls and their parents the importance of mutual supportiveness can prevent the dysfunctional person-to-person relationships that are so rigidly adhered to in adulthood. These suggestions are not meant to encourage pathological nurturance, the perversion of the sense of caring through self-neglect and abnegation in either sex. What has been dysfunctional for women would be no more functional for men. Authentic nurturance requires neither the giving up of the self nor the protection of another's fragile ego. It is, instead, the support of what is alive and growing, albeit dormant, in another. Supportiveness does not encourage unhealthy dependence, which stunts development. It is, rather, a caretaking behavior that nourishes growth-fostering human attachment.[83]

Children at Risk: Victims of Incest

Children themselves are sometimes depressed, often in tandem with a parent. In most cases, the child is likely to be female. The statistics hold true for incest victims who usually are referred for counseling because of depression symptoms. Incest victims are ten times more likely to be girls than boys. It has been estimated that one out of four women have been victims of childhood sexual assault in the family. The perpetrators appear to be primarily fathers and male guardians. Contrary to some theories, incestuous acts are not simply the end result of family dysfunction. The family profile indicates that the father rarely has a criminal record and usually has a good work history. He tends to have difficulty relating to adult women and is domineering, viewing his wife as threatening and rejecting, dependent and insecure, in need of approval and less interested in sex than he is. The profile is more typical than deviant. Experts on the subject are reaching the conclusion that incestuous assault is not an unnatural acting-out of a family interaction. Instead, it is thought to be the end result of cultural and politically sanctioned dominance vis-a-vis females.

According to recent reports, the long-held belief fostered by Freud that children fantasize and lie about being sexually assaulted is not so. If anything, children go to great lengths to cover up for their fathers, rather than accuse them. While such acts do not generally begin with threats of physical harm and corporal abuse, more subtle early coercion is common. The promise of love if they do what they are told and "keep it a secret" is the primary motivation. As sexual activity escalates, the child adapts to the situation in order to survive in the family environment. Whatever the outcome, she will blame herself. She feels guilty for what she has done and for betraying a trust. Threats of violence and loss of love and home are not uncommon — fears very real to a powerless child.

People who work with children and their families need to be clear about the reality of the child's dependence in the home, in addition to the often powerless position of the mother. One cannot explain away the sexual assault of a child as due to a lack of sexual interest on the part of the wife, or more incredibly, to excuse the behavior on the grounds of ostensible seductiveness on the part of the child. Blaming the wife for her husband's aggression and the daughter for her father's assault is another example of blaming the victim and directly or indirectly forcing compliance. At the same time, a disservice is also done to the man; to find excuses for him is to perpetuate his inability to relate to adult women as equals and to continue to engage in behavior that is destructive to himself and to others. We must join together to break the "conspiracy of silence: the trauma of incest."[84] By recognizing that the traditional powerful-powerless continuum breeds dysfunctional behavior, we all can become a force for healthful personal and environmental change.

Women and the Work Environment*

Person-environment research tells us that the work environment is as important to well-being as the family. Contrary to conventional wisdom, the work environment is as critical for women as it is for men. Leonard Pearlin's research, however, is in disagreement.[85] He suggests that job frustrations and problems are more likely to result in depression for men than for women. But his presumption that the workplace more closely regulates the psychological fate of men than of women is not borne out in other studies. His conclusion that "women withstand the strains of work with greater equanimity than do men," is a much more credible insight. The two interpretations may be mutually exclusive. It is true, though, that work of any kind outside the home appears to benefit depressed wives. Research comparing depressed housewives and depressed wives working outside the home has revealed that the latter group improved within three months. Meanwhile, the housewives continued to report impaired performance, disinterest, feelings of inadequacy, and fiscal problems. The "working wives" improved, even though their jobs were nongratifying and low level.[86] Brown and Tirril found that women's employment cut the risk of depression in half, even when other vulnerability factors were present.[87]

Still, the unsupportive, controlling working conditions of women puts vast numbers of them at risk. Many reasons are suggested as rationales for maintaining hierarchical, authoritarian work structures, but one that generally is not reported to workers is the desire to retain power over them. When that value stance is applied to women workers, the reality is even more acute. Allowing women power (control, autonomy, and authority) is not sanctioned by society. Hence, they are seldom found at the upper end of the hierarchical pyramid.[88] Controlling work environments have been found to be detrimental to women in regard to depression in the person-environment studies. Research

*Portions of this section have been excerpted by permission from Janice Wood Wetzel, "Mental Health, Working Class Women and Their Work," *Journal of Applied Social Sciences* 5, 1 (Fall-Winter 1980-1981): 1 – 13).

undertaken through the National Heart, Lung and Blood Institute in Framingham, Massachusetts, by Suzanne G. Hayes and Manning Feinlieb reaches similar conclusions. They found that the highest risk for heart disease in women is among clerical workers who have three or more children. A nonsupportive boss was an additional risk factor, but women in higher-level jobs were not at risk.

"The current phenomenon of the massive entry of women into the labor force is almost paralleled by the disgraceful lack of attention paid to the needs of working women." So testified Elizabeth D. Koontz, Chair of the National Commission on Working Women, before Senate Hearings on American Women Workers in 1978.[89] Noting that social reformers recognized their plight in the early 1900s, Koontz admonishes succeeding generations that have virtually ignored 29 million of the 36 million working women in the United States. Eighty percent of working women are in low-pay, dead-end jobs, and the earnings gap between men and women has tripled in twenty years, with the polarization increasing each year. One of the most insidious repercussions is the direct correlation between their resultant poverty and so-called mental illness.

While compliance with the "equal pay for equal work" law of 1963 is still being debated, today many believe that "equal pay for comparable worth" is their only realistic solution. The problem is not just corporate; it is systemic. Segregation by sex in the workplace is reflected in the fact that three-fourths of all women workers work in occupations that are at least 75 percent female, and 20 percent of women workers in classifications that are 95 percent female. These positions are all at the low end of the pay scale, regardless of technical skills and advanced educational requirements. Koontz argues that the problems are so great that we can no longer enjoy the luxury of theoretical discourse. We must look at the hard facts and apply realistic solutions now, for women represent the unemployed and working poor in mounting numbers, hardest hit by governmental cutbacks. The challenge quickens as the feminization of poverty becomes a reality.

The following program for change might be considered impossible or even naive. It is included because I think only those things left untried are impossible. That doesn't mean that its implementation is likely or easy. Even so, many organizations are becoming aware that the old bureaucratic ways are unproductive in contemporary America. The time for change is ripe.

Fostering Change through Participation

The promotion of noncontrolling, supportive work environments must be approached at both management and worker levels. (Ultimately, it is hoped that the concept of "levels" will be inappropriate.) While it is obvious that management needs to be "sold," the low degree of insight and aspiration typical of many low-status female employees will require vigorous efforts on their behalf. Too often their natural human propensity to master the environment has been arrested through lack of encouragement. The innate human tendency to develop competence through exploration and mastery of the environment can be blocked if it is not nurtured. So cautioned Robert White.[90] His warning is especially appropriate for depressed women. The dependence fostered in large numbers of women, coupled with the controlling, unsupportive aspects of their work environments, may have blocked their natural thrust toward growth, resulting in depression. Jack Rothman and his colleagues have conducted research on the fostering of participation and innovation for human-service professionals.[91] Their findings indicate that voluntary participation depends on the benefits directly gained from the activity. Therefore, to promote participatory management in organizations, benefits must be provided. This is true whether one must approach management or workers. Benefits important to successful cooperation are both instrumental and expressive.

Instrumental Benefits provide tangible, direct, material, task-oriented rewards. Such benefits may also be *anticipatory*, such as developing an action plan or obtaining a partial achievement such as a verbal commitment to a future goal. *Expressive Benefits* are intangible and characteristically psychological. They may be *interpersonal* rewards, such as developing new friendships, or they may be *symbolic* benefits that are personally satisfying, such as an award of recognition or approval of participatory activities. The underlying dynamics, based on behavioral principles of reinforcement (reward), can be applied to both working-class women and to management in order to encourage change through participation.

Application of Principles to Women Workers

Workers selected for a pilot project should be a representative pilot group. Do not try to involve all workers at once. Remember, when motivation is low, involving the women may be even more of a challenge than getting management to participate. Instrumental material benefits will, of course, vary with the organization, but are similar enough to make some educated guesses relevant to women's work environments. For example, the majority of women working in lower-echelon jobs must arrive and leave at specific times, regardless of whether or not their work is completed and done well. Their breaks and lunch hours are equally inflexible and personal business may not be conducted on company time. Little if any allowance is made for unusual events, individual differences, preferences, or constraints. How jobs are to be implemented is often spelled out precisely, leaving no leeway for creativity.

Attractive benefits such as more flexibility and freedom in governing time and scheduling work assignments might be suggested. Self-management work groups with collective responsibility, shared accountability for routine maintenance tasks, job variety, managerial information sharing, and appropriate rule making by workers might be implemented, to name a few possible rewards. Plans for child-care facilities and profit sharing may be suggested as anticipatory instrumental benefits. Whatever the benefits, they must finally come from the women themselves if they are to be effective motivators.

Expressive benefits regarding employee participation are multiple, including peer and employer supportiveness, as well as the development of a noncontrolling environment. Physical space and opportunity for interpersonal peer involvement are built into the ongoing process. Symbolic rewards may be added, such as reports on the activities and accomplishments of each member or group. Internal house organs and public media coverage of events all tend to reward participation. As the program progresses, newly experienced self-determination is intrinsically rewarding, leading to renewed involvement, interest in continued self-development, and community and world concern.

In order for such participatory management to flourish, remember that participation is not defined as representative, advisory, or board membership. Such participation may be incorporated in the program, but if it is the only mechanism, it only fosters alienation, owing to the inevitable gap between expected and actual responsiveness of representatives who are also, in fact, powerless. Participatory management means, instead, that workers are enabled to control the aspects of their work that intimately affect their lives. In this way, barriers to the development of competence and effectiveness are unblocked. It permits workers to achieve a sense of personal worth and importance, to be independent and self-motivating, to develop themselves, to receive recognition and approval for their work. It gives them a meaningful voice in decisions that directly affect their experience.

Application of Principles to Management

Because the successful cooperation of management requires both instrumental and expressive benefits, selected rewards must be tailored to the organization. For example, an administration that is experiencing employee hostility leading to production slow-down might be open to instrumental benefits such as more motivated, cooperative personnel. Anticipatory benefits might include a plan for increased production and profits. As for expressive benefits, congenial employee relationships reflect possible interpersonal rewards, while community acclaim and possibly media recognition may provide symbolic rewards when they are informed of the participatory involvement of employees.

In keeping with behavioral principles, it is suggested that a partial target group be selected for initial attempts to gain cooperation. One should not try to take on the entire organization at once.[92] Those administrators selected should be, whenever possible, high-status opinion leaders who are receptive to innovation and change and people with whom one has good relationships. Important, too, are qualities and qualifications of the administrator, such as motivation, education, skills, and experience. They will facilitate a successful presentation at a later date that will provide the mechanism by which innovation is transferred from a pilot project to a larger population.

The project itself also should be partialized. Initially a small-scale pilot program, it should be as reasonable and noncontroversial as possible. Now is not the time for radical change, but for laying a foundation. Ideally, whatever the innovation, the process should not be easily reversible. Gains made, however incremental, will then remain stable. By way of example, suppose a group of assemblyline women who work a 7 to 4 shift, five days a week, want a four-day work week. They also want to stagger their breaks and lunch periods so that everyone does not always have to arrive at 7 a.m. A plan might be drawn up that will address the less radical of the requests, staggering their hours, as an initial attempt at self-mastery of the environment. When management is convinced that the quantity of work will prevail and the quality of work will be improved, a written, nonreversible agreement can be drafted. In the meantime, workers can be thinking about an anticipatory plan based upon more extensive change for future implementation.

There is a contradiction between espoused democracy in our society and authoritarianism in the workplace, according to a report by the Special Task Force on Work in America to the Secretary of Health, Education, and Welfare.[93] A decrease in control and an increase in supportiveness can remedy the situation. Each working woman whose depression is correlated with unsupportive, controlling working conditions, and those who because of improved working conditions may never be troubled by depression, will be the better for it. Our knowledge of systems tells us that management, then, will also benefit. In fact, women and management may become one and the same in some instances.

Be aware, too, that management personnel can become depressed. The principles remain the same for men and women from all walks of life. When personal and/or environmental factors are dysfunctional, they too are at risk. Some of the macro interventions require concerted efforts that may not be probable in all cases. Depressed clients who are neither in work environments that are amenable to change, nor in positions of power, should be counseled to find more functional work situations whenever possible. Dysfunctional work environments are second only to unemployment as determinants of emotional dysfunction.[94] But the difficulty of such action in this era of recession, inflation, and unemployment is certainly a factor to take into consideration. When it is unrealistic to expect a more fulfilling job, possibilities for creating areas of self-control within the job situation should be explored. There may be components of a person's job description that are open to personal control and can be enhanced. Developing a work support group may itself be of help. Encouragement of avocational interests whereby people can establish control in alternative environments may also provide a positive balance in their lives.

Poor Women at Risk

Seventy-nine percent of all the poor people in the United States are women and their children. Mexican-American women are at the bottom of the financial pyramid with black and "Anglo" women not far above them. Poor women are hit harder by nearly every social problem and health concern. They have the highest incidence of mental illness, with depression their most common symptom. Theories and therapies suggested for others are also appropriate for them. They, of course, have the same human needs. Still, there are special overriding concerns that need to be addressed by counselors who work with women in poverty (and with men who are poor, also).

For unemployed working-class women, the neighborhood is the most important, sometimes the only, support system in times of stress. According to extensive research conducted by Rochelle Warren, the most supportive neighborhoods are those that are highly organized, where residents get together frequently, have many things in common, and are active in the community.[95] I would venture that this is also true for the working poor. The encouragement of such "healthy neighborhoods" is a responsibility of all mental health clinicians and community workers.

Attention should be paid to the realities of their lives — to the fact that they may be chronically underfed or poorly fed. Their physical and psychic energy is bound to be low. Even more devastating is the psychic price of a marginal living standard. It represents continual evidence that the world is uncaring and cruel. Such women are not likely to feel optimistic, respected, adequate, or secure. Rather, hopelessness, resentment, and deprivation in the face of reality are common (though a lot less common than one could rightfully expect). Psychological dependence is a natural outcome of economic dependence, for hopelessness robs people of incentive and possibility.[96] When the hope of bettering oneself is consistently cut off, the spirit that makes people want to continue to struggle for independence is cut off with it. The budget cuts for the 1980s can be expected to aggravate an already overwhelming situation.

The disposable income of poor workers is being reduced so greatly that their families will be little better off than those who rely on public assistance alone, according to a report by the University of Chicago Center for the Study of Welfare Policy. That has always been the case for welfare mothers who work outside the home. Although one-quarter of them do, they do not earn enough to support their families. Working is not the answer. *Working for a sufficient wage is,* provided high-quality child care is available. Nor is assistance the answer. More than half of all families receiving public assistance live *below* the official poverty line *after* receiving benefits. Assistance and wages must be adequate enough so that physical energy is not sapped by hunger, illness, or worry about how their family's basic daily needs can be met. Given today's social climate, it is unlikely that this will come to fruition without the help of advocates.

Those who work with poor women must guard against any behavior that implies punishment, authoritativeness, or conversely, overprotectiveness. Economic dependence need not reflect psychological dependence. Women must be included in all decisions and problem solving; they should be helped to use their own powers. Independence and self-respect will grow. They can be helped to find the necessary resources and encourage group development, which will lead to community action and a sense of support and control. Women of different ethnic backgrounds will have varying cultural needs and styles that only they can discern. Through group discussion, their issues will emerge together with an awareness of the commonalities among the members. Any misplaced sense of self-blame and guilt will be corrected in the process. This is essential to the alleviation of depression.

If you are a community volunteer, a social worker, or a caseworker overburdened with a high caseload of low-income clients, your job requires even more attention from policy makers. Inadequate salaries, insecure jobs, and unreasonably high work expectations go hand in hand with depression, burnout, and turnover.[97] Both you and your clients are at risk. They will not receive from depressed social workers the kind of support and direction that people on welfare need if they are to survive and overcome their conditions. By joining with fellow workers and clients, recognizing the commonality of your human needs, progress can be made to that end. Whether in the position of social workers or "working poor" clients, people need to feel that they are active in their own behalf and to be encouraged to move forward if they are to avoid the conditions inherent in depression — environments that paralyze motivation. Helen Harris Perlman said it succinctly in 1951; her message holds true today in this potentially less supportive and even more controlling era:

The everyday experience of every one of us helps us to know that incentive, like self-dependence, is compounded of many things other than fear and want. It is made up of the wish for status in the eyes of one's fellowmen; of the wish to occupy one's self with something that is rewarding and satisfying; of the wish for more of the good things of living than relief payments or insurance benefits will ever buy; and of the desire to be something better than what one is today. We know, too, that in order for incentive, like self-dependence, to be sustained it must be underpinned by physical and mental well-being, by basic security, by open opportunity and by some realistic grounds for looking forward with hope. Therefore, it is those conditions that make for basic human welfare and for reasonable self-dependence and for incentive that public assistance must provide and that the social worker along with every other citizen of the community must strive to attain.[98]

PREVENTION AND INTERVENTION

The person-environment model applies an ecological perspective to theory and practice. It is concerned with psychological traits — the predisposition, development, and adaptive potentialities of human beings, as well as the properties of social and physical environments that support or fail to support optimal growth. Prevention and intervention, then, focus on the advancement of the growth potential of people and the nutritive qualities of their environments. Within the ecological framework, human adaptation represents the efforts of individuals over the lifespan to reach a "goodness of fit" with the environment and vice versa, for the process is reciprocal. Human beings must respond to environmentally induced changes, but they also impact their environments, causing them to adapt in turn.[99]

Ideally, "goodness of fit" is synonymous with "mutually beneficial." Unfortunately, such is not always the case. When adaptation reflects manipulation on the part of people who are unable to take reasonable responsibility for themselves, on the one hand, or submission to unsavory situations on the other, then the concept of adaptation must be questioned. Prevention and intervention efforts, therefore, should focus on optimal development and relationship, rather than adaptation, in order to avoid the possibility of subtle coercion on the part of either the depressed person or the environment.[100] While adaptation may be immediately less stressful, it is not necessarily the optimal choice in the long run. Suggested interventions will address personality and environmental components, first in family situations, then followed by the workplace.

PERSON-ENVIRONMENT FAMILY INTERVENTIONS[101]

Table 5-1 summarizes the significant person-environment variables found to be relevant to the family. Opposite each finding are brief suggestions for appropriate intervention. They are by no means exhaustive, but are meant to be examples of appropriate ways to enhance persons and their environments so as to prevent or alleviate depression.

Conditions basic to growth must be provided. If the conditions have not been met in infancy and childhood, it is never too late to establish them. First, a feeling of safety must be present, a knowledge of basic support that leads to security. Second is the presence of tangible opportunities for self-development. And third, some regard and gratification for taking a risk for trying, even if one fails. Both children and adults are able to act on their natural propensities to reach out for new learning and growth when they are assured that their basic needs are met and opportunities are open and encouraged.[103] A therapist can encourage such family environments whether the goal is the prevention of future depression or the alleviation of present psychic pain.

The Person within the Family

Independence Training

The overwhelming majority of depressed people can be characterized as being dependent in that they are easily influenced,

Table 5-1*
Summary: Person-Environment Family Interventions[102]

Significant Family Variables Affecting Depression	Suggestions for Family Prevention/Intervention
Personality variable: Dependence at home is characterized by being easily influenced by others and was found to be the most likely personality trait of depressed people.	Development of family-related independence made possible by learning to master a desirable task; exploration, validation, and reinforcement of beliefs; learn decisionmaking and problemsolving; assertive training.
Environment variable: Lack of supportiveness was found to be the leading environmental problem for all depressed people.	Encourage mutually supportive nurturing; structure shared time and attention; teach the importance of sharing relationships.
Person × environment interaction: Dependent women in autonomous family environments that insisted on independent behavior (assertiveness, self-sufficiency, and decisionmaking) were found to be depressed. Independent women in nonautonomous family environments that did not support independent behavior were also depressed. Family responsibilities were relegated almost solely to the independent, depressed person.	Apply the Person and Environment interventions suggested above relative to both dimensions; emphasize family nurturance; encourage independence development. Encourage egalitarian family relationships and shared responsibilities; explore areas where clients can experience support for independent behaviors such as assertiveness, self-sufficiency, and decisionmaking.

*Excerpted by permission from "Operationalizing the Person-Environment Conceptual Framework for Social Work Intervention with Depressed Clients," by Janice Wood Wetzel, in *Arête 6*;2 (Fall 1980):33 – 42.

particularly in relation to their families. Those whose dependence needs are being met probably will not be motivated to develop themselves further. The desire to become independent and to develop competence, to explore and to master, can be blocked if it is not encouraged;[104] thus, even those whose needs are not being met remain unmotivated. A major step toward developmental maturity, then, is awareness of the need for such growth. Kuperman's Origin-Pawn Game,[105] based on the work of deCharms,[106] is designed for such a task. It dramatizes one's dependence, experientially dichotomizing pawn behavior which is externally caused, and internally motived origin behavior.

*Motivation Training***

The following modified version of the Origin-Pawn Game can be adapted to a group of people who have been briefed concerning the

**A description of the Origin-Pawn Game and the following three sections have been excerpted by permission from "The Work Environment and Depression: Implications for Intervention," by Janice Wood Wetzel, in John W. Hanks, ed., *Toward Human Dignity: Social Work in Practice* National Association of Social Workers, Inc., 1978), excerpt, pp. 239 – 243.

fantasy nature of the game. The initial activity involves asking the group members to play the role of sixth-grade children who are being given the opportunity to do something creative with paper and pencil. They are told that they are free to do anything they wish to do; if they prefer, nothing at all. The activity continues for fifteen minutes, at which time the facilitator, in this case a woman, makes an excuse to leave the room.

After a few minutes, the facilitator returns in the role of a substitute leader. "Now, children," she says in a loud, authoritative tone, "take everything off your desk except a pencil or pen." If there is any retort, she responds with, "No more talking. Raise your hands if you want to say something." Handing out blank paper, she continues in her role with, "The key to this exercise is being good and doing exactly what I tell you. Raise your right hand . . . . Now put both hands in your lap and sit up straight." The leader reprimands behavior, finally explicitly directing the group to draw certain lines and figures step by step, controlling every movement, keeping the group constantly under surveillance.

After a few minutes of this controlling behavior, she returns to her original role, supportively suggesting exploration of the anger, hurt, frustration, and lack of control about which the clients are now becoming explicitly aware. The exercise and follow-up discussion provide rich insights in which clients get in touch with subservient, dependent feelings in a short time, together with the anger and frustration they feel at being controlled. It is clear from the description that this exercise must be engaged in with discretion. Only well-trained facilitators and nonpsychotic clients should take part, for the emotional effect can be as intense as it is effective.

Interest in the World and Self-Development

A further dimension of awareness training that addresses the dependency issues reflected by a lack of interest in the world and self-development is sometimes called reconstructive therapy. Group members choose topics of potential interest that they agree to investigate and report on. Topics may include such diverse areas as politics, business, cooking, gardening, pet care, literature, theater, dance, sports, and so on. Participants share their information with one another, and are encouraged to plan group activities around the areas of interest whenever appropriate. Thus, interests are reinforced through positive group experience, which may then be generalized to the larger community. The exercise can be adapted to a client-therapist dyad.

Though the group influence will be lacking, the process still can be effective.

Self-Esteem Via Task Mastery and Competence

The development of self-esteem through environmental mastery and competence is appropriate to independence intervention. These strategies have been found to boost low self-concept, which in turn positively counters depressed affect.[107]

One must remember to "begin where the client is" and to be certain that first attempts, however minimal, are chosen by the client and are likely to result in success. A contract for more extensive accomplishments can follow the initial effort. Eventually, through personal experience, clients learn that they are effective people who have control over their own well-being and are not dependent on others to sustain their feelings of self-worth. When they trust their own knowledge and reasoning powers, external influence is of less importance. They will have developed a sense of responsible independence and no longer need to live vicariously through others.[108] Recall that the development of independent competence has been theoretically maintained by leading social scientists for many years. Supported primarily by clinical observation, the person-environment model provides empirical support for their position. Clients should be assured, of course, that the interim environmental stability that is congruent with their present state of dependence will be provided. Premature insistence on independence can be devastating.

Social Skills and Assertiveness

Since depressed people often lack social skills[109] and the ability to say "no,"[110] it is essential that they develop proficiency in communication and assertiveness. Such skills tend to encourage supportiveness of others, while lessening the need for support due to dependence by increasing independent functioning. These skills are described in detail in Chapters 3 and 5.

The Family Environment

Increasing Support Systems

Manswell Pattison has devised a psychosocial inventory to assess the health of one's social network, which he views as the new family social structure.[111] By applying the inventory to a national sample, it was found that a normal healthy network has about twenty-five persons with five or six people making up subgroups of the network. Pattison notes that the normal social network provides a relatively consistent set of norms for stress management. Persons can be readily mobilized to respond to a person under stress, there is a rather continuous flow of positive emotional support, the network provides ready and available emotional and instrumental (concrete) assistance, each person has more than one group with whom to interact, and finally, the network of selected persons is such that the loss or addition of any one person can be accommodated.

In contrast, the "neurotic type" of network, which may reflect that of many depressed people, is relatively impoverished and isolating. Often invested in internalized objects who are not present, they fail to interact with real people present to them.[112] Prevention and intervention can constructively focus on the development of healthy support systems as outlined below. Clients can be directed to assess their networks. Instruct them to:

   A. list all of the persons who are important to me, whether I like them or not.
   B. arrange the list in four subgroups of (1) family, (2) relatives, (3) friends and neighbors, and (4) social and work associates.
   C. specify which persons have ongoing relations between them, apart from their relationship to me. (These are the connecting links in the network. In a normal network, each person relates to about six others apart from the subject.)
   D. relate the nature and quality of interaction with each person in the network on each of the five variables listed below (pathology-free people are rated highly):

Pattison Psychosocial Inventory

   1. *Contact* — the type of interaction (face-to-face, telephone, letter).
   2. *Emotional intensity* — the degree of valued investment.
   3. *Positive emotion* for the other person.
   4. *Instrumental base* — concrete assistance to be counted on.
   5. *Symmetrical Reciprocity* — the other person, too, returns strong, positive, emotional feeling and may also count on you to provide instrumental assistance.

While it is suggested that these directives be flexibly applied, they can provide helpful insights into the supportiveness available in family and extended family systems, as well as guidelines for developing further supportive environments.

Person-Environment Work Interventions[113]

Table 5-2 summarizes the significant person-environment variables found to be relevant to the work situation. Brief suggestions for prevention and intervention are opposite each finding. Again, the suggestions are not meant to be all-inclusive.

Table 5-2*
Summary: Person-Environment Work Interventions[114]

Significant Work Variables Affecting Depression	*Suggestions for Work Prevention/Intervention*
Personality variable: Dependence at work is characterized by low self-reliance, lack of interest in the world, lack of interest in self-development, and lack of assertiveness. Such people were likely to be depressed.	Development of work-related assertiveness; learn decisionmaking and problem-solving; explore new ideas and experiences outside the work situation as well as within; become involved in the community; learn a new work related skill.
Environment variable: Lack of peer support was also found to represent the depressed groups.	Increase activities with peers at work; increase work- and leisure-related group activity; increase communication and social skills; consult in work setting regarding importance of time and physical space for informal peer interaction; foster noncompetitive work atmosphere.
Person × environment interaction: Dependence and lack of peer support were typical of a significant number of depressed women and men.	Consult with clients and in work settings regarding encouragement of decisionmaking and comprehensive policymaking, rewarding initiative, support of long-term employees' goals, increased job freedom and responsibility; explore ways clients can establish relationships with peers such as peer-supported collective bargaining, task forces, peer consciousness-raising groups, assertiveness training, open communication.
Environment variable: Controlling environments were found to be the leading work problem for all depressed people.	Explore partial aspects of work situation where client can make some task and/or policy decisions; consult in work settings regarding the dysfunctional aspects of hierarchical organizations and control of workers; encourage more flexibility and individual input into establishment of necessary rules and regulations, eliminating them where possible; reduce external supervision, establish more egalitarian atmosphere by including workers in total planning efforts (not just partialized tasks, advisory groups, or representatives).

*Excerpted by permission from "Operationalizing the Person-Environment Conceptual Framework for Social Work Intervention with Depressed Clients," by Janice Wood Wetzel, in *Arête 6*;2 (Fall 1980):33 – 42.

The Person at Work

A person who is dependent at work is characterized by a lack of self-reliance, very little interest in self-development or the larger world, and a general nonassertive stance. Such a person is very likely to be depressed, but independent people who are locked into restrictive, unsupportive job situations are also at risk. Dependence increases vulnerability, but the trait in and of itself need not cause depression. And so it is with independence; the trait does not immunize against depression; rather, it simply decreases the probability of its occurrence.

The independence training exercises suggested in the above section on Family Interventions are also appropriate in work situations. The achievement of mastery can be tailored to work tasks that have been sectioned into incremental steps to ensure success. Work-related assertion skills can be practiced, and decision making and problem solving can be enhanced in order to develop a personal sense of identity. New ideas and experiences outside the work situation can be equally important to an emerging identity. Community involvement, particularly in relation to one's developing expertise, can augment a new-found sense of autonomy. When one's peers or employers become aware of a person's abilities, they are inclined to show a new respect. That regard, in turn, reinforces one's personal feelings of competence and independence.

There are other instances when people feel relatively assured of their capabilities, but give up trying because the work environment has been unresponsive to their efforts or even consistently punishing.[115] In this case the prevailing environment would be the preferred target for intervention. In fact, environmental consultation can be an effective step toward alleviating depression, regardless of the personality attributes of the client.

The Work Environment

Peer Supportiveness

The therapist should be alert for reactions to stressful work-related situations. While the work environment can be a determinant in the promotion of mental health, it also can be a source of great stress. Peer support (and its absence), for example, is a major factor correlated with both well-being and depression in the marketplace. Management must be educated to the importance of establishing time, space, and a supportive attitude toward peer interaction at work. Rather than encouraging isolation and competitiveness, the encouragement of peer support through attitudes, policies, and time and space allotted to its enhancement also reflects sound management.[116] Workers, themselves, can assess such supportiveness, using the appropriate Moos subscale described in Chapter 11 and by applying the Pattison Psychosocial Inventory detailed in the Family Interventions section of this chapter. (Work acquaintances are included in Pattison's assessment of social networks.) Coworkers can be encouraged to reach out to their peers, to form work support groups and to develop after-hours social groups. Indeed, if not a group, then at least one other significant relationship might be developed. There is research indicating that social support from just one person important to the individual can be effective in alleviating the deleterious impact of stress at work.[117] The therapist can encourage clients to form such relationships.

Management Supportiveness

Work supervisors can be effective sources of social support.[118] While not as significant to well-being as peer support, person-environment research also indicates that lack of supportiveness by the managerial staff is highly correlated with depression. Depressed people were less likely to report experiences of managerial supportiveness than were nondepressed people. Depressed persons also reported that they were not likely to be treated with respect, to be given credit openly for their contributions, or to be encouraged to communicate to management. The employer's expectations, they said, were not liable to be considered reasonable, and supervisors did not "stand up" for their employees. Nor did depressed people feel that they were encouraged to be self-sufficient and to make their own decisions. The opposite was true for the nondepressed groups.[119] Interventions regarding lack of managerial supportiveness closely parallel those for the controlling work environment detailed below.

Promoting Noncontrolling Work Environments[120]

Those mental health clinicians and administrators who are in positions that can influence social policy and planning can apply this knowledge to constructive environmental engineering, both in their own work environments and in those in which they are management and labor consultants. When the case is made that restrictive rules and pressures are dysfunctional to all employees and, consequently, to their productivity and service, those who formulate policy may be convinced to find more rational work incentives.

Catalytic Change Model[121]

Intervention can be approached from both social-policy (macro) and clinical-practice (micro) points of view. Ideally, the two foci are not mutually exclusive, but interact. From the macro vantage point, when more than suggestion to employers is required, a catalytic change model is recommended. In such a schema, mediators facilitate a meeting of management and employees in an open exchange, discussing their different needs in relation to the problem of depressed personnel. Decreasing control while increasing staff and peer supportiveness are the focal points of concern. In such a model, high-risk groups are identified, along with relevant environmental "structures" and "sentiments." *Structures* refer to staff and peer groups and their informal and formal networks and hierarchies. *Sentiments* involve shared feelings, opinions, values, and attitudes that govern behavior within the structure. After group assessment of the needs of both management and employees, identification of those concerns that are most amenable to change and that influence high-risk, depression-prone persons are targeted. The need for managerial control and the parallel needs of employees for environmental support and personal control must be addressed. Management may also be influenced to encourage formal collaborative efforts, as well as to provide time and physical space for informal peer interaction. The discouragement of personally threatening competitiveness leading to alienation and discord is also appropriate as a strategy.

Note that facilitators do not take charge of the group. They simply act as catalysts for change, withdrawing when the members of the organization have mobilized their goals. By so doing, because they have not acted as protagonists, they are free to address new high-risk situations. Because the work environment is crucial to well-being, it is important to give it the attention it deserves. Further discussion applied primarily, though not exclusively, to women can be found in the following section.

Nursing Home Interventions*

There are more than one million people living out their lives in nursing homes in the United States. They are primarily white, gener-

*This section is excerpted by permission from Janice Wood Wetzel, "Interventions with the Depressed Elderly in Institutions," *Social Casework* 61,4 (April 1980): 234 – 239, published by The Family Service Association of America.

ally elderly, and usually poor. They are largely women who are alone in the world. In fact, three-fourths of all nursing home residents are women.[122] Experts generally agree that depression statistics would be increased considerably if the many elderly now misdiagnosed as suffering from organic brain syndrome were correctly assessed as depressed.[123] Depression is one of the most pervasive problems, reflected in the prevailing helplessness and hopelessness of nursing home residents. It is significant, then, that social scientists have found institutions to be guilty of accelerating, rather than reducing, the symptoms of helplessness and hopelessness in the elderly.[124] Since the number of institutionalized elderly women is three times greater than the number of such men, the problem looms large in any case. As for elderly men, theirs is the highest suicide rate of any group of people. Given the obvious correlation between depression and suicide, the problem of depression in nursing homes applies to both sexes.[125]

Interventions in the person dimension focus on individual personal change and development. Implicit is a developmental perspective on aging recognizing the ongoing possibilities for personal growth throughout the life span.[126] In the environmental sphere, family supportiveness should be addressed. The institutional setting must create an alternative family for most female residents, for statistics indicate that only 10 percent have a living spouse, 50 percent have no close relatives, 60 percent have no visitors at all, and only 20 percent will return to their homes in the community.[127] Loss of love objects and role loss, two of the major theories of depression, are realistic conditions in the aged woman's world.[128]

The development of quasi-families need not be viewed as second-rate substitute relationships. Research tells us that friends are much more likely to provide intimate support systems for older women than are blood relations or spouses.[129] It has been found that spouses and coworkers are more important than children to the well-being of older people.[130] Friendship is based on mutual choice and need, involving a voluntary social exchange between equals. A person's sense of self-esteem and usefulness thus appears to be more important than filial relationships. The implications are great for nursing homes. The development of social-support systems is not only imperative, but highly feasible and satisfactory.

That is not to say that existing families are not important. Group activities involving families with elderly relatives are suggested for the purpose of mutual support. The actions and reactions of families due to their own needs must not be overlooked. What is true for the elderly is no less true for their families, for we are talking about common human needs. Support of family needs will have a direct effect on the well-being of their elderly kin, while reinforcing the existing natural helping network in the family.

Independence and Aging

The development of independence and self-worth is always possible, regardless of age, for personal growth is a lifespan reality. Far too often independence is not encouraged. Never is this more of a reality than in the lives of aging men and women. Research indicates that the primary cause of low morale among older people is dependence.[131] Their negative status associated with dependence may be as important as the inconvenience caused by having to depend on another.[132]

Application of the person-environment model to an elderly sample suggests a reassessment of the compliant behavior of those aging people who are too easily influenced by others. It is important to rethink the long-range effects of such subservience. Although its reinforcement in the hectic world of the nursing home is understandable, such extremely dependent behavior is contraindicated. These are the people who are most likely to be or to become depressed, and eventually will require more care than will those who are more assertive. Research tells us that dependence in the form of persuadability (easy influence) is linked with lack of self-esteem[133] as well as with depression.

Differential Autonomy Needs

The concept of environmental autonomy must be addressed, for its application differs vis-à-vis one's dependency orientation. While steps may be taken to develop independence, such a change in orientation takes time and is on a developmental continuum at best. Support must be provided for dependence needs. While research tells us that women have been socialized to dependence, and that dependence is typical of the majority of depressed women, it is likely that many elderly women have developed a degree of independence that is not sustained by the nursing home environment. There is some evidence that women move in the direction of independence as they age, while men become more dependent, though this is only conjecture and subjective observation. It is not unusual for a nursing home staff to attest personally to the fact that many female residents are independent. For such women, whatever their numbers, autonomous milieus must be encouraged. In their absence, such women become "secondarily dependent,"[134] and are vulnerable to depression.

Youth Involvement and Life Review

Whatever the program, the involvement of youth with the elderly is an almost automatic success and one that can be influential in promoting independence. Young people are equally appreciative of the relationship, a fact that is not lost to their seniors. The long-range socialization factor should not be discounted either. Youth who learn to esteem the aged provide a natural support network that is all too often missing in this generation. They will also have a more positive view of their own aging.

While young people can effectively take part in all of the suggested interventions, a particularly relevant program is the Life Review. Life Review is the telling of one's early life history, which is often demeaned as "living in the past." Gerontologists Robert Butler and Myrna Lewis suggest that it is a life-affirming therapeutic process that is to be encouraged.[135] The sharing of oral histories with the young communicates to the older person a validation of his or her life experience and self-worth in a rapidly moving society. The young are thereby educated to the past and can relate the life knowledge of the older person to present-era conditions. If both the youth and the older person are female, they share the added benefit of mutual feminine history. Often forgotten in the pages of male-oriented history books, feminists call such valuable information "herstory." The elderly person thus provides a valuable service that is not available elsewhere. This approach can be extended to other needed services, and should be encouraged whenever possible. Populations such as children, teenagers, the physically and mentally handicapped, and even other elderly people in nursing homes all benefit from the attention of our older citizens. Such involvement develops a sense of self-worth crucial to optimal mental health.[136]

Creativity and Life Review

Gerontological research indicates that intelligence and creativity do not inevitably decline with age. In fact, insight in problem situations, creative understanding, and metaphoric processing often improve in the elderly. Evidence of retarded abilities has been found to be associated with physical and mental illness. As with younger people, for example, depression inhibits personal growth and creative interests. Creativity also can be arrested when underlying capabilities are not challenged, when people are locked into boring situations. Too often, this is the case for nursing home residents. The life reminiscences of the aged can be fashioned into journals, short stories, novels, plays and poetry, as well as visual arts and music. Even the inevitable deterioration of Alzheimer's patients may be slowed. "Metaphors of the self," familiar objects taken from the lives of the elderly and shaped into symbolic objects, permit a transcendence of death. Such transitional objects become creative alter-egos and supportive companions that will live on indefinitely.[137]

Staff Supportiveness

In a research project evaluating the effectiveness of treatment of the depressed elderly, it was found that there was a significant relationship between alleviation of symptoms and intensive involvement with residents. Such was not the case for those treated with chemotherapy or assigned to a "no-treatment" control group. Types of intervention that were most effective more fully engaged the elderly in the mental health center. Length of time spent with the clients or types of activities were not of great importance. Rather, the total number of times the social workers had casual chats, contacts, or meetings with the elderly were the critical variables.[138] We might suspect that confidante relationships were also established, a condition that had a positive effect on morale. Personal involvement on the part of personnel, therefore, should be regarded as a basic therapeutic attitude.

Peer Support/In-House Experts

Even more critical is the encouragement of peer-support groups. The emphasis of these groups should be put on mutually nurturing behavior and personalized attention. Residents can be taught the importance of such supportiveness to their comfort and happiness; it need not be a professional mystery. Whenever possible, group members should be made an active part of the decision-making, programming, and service-delivery system.

Another project that may be instituted to stimulate peer support, as well as self-development and self-esteem, is an "In-House Expert" program. Each participant is encouraged to provide expertise in one area. It may be in the world of ideas, talents, or skills. The interest may be newly developed or may have been a lifelong vocation or avocation. Whatever the case, cohorts are free to call upon one another for advice and help relative to their area of expertise. A mutual peer-support system is thereby developed and reinforced, as are individual competence and worth.

The in-house program may also provide a vehicle for attitude change among elderly men. Household types of maintenance and self-care tasks can be encouraged and supported. Research indicates that such activities, viewed as women's work, have been so negatively assessed by elderly men that they often refuse to learn how to do them, even when their own survival is at stake.[139] A peer-support program might change attitudes enough to remove these inhibitions and to develop appropriate self-reliance and esteem. Residential care might even become unnecessary in some cases. Controlling long-term care facility systems need not be perpetuated. Gerald Euster refers to the growing evidence that institutional programs for the elderly are leaving the "dark ages."[140] One of the elements critical to such progress is the need for independent control of some aspects of their lives.[141] Environmental control is an antecedent of depression, regardless of the individual's dependence or independence orientation. The elderly are as drained by rigid rules, procedures, and orders as their younger counterparts are. While efficiency is admirable in a nursing home, and control has been viewed as a prerequisite of efficiency, the toll is too great. This factor, however, probably meets with the most resistance to change.

Staff

Environmentally controlled staff who lack peer support, and who may also be dependent personalities, are as vulnerable to depression as patients. Their situations differ only in that it is possible for staff to experience a supportive environment at home. They will have a somewhat lesser chance, then, of experiencing depression. In any case, their discomfort will have environmental repercussions just as surely as does a patient's subjective discomfort. People who are controlled, and therefore lack power, may be more likely to exert control over those in a one-down position. The situation is too often a reality in institutional settings of all kinds.

The same principles are applicable to all health care personnel, whether physician or maintenance crew. The same attention to dependence and independence needs, the same encouragement of independence, the endorsement and fostering of peer support, and the subscription to the employer's support of staff are equally important to effective health care and prevention of depression.

Hospital Environments[142]

Hospital administration historically derived its model of management from the corporate organization of the labor process.[143] Recent studies, including conclusions drawn from extensive government-sponsored research in the past indicate that "significant numbers of workers are dissatisfied with the quality of their working lives."[144] The result is a decline in both physical and mental health, family stability, community participation, and productivity, and an increase in drug and alcohol addiction, aggression, delinquency, crime, heart disease, and depression. The root of dissatisfaction is the so-called "scientific management" method which breaks work responsibilities down into simple, routine steps, resulting in low-pay, dead-end jobs, while simultaneously denying knowledge of the overall process to any personnel but superiors.[145]

Hospitals have become prime examples of such employee dissatisfaction. This fact impinges on the well-being of patients, as well as health care personnel, for there is also a direct correlation between worker satisfaction and mental health and services to patients. Depressed nurses or social workers, for example, controlled by physicians and their institutions and lacking a sense of competence and worth, may in turn treat their patients in a controlling manner. They may also treat staff who come under them in the same dysfunctional way, thus perpetuating the depressing environmental conditions.

Burnout[146]

Never is supportiveness more critical than in the work settings of mental health clinicians themselves who are vulnerable to burnout. Burnout has been defined as "a wearing out, exhaustion or failure due to excessive demands made on energy, strength, or resources." It is being addressed in contemporary literature as a relatively new phenomenon, but is suspiciously analogous to old-fashioned depression related to stressful working conditions. Burnout is manifested by emotional detachment from the job, loss of human caring, and lack of self-confidence. Symptoms are most likely to be found in people who self-select to help others, who start out as hard-working, involved, and caring persons. These are the very people society cannot afford to lose. Experts in the field indicate that fully functioning support systems may be instrumental in preventing such burnout. Suggestions span family, work, and community. Those who are in private practice should also take heed, for they must go to even greater lengths to find the following preventive social supports:[147]

1. Someone who will listen to you ventilate.

2. Someone who will provide unconditional emotional support, even if he or she does not agree with you.

3. Someone whom you respect or admire and who provides positive feedback.

4. Someone who can provide constructive criticism, thereby helping you to grow professionally.

5. Someone who will provide emotional challenge, thereby encouraging emotional growth (for example, someone who will insist on

the mutual sharing of feelings will be a catalyst for a person who tends to block or shy away from the expression of feelings).

6. Someone who will provide a social comparison touchstone, who shares one's world view.

Interpersonal Therapy

While not associated with the Person-Environment Model, Interpersonal Therapy dovetails well with many of its underlying assumptions. Myrna Weissman and her colleagues at the Yale Depression Research Unit focus on the depressed person's current problems, with attention to role disputes and interpersonal communications, perception and performance. The clinician provides reassurance and clarification of feelings as well. Research findings are promising, particularly when psychotherapy is coupled with amitriptyline drug therapy.[148]

NOTES

1. The person-environment model is based upon a conceptual framework and research developed by the author. Hence, there are a number of excerpts and references from published papers.

2. Refer to Chapters 2 through 8 for conceptual variations on the dependence theme.

3. Ferster, Charles B., "Classification of Behavioral Pathology," in *Research in Behavior Modification*, ed. L. Krasner and L. P. Ullman (New York: Holt, Rinehart, and Winston, 1965).

4. Excerpted from Wetzel, Janice Wood, and Franklin C. Redmond, "A Person-Environment Study of Depression," *Social Service Review 54*, 3 (September 1980): 363 – 375; also see Chapter 4.

5. Mischel, Walter, *Introduction to Personality*, 2nd ed. (New York: Holt, Rinehart, and Winston, 1976).

6. Excerpted from Wetzel, Janice Wood, "Operationalizing the Person-Environment Conceptual Framework for Social Work Intervention with Depressed Clients," *Arete 6*, 2 (Fall 1980): 33 – 42; see Chapter 8 for a discussion of NIMH-funded bio-psychosocial studies to be completed in the mid-1980s.

7. Alexander, James, "On Dependence and Independence," *Bulletin of the Philadelphia Association of Psychoanalysis 20*, 1 (1970): 49 – 57.

8. Mischel, Walter, *Introduction to Personality*, 2nd ed. (New York: Holt, Rinehart, and Winston, 1976).

9. Hans S. Falck, Personal Communication, October 14, 1979.

10. Moos, Rudolph H., *Family Environment Scale* (Palo Alto, CA: Consulting Psychologists Press, 1974).

11. Berger, Peter L., and Thomas Luckmann, *The Social Construction of Reality* (Garden City, NY: Doubleday, 1967).

12. Lewin, Kurt, *Principles of Topological Psychology* (New York: McGraw-Hill, 1936).

13. Holland, John L., *The Psychology of Vocational Choice: A Theory of Personality Types and Model Environments* (Waltham, MA: Blaisdell, 1966); see also Lawrence A. Pervin, "Performance and Satisfaction as a Result of Individual-Environment Fit," *Psychological Bulletin 69* (1968): 56 – 68; see also Roger G. Barker, *Ecological Psychology: Concepts and Methods for Studying the Environment of Human Behavior* (Stanford, CA: Stanford University Press, 1968); see also George G. Stern, *People in Context* (New York: Wiley, 1970).

14. Wetzel, Janice Wood, "Depression and Dependence Upon Unsustaining Environments," *Clinical Social Work Journal 6*, 2 (Summer 1978): 75 – 89.

15. Wetzel, Janice Wood, and Franklin C. Redmond, "A Person-Environment Study of Depression," *Social Service Review 54*, 3 (September 1980): 363 – 375.

16. See ibid. for a discussion of the development of the Wetzel Independence-Dependence Scales.

17. Freud, Anna, "The Concept of Developmental Lines," in *The Psychoanalytic Study of the Child*, Vol. 18 (New York: International Universities Press, 1963), pp. 245 – 265.

18. Parens, Henri, and Leon Saul, Jr., *Dependence in Man* (New York: International Universities Press, 1971).

19. Berger, Peter L., and Thomas Luckmann, *The Social Construction of Reaility* (Garden City, NY: Doubleday, 1967).

20. Emerson, Richard, "Power-Dependence Relations," *American Sociological Review 22* (1962): 31 – 41.

21. Thibaut, John W., and Harold H. Keley, "Power and Dependence," in *The Social Psychology of Groups*, Vol. 7 (New York: Wiley, 1959), pp. 100 – 125.

22. Rotter, Julian, "Generalized Expectancies for Internal Versus External Control of Reinforcement," *Psychological Monographs 80*, 1 (1966): 1 – 28.

23. Rotter, Julian, *Social Learning and Clinical Psychology* (New York: Prentice-Hall, 1954).

24. See Chapter 6 for further discussion of internal and external reinforcement.

25. Alexander, James, "On Dependence and Independence," *Bulletin of the Philadelphia Association of Psychoanalysis 20* 1 (1970): 49 – 57.

26. See Chapter 3, and the discussion of psychic energy in Chapter 2.

27. Allport, Gordon, *Becoming: Basic Considerations for a Psychology of Personality* (New Haven: Yale University Press, 1955).

28. Refer to Henry Minton, in J. Tedeschi, ed., *The Social Influence Processes* (Chicago: Aldine-Atherton, 1972)100 – 150. for a comprehensive discussion of the urge toward self-determination.

29. Note that the dualistic poles of independence and the need for support, while couched in less esoteric terms, are somewhat analogous to the paradox of human uniqueness and unity described in Chapter 7.

30. President's Commission on Mental Health, *Report to the President*, Vol. 4, Washington, D.C., 1978.

31. Wetzel, Janice Wood, "Depression and Dependence upon Unsustaining Environments," *Clinical Social Work Journal 6* 2 (Summer 1978): 75 – 89; see also Wetzel, Janice Wood, and Franklin C. Redmond, "A Person-Environment Study of Depression," *Social Service Review 54* 3 (September 1980): 363 – 375.

32. Ilfield, Frederick W. Jr., "Current Social Stressors and Symptoms of Depression." *American Journal of Psychiatry*, 134, 1977: 161-166.

33. U.S. Bureau of Census, *Current Population Reports*, Series P-70, No. 349, 1979, *U. S. Crime Reports* (1979).

34. Freud, Sigmund, "Female Sexuality," (1931) in *Collected Papers*, Vol. 5 (London: Hogarth Press, 1956), pp. 252 – 272.

35. Maslow, Abraham H., *Motivation and Personality*, 2nd ed. (New York: Harper and Row, 1970).

36. Buber, Martin, *Hasidism and Modern Man* (New York: Harper and Row, 1958).

37. White, Robert, "Motivation Reconsidered: The Concept of Competence," *Psychological Review 66*(1959): 297 – 333; also see Chapter 4.

38. Excerpted from Janice Wood Wetzel, "Mental Health, Working Class Women and Their Work," *Journal of Applied Social Sciences 5*, 1 (Fall/Winter 1980 – 1981): 1 – 13.

39. Markham, William T., Charles M. Bonjean, Judy C. Tully, and Sandra L. Albrecht, "Self-Expression at Work: An Approach to Testing Personality and Organization Theory," paper presented at the Annual Meeting of the Southwestern Social Science Association, March 1975.

40. Kornhauser, Arthur, *Mental Health of the Industrial Worker* (New York: Wiley, 1965), abridged in V. H. Vroom and Edward L. Deci, eds., *Management and Motivation* (New York: Penguin, 1970).

41. Payne, Roy, and Derek Pugh, "Organizations and Psychological Environments," in *Psychology at Work*, ed. Peter B. Warr (Baltimore: Penguin Books, 1971), pp. 374 – 401.

42. Likert, Rensis, *The Human Organization: Its Management and Value* (New York: McGraw-Hill, 1967).

43. Ahrens, Lois, "Battered Women's Refuges: Feminist Cooperatives vs. Social Service Institutions," *Radical America 14* 3 (May – June 1980): 41 – 47.

44. Ouchi, William G., *Theory Z* (New York: Addison-Wesley, 1981).

45. Taylor, F. W., *The Principles of Scientific Management* (New York: Harper and Row, 1911); see also Amital Etzioni, *Modern Organizations* (Englewood Cliffs, NJ: Prentice-Hall, 1964); Chris Argyris, "Personality and Organization Theory Revisited," *Administrative Science Quarterly 18* (1973): 141 – 167; Harry Braverman, "Labor and Monopoly Capital: The Degradation of Work in the Twentieth Century," *Monthly Review, 26*, 3 (July – August 1974).

46. Wolman, Jonathan, "Worker Participation Changing Traditional Job Situations," Associated Press, August 27, 1978.

47. Toffler, Alvin, "Adhocracy — The Coming of Contemporary Organizations," in *The Future of Work*, ed. Fred Best (Englewood Cliffs, NJ: Prentice-Hall, 1973).

48. U.S. Department of Health, Education and Welfare, *Report on a Special Task Force on Work in American* (Cambridge, MA: Massachusetts Institute of Technology, 1971); also refer to Chapter 4 for a discussion of power.

49. Early, Sandra, "Your Job Can Drive You Crazy," *The National Observer*, May 2, 1977.

50. de Beauvoir, Simone, *The Second Sex* (New York: Alfred A. Knopf, 1953).

51. Janeway, Elizabeth, *Man's World, Woman's Place: A Study in Social Mythology* (New York: William Morrow and Co., 1971).

52. Oakley, Ann, *Sex, Gender and Society* (New York: Harper and Row, 1968).

53. Spence, Janet T., and Robert L. Helmreich, *Masculinity and Femininity: Their Psychological Dimensions, Correlates, and Antecedents*. (Austin TX: University of Texas Press, 1978).

54. Turner, Francis J., *Psychosocial Therapy* (New York: Free Press, 1978).

55. Bem, Sandra L., "Sex-Role Adaptability: One Consequence of Psychological Andorgeny," *Journal of Personality and Social Psychology 31*, (1975): 634 – 643.

56. Laws, J., "A Feminist Review of Marital Adjustment Literature," *Journal of Marriage and the Family 33* (August 1971): 483 – 516.

57. Miller, Jean Baker, *Toward a New Psychology of Women* (Boston: Beacon Press, 1976) p. 71.

58. Janeway, Elizabeth, *Man's World, Woman's Place: A Study in Social Mythology* (New York: William Morrow, 1971), p. 284.

59. Macoby, Eleanor E., and Carol N. Jacklin, *The Psychology of Sex Differences* (Stanford, CA: Stanford University Press, 1974).

60. Hovland, Carl, and I. L. Janis, eds., *Personality and Persuasability*, Vol. 2 (New Haven: Yale University Press, 1959).

61. Horney, Karen, *Feminine Psychology* (New York: Norton, 1973).

62. Radloff, Lenore Sawyer, "Risk Factors for Depression," in *The Mental Health of Women*, Marcia Guttentag, Susan Salasin, and Deborah Belle, eds. (New York: Academic Press, 1980), pp. 93 – 110.

63. Symonds, Alexandra, "Phobias after Marriage: Women's Declaration of Dependence," *American Journal of Psychoanalysis 31*, 2 (1971): 144 – 152.

64. Miller, Jean Baker, *Toward a New Psychology of Women* (Boston: Beacon Press, 1976), p. 71.

65. Weissman, Myrna M., and Eugene Paykel, *The Depressed Woman* (Chicago: University of Chicago Press, 1974).

66. Weinberg, Jon, "Counselling Recovering Alcoholics," *Social Work* (July 1973), pp. 84 – 93.

67. Kintner, Susan, "So What's So Different about Women Who Drink?" in *Bottled Up Women* (New Britain, CT: Prudence Crandall Center for Women, 1977).

68. Thibaut, John W., and Harold H. Kelley, "Power and Dependence," in *The Social Psychology of Groups*, Vol. 7 (New York: Wiley, 1959), pp. 100 – 125.

69. Weissman, Myrna M., Gerald Klerman, and Eugene Paykel, "The Clinical Evaluation of Hostility," *American Journal of Psychiatry 128* (September 1971): 261 – 267; see also Myrna M. Weissman and Eugene Paykel, *The Depressed Woman* (Chicago: University of Chicago Press, 1974).

70. Lewinsohn, Peter M., Martin Shaffer, and Julian Libet, *A Behavioral Approach to Depression*," Unpublished manuscript, University of Oregon, 1969.

71. Wetzel, Janice Wood, "Depression and Dependence upon Unsustaining Environments," *Clinical Social Work Journal 6*, 2 (Summer 1978): 75 – 89.

72. Moos, Rudolph H., *Family Environment Scale* (Palo Alto, CA: Consulting Psychologists Press, 1974).

73. See Chapter 4 for further discussion of women's dual roles; see also Bureau of the Census, *Statistical Portrait of Women in the U.S.*, Special Studies, Series P. 23 1978; see also M. M. Poloma and T. N. Garland, "The Myth of the Egalitarian Family," in *The Professional Women*, ed. A. Theodore (Cambridge, MA: Schenkman, 1971); Myra Ferree, "The Confused American Housewife," *Psychology Today* (September 1976), pp. 76 – 80; Juanita Williams, *Psychology of Women: Behavior in a Biosocial Context* (New York: Norton, 1977).

74. Bart, Pauline, "Depression in Middle-Aged Women," in *Women in Sexist Society*, ed. V. Gornick and B. Moran (New York: Basic Books, 1971), pp. 99 – 117.

75. Rotter, Julian, "Some Problems and Misconceptions Related to the Construct of Internal versus External Control of Reinforcement," *Journal of Consulting and Clinical Psychology 43*, 1 (1975): 56 – 67.

76. U.S. Bureau of Census, *Current Population Reports*, Series P-70, No. 349, 1979. *U. S. Crime Reports* (1979).

77. Federal Bureau of Investigation, Uniform Crime Reports for the U.S. and its Possessions (Washington, D.C.: U. S. Government Printing Office, 1976).

78. Excerpted from Janice Wood Wetzel, Redefining Concepts of Mental Health," in *Women, Power, and Change*, ed. Ann Weich and Susan T. Vandiver, (Washington, DC: National Association of Social Work, 1981).

79. Van Gelder, Leslie, "An Unmarried Man: Report on a New American Syndrome," *Ms. 8*, 5 (November 1979): 51 – 52, 73 – 75.

80. Bernard, Jesse, *The Future of Marriage* (New York: Bantam Books, 1973).

81. Wetzel, Janice Wood, "Preventing Mental Illness through Existential Principles," *Journal of Religion and Health 19*, 4 (Winter 1980): 268 – 274.

82. Bernard, Jesse, "The Good Provider Role: Its Rise and Fall," *American Psychologist 36* 1 (January 1981): 1 – 12.

83. Sable, Pat, "Differentiating between Attachment and Dependency in Theory and Practice," *Social Casework* (March 1979), pp. 138 – 144.

84. Butler, Sandra, *Conspiracy of Silence: The Trauma of Incest* (San Francisco: New Glide Publications, 1978).

85. Pearlin, Leonard, "Sex Roles and Depression," in *Life-Span Developmental Psychology Conference*, 4th, ed. Nancy Daton and Leon Ginsberg, West Virginia University, 1974 (New York: Academic Press, 1975); see Chapter 4 for reference to Pearlin's sex-role research on depression.

86. Mostow, E., and P. Newberry, "Work Role and Depression in Women: A Comparison of Workers and Housewives in Treatment," *American Journal of Orthopsychiatry, 45*, (1975): 538 – 548.

87. Brown, George W., and Tirril Harris, *Social Origins of Depression* (New York: Free Press, 1978).

88. Acker, Joan, and Donald R. Van Houton, "Differential Recruitment and Control: The Sex Structuring of Organization," *Administrative Science Quarterly 17*, (1972): 177 – 125; see also Wendy C. Wolf and Neil D. Fligstein, "Sexual Stratification: Differences in Power in the Work Setting," (Institute of Research on Poverty, Discussion Papers, No. 429, 1977).

89. Koontz, Elizabeth D., *American Women Workers in a Full Employment Economy*, September 17, 1977 Senate Hearings (Washington, DC: U.S. Government Printing Office, 78-26765, 1978).

90. White, Robert, "Motivation Reconsidered: The Concept of Competence," *Psychological Review 66* (1959): 297 – 333.

91. The following plan has been adapted from research and program development of Jack Rothman, Joseph G. Teresa, and John L. Erlich, *Fostering Participation and Promoting Innovation: Handbook for Human Service Professionals* (Itasca, IL: F. E. Peacock, 1978).

92. See Chapter 6 for an understanding on behavior modification principles.

93. U. S. Department of Health, Education and Welfare, Special Task Force on Work in America, 1971.

94. President's Commission on Mental Health, *Report to the President*, Vol. 4, 1978.

95. Warren, Rachelle, and Donald Warren, *The Neighborhood Organizers Handbook* (Notre Dame, IN: University of Notre Dame Press, 1977).

96. This section is largely influenced by Helen Harris Perlman, "Are We Creating Dependency?" *Minnesota Welfare* (June 1951); also see Deborah Belle, ed., *Lives in Stress: Women and Depression* (Beverly Hills: Sage, 1982) for an excellent study of the impact of poverty on women in regard to depression.

97. See the section of this chapter on burnout.

98. Perlman, Helen Harris, "Are We Creating Dependency?" *Minnesota Welfare* (June 1951).

99. Germain, Carel B., ed., *Social Work Practice: People and Environments* (New York: Columbia University Press, 1979).

100. See Arieti and Bemporad's view of Adaptation and the Dominant Other in Chapter 2 for further discussion of adaptation.

101. Wetzel, Janice Wood, and Franklin C. Redmond, "A Person-Environment Study of Depression," *Social Service Review 54*, 3 (September 1980): 363 – 375.

102. Wetzel, Janice Wood, "Wetzel Independence-Dependence Scales," copyright 1975, reported in Janice Wood Wetzel and Franklin C. Redmond, 1980.

103. Perlman, Helen Harris, "Are We Creating Dependency?" *Minnesota Welfare* (June 1951).

104. White, Robert, "Motivation Reconsidered: The Concept of Competence," *Psychological Review 66* (1959): 297 – 333.

105. Kuperman, Arnold, "Relations between Differential Constraints, Affect, and the Origin-Pawn Variable," Unpublished Doctoral Dissertation, Washington University, St. Louis, MO, August 1967.

106. de Charms, Richard, *Personal Causation: The Internal Affective Determinants of Behavior* (New York: Academic Press, 1968).

107. Refer to the President's Commission on Mental Health, Report to the President by the Task Panel on Women, Vol. 4, 1978; also see Chapter 6 for a theoretical and operational understanding of self-esteem through mastery.

108. See Social Role Theory and Depression in Chapter 4 for further interpretations of vicarious living.

109. Stuart, Richard B., "Casework Treatment of Depression Viewed as Interpersonal Disturbance," *Social Work 12*, 2 (1967): 27 – 36.

110. Weissman, Myrna M., and Eugene Paykel, *The Depressed Woman* (Chicago: University of Chicago Press, 1974).

111. Pattison, E. Manswell, "Religious Youth Cults: Alternative Healing Networks," *Journal of Religion and Health 19* 4 (Winter 1980): 275 – 286.

112. See Chapters 2 and 4 for further discussion on internalization and depression.

113. Wetzel, Janice Wood, and Franklin C. Redmond, "A Person-Environment Study of Depression," *Social Service Review 54* 3 (September 1980): 363 – 375.

114. Wetzel, Janice Wood, "Wetzel Independence-Dependence Scales," copyright 1975, reported in Janice Wood Wetzel and Franklin C. Redmond, ibid.

115. Bandura, Albert, "Self-Efficacy: Toward a Unifying Theory of Behavioral Change," *Psychological Review 84*,2 (March 1977): 191 – 215.

116. Wetzel, Janice Wood, "Prevention and Treatment of Depression in Hospital Patients and Staff," selected papers, *Stress/Distress in Health Care Settings* (Galveston, TX: University of Texas, Medical Branch, September 1979), pp. 179—188.

117. President's Commission on Mental Health, *Report to the Presidents*, Vol. 2 (Washington, D.C., 1978).

118. President's Commission on Mental Health, *Report to the President*, Vol. 2 (Washington, D.C., 1978).

119. Wetzel, Janice Wood, and Franklin C. Redmond, "A Person-Environment Study of Depression," *Social Service Review 54*,3 (September 1980): 363—375.

120. The preceding and following sections regarding work have been largely excerpted from Janice Wood Wetzel, "Mental Health, Working Class Women and Their Work," *Journal of Applied Social Sciences 5*,1 (Fall/Winter 1980—1981): 1—13.

121. Cardoza, Victor G., William C. Ackerly, and Alexander H. Leighton, "Improving Mental Health Through Community Action," *Community Mental Health Journal 11* (Summer 1975): 215—227; see also Janice Wood Wetzel, "Depression and Dependence upon Unsustaining Environments," *Clinical Social Work Journal 6*,2 (Summer 1978).

122. Wetzel, Janice Wood, "Interventions with the Depressed Elderly in Institutions," *Social Casework 61*,4 (April 1980): 234—239.

123. Butler, Robert N., and Myrna S. Lewis, *Aging and Mental Health: Positive Psychosocial Approaches* (St. Louis: C. V. Mosby, 1973).

124. Euster, Gerald L., "A System of Groups in Institutions for the Aged," *Social Casework 52* (November 1971): 523—539; see also Gerald L. Euster, "Humanizing Institutional Environments for the Elderly: Some Social Interaction Perspectives," *Arete 5* (Spring 1978): 1—10.

125. See Chapter 10 for a detailed discussion of elderly men at risk.

126. Manney, James, *Aging in American Society* (Ann Arbor: University of Michigan Press, 1975).

127. Moss, Frank E., and Val J. Halamandaris, *Too Old Too Sick Too Bad* (Germantown, MD: Aspen Systems Corp., 1977).

128. See Chapters 2 and 4 for further discussion of loss and depression.

129. Lowenthal, Majorie F., and Clayton Haven, "Interaction and Adaptation: Intimacy as a Critical Variable," *American Sociological Review 33* (February 1968): 20—30; see also Marilyn R. Block, Janice L. Davidson, Jean D. Grambs, and Kathryn E Serock, *Uncharted Territory: Issues and Concerns of Women over 40* (Center on Aging, College Park: University of Maryland, 1978); Stanley E. Goldstein, "Depression in the Elderly," *Journal of American Geriatrics Society 27*,1 (January 1979): 38—42.

130. Blau, Zena Smith, *Old Age in a Changing Society* (New York: Franklin Watts, 1973).

131. Clark, Margaret, and Barbara Anderson, *Culture and Aging* (Springfield, IL: Charles C. Thomas, 1967).

132. Atchley, Robert C., *The Social Forces in Later Life* (Belmont, CA: Wadsworth, 1977).

133. Hovland, Carl, and I. L. Janis, eds., *Personality and Persuasability*, Vol. 2 (New Haven: Yale University Press, 1959).

134. Alexander, James, "On Dependence and Independence," *Bulletin of the Philadelphia Association of Psychoanalysis 20*,1 (1970): 49—57.

135. Butler, Robert N., and Myrna S. Lewis, *Aging and Mental Health: Positive Psychosocial Approaches* (St. Louis: C. V. Mosby, 1973).

136. Jung, Carl G., ed. (and M. L. von Franz after Jung's death), *Man and His Symbols* (Garden City, NY: Doubleday, 1964); see Chapter 7 for a discussion of independence and authenticity, especially appropriate to the elderly who are often attuned philosophically; see also Chapter 9 for a discussion of elder female development and spirituality.

137. Collins, Glenn, "Exploring the Past: Creativity in Old Age," *New York Times*, Section A, March 2, 1981, p. 16.

138. Galper, Jeffry, and Seymour Kornblum, "Depression and the Jewish Elderly: Identification and Treatment," *Research Digest* (Philadelphia: Florence G. Heller — JWB Research Center, 1977), pp. 1 – 24.

139. Bikson, Tora Kay, and Jacqueline K. Goodchilds, *Old People and New Ideas: Receptivity and Rigidity* (Santa Monica, CA: Rand Corporation, August 1979); also see Chapter 4 for further discussion of dysfunctional sex roles.

140. Euster, Gerald L., "Humanizing Institutional Environments for the Elderly: Some Social Interaction Perspectives," *Arete 5* (Spring 1978): 1 – 10.

141. Gottesman, Leonard E., and Jane Barney, "Innovations in Institutional Settings: Some Suggested Approaches," in *Housing and Environment for the Elderly*, ed. Thomas O. Byerts (Washington, DC: The Gerontological Society, 1970), pp. 135 – 136.

142. Wetzel, Janice Wood, "Interventions with the Depressed Elderly in Institutions," *Social Casework 61*,4 (April 1980): 234 – 239.

143. San Francisco General Hospital, "Workers' Report on the Conditions of Labor and Their Effect on Patient Care at San Francisco General Hospital" (Institute for the Study of Labor and Economic Crisis, March 1979).

144. U. S. Department of Health, Education and Welfare, *Report on a Special Task Force on Work in America* (Cambridge, MA: Massachusetts Institute of Technology Press, 1971).

145. Patry, Bill, "Taylorism Comes to the Social Services," *Monthly Review* (October 1978).

146. The following information on burnout is largely adapted from Holly Henderson, "Burn Out," *Selected Papers: Stress/Distress in Health Care Settings* (Galveston, TX: University of Texas, Medical Branch, 1979); see also Barry A. Farber, ed., *Stress and Burnout in the Human Professions* (New York: Pergamon Press, 1983).

147. Pines, A., and E. Aronson, "Coping with Burn Out," paper presented at Third National Conference on Perinatal Social Work, San Diego, May 1979.

148. Refer to the Yale Depression Research Unit or NIMH for a report on Interpersonal Therapy. See also *Special Report on Depression Research* (Washington, DC: U.S. Department of Health and Human Services, National Institute of Mental Health, DHHS Publ. No. ADM 81-1085, 1981). See also Life Events Models, Chapter 4, and see Biochemical Theories, Chapter 8, for a discussion of drug therapy.

Chapter 6
Cognitive-Behavioral Theories

> One way of getting an idea of our fellow
> countrymen's miseries is to go and look
> at their pleasures.
> George Eliot, *Felix Holt, The Radical*

The behavioral model is concerned with the relationship between behavior and the events that occur immediately prior to that behavior. The emphasis is on observable, countable actions and their measurement. Behaviorists make no distinction between normality and abnormality, for all behavior is considered to be governed by the same principles — primarily, the law of reinforcement.[1] Those behaviors that are accompanied — or closely followed — by rewards are said to be positively reinforced; the rewarded behaviors are strengthened, and the probability of their occurrence is increased. Controversy between behaviorists and cognitivists continues regarding the sufficiency of external reinforcement to explain complex human behavior versus the influence of thoughts and feelings. Most contemporary behaviorists, however, incorporate cognitive theory in their interpretation of depression, while cognitivists are well versed in behavioral principles concerning the phenomenon.

BEHAVIORAL THEORY

For the behaviorist, environmental rewards — reinforcers — shape both affect and behavior. Depression is considered to be a learned response, the result of a "low rate of response-contingent reinforcement," in behavioral terms. The behaviorist is simply referring to the inadequate or insufficient personal gratification that comes about in connection with the depressed person's behavior. Conjecture as to how that deprivation occurs may focus on the environment or on the depressed persons themselves, depending on the theorist. Some note that few reinforcing events are available in the depressed person's environment, while others suggest that people who become depressed elicit few responses that are likely to be rewarded by others. The amount of reinforcement, the importance of the rate at which rewards occur, as opposed to one's control of that rate, are also dimensions debated and researched by behaviorists. However, most behavioral theorists agree that frequency, duration, and intensity of depressed and nondepressed behaviors are essential measures of assessment.

Functional Analysis

The clinical observations of Charles Ferster, one of the earliest researchers to apply the behavioral framework to depression, conclude that depressed persons are passive and react to the environment indirectly and reflexively, instead of acting in a direct, reciprocal way with people.[2] They react to someone else's initiatives and commands, for the passive, depressed person lacks positive control. Ferster's functional analysis suggests that aversively controlling physical and social environments are responsible for creating the stressful conditions that reduce positively reinforced behaviors. In short, daily existence is not pleasurable or otherwise rewarding for depressed persons. When satisfying activities occur in their lives, the activities are more likely to be appropriate to others than to themselves. To illustrate, a man who has no interest in detective films repeatedly accompanies his mystery-buff friend. This dynamic is characteristic and may be due in part to his passive, uninvolved attitude, or possibly to the aggressive control by his friend. It is not unlikely that the two realities coexist. In any case, depression is the final response.

Reduced-Reinforcement Model

A reduced-reinforcement model argues that depression can be reinforced socially. In such cases, the environment is the reinforcer of a low level of activity or even of depressed behavior itself. Peter Lewinsohn outlines three conditions that are subsumed in this analysis:[3]

— There are few available potentially reinforcing events related to personal characteristics.

— There is little availability of reinforcement in the environment.

— There are few effective behaviors and skills available to the individual.

This low rate of positive reinforcement reduces even further the person's activities and the expression of behaviors that might be rewarded. Consider, for example, the case of a bereaved woman. Ordinarily her friends would smile, be pleasant, and generally show her positive attention when she is behaving congenially. Because of her bereavement, however, they forgo their accustomed conditions for positive responding. Instead, they smile, are pleasant, and generally show her positive attention regardless of her depressed mood, withdrawn behavior, or even irritability. Because of well-meaning dispensations, her depressed behavior may be reinforced unwittingly. The obvious difficulty in correcting this dynamic is the possibility of conditionally qualifying human caring and sympathy. The subject is a delicate one that must be considered with sensitivity and balance.

Extinction Trial Behavior

Depressive "self-punishing" symptoms also may be viewed as instrumental behaviors that are themselves responses to aversive and controlling conditions.[4] When individuals are under stress that leads to an increased need for support, depressed symptoms are designed to increase that support. The persistence of the demands may cause guilt and hostility in others; often only partially suppressed, depressed persons reinforce their own aversive environments.[5] Arnold Lazarus uses the metaphor of "extinction trial" to explain depressed persons' tendencies to induce others to withdraw their voluntary support even though they need and want attention and nurturance.[6] Positive reinforcers are extinguished (withdrawn) since the depressed person reinforces negative responses and has such a poor repertoire for eliciting positive responses. Thus, the depressed college student who calls his friend in order to receive support, finds his friend's attention waning after the third needful call within two days' time. From a behavioral perspective, the depressed student lacks social skills. This is defined as the complex inability to emit behaviors that are positively reinforcing, as well as the inability to refrain from emitting negatively reinforcing behaviors. Deficient communication skills are viewed as the underlying cause of such social ineptitude.

COGNITIVE THEORY

While positive external reinforcement is the bedrock of behavioral theory, it has become increasingly clear that internal cognitions are also important reinforcers. What people "tell themselves" also alters their behavior. Those cognitive processes we call "thought" or "thinking" carry affective-emotional content. Thought is often heavily endowed with feeling — sometimes its product and sometimes its catalyst. Long aware that the emotions affect thought, we have tended to overlook the converse. Our feelings and actions are shaped and colored by internal cognitions. Whether based on beliefs, notions, convictions, or facts, feelings and thoughts are in constant interchange, the one affected by and simultaneously affecting the other.

While clinicians tend to elicit, explore, and attend to feelings with sensitivity and compassion, in the past short shrift has been given to the thought content and processes that might have been the cause, as well as the consequence, of such affects.[7] The assumption has been that cognitive distortions common to depressed people are the product of affective disturbance. While sometimes valid, it is also true that ideas based on incorrect and insufficient information may rouse or create emotional depressive reaction of considerable intensity. Depressed persons, for the cognitive theorist, are depressed personalities reflecting a particular personality style. They typically harbor negative cognitions based on attitudes and assumptions from past experience. Sometimes verbally expressed, often only visualized, cognitive elements in depression have even been found in the thematic analysis of dream content. In controlled studies, it was discovered that depressed patients had a higher proportion of masochistic dreams and consistently saw themselves as losers.[8]

Negative Cognitive Set[9]

Aaron Beck has concluded that a negative cognitive set is primary and that depressive affect is secondary to depression. The "cognitive triad" at the core of his model reflects the depressed person's constellation of negative perceptions of the self, the world, and the future. Motivational, emotional, and behavioral changes flow directly from this triad. These errors in thinking are called characteristic sets, disposing the depressed person to interpret events within a schema of self-depreciation and self-blame. This assessment of self appears as truth to the client, even though clearly a distortion when balanced against the perception of others. Errors of logic may include arbitrary inference, selective abstraction, overgeneralization, and magnification or minimization. They are defined as follows:

Arbitrary inference is reflected in conclusions drawn without adequate evidence.

Selective abstraction refers to conclusions drawn on the basis of a single element among many possibilities.

Overgeneralization represents sweeping conclusions based upon a single event.

Magnification and minimization are gross evaluation errors with little or no basis in reality.

Depressed persons are victims of their own self-distortions, according to cognitive theory. Treatment, then, is devoted to a reversal and realignment with reality of the clients' "personal paradigm."

Learned Helplessness Model[10]

"Learned helplessness" represents an application of a cognitive-behavioral framework based primarily on animal research. The experimentation of Martin Seligman and his colleagues with dogs led them to conclude that uncontrollable traumatic events can significantly debilitate organisms. The events produce passivity in the face of emotional stress, and the inability to learn the effectiveness of responding. Learned helplessness is defined as an interference with adaptive responding, produced by trauma. Considered to be analogous to extinction views of depression where reinforcement is withdrawn altogether, the depressed person has had repeated occasion to learn that his or her response and lack of response no longer elicit reward.[11] In short, responding either way doesn't change anything. The learned helplessness model incorporates the extinction view and adds an essential behavioral insight: even when positive reinforcers are present, if they are independent of one's behavioral response, even rewards will increase vulnerability to depression. One must feel in control of one's own environment, for self-esteem and a sense of competence cannot be perceived without that sense of control. To the degree that controllable events occur, a sense of mastery will result and concomitant resistance to depression.

While the original learned helplessness research concerned animals, studies have continued with human beings. It is thought that people learn to be helpless in three different ways. Those who have been overprotected and have never had the opportunity to master the environment are at risk, as are those who have never encountered failure at all. I would guess that there are relatively few such people. Those who have experienced past trauma without having been able to control the negative events of their lives are particularly vulnerable to depression. These conditions all predispose individuals to learned helplessness, according to Seligman. Other social scientists generally agree that environmental mastery is essential to human well-being.[12] Credibility for the model has been reinforced by biochemical studies that indicate parallels between depressed people and dogs who are rendered helpless by uncontrollable shock.

WOMEN AT RISK

Behavioral Theories

Researchers who observe depressed women's behavior note their dependence on others for reinforcement, their lack of communication skills and manipulativeness, their tendency to be more easily influenced or more "shapeable" in behavioral terms, and their nonassertiveness. This hodge-podge of observations may indicate that depressed women are simply lacking in social skills. Lewinsohn came to this conclusion based on observations of depressed people in their home environments. Primarily women, they gave many positive reinforcements to their families but received few, if any, in return. He conjectured that their timing was off because they did not elicit positive reinforcements following closely upon the desired behavior.[13] (Lewinsohn's discussion was not sex-specific; the connection to women is mine.)

Cognitive-Behavioral Theories

The issues may be related more closely to the problems inherent in reinforcement principles. In order for something to be conceived of as a reward, the receiver of that reward must view it as such. One might say, "Reward is in the eye of the beholder." There is also a correlation between one's perception of a reward and the person offering it. Rewards given by a person who holds little respect, however well timed, will not elicit positive reactions. Rather, the "rewards" will be ignored or even rejected as unwanted. This may be the case for many depressed women, for despite protestations to the contrary over the last seventy-five years, the role of housewife and mother is seldom esteemed in our society.[14] The aversive control that Charles Ferster observed is applicable to the powerless condition of many of these women.[15] Socialized to please others, they learn to be attuned to those things that interest their mates and their children, never considering what might please themselves. Since they too have needs, their dependence on others for happiness often results in manipulative behavior in order to get those needs met. Their lack of interest in the world or in self improvement are directly related to that same dependence.[16] It is important to be aware of these possibilities when clients are female. The long-noted covert hostility and overt rage of depressed women toward their husbands and their children may be directly related to their low status and frustrating conditions both in the home and in the larger society.[17] It may also be that the "rewards" offered by some women are accurately perceived as manipulative by their families. Since love with strings attached is seldom welcome, it understandably does not receive a warm response.[18]

Negative cognitions are particularly pertinent to women's perceptions of themselves. There is no doubt that modification of their personal paradigms is crucial, but cognitive therapists must guard against a single conception of depression based on self-distortion. In so doing, it is possible to overlook the reality of external oppression. To locate the initial cause of women's depressions solely within themselves only reinforces self-blame. Their inferior position in society leads them to perceive of themselves in the same guilty manner. Self-depreciation, unfavorable comparison, distrust of self, and perceptions that others negate them are all extensions of the culturally reinforced negative cognitions of women. Their lifestyles reflect this negation in that they often choose and remain in inferior jobs even when exceptionally well qualified. They are likely to choose marital partners who are incompatible, have lesser interests, and disparage them.[19] Women typically anticipate nothing more favorable than their present existence, and take the blame for the trauma in their lives. The battered woman, like the depressed female, is a perfect example of this tendency. In the face of overwhelming evidence to the contrary, she typically places the blame for her attack on herself. This self-devaluation, replicated in the life of the sexually abused child and the raped woman, is more than coincidental.[20]

The paradoxical tension between lack of environmental control and the belief that one is unrealistically responsible for events has confused cognitive-behaviorists. The confusion is both perceptual and semantic, a not surprising combination considering that language reflects our social reality. If one considers that women's perception of powerless-

ness represents a realistic condition, their self-blame, reinforced by
society, creates a devastating double bind, rendering them immobile
and depressed. Responsibility without possibility is a depressing cognition in and of itself.

Intrinsic Motivation

Research on intrinsic motivation is an important addition to a
discussion of women's perceptions of control. Edward Deci and his
colleagues have developed a Cognitive Evaluation Theory of intrinsic
human motivation based upon empirical studies.[21] External feedback
that is considered to be controlling, however superficially rewarding,
does not positively reinforce behavior that is essentially internally
motivated. To illustrate, when someone does something for the sheer
joy of doing it, rather than for the approval of others, it is thought to be
intrinsically motivated, as opposed to extrinsically motivated behavior
that responds to external rewards.

Studies reveal that behavior motivated from within stops when
women are given positive verbal feedback, probably because that feedback is perceived by them to be judgmental and externally controlling.
Men, however, interpret the same compliments as information that
they are competent and effective, so they continue in their self-moti-
vated activities. It is conjectured that female socialization is so inundated with aspersions concerning their goodness and badness that
they perceive commentary of any kind as judgment. Even if they are
complimented for an action, it implies judgment, leaving open the
possibility that they might be faulted at another time. Their intrinsic
pleasure is thereby diminished. Were positive feedback considered to
be informational rather than judgmental, as is the case for men, then
feelings of competence and self-determination would be enhanced and
intrinsic motivation would not decrease. Every reward, therefore, has
two aspects, a controlling element and an informational element that
provide the recipient with feedback about his or her competence and
self-determination. If the controlling aspect is more salient, it will not
be a positive reinforcer.

Learned Helplessness

Aaron Beck and Ruth Greenberg compare female socialization to
learned helplessness.[22] They believe that women tend to see themselves as needfully dependent, helpless, and repressed. Women, they
observe, have a culturally induced tendency to see themselves as

powerless. Rather than selecting an uncensored set of expectations, they respond habitually. Women's personal worth and survival have depended on their appeal to men, rather than their effective response to life situations. In other words, because it is not what *they do* that counts, they have no direct control over circumstances. Like Seligman's animals, they lose their ability to respond effectively and to learn that such responding produces relief. The suggestion is that women see themselves as shackled long after the shackles have been removed. This may be true for some. But the fact is that cultural shackles still exist for many women.

The reverse situation also may be true. There is evidence that people who believe themselves to be in control of the environment when in fact they are not, are subject to trauma.[23] The implications are clear that women must perceive themselves differently, but they must also be helped to see their world realistically, as it truly is, and to work for change in order to develop control over it. Internalized cultural expectations and reality are often one and the same.

Lenore Radloff and Mimi Monroe advocate prevention and treatment of depression through remedial "helplessness training" and the analyses of education, childbearing practices, and the media,[24] which reinforces their learned helplessness. Programs should encourage contingent reinforcement of instrumental (as opposed to affective) responses in women. And, they point out, the culture must stop collaborating by punishing their successful actions.

Assertion Training and Cost-Benefit Analysis[25]

While certainly not limited to women, assertion training has become closely associated with them because of its relevance to female socialization. Societal pressures continue to mitigate against women's assertion, providing them with conflicting values—one to please others and feel loved, and another to develop themselves more fully. In assessing their situations, deciding whether or not to become assertive, female clients can weigh the pros and cons through a "cost-benefit analysis," asking themselves the following questions:

- Do I gain something from staying nonassertive? If so, what?
  —Protection?
  —Praise for meeting others' expectations?
  —Maintenance of a familiar behavioral pattern?
  —Avoidance of responsibility?
  —Avoidance of accepting feelings of conflict, rejection, and anger?

- Would I give up any of these "gains"? If so, which ones?
- Do I lose anything from being nonassertive? If so, what?
  —Independence?
  —Power to make decisions?
  —Honesty in relationship?
  —Respect of my rights by others?
  —Loss of emotional control when I finally blow up?
  —Relaxation and inner peace?
  —Ability to influence others, particularly in regard to their relationship to me?
  —Satisfaction of planning and reaching goals?
- What is the cost-benefit ratio?
  —Do the gains of staying nonassertive outweigh what I am losing? Why or why not?
  —Can I enlist the support of others in my decision to remain the same or change?
  —What are my short-term goals, personally and in relationship?
  —What are my long-term goals?
  —How does assertiveness help or hinder reaching my goals?

Using this outline, which is based on the work of Lynn Bloom, Karen Coburn and Joan Pearlman, therapists and their clients can better evaluate behaviors and thoughts in the light of reality, both present and future. They do, after all, reserve the right to be nonassertive if they so choose. That decision, however, can only be made honestly, when their options are clear to them.

Commentary on Cognitive-Behavioral Theories

Cognitive-behavioral theories are supported by more empirical data than most conceptual frameworks. Many theorists who may otherwise disparage the model for its seeming lack of depth and sophistication often employ the methods when faced with a depressed client. The fact is that cognitive-behavioral interventions are more likely to be effective than many apparently richer constructs. Respect for cognition has emerged from an array of seemingly disparate ideologies. Not only has the behavioral field incorporated the concept, but ego-psychology and existential and spiritually oriented therapies are strong supporters. Even biochemists and biophysicists are emerging as cognitive advocates. There is something encouraging in the discovery that scientifically oriented cognitive-behaviorists are using parallel treatment methods to those of the ethereal Eastern philosophies. Imagery and its influence on positive cognition is a case in point.[26]

Regardless of one's ideology and practice, behavioral principles must be kept in mind because they are surely operating. For that reason, all clinicians must guard against possible abuses rooted in laws of reinforcement. While these principles are most effective when clients cooperate, they also function independently. Persons, for example, can be reinforced for desired activities without their knowledge. The values of the clinician may reinforce choices and practices that are not in the best interest of the client. While few clinicians would be so unethical, many may do so because of lack of knowledge and insight concerning the problems of people in transition in our transitional world. It may not be ethical to reinforce the norms of yesterday when they don't reflect the needs of today and tomorrow. Our growing knowledge concerning women and men, people of all ages, classes, and sexual preferences, persons of differing racial and cultural backgrounds are all in transition between old traditions and new realities, and all require more than a conventional response rooted in obsolete mores. This respect for the importance of perception and the reinforcement of attitudes and behaviors is in keeping with the principles of the cognitive-behavioral paradigm. Clinicians must take care to maintain congruence between theory and practice.

Behavioral Prevention and Intervention[27]

Depression is viewed as a function of inadequate or insufficient positive reinforcers.

Basic Principles of Positive Reinforcement

The aim of behavioral clinicians is to change their client's behavior so as to elicit more positive reinforcements because all behavior is considered to be based on its presence or absence. Including the client in the treatment plan is inherent in behavioral therapy, for the demystification of psychotherapy is an underlying principle. This is an especially important value for people who have been viewed, and view themselves, as powerless and of inferior status. The following basic principles enlighten clients to this end:

All techniques focus on the positive, since there is more power in the strengthening of positive responses than in the weakening of negative ones.

Never try to eliminate a destructive behavior without providing a constructive substitute.

The timing of rewards is critical. The immediate reward of behaviors is to be encouraged.

Establish desired behaviors initially by continuously reinforcing them; all behaviors are consistently followed by positive consequences.

Successful maintenance requires movement from a continuous schedule to an intermittent reinforcement schedule because habits are increased by infrequent rewards. Also, it is more typical of real life situations. Intermittent reinforcement is accomplished by providing positive consequences only after every second desired behavior, then every fourth behavior, and so on.

If the desired behavior decreases substantially, return temporarily to a continuous reinforcement schedule.

Persistence of behavior change may be enhanced by introducing increasingly longer periods of time between the behavior and the reinforcer.

Isolated positive behavior can be reinforced and generalized to other people, places, or events. For example, a lonely, depressed teenage girl may have an effective social repertoire with her relatives but remain aloof from her peers. Her positive behaviors with relatives can be generalized to her peer group.

The principles behind extinction trials should be clarified for clients, to show them how they sabotage their needs through negative reinforcement of the very responses they wish to encourage.

Apply the Premack Principle, whereby high-frequency behaviors reinforce desired low-frequency behaviors. To illustrate, the person you want to influence is a withdrawn, lonely man who has difficulty interacting socially. Probing for interests, you find that he enjoys swimming each morning at the local YMCA. The Premack Principle can be put into effect in two ways: (1) contract with him to take someone along when he swims, or (2) contract with him to make an arrangement to do something with another person. Only then can he reward himself by swimming. In either case, the pleasurable activity, swimming, has a high probability of occurring. By making a social encounter contingent on swimming, the likelihood that social activity will occur is increased.

Contracting

Though the behavioral approach to treatment is directive, it is egalitarian. The behavioral therapist and client together decide on a plan of action, spelling out their separate and mutual expectations and responsibilities. There should be open discussion of the conditions under which a desired behavior is expected to occur. The contract is noncoercive, its contents perfectly clear to both parties.

Establishing a Base Rate

Establishing a base rate is an essential part of the contract. This is a measure of frequency, intensity, and duration of the behavior that is to be changed. The client's present activity is recorded for the purpose of assessing future change. The base rate is determined by a relatively simple procedure that involves assessing how often a client does the behavior (the frequency), how pleasant the activity is on a continuum (the intensity), and over what length of time the action occurs (the duration). An example of a base rate of social time spent with other people would be:

Frequency: 3 times per week.
Intensity: 2 on a 5-point scale with 1 representing very unpleasurable and 5 representing very pleasurable.
Duration: an average of 30 minutes each time.

Increasing Social Skills

In keeping with the principles of positive reinforcement, emphasis is on strengthening social skills, rather than on weakening undesirable behavior. Since depressed people are less likely to interact socially with others, they can be encouraged to make and sustain social contacts. To begin, the client can survey social interests and community resources, and choose a promising activity. That activity can be broken down into graduated performance tasks in order to promote social engagement. For example, the therapist and client decide together what incremental steps need to be taken in order to meet someone and establish a friendship. It may be that the client will plan to find out where a meeting is located and go to it, speak with people there asking them about their interests and telling them something about his or her own, then inviting them out for coffee. This attention to incremental detail is not to be discounted, for it is essential to success. The assignment is preceded by a behavioral rehearsal in the treatment setting, and the program is reviewed regularly. When special training is required to implement the plan, it should be incorporated. Assertion training, for instance, is often a prerequisite for the depressed person who is lacking in communication skills and the self-assurance needed to develop them.

Assertion Training — Behavioral Procedures[28]

Assertion training is based on behavioral principles. It is a highly effective tool for prevention and intervention since depressed people have been shown to be nonassertive, at times manipulative, and often lacking in communication skills. These qualities are directly related to their dependence and consequent feelings of inadequacy and inability to act directly. Such behavior is related expressly to fear of vulnerability and loss of control over others. Assertive behavior increases control over one's self, resulting in self-confidence and reduced vulnerability. That vulnerability may include depression. While traditionally used in small groups, assertion-training methods also may be used with individuals.[29]

To begin, clients must be taught the difference between assertive, nonassertive, and aggressive behavior. *Assertiveness* refers to standing up for one's personal rights and expressing oneself in an appropriate, direct, and honest manner in such a way that the rights of others are not violated. *Nonassertiveness* implies deference and lack of self-respect. It involves violating of one's personal rights in order to appease others and avoid conflict. This is the behavior generally attributed to depressed people. Still, it is not unusual to find the frustrated, passive person becoming manipulative, or occasionally exploding with aggressive behavior. While *aggressiveness* includes standing up for personal rights, the standing up is done at the expense of another. Domination, winning, and forcing subservience are usually accompanying attitudes. *Passive-aggressiveness* is a less direct, manipulative kind of behavior whereby a person appears to be nonassertive, but controls others in a subtle, underhanded fashion. Here again, depressed persons may be found. Dependent and unable to act directly, they must manipulate the environment indirectly in order to get what they want or need.

Behavioral Rehearsal Techniques

Assertive behaviors can be rehearsed by using the following behavioral techniques:

Modeling — clients model their own actions after the actions of others that they may observe in person or on film.

Role playing — clients practice the behaviors they wish to carry out in reality, while the facilitator or group members take on the roles of others.

Role reversal — clients take the non-assertive role, experiencing the interaction from this viewpoint, while the facilitator or group member models assertive behavior.

Positive reinforcement — the facilitator and group members compliment improved assertive behavior.

The following skills have been compiled from a number of assertion-training references.[30] They are an integral part of practice sessions and homework assignments.

Free information is information that helps one learn about another's interests in order to encourage conversation. It is reflected in the giving and receiving of genuine compliments and other cues informally offered in social interactions. The person can be taught to listen for these cues and to offer them to others. For example, when a person comments in passing that she is reading a book about the environment, a conversation about her interest in the subject might be pursued.

Self-disclosure is the easy presentation of both positive and negative aspects of oneself to enhance social communication by reducing manipulative behavior. While assertion training teaches acceptance of the negative aspects of one's personality, it also must reinforce the positive aspects if it is to be a successful tool for alleviating depression.

"Broken record" is the unruffled, persistent repetition of an assertion which enables the client to ignore manipulative pressure and arguments while remaining clearly focused. A firm, repetitive "no" will suffice.

"Fogging" is the calm acknowledgment of the probability of a partial truth in a criticism by another that is manipulative. The client thus retains the right to judge his or her behavior by accepting criticism without anger or defensiveness. For example, in response to repeated criticism that one is a spendthrift, one could assert, "Yes, I do tend to spend too much money." Motivation to change that reality is not a necessary component. Control is retained while the aggressor is defused.

Negative assertions fully acknowledge one's negative qualities. A negative assertion allows the client to accept and recognize personal shortcomings. This skill is especially relevant to depressed people who are often perfectionists who can't tolerate defects in their character and try to hide them from themselves as well as others.[31]

Negative inquiry is the active encouragement of the expression of another's honest, critical feelings about oneself. Open, nonmanipulative communication is improved when one can sincerely accept the possibility of fault without resorting to self-recrimination or depression. Negative inquiry, in moderation, can be very useful in changing the manipulative behavior of dependent, depressed people who fear open dialogue.[32]

Learning to say no is essential to assertion training with depressed people; the inability to do so is a typical characteristic. Such people feel they must please others at all times in order to be worthy.[33] Myrna Weissman and Eugene Paykel, for example, have found that depressed married women had not said "No" to their husband's sexual advances even though they had no interest or desire for sexual relations.[34]

Time out is the purposeful withdrawal from encounters that are more than people feel they can handle. They may need five minutes to stop crying, five days to be separate from another person, or even five weeks to prepare for a difficult discussion. It is their right to do so.

Workable compromises when self-respect is not affected are an integral part of assertiveness. The freely chosen decision *not* to be assertive is as important as one's ability to do so, for assertiveness is not a behavior to be applied indiscriminately. There are times when a behavior may be a self-destructive action, or when assertiveness may hurt others unnecessarily. Assertiveness directed toward each and every issue may be a clear waste of energy. These are areas to be explored in open discussion. The important point is that the decision to be assertive is within the participant's control. This recognition of choice is as important to depressed persons who experience little personal control over their lives as is their ability to implement assertive behavior.

In the early phases of assertion training, there is a natural tendency to go overboard — to be more aggressive than assertive. After years of subservience, once permission to be assertive is accepted, former shrinking violets may overreact. The facilitator is cautioned though, not to overuse the label "aggressive" when the tendency is to label any behavior that is not subservient as aggression. This warning is especially relevant with people of color, the poor, and/or female clients whose behavior is often mislabeled even within their own families. It is not unusual, for example, to find that people who fit these descriptions are carefully taught in the home to be nonassertive so as not to bring attention to themselves. Such is the nature of survival. The family, therefore, needs to be educated to the importance of assertiveness in preventing and alleviating depression.

Learning to take responsibility is inherent in the behavioral approach to depression and assertiveness intervention. Nonassertiveness implies that one is unable or unwilling to take responsibility; aggressiveness reflects irresponsibility and a lack of concern for others. The following concepts, couched in a reality therapy framework, are congruent with the thesis.

Reality Therapy—A Behavioral Approach[35]

William Glasser has developed a treatment intervention based on behavioral principles, focusing on learning to take responsibility for one's own behavior. Glasser believes that the client is in control of being depressed. To emphasize their active participation, he uses the verb "to depress," rather than "to be depressed" which might imply an external referent or a chemical influence. The following eight steps briefly outline the process of reality therapy.

1. Since the relationship between client and therapist is at the core of this model, rapport is an essential prerequisite. The therapist spends time asking clients what they want. That "want" is clarified as a goal that might be reached were the clients not depressed.

2. According to the goals clarified in the first step, depressed clients are asked, "What are you doing now?" and "Why are you depressing?" They are encouraged to focus on their depressed behavior, but not on their depressed feelings, for that would reinforce the undesired activity.

3. Clients are encouraged to look at the unrealistic incongruence between their wished-for goals and their own behavior. They are asked, "Is what you are doing helping you get what you want?" This places the responsibility and the control with the client.

4. The clinician and client collaborate, mutually developing a plan that promises to be successful. Incorporating behavioral procedures, the plan can include incremental tasks toward the goal. Keeping a daily log is also suggested for ongoing personal assessment as well as positive reinforcement.

5. A behavioral contract is drawn up founded on the client's commitment to work toward changing "unrealistic" behavior.

6. When the client fails to follow the plan, excuses are neither made nor accepted. The client has not failed; the plan has. A new plan is developed in a matter-of-fact manner, improving on the previous one.

7. The client is never "punished" in any way for not carrying out the agreement, because punishment will only reinforce failure. At the same time, unpleasant consequences that evolve naturally from irresponsible behavior are not interfered with. The client's part in controlling the outcome is thus understood.[36]

8. The therapist's commitment to the client is essential. "Never give up" is not only a slogan, but a belief in the client's possibility to become a responsible person. The depressed person's self-image thus changes from that of a dependent, helpless, depressed individual.

There may be a tendency for clinicians to overlook Glasser's emphasis on the relational aspect of reality therapy, mistakenly taking on a "pull yourself up by your bootstraps — it's your own fault" attitude. There is nothing more destructive to depressed persons who already have little or no self-esteem. There is a fine line between positively reinforcing a sense of healthful autonomy and control, and manipulative coercion. The reality therapist, therefore, must make considerable effort to provide the former reality and avoid the latter abuse. The reader may find the discussion on Reality Therapy in relation to loneliness helpful to this end.[37]

Most contemporary behaviorists incorporate cognitive theory in their work. Cognitive therapists are equally respectful of behavioral principles, generally applying them to their interventions. Thus, both external and internal reinforcement are acknowledged.

COGNITIVE PREVENTION AND INTERVENTION

While the goal of cognitive therapy is to relieve depressive symptoms, the means is attending to clients' misinterpretations, dysfunctional attitudes, and self-defeating behavior. Because both behavior and affect of individuals are largely determined by the way in which they structure the world, the frame of reference of depressed people, their own interpretation of events, must be incorporated into treatment. The therapist must continually address the cognitive antecedents or accompaniments of feelings, opening the opportunity for a corrective cognitive grasp of their dilemma. The way is thus paved toward the much valued, "corrective emotional experience."

Cognitive therapy is best applied during depressed periods, according to a state-dependent learning concept. What one learns in a particular state, such as depression, is more likely to generalize to that specific state at another time. The best time to gain objectivity toward automatic negative responses, then, is when the client is engaged in the behavior. Still, severely depressed persons may be unable to function, so only minimal improvement can be expected until their deep despair is alleviated. Because depressive episodes are self-limited, such people can be assured of some improvement in a few weeks.[38] In the meantime, the cognitive-behavioral approach will facilitate the process of recovery. During nondepressed periods, cognitive interventions can be preventive, since their continued application reinforces a positive cognitive set, reducing future vulnerability. The cognitive approach, then, is appropriate under any conditions. While there are nuances of differences between cognitive theoreticians, there is little reason to believe that treatment goals conflict.

Seligman suggests that the most effective way to break up depression caused by learned helplessness is the forced exposure to the fact that responding produces reinforcement. Repetitive learning and new perceptions are key. Clearly, negative cognitions are inherent in learned helplessness. Beck and his colleagues have provided a congruent treatment model that calls for the empirical investigation of the client's automatic throughts, inferences, conclusions, and assumptions. By the time these areas have been explored, repeatedly correcting perceptual distortions, the depressed person has been exposed to the fact that responding produces reinforcement. In addition, the client also learns which responses produce positive reinforcement and which elicit negative reactions.

Changing a Negative Cognitive Set[39]

The following points are suggestions for changing a negative cognitive set:

Prevention and intervention techniques are carefully taught to clients, as in behavioral therapy, and instruction is clear, direct, and without mystery. Clients learn how to stop negative thoughts by recognizing and correcting them and then substituting more realistic ones.

Clients are taught how to recognize when they are ignoring the positive by exaggerating and overgeneralizing the negative. By using humor as an effective tool, a casual "There I go again" attitude is fostered which can do much to alleviate judgment and hasten positive change.

The informal self-monitoring of thoughts, checking for mood and behavioral effects, teaches clients cognitive control. They record only successful attempts, thus reinforcing the positive.

Clients who are unable to suppress negative thoughts can begin by using temporal control (suppressing them for a specified time period) or geographic control (suppressing them in a specified area).

Apply a graduated performance principle by decreasing task demands and thereby increasing success. Tasks are accomplished in small incremental units, along with the gradual expansion of temporal and geographical limits.

Teach clients how to give themselves positive verbal feedback. By "positive scanning," a quick inventory of personal assets, strengths, and accomplishments can be made, thereby reinforcing positive self-cognitions.

Life Values Workshop[40] (Four Sessions)

Depressed people are often not aware of what pleases or displeases them, what they do well, or what they enjoy. This profile parallels that of most powerless people. They are other-oriented — keenly aware of the values, needs, and aspirations of others, but seldom of their own.[41] A Life Values Workshop can remedy this cognitive void that is so conducive to depression. While group dynamics are inherently reinforcing, the exercises also are effective when working alone with individuals, or even for self-help. The workshop is comprised of four sessions that can be interpreted as hourly meetings or all-day sessions. Depth, of course, will be influenced by length of time. If taking a workshop approach, Mastery-Pleasure Schedules can be the focus of the first session, with time allotted for discussion at subsequent meetings.

Session 1: Mastery-Pleasure Schedules[42]

Because depressed people often are unaware of pleasurable feelings of accomplishment even when they have achieved something, they typically do not experience success and pleasure. Mastery-Pleasure Schedules are designed to remedy the problem by reinforcing their positive self-cognitions through the accumulation of successes and increased awareness of gratification. The perception of mastery itself has been found to alleviate depression, and even mild satisfaction may help to restore morale. The two entities, mastery and pleasure, are on a continuum, not necessarily interrelated. It is especially important that the concepts be recognized in the context of the client's depression, as well as prior to the onset of symptoms. Since success and enjoyment are at a low ebb for the depressed person, reaching even a minimal goal can be regarded as an achievement.

In some cases, it will be difficult to elicit any response because of the absence of a history that entertained the concept of personal pleasure. This is often particularly true about females. It may be helpful to return to childhood for ideas, or to develop future interests through the questions asked. Mastery-Pleasure Schedules initially are constructed by recording one's usual activities. This reinforces the importance of mastering and enjoying activities and allows the clinician to obtain baseline data. Aaron Beck and his colleagues suggest discussion of the following areas that may help to generate potential activities. The client can select and rank them according to their difficulty and their satisfying qualities:

— Learning activities enjoyed prior to being depressed.
— Day trips enjoyed.
— Things that might be enjoyed if one had no inhibitions.
— Things previously enjoyed alone.
— Things previously enjoyed with others.
— Things that were enjoyed that are free.
— Things that were enjoyed that cost less than $5.00 ($10.00 for inflation years?).
— Things that were enjoyed *when* money was no object (or *were* money no object).
— Activities enjoyed at different times of the day, the week, seasonally, and so on.

Mastery-pleasure activities can be selected by specifically asking what might be done at a particular time to gain satisfaction. When this is not productive, activities that might provide a sense of mastery can be devised by asking clients what things they presently are unable to do because of their depression. After mastery activities are identified, they are hierarchically arranged from the client's perspective relative to degree of difficulty. The most easily performed activity is assigned. Records are written and maintained by clients to reinforce the perception of self-mastery. Homework, too, will help them shape their own behavior by increasing their participation in the treatment process. Assignments may include readings on depression and cognitive behavior modification, the exposition of ideas, creative self-development, or any other self-selected relevant activity. By implementing successful strategies, the self-perception of competence and mastery is reinforced.

Session 2: Values Clarification

Values-clarification exercises can be helpful in bringing personal cognitions to awareness. The acknowledgment of anger, previously denied expression or even recognition, is an important component. The facilitator directs participants to respond quickly (verbally or in writing) to each of the following inquiries. Discussion should follow each question to provide insight formerly ignored or only peripherally recognized. The last two questions are action oriented, a first step toward future goal planning:

What do you like?	....	What do you dislike?
What makes you angry?	....	What frightens you?
What makes you happy?	....	What makes you sad?
What do you need?	....	What do you want?

What did you want to do when you were young?
What do you want to do now?

Session 3: Life Inventory

Mastery, action, and control can only evolve when people are secure in their assessment of their attributes and experiences. Without personal knowledge, one can have no real sense of accomplishment or possibility. To this end, the following inventory provides an appropriate tool for people in transition. Participants are asked to respond briefly and specifically to each of the following items:

— The greatest experience I've ever had.
— Things I do badly.
— Things I would like to stop doing.
— Things I do well.
— Things I would like to learn to do well.
— The one thing I most want to accomplish in the future.
— The one experience I most want to have.
— Forgetting restrictions such as money, education, or responsibilities, what would I like to do more than anything else?

Session 4: Valuing Process[43]

Participants should be given the opportunity carefully to explore and define old values to be discarded or retained, together with new values to be developed. A cognitive-behavioral approach to the valuing process combines the perception of values with their reinforcement. To that end, the following ideas are included for discussion:

- Choosing freely and from among alternatives. If something is to guide one's life, it must be coercion-free and something to choose from. Without reasonable alternatives, there is no real choice.
- Prizing and cherishing is to respect and esteem something gladly.
- Affirming choices is to value them openly. To keep them hidden negates them as values.
- Acting upon choices means one's life must be affected by them; talking about them is not sufficient. In order to create a life pattern, actions that are valued must be reinforced by repeating them often.

Once an individual's values have been explored, goal-setting procedures unfold quite naturally. The following inquiry can be made available to participants, helping them to think through their self-cognitions, applying their perceptions to the evolving mastery and development of competence. It, too, can be incorporated into a workshop or accomplished on a one-to-one or individual basis.

Goal-Achievement Workshop (Three Sessions)

Session 1: Goal Setting[44]

Ask participants to consider the following:

Are my goals consistent with my personal characteristics, abilities, and opportunities?

What is the relationship between my immediate goals and my distant goals?

What is the time limit necessary to reach my immediate goals? Can I do it?

Goals I want to accomplish:

Short-term goals —

Things I want to do starting immediately. Be specific — how, when, where.

Long-term goals —

How do I get started?

In reaching my immediate goals, is there anything I can do before tomorrow?

What can I realistically have accomplished by one week from today?

What, specifically, can I do within one month to implement or reach my goals?

What do I contract to do?

Women and people of color will find this very pragmatic approach to the treatment of depression particularly beneficial. Because of their socialization, there may be a tendency within these populations to talk about future aspirations without realistically assessing what it will take to actualize them. There is often no serious evidence of goal planning, for they have learned early in life that response does not make a difference. The following exercises are provided to teach them (and others that require the skills) further decision-making and problem-solving methods that will reinforce their perception of personal control and self-mastery.

Session 2: Decision-Making and Problem-Solving Processes

1. Identify the problem in general abstract terms.
2. Specify the exact problem in precise terms.
3. Prioritize problems if more than one emerges. Choose the first problem based on the following criteria:
   a. Degree of crisis and/or distress.
   b. Possibility for success. *It is extremely important* that the exercise be successful in order to reinforce the activity positively.
4. Brainstorm: quickly list alternative solutions noncritically.
5. Specify, in general terms, the necessary procedures for each solution.
6. Evaluate anticipated outcomes of each of the would-be solutions in terms of critical variables (for example, cost, time, who is affected, and short-versus long-term beneficial effects).
7. Eliminate unreasonable or undesirable solutions.
8. By the process of elimination, choose one solution (the first goal) and one alternative as a backup.

Session 3: Goal-Attainment Process[45]

Once a decision concerning a goal that will be pursued has been made, the next step involves attaining that goal. The following cognitive-behavioral procedure details the process that participants will engage in:

1. Make the goal behavioral and therefore observable.
   a. What specific things will I be doing or saying when I reach my goal?
   b. What specific thoughts and feelings will I be experiencing when I reach my goals?
   c. To whom or with whom will I be saying or acting what my goals entail?
   d. In what situation or circumstances will I be accomplishing my goal?
2. Establishing my base rate of progress on this goal: how well do I accomplish it right now?
   a. What do I do and say right now, specifically in regards to my goal?
   b. To whom or with whom do I say it or act it?
   c. In what situations or circumstances do I carry out my present level of accomplishment with the goal?
3. Criteria of failure for my goal: suppose I don't reach my objectives. How will I be behaving? Include:
   a. Words and/or actions.
   b. Person(s) involved.
   c. Situation and/or circumstances.
   d. Feelings and thoughts inside as I fail.
4. Assess the reality dimension of accomplishing my goal: how likely is it that I can accomplish this goal in terms of:
   a. My present behavior with the goal.
   b. My motivation to change.
   c. My capacity to change.
   d. Whether external circumstances in my social environment will help or hinder my trying.
5. Plan for action translation of my conceived goal. Plans include actions not specifically described in my goal formulation but called for to reach goal attainment.
6. Implement the first step of the plan.
7. Monitor daily performance.
8. Follow step by step, monitoring daily.

If the achievement exercises have been incorporated into a workshop format, one or more follow-up sessions are recommended for clarification and reinforcement purposes. Although the procedure has been simplified for self-instruction, it is more likely to be implemented with the encouragement of a facilitator or group participants. Once success has been achieved, it will be self-reinforcing, in keeping with cognitive-behavioral principles.

Restructuring Cognitions—Rational Emotive Therapy[46]

By becoming aware of their ineffectual behavior that results from thought patterns that are dysfunctional, depressed people can learn to restructure their irrational cognitions. The three fundamental steps are:

1. Clear identification of the specific thought and situational context.
2. The employment of cognitive-behavioral intervention techniques.
3. Identification of one's rights in a given situation.

Albert Ellis's Rational Emotive Therapy(RET) provides a conceptual base for these interventions. This is a cognitive-behavioral model based on the belief that irrational ideas cause emotional disturbances. The depressed person doesn't respond just to an event, says Ellis, but to a belief system surrounding that event. The young woman who is alone on a Saturday night does not respond only to the fact that she is alone, then, but to the idea that her aloneness means that she is a terrible person and unloved. Her negative perceptions increase as she judges her depressed mood even more harshly. She berates herself endlessly with thoughts such as, "I am a weak person because I feel depressed, and I should not feel depressed." The Activating event (*A*) is thus joined to the emotional Consequences (*C*) via the intervening Belief (*B*).

Employing the *A-B-C* paradigm, the client collaborates with the therapist to determine the irrational beliefs connected to their behaviors. More rational beliefs are substituted and practiced. A few of Ellis's irrational notions to be unlearned, selected for their relevance to depression, are listed below:

—One must have love and approval almost all the time from all significant others.

—One must prove oneself to be thoroughly competent, adequate, and achieving or at least have real competence in something important.

—When things do not go as one wishes them to, life is "awful" or catastrophic.

—One has little ability to control one's feelings or rid oneself of depression and hostility.

—Because something once strongly influenced one's life, it has to keep determining one's present feelings and behaviors.

These notions are not foreign to any of us. They provide an ideal forum for discussing shared experiences. A light touch—adding a little humor concerning our common irrationalities—can help people to accept their skewed ideation more readily. Those who are interested in more in-depth knowledge of RET should consult Ellis and Harper, *A New Guide to Rational Living*.

M.C. Maulsby has developed similar techniques for changing irrational beliefs through a process he calls Reattribution.[47] This technique focuses on characteristics that are unrealistically attributed to personal deficiency, reattributing them properly. This is especially applicable to depressed people. Recall that they tend to take the blame for events over which they have no responsibility. They translate this sense of responsibility as "my fault," rather than "I am in control of my life."

Assertion Training—Cognitive Component

Assertion training encompassing a cognitive component is an appropriate method for unlearning old dysfunctional ideas and learning new constructive ones. Cognitions play an essential part in the development of assertiveness, in that it is one's belief system that supports and reinforces assertive behavior. That belief system is necessary to strengthen and sustain individuals in their right to act assertively even when unjustly criticized for doing so. At its core is the acceptance of certain basic interpersonal rights, all of which have limitations and responsibilities and are in all likelihood unknown to the nonassertive person. This is often true of people who are taught to discount their own needs and fulfill those of others. Such emphasis on self-sacrifice reinforces nonassertive behavior as well as guilt that emerges when one's natural propensity to stand up for oneself breaks through the inhibiting barrier. It is important to counteract irrational guilt that occurs as a result of assertion, and to create feelings of pride in assertive behavior even if no one else is pleased with it.

Accepting Basic Interpersonal Rights

The repetition and assertion of the following list of interpersonal rights can be enlightening:[48]

• I have the right to be treated as a competent person.
• I have the right not to be labeled, but to be treated as an individual.
• I have the right to have my feelings and opinions respected.
• I have the right to change my mind.
• I have the right to make mistakes.
• I have the right to feel anger.
• I have the right to demand that others change their behavior when it violates me.
• I have the right to refuse requests without feeling guilty or making excuses.
• I have the right to ask for what I want.
• I have the right to make decisions regarding my own life.
• I have the right to say, "I don't know."
• I have the right to recognize that my needs are as important as others' needs.

While this list of rights seems simplistic, their application is fraught with emotion, for the balance of power may be equalized between the haves and have nots, the dominant and the submissive, the powerful and the dependent. No matter what one's status, rights are the same,[49] and with each of them comes the responsibility to treat others with respect. To act aggressively suppresses others and decreases the self-respect of the aggressor as well. But to act nonassertively denies others the opportunity to respond to one's needs.

It may take time to accept these rights and attendant responsibilities without conflict. Role playing is a technique that facilitates the process. The participant can play the part of the self that wants to accept the right while the facilitator or group member acts out the self that does not want to accept it, reversing roles for further insight. Another method is based on Fritz Perls' empty-chair technique.[50] This is a gestalt approach in which the client takes one position and uses an empty chair to represent the conflicting position, changing seats as the dialogue-with-self develops. Both methods bring issues to the surface, enabling clients to confront and resolve their conflicting attitudes and beliefs.

Nonassertive behavior results in anxiety, hurt, low self-esteem, avoidance, and denial. It is often viewed as manipulation because the relinquishment of rights is an attempt to influence another to act a certain way. Typically, self-denial is taken for granted or ridiculed, the manipulation fails, and the person feels cheated. The outcome is depression.[51]

An important by-product of assertion training is learning what is important to oneself rather than what "should" be important. The helper must be aware of the dichotomy between the individual's verbal and nonverbal cues, which may communicate opposite messages. The woman who insists that her rights have not been infringed upon can be helped to recognize her true feelings through increased awareness of body clues. For example, if her body tenses, her stomach feels queasy, or she feels resentful or angry, regardless of how trivial others think the situation, her rights have probably been violated.[52]

Reducing Anxiety and Fear

Anxiety is an affective component of depression, a response that is in proportion to perceived fear. The following techniques are used in cognitive treatment to correct faulty, maladaptive ideas:

Perception: Change the client's thinking through awareness that one's emotional state gives credence to felt anxiety. "Since I'm so afraid," goes their logic, "this must really be a dangerous situation." Often people are unaware of their silent assumptions because they have avoided the painful anxiety-producing situations.

Constructive anger: Emotionally attack fears with an assertion such as, "I refuse to be afraid."

Communication skills: Practice "I messages," allowing the client to be assertive even when angry. An "I message" is simply a direct statement that identifies the undesirable behavior of another while declaring how one feels: "When you don't let me know that you'll be late, I feel discounted."[53]

Emotive imagery: Cognitively reinforce positive self-images and diminish anxiety by creating imagery that arouses confidence, affection, laughter, pride, and self-worth in an encounter.

Relaxation training: Apply progressive relaxation techniques, including relaxing thought and ideation. Clients desensitize themselves to anxiety-provoking stimuli.[54]

Confrontation: Challenge the client's "poor little me" behavior; this also confronts anxiety.

Imagining: Imagine carrying out an assertive behavior that will diminish anxiety.

Bioenergetic techniques: Alexander Lowen and Leslie Lowen's exercises help clients reexperience and accept their feelings; as a result, anxiety wanes.[55]

Anticipation Training[56] (Six Sessions)

Anticipation training is a cognitive-behavioral intervention, developed by Jane Anton and her colleagues, that has proven successful in the individual, dyadic, and group treatment of depression. Anton developed her interventions, because of her awareness of the sense of hopelessness that pervades depressed persons. They anticipate nothing more pleasurable than the status quo, leaving them with nothing to look forward to. Research indicates that they engage in fewer pleasant activities than nondepressed people, their potential and availability for reinforcement is limited, as is their knowledge of behaviors to elicit reinforcement.[57] Anticipation training increases the number of pleasant events the person experiences, thereby increasing their reinforcement potential. Self-control over depressed feelings also is strengthened by modifying negative anticipations and perceptions. The training, detailed below, takes place in six sessions spanning a two-week period.

Session 1

During the first session, rapport is established and the principles of treatment are described. Clients are instructed to keep a daily activity log in which they rate, from their own perspective, the eight most important activities of the day. Each day they assess the activities nonjudgmentally on a 7-point scale, regardless of how they compare with other days. (1 is Extremely Unpleasant and 7 is Extremely Pleasant.)

Session 2 (one week later)

The second session focuses on arranging an increase in pleasant events in the client's life, as well as beginning training in the self-control of negative anticipations. The activity log is discussed and the client is instructed to continue it. Clients are told that they will select and schedule six pleasant activities during the next two weeks. Three will be carried out alone and three with at least one other person. These activities are to take more than ten or fifteen minutes, but should be completed easily within a day. Each activity is to be something that the person expects to enjoy, and that is potentially reinforcing.

The first two activities are selected and scheduled with the clinician's help, the first to occur before the third session, which is slated three or four days later. The second activity is scheduled for shortly after the third session. Clients are encouraged to select and schedule the remaining events themselves. They may need assistance in constructing three positive anticipation statements for each of the first two activities. Each statement should begin with "I will enjoy — " and contain a specific description of some aspect of the activity.

Participants are then asked to close their eyes, relax, and imagine the first activity as though it were actually happening. (They may need assistance in creating vivid imagery.) They are instructed silently to rehearse each of the three statements regarding the activity and to create a vivid image for each statement. They are to continue repeating the statements and imagining the activity until they can identify a positive feeling while doing so.

They are then instructed to repeat each statement and review each image for both of the first two activities at least three times a day at home, until the activities are completed. It is helpful to decide on specific times for daily review.

Session 3 (3 – 4 days following Session 2)

The activity log is discussed and continued, and the completion of the first planned activities is reviewed, along with any problems in performing the anticipation sequence. Help participants to construct the third activity and ask them to develop the fourth themselves. The process is repeated as in Session 2.

Session 4

Repeat the process outlined in Session 3, but also apply the anticipation format to daily logged activities. Discuss this in detail.

Session 5

Repeat as in Sessions 3 and 4, also suggesting alternative ways of developing uses for the positive anticipation format. For example, if clients have difficulty motivating themselves in particular tasks, suggest that they imagine how they will feel when the task is finished, visualizing the completed event while they think about it.

Review participants' use of Anticipation Training and their evaluation of the training procedure in general. The activity logs can provide an overview for review, making plans for future use.

The following suggestions will help to make Anticipation Training a successful treatment method:

— Avoid activities that require the reactions of others in order to make it pleasant; they may be disappointing. The fact that someone else also enjoys the activity should be viewed as a bonus, not as an essential. Recall that satisfactions are typically more likely to be appropriate to others than to the depressed persons. This dysfunctional pattern must not be reinforced further.

— Avoid choosing activities about which people have insufficient information in regard to predicting enjoyment.

— It is important, especially in early sessions, to teach participants to maximize the probability of success and enjoyment. Failure at this time can be a negative reinforcer.

— If the planned activity is contingent on the weather, be sure that a backup plan is included.

— A before, during, and after self-monitored assessment of depression may be helpful in reinforcing the observation of improved well-being.[58]

Anton has also used a "buddy system," training the depressed person together with a selected friend. This concept is especially helpful in that generalization of progress made in therapy to the larger environment is a universal problem for behaviorists and their clients. From the friend's point of view, the knowledge required alleviates the frustration and guilt inherent in dealing with a depressed person. The reality of extinction behavior, fraught with emotion from the point of view of both the depressed persons and their friends, makes Anticipation Training a boon to both parties.

Sleep Problems and Stimulus Control[59]

The cognitive-behavioral approach to the treatment of sleep difficulties, so common to depression, emphasizes self-management. Individuals take an active role in identifying the exact nature of their complaint, and a baseline provides a doublecheck on their verbal reports. Information on related antecedents and consequences is gathered in the process. Education is as important to the subject of sleep as it is to other targets of behavioral intervention. Some people have exaggerated beliefs concerning the ill effects of lost sleep that can be changed by suggestion alone. Effective procedures to relieve sleep deficits also include progressive relaxation training,[60] stimulus and temporal control. All have been substantiated by research, but the combination of relaxation with stimulus control appears to be most effective. People often use bedtime as a cue for thinking about the problems of the day, worrying about sleep, and thinking about how miserable they will feel when they get up in the morning, all of which is incompatible with falling asleep. Stimulus-control procedures are designed to interrupt this influence. Because it is easier to develop new patterns of behavior in new situations, clients are encouraged to rearrange their bedrooms. They are asked to avoid napping during the day since this decreases the need for sleep at night, and also because sleep is then associated with inappropriate temporal and physical events. Clients are asked to reduce distracting light and noise at bedtime, but to remain in bed no longer than ten minutes if they do not fall asleep. At such times, they are to get up and do something else that is not associated with past sleep difficulties. The cues for falling asleep are thus separated from cues for other activities. The process is repeated when they feel sleepy again — returning to bed, but getting up if they don't fall asleep in ten minutes. Finally, replacing worrisome thoughts with positive fantasies and self-instructions also increases the probability for a good night's rest. In my experience, meditation while lying down is one of the fastest ways to insure both positive self-messages and sleep. (Meditation in the sleep position is contraindicated when sleep is not the end goal.)[61]

NOTES

1. Gambrill, Eileen D., *Behavior Modification: Handbook of Assessment, Intervention and Evaluation* (San Francisco: Jossey-Bass, 1977).

2. Ferster, Charles B., "Classification of Behavioral Pathology," in *Research in Behavior Modification*, ed. L. Krasner and L. P. Ullman (New York: Holt, Rinehart, and Winston, 1965); see also Charles B. Ferster, "A Functional Analysis of Depression," *American Psychologist* 28 (October 1973): 857–870; and Chapter 7 for similar observations of depressed people as reactors.

3. Lewinsohn, Peter M., "The Behavioral Study and Treatment of Depression," in *Progress in Behavioral Modification*, ed. M. Hersen (New York: Academic Press, 1975).

4. Forrest, M. S., and J. E. Hokanson, "Depression and Autonomic Arousal Reduction Accompanying Self-Primitive Behavior," *Journal of Abnormal Psychology 84* (1975): 346 – 357.

5. Coyne, J. C., "Depression and the Response of Others," *Journal of Abnormal Psychology 85* (1976): 186 – 193; see also J. C. Coyne, "Toward an Interaction Description of Depression," *Psychiatry 39* (1976): 28 – 40.

6. Lazarus, Arnold, "Learning Theory in the Treatment of Depression," *Behavioral Research Therapy 6* (February 1968): 83 – 89.

7. Perlman, Helen Harris, "In Quest of Coping," *Social Casework 56* 4 (April 1975): 211 – 225.

8. Beck, Aaron T., A. John Rush, Brian F. Shaw, and Gary Emery, *Cognitive Therapy of Depression* (New York: Guilford Press, 1979).

9. Beck, Aaron T., and Ruth L. Greenberg, "Cognitive Therapy with Depressed Women," in *Women-in-Therapy*, ed. Violet Frank and Vasanti Burtle (New York: Brunner/Mazel, 1974): 113 – 131; The Cognitive Theory section is largely adapted from the work of Beck and his colleagues.

10. Seligman, Martin E. P., *Helplessness* (San Francisco: W. H. Freeman, 1975).

11. Refer to the Behavioral Theory section of this chapter in regard to extinction trials.

12. See Chapter 5 for a detailed discussion of environmental mastery.

13. See Chapter 8 for further discussion of sleep difficulties.

14. Lewinsohn, Peter M., Martin Shaffer, and Julian Libet, *A Behavioral Approach to Depression* Unpublished manuscript, University of Oregon, 1969.

15. See the discussion of Role Theory in Chapter 4.

16. Ferster, Charles B., "Classification of Behavioral Pathology," in *Research in Behavior Modification*, ed. L. Krasner and L. P. Ullman (New York: Holt, Rinehart, and Winston, 1965); see also Charles B. Ferster, "A Functional Analysis of Depression," *American Psychologist 28* (October 1973): 857 – 870; and Chapter 7 for similar observations of depressed people as reactors.

17. See Chapter 5 for a detailed discussion of dependence and environmental control.

18. Weissman, Myrna M., and Eugene Paykel, *The Depressed Woman* (Chicago: University of Chicago Press, 1974); see also George W. Brown and Tirril Harris, *Social Origins of Depression* (New York: Free Press, 1978).

19. See the discussion of the empty-nest syndrome and role loss in Chapter 4.

20. Missildine, W. Hugh, and Lawrence Galton, *Your Inner Conflicts—How to Solve Them* (New York: Simon and Schuster, 1975).

21. *Aegis: Magazine on Ending Violence against Women* (Summer/Autumn, 1980); also see Chapters 2 and 5 for discussions of violence against women.

22. Deci, Edward L., *Intrinsic Motiviation* (New York: Plenum Press, 1975).

23. Beck, Aaron T., and Ruth L. Greenberg, "Cognitive Therapy with Depressed Women," in *Women-in-Therapy*, ed. Violet Frank and Vasanti Burtle (New York: Brunner/Mazel, 1974).

24. Rotter, Julian, "Some Problems and Misconceptions Related to the Construct of Internal versus External Control of Reinforcement," *Journal of Consulting and Clinical Psychology 43*, 1 (1975): 56 – 67.

25. Radloff, Lenore, and M. M. Monroe, "Sex Differences in Helplessness: With Implications for Depression," in *Career Development and Counselling of Women*, ed. L. S. Hasen and R. S. Rapoza (Springfield, IL: Charles C. Thomas, 1978).

26. See Chapters 2, 5, 7, 8, and 9 for references to cognitions and perception which effect depression.

27. For a comprehensive reference on behavior modification, see Eileen D. Gambrill, *Behavior Modification: Handbook of Assessment, Intervention and Evaluation* (San Francisco: Jossey-Bass, 1977).

28. Lange, Arthur J., and Patricia Jakubowski,*Responsible Assertive Behavior: Cognitive/Behavioral Procedures for Trainers* (Champaign, IL: Research Press, 1980).

29. Refer to the Cognitive Theory section of this chapter for discussion of assertiveness relative to cognitions.

30. Luzader, Marthanne, ed., *An Introduction to Assertive Skills Training* (Austin: Assertive Skills Trainers of the Austin Women's Center, 1980; may be purchased singly or in bulk from the editor: 1401 St. Edwards Drive, 280, Austin, Texas 78704); also refer to Manual Smith, *When I Say No, I Feel Guilty* (New York: Dial Press, 1975).

31. See the discussion of ego-state conflicts and depression in Chapter 2.

32. Stuart, Richard B., "Casework Treatment of Depression Viewed as Interpersonal Disturbance," *Social Work 12*, 2 (1967): 27 – 36.

33. Smith, Manual, *When I Say No, I Feel Guilty* (New York: Dial Press, 1975), for a detailed overview of assertive skills.

34. Weissman, Myrna M., and Eugene Paykel, *The Depressed Woman* (Chicago: University of Chicago Press, 1974).

35. Glasser, William, *Reality Therapy: A New Approach to Psychiatry* (New York: Harper and Row, 1975); see also William Glasser, "The Basic Concepts of Reality Therapy," diagram created by William Glasser, revised 1979, available through Reality Therapy, 11633 San Vincente Blvd., Los Angeles, CA 90049.

36. McLean, Peter D., "Depression as a Specific Response to Stress," in *Stress and Anxiety*, Vol. 3, ed. I. G. Sarason and D. Speilberger (New York: Hemisphere, 1976), pp. 297 – 323.

37. See Chapter 4 for a discussion of Reality Therapy in relation to loneliness. Also refer to Chapter 7 for a discussion of loneliness and solitude.

38. See Chapter 8 for further explication of organic considerations of depression.

39. Beck, Aaron T., A. John Rush, Brian F. Shaw, and Gary Emery, *Cognitive Therapy of Depression* (New York: Guilford Press, 1979).

40. Thibaut, John W., and Harold H. Kelley, "Power and Dependence," *The Social Psychology of Groups*, Vol. 7 (New York: Wiley, 1959) pp. 100 – 125; see also Charles B. Ferster, "Classification of Behavioral Pathology," in *Research in Behavior Modification*,ed. L. Krasner and L. P. Ullman (New York: Holt, Rinehart, and Winston, 1965); Mary Teague, material incorporated in Janice Wood Wetzel's workshop on *Depression: Theory and Treatment*, Texas Department of Human Resources, April 1978 through July 1980.

41. Hall, Mary, *A Social Worker's Critique of the Afro-American Experience*, Unpublished manuscript, Boston University, 1981.

42. Beck, Aaron T., *Depression: Clinical Experimental and Theoretical Aspects* (New York: Harper and Row, 1967); see also Aaron T. Beck and Ruth L. Greenberg, "Cognitive Therapy with Depressed Women," in *Women-in-Therapy*, ed. Violet Frank and Vasanti Burtle (New York: Brunner/Mazel, 1974), pp. 113 – 131; the Cognitive Prevention and Intervention section is largely adapted from the work of Beck and his colleagues.

43. Luzader, Marthanne, ed., *An Introduction to Assertive Skills Training* (Austin, TX: Assertive Skills Trainers of the Austin Women's Center, 1980); also

refer to Louis Rath, Merrill Harmin, and Sidney Simon, *Values and Teaching* (Columbus, OH: Charles E. Merrill, 1966).

44. Luzader, Marthanne, ed., *An Introduction to Assertive Skills Training* (Austin, TX: Assertive Skills Trainers of the Austin Women's Center, 1980); also refer to Louis Rath, Merrill Harmin, and Sidney Simon, *Values and Teaching* (Columbus, OH: Charles E. Merrill, 1966).

45. Teague, Mary, material incorporated in Janice Wood Wetzel's workshops on *Depression: Theory and Treatment*, Texas Department of Human Resources, April 1978 through July 1980.

46. Ibid.; also see Chapter 4 for further discussion of life planning and goal setting.

47. Ellis, Albert, and Robert A. Harper, *A New Guide to Rational Living* (North Hollywood, CA: Wilshire Book Co., 1975); also refer to Arthur J. Lange and Patricia Jakubowski, *Responsible Assertive Behavior: Cognitive/Behavioral Procedures for Trainers* (Champaign, IL: Research Press, 1980), for a comprehensive discussion of Rational Emotive Therapy and Assertiveness Training.

48. Maultsby, M. C. Jr., *Help Yourself to Happiness* (New York: Institute for Rational Living, 1975).

49. See Chapter 7 for further discussion of assertions, called affirmations.

50. Lange, Arthur J., and Patricia Jakubowski, *Responsible Assertive Behavior: Cognitive/Behavioral Procedures for Trainers* (Champaign, IL: Research Press, 1980), for a comprehensive discussion of Rational Emotive Therapy and Assertiveness Training.

51. Perls, Frederick S., *Gestalt Therapy Verbatim* (Lafayette, CA: Real People Press, 1969).

52. See Chapter 3 for further discussion of the relinquishment of self; also refer to Chapter 7 and to Chapter 9 regarding letting go of the ego.

53. Jakubowski-Spector, Patricia "Facilitating the Growth of Women through Assertiveness Training," *The Counselling Psychologist 4*, 1 (1973): 75 – 86.

54. Gordon, Thomas, *Parent Effectiveness Training* (Reading, MA: David McKay, 1970).

55. See Chapter 7 for further explication.

56. See Chapter 3 for explication of Bioenergetics.

57. Anton, Jane, L. Dunbar, and L. Friedman, "Anticipation Training in the Treatment of Depression," in *Counselling Methods*, ed. J. D. Krumboltz and C. E. Thoresen (New York: Holt, Rinehart, and Winston, 1976).

58. Lewinsohn, Peter M., and Julian Libet, "Pleasant Events, Activity Schedules, and Depression," *Journal of Abnormal Psychology 79* (1972): 291 – 295.

59. See Chapter 7 for a discussion of relaxation techniques.

60. Gambrill, Eileen D., *Behavior Modification: Handbook of Assessment, Intervention and Evaluation* (San Francisco: Jossey-Bass, 1977).

61. See Chapter 7 for a discussion of relaxation techniques.

Chapter 7
Existentialism and Spiritual Healing

Hail divinest Melancholy.
"John Milton, II Penseroso"

Existentialism is not a single school of thought but a philosophical focus on the meaning of existence. The existential approach to the understanding of human beings is best conveyed by the phrase, "existence precedes essence." Persons, before all else, are centers that radiate and exude meaning. A person already "is" before he or she is defined by characteristic traits, roles, powers, and limitations. Beyond these premises, existential thinkers have focused on a variety of fundamental questions about human existence. Many are spiritually oriented, while others fall on a continuum between a neutral stance and atheism. Those who tend toward more secular positions search within humanistic values for those attributes that others interpret theologically. While this chapter incorporates views concerning depression from a broad range of existential perspectives, the central focus is on spiritual healing. This decision was made purposefully, since it will provide a significant and compelling viewpoint otherwise absent in this book. Also addressed is the special relevance of spiritual healing in the lives of women.

The earliest and most thorough existential theorist was Soren Kierkegaard, a spiritually oriented philosopher who continues to influence contemporary thought.[1] He speaks of the paradoxical duality of the human condition — the conflict between animal finiteness and infinite spirituality. This is the contradiction at the center of one's being which results in despair when it is denied. It is the spiritual self that is sacrificed, generally in response to a profound fear of being alone in the world. Half of one's humanness is closed off in this desperate identi-fication with amorphous crowds.

To accept the perpetual tension between the two polarities is to accept both the infinity and the finitude of humanity. Kierkegaard tells us that we must mediate between aesthetic human potentiality and the mundane reality of actual accomplishment. Existential guilt results from being less than one's lofty possibility. Though this guilt is inevita-ble owing to earthly limitations, not to venture brings only "a sickness unto death" — depression, a sickening from unrealized potentials. Despite anxiety, the only way out of this human dilemma is to risk. One becomes great in proportion to one's expectation, for only by passion of thought and action can the chasm of the center of being be spanned. For the spiritual existentialist, God calls each person to his or her true vocation; each person's purpose is to be fully oneself, an authentic being.[2]

AUTHENTICITY AND ALIENATION

Existentialists view depression as the result of alienation from the authentic self, as well as of alienation from other human beings. Play-ing out social roles, motivated to belong and not to be "different," individuals lose touch with those qualities that make them truly unique and special. Their authentic qualities, a synthesis of attributes that are unprecedented and never to recur, are often hidden from themselves, having been suppressed for so long. Often their behavior is stereotyped, rigid, and exploitative, for it is based on fear and insecurity. Factors that may predispose a person to feelings of aliena-tion and inauthenticity may begin in childhood. Growing up around people who value only *some* aspects of them, believing in social roles and biological needs as the only important pressures to be faced, such people learn to deny their very existence early in life.[3] Estranged from themselves, their task is to rediscover their true nature if they are to confront depression and transcend it.

The charge is complex because the human self does not exist in isolation. Depressed people often are alienated from others; they are typically nonparticipant spectators to life.[4] Their superficiality and facade obviate living in dynamic relationship. Instead, they are con-cerned with protecting the ego from attacks.[5] And here the existential-ists note a poignant human paradox, for people must exist in relationship, at the same time recognizing that they are alone in the universe. To be aware that they are separate from others, different from them in experience, interests, views, and tastes also leads to a painful sense of alienation and aloneness. The reconciliation between alone-ness and relationship is the atonement (at-one-ment) of persons and God, according to spiritual interpretation. While human beings are as alone as they are unique, they are also paradoxically one with the universe and each other. Metaphorically, human beings are envisioned as "the wave that is the ocean." Each is indeed a separate entity, but joined to make a whole that would not exist without the component parts.[6] How this principle is conceptualized varies with the spiritual or secular orientation of the theorist. Theologians have created a multi-tude of metaphors: the expression of a Higher Power, the God in Us, a Divine Spark, Cosmic Center, a Heavenly Force, the Holy Spirit, and Transcendence, to name a few. Others refer to creative energy and speak to analogous secular issues. Whatever the terminology, people create a proliferation of defenses against acknowledgment of the ulti-mate paradox of the human condition — that of finitude and the dualis-tic possibility of transcendence. The avoidance of such responsibility for one's actions results in "default on the task of becoming a self."[7] It also results in depression, according to existentialists, representing the absence of creative energy, or a blocking of the way of the spirit — or both.

BEING-IN-THE-WORLD[8]

Being-in-the-world, called *Dasein*, is a fundamental concept of exis-tential psychology developed by philosophers Ludwig Binswanger and Medard B. Boss. Their notions do not represent a person-in-situation perspective. Nor is this another way of saying that human beings and the environment interact; such views would suggest two separate entities. Rather, *Being* and the *World* are one, a shared entity, in which persons are thought to exist in three hypothetical "regions." The first is the *Umwelt*, the experiential, biological, physical surround-ings. The second is the *Milwelt*, the human environment. And the third region is the person him or herself, including the body, called the *Eigenvelt*. While the German labels may lend mystery to the construct, the ideas put forth are not, in fact, intangible. Only that which can be seen or experienced is considered real, so cause and effect between the three-part regions do not exist. Phenomenon (that which exists) is simply what it is in all its "here and now" immediacy; neither prejudgment nor prediction have a place.[9] Because mature human qualities exist as a given reality, the traditional notion of development is inappropriate. Existential analysis, then, is concerned with the realization of these already existing qualities made apparent through awareness.

WOMEN AT RISK

The Experience of Nothingness

If it is true that women's early socializing experience results in their propensity to merge with others, it may have a profound positive effect on their later experience.[10] While undifferentiation with the mother in early infancy is generally perceived to be a necessary forerunner to autonomous maturity and individuality, it may also provide a nutritive environment in which the possibility of merging not only with other human beings but with a higher power is enhanced. Since females are more likely to retain vestiges of undifferentiation because they are raised by a person of the same sex, they are likely candidates for mystical fusion. Women generally translate their spiritual experience as a universal communion with nature, a sense of oneness with a higher power while men characteristically speak of the surrender of the ego to a higher power. Carol Christ points out that the male expression may be a reflection of their secular reality, for they are more apt to require giving up of the ego to arrive at a state of nothingness.[11] Conversely, women's openness to mystical, spiritual experience may be a component of their quest for identity. Christ summarizes the insights of Mary Daly[12] and Adrienne Rich,[13] who note that women's spiritual journey begins in an experience of worldly nothingness, a climate conducive to mystical experience. By shattering the superficial facades of conventional society that create a false sense of self, they open themselves to the revelation of deeper sources of value and power. This awakening through mystical identification may be easier for them to experience. It may be that they are closer to true Being because of their biological attunement to nature and the essentials of life.

While this may well be true, I would caution against broad interpretations that could be detrimental to women in the long run. History is replete with spiritual profiles of women as humble, virtuous creatures placed above "animal man," thus providing a rationale for exempting them from the more tangible rewards of life. At the same time, their unassuming position in the world has been touted as destiny not to be tampered with. The "experience of nothingness" thus turned in on itself, to my mind, may result in a distortion of principles.

Solitude Versus Loneliness

Existential loneliness, the perception of one's basic separateness from other human beings is an area of growing awareness for women. Their aloneness is often a physical reality that adds credibility to feelings that prevade all human beings. Over ten million women of all ages live alone in this country, and unlike their male counterparts, 79 percent of all women are living alone at the time of their death, many for a quarter of a century or more.[14]

Laura Primakoff has investigated patterns of living alone, assessing some of the dysfunctional behavioral and cognitive aspects of aloneness that result in feelings of loneliness.[15] Also concerned with contented aloneness, Primakoff interviewed a sample of people living alone who enjoyed such a lifestyle, inquiring into their actual coping behavior. Her study suggests that there is a shift in our values, whereby singleness as a legitimate lifestyle is becoming accepted and enjoyed by many. Moreover, short-and long-term experiences of solitude may provide unique benefits. Living alone contentedly involves the ability to create a pleasurable and satisfying internal as well as external world. There are indications that people who do so, experience a fundamental shift from an externally oriented traditional commitment, to modes of living that involve an aesthetic, ethical, or spiritual dimension.

If one views emotional development as a process of separation from external objects, partly through symbolic incorporation, and partly through reflectively giving love to oneself, then contented aloneness may be perceived as individuation at a higher developmental level.[16] Again, there appears to be an inherent conflict between relationship and aloneness as healthful dynamics. The relational capacities and socialization of women are often noted and lauded. Yet, these qualities do not obviate the need for lonely depressed women to develop solitude skills. These skills focus on the reality of being alone and the positive possibilities to be found in that reality. Women learn that life can be lived fully even though one is not in an intimate relationship.[17] Primakoff suggests that women who live alone practice treating themselves as if they were their own lover. They must learn to love themselves and do for themselves what they would do for very special others. This may be played out in a candlelight dinner, a Sunday in bed, an afternoon of music, or fresh flowers — whatever the imagination can evoke as pleasurable.[18] Aloneness, once feared, can be experienced as welcome solitude.

Journal Writing and Dreams

Seldom has the need for solitude been better depicted than in Anne Morrow Lindbergh's *Gift from the Sea*, in which the author describes her seaside retreat.[19] As she thinks through her personal pattern of living, she records her thoughts and insights, her feeling of increasing closeness to others though separated from them physically. It is spiritual isolation that truly alienates, she discovers, for when one is a stranger to oneself, one is also estranged from others. Conversely, when one is connected to one's core, which is found through solitude, one can be connected to others. Lindbergh chose the beach and the sea as her haven. Other women may find a different habitat for the same purpose. Usually the woods, the mountains, a stream, a garden or field, a quiet corner are thought to provide the essential climate for growth. It may be, however, that the journey inward for some women is less stereotypic. There are no rules. Neither nature nor quiet are prerequisites.

The journal, which was the precursor of Lindbergh's book, has been a technique for exploring solitude long used by literary women. May Sarton's *Journal of a Solitude* is a more recent version.[20] Aptly, she speaks of poetry writing as a soul-making tool enabling her to learn to let go. The journal is a powerful method of self-healing and self-guidance. Problems released and confronted allow negative energy to be transformed into constructive energy that moves one forward. Energy theories are clearly compatible with this notion, and existential and cognitive theories also find common ground again. While Jungians, for example, have always asked their patients to record their dreams and keep diaries,[21] a journal of sorts is also used as a cognitive tool for depressed clients.[22]

The journal, as a vehicle for "working through" emotions, can be used creatively in a number of ways. One effective means entails writing a dialog with an unhappy event or sorrow and one's inner wisdom concerning it. Or people can write about change in their lives that was brought on by a painful incident, from the perspective of the ending of one phase and the beginning of a new era. Another approach increases self-understanding. Tristine Ranier suggests that most hurt feelings come about from the part of the self that responds as one did as a powerless child. To gain insight into inappropriate ideas, one must write about feelings, freely, as if still a child, and then gain a perspective by writing objectively as an adult on the same subject.[23]

Ranier tells us that loneliness often indicates a division within the self, a loneliness for union with the authentic self. Diary writing can help people who fear being alone, helping them to experience solitude as an opportunity for communion with the self. Loneliness is a sensation that tells us that self-love and self-nourishment are needed; the diary or journal can provide that spiritual food. Depression will be dispelled when the intuitive right side of the brain is tapped through catharsis, imagery, and free-intuitive writing. These techniques bypass the rational intellect of the left cerebral hemisphere that is often responsible for keeping the causes of depression from recognition.[24] When one is depressed, most of one's energy goes into resisting conscious awareness of unwanted emotions. Acknowledgment of these feelings in writing can redirect the released energy back into one's life.[25] But even more important, the rereading of one's journal over time is a process for uncovering the unique meaning of one's life. Ranier describes this experience as the continuity of the spirit through time. The depressed woman who is encouraged to explore her depths will no longer be a passive, isolated self. Instead, she will become a full participant in life. It is generally believed that there may be a female propensity for introspection, whether socialized or innate. If it is indeed so, it will become a major strength to facilitate her journey into health. If it is not so, the attribute may be developed with practice.

The process of introspection and journal recording can be applied effectively to dreams, although the practice requires even more discipline. If insomnia is a problem, I don't recommend it, for it necessitates waking in the middle of the night, or writing immediately upon wakening in the morning. In appropriate cases, however, the interruption may be well worth the discomfort. As one becomes accustomed to recording dreams, it is increasingly easier to recall their details. The dreams should not be analyzed, although events and associations that amplify and reflect on them are welcome. It is the act of careful and honest description made tangible through the written word that is essential. Insight and clarification occur naturally and spontaneously as time goes on. What one may have interpreted intellectually before may prove to be incorrect later, hence the concerted effort to refrain from doing so prematurely. It is helpful, however, to realize that one often dreams the same message, in at least three different symbolic guises, during one night's sleep. It is as if we are destined to dream something until it finally "gets through" to our conscious selves.[26]

Feminism and Existentialism

Feminism is a single standard system wherein all human beings have personal power to be fully human and authentic without adherence to preordained roles and facades. Existentialism is not at odds with this definition, with its emphasis on authenticity, awareness of self, and the full development of inherent potentialities. While neither feminists nor existentialists represent a homogenous group, many would agree that women who hide behind subservient masks of inferiority and men disguised by images of superiority, are both inauthentic. Both are alienated from themselves and others, and are vulnerable to depression when the mask begins to slip.

Allegiance to traditional mores that restrict personal development and possibilities may be grounded in the secular principle of scarcity — the fear that there is not enough to go around. According to this line of reasoning, "if women are allowed to develop, men will not be." It is a dual standard of logic based on conflict and power differentials and it is likely to be a competitive male model. Feminists urge the adoption of a single standard system whereby the existential principle of abundance is applied to relationship. Competence need not be a rationed commodity too scarce to share, for there is no lack.[27] To develop oneself is not to diminish another. Rather, the perception of abundance dispenses with competitive striving and encourages mutual supportiveness and shared responsibility in the home and in the larger world.[28]

Feminism and existentialism both incorporate achievement and service. Jean Baker Miller suggests that "to serve and yet not be subsevient" is the major issue and essential quality necessary for the mutual growth of women and men.[29] Women's strength centers on her propensity to serve others, while her inability to serve herself inhibits her development and places her at risk for depression. Men who have focused solely on their own development are denied the highest necessities for human life and growth in that they lack the sensitivity to serve responsively, while requiring the subservience of others. To do otherwise is to be feminine, thought to be an undesirable condition due to the universal repudiation of femininity. Both women and men lose in the process.[30]

Subject-Loss

In a theoretical study synthesizing existential philosophy, feminist theory, and psychoanalysis, Linda Thomas concludes that depression in women is caused by subject-loss (in contrast to object-loss, the psychoanalytic paradigm). Subject-loss depression, she argues, is not an internal deficit, but a condition that arises from the values prioritized in the dominant male culture.

Those attributes generally developed in women — affiliation, confirmation, attunement, and receptivity — have been culturally ignored, labeled pejoratively, or reframed as female virtues not to be emulated by males. Thomas suggests that these attributes represent the highest level of ego-organization. She points out that the emerging developmental psychology of women views them as psychological strengths rather than weaknesses. They, in fact, are highly prized by existential philosophers as well. Existentialists lament that these characteristics have been "lost to man" over the centuries, creating an existential void. Therein lies woman's "subject-loss," for these traits have not been lost to *her*. It is their recognition and respect in the world that is missing. There is a kinship between existentialism and a feminist perspective that one cannot ignore. The following schema developed by Thomas parallels the two perspectives, illuminating their common values:

EXISTENTIAL TRAITS "LOST TO MAN"	FEMINIST VALUES
Integrity	Dependability
Subjective receptivity	Active receptivity
Community versus existential authenticity	Attunement to others and service to others
Restoration of being	Confirmation of being
Existential connectedness	Affiliation as self-enhancement
Openness to experience	Vulnerability as strength
Morality as related to context	Morality as related to context
Forgiveness through caring	Forgiveness through caring
Self-mastery and belongingness	Self-mastery and belongingness
Restoration of feeling	Emotional frankness
Interdependent orientation	Interdependent orientation
Making connections through context and synthesis	Making connections through context and synthesis

If a depressed woman is to return to healthy functioning, the possibility of a highly evolved ego-formation must be considered and validated. If her strengths are ignored or devalued, as is often the case, she will continue to believe that she must have the dominant culture's characteristics before she is considered mature or healthy. Such a woman unknowingly collides with society, keeping herself from noticing how strong she really is. Her depression will reflect the illusion rather than the reality of her personal development. Muriel Rukeyser[32] expressed the same message, as only a poet can, in "The Six Canons". These canons urge women to:

> Seize structure:
> Correspond with the real.
> Fuse spirit and matter.
> Know your secrets.
> Announce your soul in discovery.
> Go toward the essence, the impulse, the creation.

PREVENTION AND INTERVENTION

Depression is viewed as alienation from the authentic self and others in the world.

Awareness and Authenticity

Through total awareness (consciousness) one becomes authentic and more fully alive. For existentialists, these qualities are synonymous with freedom — the freedom to create and to be cognizant of human meaning. When genuine alternatives in life and behavior are acknowledged, human action becomes ethical and often even religious; such insight is said to be "innersight." Conversely, the more awareness is distorted, the more likely one is to be alienated from one's self and others, and the greater the vulnerability to depression. The remedy is not in striving to do something to overcome depression or to become a "better" person; rather, the cure is in awareness and authenticity — becoming aware of who one already "is" in truth, beneath the mask. Human beings are not the product of their search for identity, but the process itself.[33]

The process of being aware is itself a creative, growth-producing, healing process. Authentic qualities are brought into existence through the knowledge of one's essential quality and inclination, revealed, says Martin Buber, as one's strongest feeling, the central desire that stirs the innermost being.[34] The courage to be truly oneself in the face of fear, then, is the courage that is needed to become fully alive. Existentialists believe that it requires a faith that is lacking in depressed persons.[35] Their anxiety stems from the possibility of nonbeing — the common human fear of finding their lives are meaningless. By making the ultimate choice to participate in life, to find their unique purpose in the world, their courage "to be" is activated. Existential dynamics are most clearly reflected in the decision-making process that begins with this core resolution. The identification of what Jean-Paul Sartre calls the person's fundamental project[36] is the task of the existential healer and depressed person, working together.

Using the process of full awareness as a guiding principle, James Bugental provides a secular existential approach to decision making and problem solving.[37] It can be readily applied to the search for authenticity:

1. Whatever the problem, do not try to solve it. Instead, instruct people to "soak in" the issues for quite a while. Consider them from all angles and experience the feelings that accompany their thoughts.

2. Encourage people to share their thoughts with you or another person, but do not respond except to encourage further communication. If no one is available, direct them to write with the same uncensored freedom.[38]

3. The process will lead to new perspectives as the depressed person opens up. What appeared to be hopeless in the beginning now has possibilities.

4. The changing process leads to an awareness that something new has been created. The real work of problem solving has been done, for it is the process itself that is a healing, self-actualizing force, according to existentialists.

The Spiritual Power Within

From a metaphysical perspective, the authentic self is the divine Self that exists in all creatures. In every human being there is a spark of divinity that is at one with the divine spark in others, a transcendence paradoxically at one with human limitation.[39] Meister Eckhart, philosopher and theologian, teaches that our only real task in life is to "let God be God" in us.[40] For spiritual existentialists, this premise represents limitless potential for healing. The existential separation revealed in depression is the separation from one's true divinity, the suppression of the creative spirit within, as well as separation from the spirit in others. Treatment entails opening one's mind to accept that internal spirit not only as existing within, but also as inherently *of* the individual. To be healed, full acceptance of this doctrine is required, an acceptance reflected in a risk of faith, the letting go of all striving and all goals, with the assurance that a higher power will prevail. It is said that those who seek are unable to find, for they see only that which they seek, blind to the reality of the existential message. That message reveals that the world is not slowly evolving toward perfection as so often thought, for perfection already lies within, waiting to be released. There need not be, indeed *cannot* be, an effort made. The miracle lies in "letting go."[41]

The Paradoxes of Ego and Non-Ego

It is no surprise that the dual relinquishment of control and receptivity to a divine force is not as effortless as it might sound. Human beings go to great lengths to protect the ego, to retain control at all costs. Is it any wonder when letting go is like letting go at the edge of a precipice? Relinquishing ego-control also is paradoxical. Inadequate ego-development and lack of control and mastery are shown to be central to depression from most theoretical perspectives.[42] Surely existentialists do not ignore human needs. The remainder of this chapter will focus on a possible explanation and resolution of this paradox.

There is an apparent discrepancy between the concepts of having power over one's life and relinquishing oneself by giving up all striving, allowing a higher power within to manifest itself. There need not be, for both lessons may be essential to optimal functioning and development. It is the premature relinquishment of oneself that may lead to depression, for one cannot give up what one does not have. Before saying "yes" to renunciation, one must dare to say "no." An analogy between life and the trapeze has been suggested by the existential theologian, Paul Tournier. One can let go safely, he cautions, only when life is in full swing.[43] The development of the self through mastery and assertiveness sets the process in motion. Mastery and assertion training, discussed in Chapter 6 as cognitive-behavioral interventions, are appropriate in the early phase of existential intervention. Only when these attributes are an integral part of life; only when persons are secure in their control of self, only then is renunciation of the ego in order. Adults must not be asked to do what they are not ready to do, any more than one would insist on a child's premature relinquishment of age-appropriate behavior. Such untimely self-denial is often mandated by well-meaning religious groups who exhort their followers stoically to give themselves up to the service of others and the larger good. In most cultures, in fact, there are groups of people who are singled out to subordinate themselves selflessly. The end result is likely to be depression, for to deny the mandate is to believe oneself a sinner, to feel guilt and inadequacy at best, and consumed by the devil at worst. Those who do abdicate themselves are no better off, for they are the depressed people who have given themselves up to living vicariously through others.[44]

Once self-development is progressing well and people show indications of a need for further enlightenment, it is time to embark on the process of self-relinquishment. This does not necessitate giving up one's skills and personal power, as is often suggested. It is, instead, a commitment to a higher power and the promise that removing barriers to that force will allow one's uniquely potent gifts to emerge. This is a time of transition in which people understandably need tremendous support in order to make this leap of faith. To let go of what one has acquired, to leave one place to find another, to turn one's back on the past and take responsibility for the unknown future all require great strength.[45] Such faith is not just an opinion, it is a way of existing. It is the role of the therapist to help the client who is ready to risk—to be drawn out of the crowd, out of a subjective perspective, and into a life of trust and wholeness.

Surrender and Nonattachment

Complete nonattachment — surrender — is the ultimate faith, according to existentialists. It cannot be acquired, attained, or developed through perseverance or practice, except insofar as such efforts prove the impossibility of acquiring it. As people struggle with this reality, they must give up, one by one, every trick or device for letting go, including "giving up" as something one does to get it.[46] When people realize that letting go is beyond all their powers of action or inaction, that it comes only through desperation, "that is the mighty self-abandonment that gives birth to the stars."[47] Just as letting go and accepting oneself can never be a deliberate act, neither can the rejection of the self. The wholeness of oneself as an inescapable fact is revealed as people learn to stop defending against themselves. They come to recognize that they are not their egos, for the ego, too, is learned. Ultimately, they cease to identify themselves with their egos altogether.[48]

Within this model, healing comes through the dual acceptance of one's frailties and faults, and the divinity residing in oneself. In this contradictory totality, one is free to be oneself, or more profoundly, One's Self, without struggle. By accepting both the evil and the good, the depths and the heights in humanity, there is no longer a need for attachment, to hold on to one's false image, and the frustration and anxiety inherent in trying to save and control the self. When people reach this point, they stop seeking and clinging to life and start living it. Secure in the wisdom that life is the immediate now, and now is the goal of life fulfillment, there is no need to strive relentlessly for survival. Severely depressed persons are more receptive than most to this transformation. Having recognized that striving for perfection and trying to conform have failed, they are in ideal circumstances for completely letting go. When they do, they are released from the prisons of their egos.[49]

Affirmation and Visualization

Taking a closer look at some of the phenomenological notions present in spiritually oriented healing, one can find common denominators in the more empirical discipline of cognitive-behavioral psychology. Such seemingly disparate fields are finding the same basic truths, couched in deceptively diverse theoretical constructs. Existentialists who speak of the importance of positive thought as a creative, healing force are essentially in agreement with cognitive-behavioral theorists who hold that a negative cognitive set predisposes one to depression. Thought, according to existentialists, sets in motion the law of the mind which is reflected in action. The conscious mind controls one's fate by furnishing the subconscious with thought that will be accomplished exactly as directed. Thoughts that are accepted as true automatically find expression. We reap what we sow and the seeds are our thoughts. To control depression, one must control negative thoughts.[50] Ideas, then, for both existentialists and cognitive-behaviorists, are the generating energy underlying existence. The common message is that human beings can control ideas and, in turn, their lives.

Whether interpreted existentially or conceptualized from a social-learning perspective, the repetition of positive self-statements (affirmations) is a powerful tool for changing depressive negative thought patterns. Control one's thoughts and effects are also controlled.[51] To begin, people can be taught the following fundamental principles:

First, recognize your ability to control your own life.

Second, visualize that which you want manifested.

Third, affirm yourself and hold a positive image of your actualized desire, in spite of apparent disparity.

The most important rule is to ignore outward appearances; the desired state must be affirmed as an already existing reality.[52] One attracts what one affirms, for like attracts like. According to existentialists, the following affirmations will reinforce positive spiritual self-concepts, establishing a broad, conscious understanding upon which all life and existence depends.[53]

Affirm: "I am open and receptive to the inflow and the outpouring of all there is in the universal, creative force."

Affirm: "I keep my thoughts centered upon those things that I want to see manifest in my life."

Affirm: "I see the world, not as it is, but as I AM, and I AM in spiritual unity with a higher power." (This means that God, the I AM and I are One.)

Affirm: "I am a radiating center of peace and love."

These affirmations should be repeated at regular specified intervals. While the principles are spiritual, they are also cognitive-behavioral. Learning theorists would agree that concentration should be centered on the positive, what is wanted, rather than on what is not wanted. They have shown empirically that positive reinforcement is the primary conditioner.[54] With that in mind, the existential mandate to see oneself as divine spirit, resulting in a spiritual awakening, is even more credible.

Everything is first invisible to the eye and must be imaged or imagined in order to be brought to fruition. Positive imagery as a therapeutic technique is a common practice for contemporary cognitive-behavioral therapists.[55] For Christian existentialists, the idea is expressed in the directive, "Ask and you shall receive." The petition first must be visualized in order to put the undeviating law of cause and effect into operation. It must, above all else, be wanted "with all one's mind and heart and strength," and its manifestation must not be questioned. One should not say, "I'd like to have," but rather, "It is already mine."[56] This is reinforcement at its most positive, for one does not seek that which is already found. While existential faith might be optimal, knowledge of cognitive-behavioral principles may convince a most unlikely depressed client to apply these universal laws. What is desired must be visualized as an already accomplished fact, whether endowed with mystical etiology or cognitive-behavioral principles. In this sense there is no supernatural miracle. There is instead the application of the same universal laws applied on many levels (or perhaps that *is* the miracle).

Contemplation and Meditation

The divine quality of human selflessness is regarded as the final truth in all religions throughout the world.[57] To this end, contemplative practices are employed universally. To know oneself is to forget oneself by allowing the body and mind, and those of others, to fade into the background. This is the action of no-action which is a simultaneous process of decreasing the secular self, the ego, and increasing the divine self. It is fitting that this process often is expressed in terms of death and rebirth.[58] It is not uncommon for this transcendent experience to be preceded by pain, depression being an expression of that pain. The cataclysmic annihilation and transformation of the ego that requires overcoming powerful forces of resistance cannot be accomplished without discomfort.[59]

This discomfort is transcended in meditation, the method of centering, the process of clearing the mind to allow the self to emerge. The process is facilitated through the healing sound of mantric syllables that are sung or recited inwardly. The Asian mantra, "OM," corresponds to the Western "AMEN" and the Moslem "AMIN." Considered to be one of the most important, OM is divided into three phonetic components. When slowly pronounced as $\breve{A}\breve{U}\breve{M}$, with each letter sounded, the whole frequency range of human speech is utilized according to experts on the subject.[60] A, they conjecture, represents consciousness, U is dream consciousness, and M is deep sleep consciousness. Together, as OM, they are an expression of the "highest consciousness." While the sound of OM may be healing, its power is not physical, it has no effect on those ignorant of it. Rather, its power is in belief. Again, perception is all. And so it is that even a meaningless but pleasing sound (such as "tha-ring") can be an effective mantra. While some think the utterance should have no distracting connotation, others believe that taking a thought like "love" into the innermost mind is by far more effective. Whatever one's personal preference, a mantra should be selected prior to meditating.

While there are countless methods of meditation, the simplest may be as helpful as the most stringent. All hold commonalities reflected in the following suggestions for meditating[61]

Sit with a straight spine, the lower back out and the abdomen relaxed, in a comfortably heated room — not too warm or too cold. Be sure that clothing is not constricting.

Hold hands palms up in one's lap, thumbs lightly touching. If right-handed, the left hand is placed over the right; reverse if left-handed.

The less active side of the body is thus placed in the superior position, to equalize both halves of the body.

Close the eyes or lower them, focusing but not concentrating on specifics.

Relax all parts of the body. Feel the feet and ankles getting heavy, followed by knees, hips, and midsection; then hands, arms, shoulders, neck, jaw, eyes, forehead, and even tongue. The important thing is to feel natural and comfortable.

Close the mouth easily without clenching the teeth. Breathe comfortably through the nose. Observe the breathing, concentrating on exhaling.

Silently think a mantra at regular intervals (for example, at each exhale, or whenever it is more spontaneous and natural).

As you become aware that thoughts have come into the mind, gently brush them aside without frustration and continue with the mantra. The important thing is to keep alert and relaxed. Do not make a deliberate effort not to think. I join with those who believe than an attitude of "listening" to the Stillness within is Key.

Meditate for up to twenty minutes, twice daily. Start with as many minutes as is comfortable, working up to the full twenty minutes. Any time of the day is suitable, except right after eating or drinking. The digestive process is an active one, directly opposed to the desired inactivity.

The Shadow[62]

Though seldom noted, it is important to provide a support for people who are new to meditation. This is especially true for those who become even more depressed as deep-seated conflicts and repressed negativity rise to the surface of consciousness in meditation. As these cognitions come to the fore, they can be dispelled by quietly accepting their existence. These are the hidden, repressed, and unfavorable aspects of the personality which Carl Jung called the ever-present shadow. This darkness is not just the flip-side of the ego. Just as the ego contains negative attitudes that are destructive, so the shadow has positive qualities — creative impulses and normal instincts. Ego and shadow though separate, are inextricably linked. Still, Jung refers to the shadow's conflict with the ego as "the battle of deliverance." As the client accepts the shadow when it comes to consciousness in the process of meditating, the ego can cease its constant defense in readiness for healthy surrender. The surrender is not to the shadow as enemy, but to the higher power, the authentic Being that lies within. Realistically, the process can be described more easily than it can be realized. The support and guidance of the therapist are essential, for the facts brought to consciousness can be painful. Because the depressed person's ego is often invested in perfection, the emergence of this "dark force" is particularly distressing. It may, in fact, be the cause of the depression. What is more, every situation that contains a charge of strong affect, whether excessive anger, anxiety, depression, or even delight, must be considered. It is possible that the extra investment may be coming from the unconscious in the form of a shadow projection.

Only the shadow brought to light can be corrected. The depressed person must be able to express negativity before moving on to positive perceptions and relationships, and finally letting go.[63] In existential terms, the ego must be allowed to function before it can be surrendered. The surrendering of the ego is the realization that one gives away in order to keep. Another paradox, such giving does not represent sacrifice or loss, for generosity of this nature arises out of Self interest (that is, the authentic spiritual Self). Threats disappear, the world is forgiven, restored, and welcome. What appeared dull, lifeless, and depressing is now perceptually changed. Existentialists agree that the journey is as difficult as it is wonderful. They also caution about impatience, for it is a lifetime pilgrimage. The shadow, once recognized, cannot be laid to rest, for it will emerge in disguised form again and again. Though the process takes a lifetime, a person can learn to look within and to reflect on what is found with honesty and courage. Remember, the process itself is the healing agent.

Mystical Experience

Light Visions

A discussion of existential principles and metaphysical phenomena would be incomplete without a consideration of the understanding of mystical experience and light. Reference to light as a healing quality is common to most major religions and philosophies,[64] while others who are less esoterically inclined interpret light phenomena in terms of electricity and energy. The spiritual and the secular appear to be reaching similar conclusions, though ostensibly traveling different paths. Scientists, too, are finding evidence that light is a universal healing energy, a built-in capacity for health. While a great deal of metaphysical, phenomenological research is being conducted, we have not given it the respect in our culture that we give the "hard" sciences. It may be physical scientists, therefore, who will provide the empirical support demanded by more skeptical disciplines.[65]

Light visions are likely to be experienced when the mind is empty of all purpose. When the mind is totaly disinterested, God is compelled to come to it, according to existential theologians.[66] And so it is with light, for the best conductor of electricity is that which is least resistant to the flow of electricity. We must be open to the possibility of such experiences, being careful to differeniate light visions from hallucinatory delusions.[67] It is better to err on the positive side of the question.

Light as mystical experience is more radiant and more luminous than any light known, yet it does not offend the eyes, according to those who report the phenomenon. It is usually pure white or golden and it may seem to merge with the solar plexus, which appears not to be just coincidentally translated as the sun center. The sensation is one of unimaginable peace, stillness, and love, an awesome, never to be forgotten sense of at-one-ment with the universe. It represents a "plugging in" to a creative force that harnesses unlimited inner potential.[68] Not only is personal creativity increased, but the ability to commit oneself to a chosen field also increases. Mystical experience is neither limited to light visions, nor at all essential to existential healing,[69] but it is important to recognize the universality of the experience and to understand the profound impact on the persons involved.[70] The phenomenon may occur to depressed people who have struggled with the spiritual paradoxes of life, experiencing deep frustration, insecurity, and intense emotion. Through the "dark night of the soul" when all else has failed and there seems to be no way out of despair, the eternal self is rediscovered. Exhausted, they have turned to a higher power, surrendering themselves totally. Their surrender is a personal giving up that is more than giving in. It is letting go in the most profound sense. The experience appears to be commonplace although it cannot be willed. Still, visual exercises that are a source of relaxation and energy renewal in themselves may provide a receptive frame of mind.[71] As a facilitator, instruct your clients as follows, not to "hope for" light vision experiences, but to make the most of that which we have recognized as growth enhancing:

Visual Imagery

— Close the eyes and take several slow, very deep breaths, breathing from the abdomen.

— With each inhalation, imagine that energy is being taken in from the universe.

— With each exhalation, imagine the entire body becoming more and more relaxed.

Breathing Light

— Now imagine that the inside of the body, from your center out, is becoming brighter and brighter, radiant and illuminated.

— Allow yourself to enjoy this feeling for several moments. You are relaxed and full of energy.

— Open your eyes.

Expanding Auras

— Now imagine that a thin aura of light surrounds the entire body. It can be any color you wish it to be.

— With each exhalation of breath, imagine this aura becoming brighter and brighter, more and more colorful, extending out from the body further and further.

— Imagine the aura filling the space around you, and extending out as far as you want it to reach.

— Allow yourself to enjoy this experience for several moments.

— You are now relaxed and full of energy.

— Open your eyes.

Imaging with Music[72]

Healing through musical sound is centuries old and crosses many cultures. A German composer and international expert on the subject, Peter Hamel, finds that most methods are group-circle exercises. Under the influence of music, participants exchange and analyze the inner pictures that they have found supported or intensified by music. Thought to help the "healthy" as well as those who are emotionally troubled, day-dreamed images deepen self-discovery and clarify personal identity. By "listening with the heart," both ancient and contemporary music can be powerful healers, probably because music has the power to transform perception.

Psychosynthesis[73]

Roberto Assogioli developed an extensive imagery therapy called psychosynthesis designed to expedite personal and spiritual well-being. Therapeutic goals include the harmonious integration of all human functions and the substitution of healthy response tendencies.

The capability of contacting an inner self that is the source of wisdom, intelligence, direction, and purpose is assumed. By experiencing the higher self, self-actualization is possible. The therapist acts as a facilitator to that end, providing symbolic exercises that are considered to be diagnostic as well as psychotherapeutic. The "Blossoming of the Rose," a visual exercise particularly appropriate for depressed people, is detailed below. A person with repressed hostility may visualize a rose with many thorns, a withdrawn person may have difficulty envisioning the unfolding of the petals, and an impulsive, impatient person may rush the process altogether. Whatever the psychodiagnoses, the depressed client's awareness of him or herself as a divine being is facilitated.[74] The exercise is presented as a group acticity, but can be experienced in individual treatment as well.

Blossoming of the Rose Exercise[75]

Ask clients to sit quietly, hands resting in the lap, much as they would do in meditation. Then tell them you are taking them on an imaginary journey into the Self. Begin as follows:

Imagine you are looking at a rosebush. Visualize one stem with a rosebud and leaves. The sepals are closed and the bud appears to be green. At the very top, the tip of the bud can be seen. Visualize this vividly, holding the image clearly in your mind.

Now watch while the green sepals start to separate slowly one by one, their points turning slowly outward revealing the colored petals which remain closed. The sepals continue to open until all of the tender bud can be seen.

Now the petals follow suit, slowly separating until a full-blown rose is in view.

At this stage, smell the perfume of the rose, inhaling its delicate, delicious, sweet scent with delight.

Now expand your visualization to include the entire rosebush. Imagine that the life force that arises from the roots to the blossom causes the process of opening.

Finally, identify yourself with the rose itself. Symbolically, you are this rose. As Assogioli explains: "The same life that animates the universe and has created the miracle of the rose is producing in us alike, an even greater miracle — the awakening and development of our spiritual being and that which radiates from it."

Close the exercise by quietly asking participants to open their eyes when they feel comfortable. A discussion of their experience should follow. When met with resistance, their reactions can be explored and the exercise repeated. Reactions will range from a profound sense of awe and relief, at having experienced the introjected rose as a living symbol, to that of frustration due to the realization that they are blocking their creativity and inner power. The message, however, remains the same and in it a positive outcome is assured, for the inner flowering of the human being has been activated.

Relationship and Action

Introspection and contemplation are essential to well-being, but not for their own sake. Its purpose is the active journey outward in relationship to others in the world.[76] Inaction, then, leads to action, not to eternal do-nothingness. Relationship can be experienced at many levels. One way is in the encounter — that moment when another becomes directly alive to us on a very different level from that previously known.[77] This way of knowing another is a profound experience that implies presence, being with the other totally. The existential therapist enters into this relationship in a disciplined, purposeful manner through active involvement. So, too, does the evolving client. The separation, isolation, and despair of human beings is overcome through the recognition of love and tenderness. When clients experience the acceptance of their being rather than their achievements, they are able to become more open and accepting of the incompleteness in others. Their relationship with the therapist may be the first of many in which the client learns to accept the coexistence of flaws and wonder in another human being.[78]

Responsibility and Vocation

Finally, the inward journey leads outward to responsibility and a sense of vocation. Here we again are reminded of Martin Buber's advice to be in touch with one's strongest feeling, one's central wish that stirs the innermost self.[79] Together with an honest appraisal of potentialities and opportunities, decisions can be made to live one's life through sevice to the community by actualizing one's combination of attributes that are unprecedented and never recurring. Decisions can be made through the existential process described earlier, or by applying more concrete methods at this stage.[80] Note that purposeful development in the early phases of intervention was focused on personal growth, leading to development in the final stage, which results in commitment to others. Ultimately, the depressed individual is healed by healing others, but the process must not be rushed or reversed. Too often, depressed persons are "helping types" who have not yet developed themselves. This does not imply, of course, that people should not learn to help one another early on in life. I am speaking here of pervasive behaviors and attitudes to the exclusion of others.

NOTES

1. Kierkegaard, Soren, *Philosophical Fragments* (Princeton, NJ: Princeton University Press, 1946).

2. Sartre, Jean-Paul, *Existentialism (New York: Philosophical Library, 1947); see also Albert Camus, The Rebel* (New York: Vintage, 1956); also refer to Charles Hampden-Turner, *Maps of the Mind* (New York: Macmillan, 1981), for a comprehensive overview of personality constructs.

3. Maddi, Salvatore, "The Existential Neurosis," *Journal of Abnormal Psychology* 72 (August 1967): 311 – 325.

4. MacMurray, John, *Persons in Relation*, Vol. 2 (New York: Harper and Row, 1961).

5. Schact, Richard, *Alienation* (Garden City, NY: Doubleday, 1971).

6. Foundation for Inner Peace, *A Course in Miracles* (Huntington Staton, NY: Coleman Graphics, 1975); see also Laura Primakoff, "Patterns of Living Alone and Loneliness: A Cognitive-Behavioral Analysis," Unpublished doctoral dissertaion, University of Texas at Austin, August 1981.

7. Heidegger, Martin, *Being and Time* (New York: Harper and Row, 1962).

8. Binswanger, Ludwig, *Being-in-the-World: Selected Papers of Ludwig Binswanger* (New York: Basic Books, 1963); see also Medard Boss, *Psychoanalysis and Daseinsanalysis* (New York: Basic Books, 1963); also refer to Calvin S. Hall and Gardner Lindzey, "Existential Psychology," *Theories of Personality*, 2nd ed. (New York: Wiley, 1970), pp. 552 – 581, for a general discussion of existentialism.

9. Tournier, Paul, *A Place for You* (New York: Harper and Row, 1968).

10. See the discussion of Object-Relations Theory and undifferentiation in Chapter 2.

11. Christ, Carol P., *Diving Deep and Surfacing* (Boston: Beacon Press, 1980).

12. Daly, Mary, *Beyond God the Father* (Boston: Beacon Press, 1974).

13. Rich, Adrienne, *Diving into the Wreck* (New York: W. W. Norton, 1973).

14. U.S. Department of Health, Education and Welfare, *Facts About Older Americans* (Washington, DC: Office of Human Development, Administration on Aging. National Clearinghouse on Aging, DHEW Pub, no. (OHD) 77-20006, 1976); see Chapter 5 for interventions regarding aging women who are alone.

15. Primakoff, Laura, "Patterns of Living Alone and Loneliness: A Cognitive-Behavioral Analysis," Unpublished doctoral dissertation, University of Texas at Austin, August 1981.

16. This interpretation of separation-individuation is apropos to Object-Relations Theory, so it might have been included in Chapter 2 as well.

17. Ephron, Doris, "Loneliness: Living Alone? Do it Right," *New York*, March 20, 1978.

18. See Chapter 6 for a discussion of pleasant activities as an intervention.

19. Lindbergh, Anne Morrow, *Gift from the Sea* (New York: Pantheon Books, 1955).

20. Sarton, May, *Journal of a Solitude* (New York: W. W. Norton, 1973).

21. Centerpoint I, Extention Course on Jungian Thought. St. Louis, MO, 1980.

22. See Chapter 6 and Beck's Mastery-Pleasure Schedule.

23. Ranier, Tristine, *The New Diary* (Los Angeles: J. P. Tarcher, 1978; see also Ira Progoff, *At a Journal Workshop* (New York: Dialogue House Library, 1981).

24. Refer to Charles Hampden-Turner, *Maps of the Mind* (New York: Macmillan, 1981), for a concise discussion regarding energy and depression.

25. See Chapter 3 for further discussion regarding energy and depression.

26. Centerpoint I, Extention Course on Jungian Thought. St. Louis, MO, 1980.

27. Blankney, Raymond B., *Meister Eckhart: A Modern Translation* (New York: Harper and Row, 1941).

28. Wetzel, Janice Wood, "Preventing Mental Illness Through Existential Principles," *Journal of Religion and Health* 19, 4 (Winter 1980): 268–274; also see Chapter 4 for further discussion in relation to depression.

29. Miller, Jean Baker, *Toward a New Psychology of Women* (Boston: Beacon Press, 1976), p. 71.

30. Freud, Sigmund, "Some Psychological Consequences of the Anatomical Distinction between the Sexes" (1925), in *Collected Papers*, Vol. 5 (London: Hogarth Press, 1965), pp. 186–197.

31. Thomas, Linda, "Depression and the Dominant Culture: A Study of Subject-Loss," Unpublished master's thesis, Smith College School for Social Work, Northampton, MA, 1981.

32. Rukeyser, Muriel, "The Six Canons," *The Speed of Darkness* (New York: Random House, 1968), p. 12.

33. May, Rollo, ed., *Existential Psychology*, 2nd ed. (New York: Random House, 1969).

34. Buber, Martin, *Hasidism and Modern Man* (New York: Harper and Row, 1958).

35. Tillich, Paul, *The Courage to Be* (New Haven: Yale University Press, 1959).

36. Sartre, Jean-Paul, *Existentialism* (New York: Philosophical Library, 1947); see also Albert Camus, *The Rebel* (New York: Vintage, 1956); see Chapter 4 and 6 for methods of "discovering" one's interests.

37. Bugental, James F. T., *The Search for Existential Identity* (San Francisco: Jossey-Bass, 1976); see also Irvin D. Yalom, *Existential Psychotherapy* (New York: Basic Books, 1980).

38. Note the similarity between the process of existential conscious awareness and Freud's theory of the unconscious and free-association as discussed in Chapter 2.

39. Hesse, Herman, *Siddhartha* (New York: New Directions, 1951); also refer to Foundation for Inner Peace, *A Course in Miracles* (Huntington Station, NY: Coleman Graphics, 1975).

40. Blakney, Raymond B., *Meister Eckhart: A Modern Translation* (New York: Harper and Row, 1941).

41. Butterworth, Eric, *Discover the Power within You* (New York: Harper and Row, 1968).

42. See Chapters 2, 3, 5, 6 and 9 for discussions concerning ego-development, mastery, and control.

43. Tournier, Paul, *A Place for You* (New York: Harper and Row, 1968).

44. See the discussion of Role Theory in Chapter 4 and of Bioenergetics in Chapter 3 for further discussion of depressed people who give up themselves to live vicariously through others.

45. Watts, Alan W., *Beyond Theology* (New York: Meridian Books, 1967).

46. See the "letting go" exercises in the bioenergetics section of Chapter 3.

47. Watts, Alan W., *Psychotherapy East and West* (New York: Ballentine Books, 1970).

48. Watts, Alan W., *The Book: On the Taboo against Knowing Who You Are* (New York: Collier Books, 1966).

49. Bloodworth, Venice J., *The Key to Yourself* (Los Angeles: Scrivener, 1965).

50. Beck, Aaron T., *Depression: Clinical Experimental and Theoretical Aspects* (New York: Harper and Row, 1967); see also Aaron T. Beck, A. John Rush, Brian F. Shaw, and Gary Emery, *Cognitive Therapy of Depression* (New York: Guilford Press, 1979).

51. See Chapter 6 for a discussion of assertions (affirmations) from a cognitive-behavioral perspective.

52. Bloodworth, Venice J., *The Key to Yourself* (Los Angeles: Scrivener, 1965).

53. Affirmations have been adapted from Eric Butterworth, *Discover the Power within You* (New York: Harper and Row, 1968), who bases his ideas on Jesus' Sermon on the Mount (Matthew, 5 – 7; Luke, 6:17 – 49).

54. Beck, Aaron T., A. John Rush, Brian F. Shaw, and Gary Emery, *Cognitive Therapy of Depression* (New York: Guilford Press, 1979).

55. See the discussion of Anticipation Training in Chapter 6 for an example of imagery intervention with depressed clients.

56. Bloodworth, Venice J., *The Key to Yourself* (Los Angeles: Scrivener, 1965).

57. Kaufman, Walter, *Religions in Four Dimensions* (New York: Reader's Digest Press, 1976).

58. Bando, Shojun, "The Dual Aspect of Faith," in *Contemplation and Action in World Religions,* ed. Yusaf Ibish and Ileana Marculescu (Seattle: University of Washington Press: Rothko Chapel Book, 1978), pp. 16 – 27.

59. Ibish, Yusuf, and Ileana Marculescu, *Contemplation and Action in World Religions* (Seattle: University of Washington Press: Rothko Chapel Book, 1978).

60. Hamel, Peter M., *Through Music to the Self* (Boulder, CO: Shambhala, 1979).

61. Mahesh Yogi, Maharishi, *Transcendental Meditation* (New York: New American Library, 1968); these instructions combine Zen, Transcendental, and Relaxation Meditation techniques.

62. Jung, Carl G., ed. (and M. L. von Franz after Jung's death), *Man and His Symbols* (Garden City, NY: Doubleday, 1964).

63. See the Bioenergetics section of Chapter 3 for exercises appropriate to the venting of anger.

64. Emmons, Michael, *The Inner Source* (San Luis Obispo, CA: Impact, 1978).

65. Morowitz, Harold, *The Wine of Life and Other Essays on Societies, Energy and Living Things* (New York: St. Martin's Press, 1979).

66. Blakney, Raymond B., *Meister Eckhart: A Modern Translation* (New York: Harper and Row, 1941).

67. Refer to Kenneth R. Pelletier and Charles Garfield, *Consciousness: East and West* (New York: Harper and Row, 1976), for a comparison of the visionary state, the schizophrenic's experience, and normal inspiration.

68. See Chapter 3 for further discussion of energy as a life force; also see a discussion of psychic energy according to Freud in Chapter 2.

69. Kung, Hans, *On Being a Christian* (Garden City, NY: Doubleday, 1976).

70. Golden, L. Gene, "Mystical Experience: Individuation as Undifferentiation at its Highest Spiral," Unpublished master's thesis, Smith College School for Social Work, Northampton, MA, 1981.

71. Samuels, Michael, and Harold Z. Bennett, *The Well Body Book* (New York: Random House, and Berkeley, CA: The Bookworks, 1978).

72. Hamel, Peter M., *Through Music to the Self* (Boulder, CO: Shambhala, 1979).

73. Assogioli, Roberto, *Psychosynthesis* (New York: Viking Press, 1971).

74. Pelletier, Kenneth R., and Charles Garfield, *Consciousness: East and West* (New York: Harper and Row, 1976).

75. "Blossoming of the Rose" has been adapted from Roberto Assogioli, 1971.

76. O'Conner, Elizabeth, *Journey Inward, Journey Outward* (New York: Harper and Row, 1968).

77. May, Rollo, ed., *Existential Psychology*, 2nd ed. (New York: Random House, 1969).

78. See Chapter 4 for further discussion of relationship, and Chapter 5 regarding supportiveness and relational qualities of women.

79. Buber, Martin, *Hasidism and Modern Man* (New York: Harper and Row, 1958).

80. See Chapters 4, 5, and 6, regarding life planning; see also Ira Progoff, *At a Journal Workshop* (New York: Dialogue House Library 1981) See also Irvin D. Yalom, *Existential Psychotherapy* (New York: Basic Books, 1980).

Chapter 8
Biochemical Theories

...health has its science as well as disease.
Elizabeth and Emily Blackwell, *Medicine as a Profession for Women*

Biochemical theories hold that depression is caused by an imbalance of chemicals in the brain. It is unclear whether this imbalance is the result of gene transmission (heredity), or abnormalities in brain chemistry that predispose a person to a vulnerability to life stress and depression. Biochemical interpretations may also be generalized to include secondary affective disorder, which is depression that is a secondary symptom resulting from another major psychological or physiological problem.

Biochemical/genetic theories are being included in this otherwise psychosocial handbook on depression because research-based information in this area is significant to all of us. Clinicians who are not medical doctors often refer clients for medication, or they work in interdisciplinary cooperation with a biochemically oriented physician. It is important to understand the theories and research on which chemotherapy is based. It is equally essential that professionals from a biochemical orientation work cooperatively with psychosocial disciplines on behalf of their clients. These perspectives need not be polarized, for body chemistry and psychological and social stresses are undoubtedly intermeshed. The aim of this chapter is to inform both disciplines, not presumptuously to coopt an organic area in which I, as a clinical social worker and social scientist, am admittedly a visitor.

Genetic and biogenic amine hypotheses will be reviewed, together with chemotherapies, electroconvulsive (electroshock) treatment, and psychosurgery. Controversial issues will be addressed, including iatrogenic depressive illness which occurs as a result of prescribed medication. The section on Women at Risk will encompass these subjects, together with female endocrine physiology and substance abuse in women.

GENETIC THEORIES

Viewing depression as a biological disorder, genetic theorists contend that genes transmit depression. While most of the research has been concerned with bipolar probands (manic-depressive subjects), unipolars (depressed people who have never experienced mania) have also been studied to a limited extent. Genetic research centers on family aggregation studies comparing illness rates within and between generations of a given family, twin concordance data comparing illness rates in monozygotic (identical) twins with dizygotic (fraternal) twins, and chromosome linkage studies investigating known genetic traits and their possible linkage with depression. Reports continue to be inconsistent, although there appears to be more support for inherited contributions to risk for bipolars.[1] Because genetic researchers have usually relied upon family histories of similar disorders as their evidence of psychiatric illness, their work has been questioned. Psychosocial theorists argue that family members in close association learn the same behavior; or, they contend, shared social stresses and experiences may result in similar symptoms.[2]

The twin concordance model has been faulted on the same grounds. Marc Schuckit has made attempts to deal with the learning and social similarity arguments in populations of alcoholics, providing a guideline for study. He compares full and half siblings who have a diagnosis of alcoholism and who have been reared with one another, with those who have been reared away from one another.[3] The number of twin subjects that are depressed and who have twin siblings who have been reared away, however, is too limited to reach any consensus. To date, most researchers who have studied monozygotic twins who have been reared apart or have reanalyzed existing twin study data,[4] conclude that it is meaningless to try to determine "how much" heredity influence development. Instead, the task is to understand the multifaceted complexity of interactions through which human individuality evolves. Genetic inheritance is one facet. Certainly, there is strong support for at least familial influence.[5]

Linkage studies hypothesizing that mania, in bipolar depression, is due to an X-linked recessive gene (like color blindness) have been supported empirically.[6] The same support had not been found for unipolar depressions until a breakthrough reported in 1981. Scientists at the University of Rochester Medical School found evidence to support the hypothesis that depression is associated with the short arm of chromosome 6, which carries human leukocyte antigen (HLA) genes. An analysis of blood samples from thirty-four pairs of depressed siblings found those with two identical HLA genes to be five times as numerous as siblings with dissimilar HLA genes. This indicates that two parents who carry susceptibility genes increase the risk of depression occurring in their offspring.[7] Still, the riddle is not yet solved. We do not know if the search for primary causes has been successful as yet. Prior to the Rochester study, all of the biological traits identified as possible genetic defects disappeared with recovery.[8] Tatrelli and his colleagues contend that as long as genetic research employs diagnoses rather than symptoms as the point of reference (whether in regard to screening or research conclusions), it will remain an uncertain instrument.[9] Should the new data be validated, which would indicate that the presence of particular genes predisposes some people to depression, exactly how the environment impacts on predisposition will have to be clarified. At this time, the question remains unanswered.

Biogenic Amine Theories

The hypothesis that depression is the result of a possibly inherited deficiency of particular brain substances called neurotransmitters has been studied for well over twenty years. The biogenic amine hypothesis incorporates a number of theories, all of which are based on the differential actions of antidepressant drugs. Research into the action of these drugs on the brain indicates that they increase the availability of certain neurotransmitters at critical receptor sites. Biogenic amines are chemicals in the brain and other parts of the central nervous system that are involved in the transmission of nerve impulses. One of these neurotransmitters is norepinephrine (NE), a catecholamine, and another is serotonin (5-hydroxytryptamine or 5-HT), an indoleamine. The following summaries are theoretical variations on the catecholamine-indoleamine theme:

1. The catecholamine theory hypothesizes that norepinephrine depletion causes depression. This brain system is associated with positive action, pleasant circumstances, and arousal.

2. The indoleamine theory hypothesizes that serotonin depletion causes depression. This brain system is associated with sleep, unpleasant or painful circumstances, and decreased responsiveness.

3. The permissive theory hypothesizes that depletion of both norepinephrine and serotonin causes depression.[10]

4. The two-disease theory hypothesizes that: (a) norepinephrine depletion coupled with a normal level of serotonin causes depression, and (b) serotonin depletion with a normal level of norepinephrine causes depression. This new emphasis is less on individual neurotransmitters, and more on interdependent relationships.[11]

Serotonin is found in the blood, pineal gland, and intestines. In the brain it serves as a communication device between nerve cells or neurons. Made in the body by the action of two enzymes on the compound tryptophon (contained in the food we eat), it is clear that serotonin levels are partly determined by diet. Knowledge concerning a remedial diet, however, is unclear. We do know that serotonin is eventually excreted in the urine. Physiological investigators continue to study the blood levels of serotonin and enzyme activity involved in its synthesis and degradation.[12]

The catecholamines have been far more extensively studied, but with more meager and inconsistent results. One of the few consistent relationships observed is a fall in the urinary compound 3-methoxy-4-hydroxyphenylethylene glycol, commonly called MHPG, when depression is present. It returns to normal levels upon recovery, or upon a shift into a manic phase. However, inactivity can also decrease MHPG levels. Since depressed people are typically less active than others, low levels might occur after the onset of depression rather than before.

Because the neurotransmitters can only be measured indirectly, and because findings have been inconsistent from study to study, the accuracy and results of biogenic amine research are highly controversial. Ross Baldessarini points out that the inductive logic used over the past two decades appears to be rational, but in fact is not when applied to pathophysiology or etiology. It does not follow, for example, that replacing norepinephrine will reduce depression, although antidepressant drugs that increase the output of norepinephrine alleviate symptoms. Such a conclusion may be no more logical than assuming a penicillin deficiency state in cases where the drug helps an illness.[13] But despite inadequate testing techniques and lack of homogeneity among groups of depressed people who are studied, important research continues. Alternative hypotheses involving acetycholine and dopamine neurotransmitters are also being explored.[14]

THE DEXAMETHASONE SUPPRESSION TEST

Bernard Carroll and his colleagues, among others, have recently established the Dexamethasone Suppression Test (DST) as a relatively simple diagnostic tool.[15] This test, comparably speaking, has both specificity and power, and is equivalent to or exceeds the usefulness of many "standard" laboratory tests. People with severe depression secrete a natural steroid called cortisol. Contrary to "normal" people (who react by suppressing the secretion of cortisol when dexamethasone is administered to them), the cortisol levels of depressed persons increase after a brief suppression of the adrenal secretion. Conditions other than depression, however, can also alter the results of this test. The DST is being standardized and can often detect both unipolar and bipolar cases (although bipolars, like other biochemical studies, have more positive rates). A family history of a major mood disorder can increase the rate of positive tests from 60 percent to as high as 80 percent or 90 percent. Even more important, negative DST (or dex test) results almost certainly exclude the diagnosis of manic-depressive illnesses. Studies supporting the DST have been replicated in a number of American and European psychiatric centers, involving almost one thousand depressed patients. Other studies question the use of the DST. While more research correlation with other biological measurements is needed, the use of DST as a predictor of depression is a real breakthrough. Still it is important to note that the DST alone can neither rule in nor rule out depression.

NEW DIRECTIONS: PEPTIDES

Other biochemical researchers in recent years have taken a new turn. Studies indicate a significant correlation between lumbar CSF (cerebrospinal fluid) endorphin levels and the depth of self-reported depressive symptoms. Endorphins (like enkophalins) are peptides, natural opiates in the body that respond to pain. Bela Almay's research analyzed such opiate receptor-active endorphins, concluding that this field of study provides new directions for neurologic/psychiatric depression researchers, for peptides are not neurotransmitters.[16]

Those who are particularly interested in the details of biomedical research can find concise, comprehensive overviews of research findings referenced under "Notes" in this chapter.[17]

WOMEN AT RISK

Female Endocrine Physiology[18]

Myrna M. Weissman and Gerald Klerman's extensive review of the research on female endocrine physiology dispels a number of myths concerning the relationship between female sex hormones and depression. The authors conclude that there is good evidence that premenstrual tension and use of oral contraceptives have what appears to be a very small effect on increased rates of depression. Francis Kane notes that women who take oral contraceptives and are most at risk seem to be those with a history of previous psychiatric illness, particularly when the illness was related to postpartum depression.[19] Kane sees the problems as iatrogenic, while Weissman and Klerman tell us that there is excellent evidence that the months following childbirth, the postpartum period, induce an increase in depression. The stresses of caring for newborn infants also may be a causal factor. The presence of children in the home as a concomitant of depression has recently been empirically validated.[20] Because women continue to have the lion's share of child-rearing responsibility, there is reason to believe that they become more vulnerable to depression.[21]

Contrary to popular opinion, Weissman and Klerman cite a number of studies that show that there is no evidence that women are at greater risk during the menopause. DSM III, an internationally respected diagnostic manual, has eliminated the diagnostic category, involutional melancholia, that had been associated with menopause.[22] While some sex differences in depression may be explained by endocrinology, Weissman and Klerman conclude that it is not sufficient to account for the high rate of depression in women. Instead, psychosocial explanations are advanced, particularly in relation to the female role.[23]

Electroconvulsive Therapy and Psychosurgery

It has been reported that a disproportionate number of women are treated by ECT and psychosurgery as compared with men. While some decry a malicious intent, others argue that the statistics reflect an unconscious cultural bias against women.[24] The Medical Committee for Human Rights notes that the evaluation of a psychosurgeon's success is controversial.[25] Patients are usually considered well, symptom-free, cured, or adjusted when they are capable of holding a job. The more menial and less intellectually demanding the job, the higher the chances for cure. It follows that the highest success rate is for women. Psychiatrists who have made a case for psychosurgery, for example, reported excellent results for ten of eighteen lobotomized females with prior symptoms of agitated depression.[26] Follow-up information upon which their conclusions were based cited seven of the ten women as: "able to do housework," "keeps house," "good housewife," and the like. Two of the remaining women who showed excellent results did not work outside the home, and one was said to be "happy and cheerful seventeen years later and busy in an old folks home." She was fifty-nine years old. Conclusions appear to be based upon traditional cultural roles. That societal roles and status may have had negative impact upon these depressed women was not addressed. In all fairness, the degree of distress prior to lobotomy was of such overwhelming intensity as to convince these psychiatrists that lobotomy was the treatment method of choice in carefully selected patients.

Those who support either the use of ECT or psychosurgery (and they are, of course, supported differentially) insist that these procedures can be highly therapeutic and often life-saving.[27] The fact that women are usually the recipients of treatment may only reflect statistical realities regarding the prevalence and incidence of depression in women. Still, the large numbers of women cannot be ignored. Our increasingly comprehensive insights regarding depression in relation to the position of women in society must be incorporated in professional decision making. The fact that lay people, who lack full understanding of treatment methods, must give prior written permission to undergo such treatment is meaningless when their knowledge of the issues is limited and psychic pain skews their perception.

Substance Abuse

A study published in 1972 reports that 71 percent of all antidepressants prescribed in 1967 were for women, as were 80 percent of all amphetamines.[28] This figure is even more alarming today, since the medical profession now questions even occasional use of amphetamines to achieve mood elevation. The drug dependency of women may in fact represent an iatrogenic disorder. Naomi Gottlieb's review of research on female drug dependency concludes that their addictions have developed through the pervasive prescription of drugs by physicians.[29] All too often physicians prescribe tranquilizers, for example, without assessing the psychosocial factors perpetuating women's symptoms. Because the symptoms of depression and anxiety reported by women are not understood, the mood-modifying drugs prescribed for them have far-reaching consequences. Gottlieb also concludes that the sexist drug advertisements in leading medical journals, analyzed by Jane Prather and Linda Fidell over a five-year period, fall on receptive ears.[30] She points out that the drug solution does not address the problem of societal expectations and women's dysfunctional life situation.[31]

The problem is not just a modern phenomenon; the higher prevalence of female drug addicts between the pre-Civil-War era and World War I has been attributed historically to the restricted lives of women during that period and the free prescription of opiates to them.[32] The abuse of barbiturate depressants appears to be paradoxically related to depressed women who are prescribed the drugs to reduce anxiety and induce sleep. Since anxiety and insomnia are two major symptoms of depression, the desire for barbiturates to relieve distress is as understandable today as it was a century ago. The National Survey on Drug Abuse indicates that one to two million women have problems because of their use and misuse of prescription drugs. The same explanations are applicable to female alcoholics. Because alcohol is a psychic pain killer that is also a depressant, habit forming, and addictive, it also has painful consequences. Moreover, the severely alcoholic woman is often dependent on more than one drug because the physician she consults often prescribes an antidepressant or amphetamine.

The similarities between alcoholism and depression are so great that some genetic researchers suggest that each condition may mask the other. Mark Schuckit and George Winokur report greater success in the treatment of the secondary affective disorder alcoholic, wherein the depressed woman has a history of depression.[33] Before the rising rates of female alcoholism came to the fore, Winokur conjectured that the increased frequency of depression in females might be explained by its greater likelihood to manifest itself as depression in women, while alcoholism was more likely to affect men (the male manifestation of the same problem.)[34] Does depression contain two or more subcategories, it was asked — females meeting the criteria for depression and males for alcoholism?[35] Or is the greater frequency of depression in women explained by X-linkage? According to these researchers, if the trait is dominant, females may be more likely to be affected because they have two X chromosomes. If such is the case, the appearance of X-linked dominant and recessive traits in parents of children of affected males and females should be predictable. To date, the findings continue to be inconsistent.[36] Even so, many studies support the model and must not be discounted as possible evidence of genetic transmission, however insufficient at this time.

The rising rates of alcohol abuse among women in recent years indicate that social expectations regarding the historically restricted use of alcohol for women may have had a greater influence over its use in the past. This appears to be especially relevant to lesbians who are reported to be directly affected by alcohol problems at a staggering rate of 25 to 35 percent of the known lesbian population.[37] They appear to be particularly vulnerable to the problem for three major psychosocial reasons. First, the lesbian community is a minority that is oppressed by all cultures; second, the lesbian bar is often the only available public setting for social activities; and third, services for alcoholism are unresponsive to lesbians.[38]

Emerging research indicates that chemically dependent women, whether drug or alcohol related, have needs and problems that are distinctive from men. New programs for women focus on their full development, rather than on their drug dependence alone. The inclusion of child-care services, female support groups, reeducation of professional staff, and enhancing the lifestyles and work options for women constitute an effective beginning.[39] While there is research to suggest the possibility of genetic, biochemical links to alcoholism, interventions must encompass psychosocial therapies.

Samuel Guze reports that long-term follow-up research is being conducted at the Washington University National Alcoholic Research Center. Women alcoholics, their nonalcoholic female siblings, and other nonalcoholic controls are being studied, while a similar investigation of depressed women is being conducted concurrently. Medical and psychological histories of the women are being collected, as well as personal and family information. An attempt is being made to distinguish between the alcoholic and the depressed women, as well as between alcoholic women and men.[40] The results should be illuminating from a combined biochemical, psychosocial perspective, particularly if the researchers have an encompassing orientation themselves. Respect for and knowledge about a given point of view, of course, influence what questions are asked and of whom, and how data are interpreted and reported. These factors will hold true for the remaining interdisciplinary research on the etiology of depression being conducted at major universities throughout the nation under the aegis of the National Institute of Mental Health.[41] Whatever the outcome, and whatever one's theoretical point of view, biochemical etiology of depression must be incorporated into psychosocial models. The organic arenas provide insights that will eventually have a positive impact on the future prognosis of depression, much as the "psychotropic revolution" following World War II did. Still, advancement will be tempered, in my view, by the degree to which the organic school incorporates psychosocial realities.

PREVENTION AND INTERVENTION

Biochemical theorists contend that depression is caused by chemical imbalances in the brain. Interventions vary in accordance with varying theoretical perspectives, just as they do in psychosocial disciplines. This section will briefly detail some of the more common

Tricyclic Antidepressants (Antipsychotic)[43]

Generic Names	Brand Names (USA)
Amitriptyline	Elavil Endes Etrafon Triavil
Desipramine	Norpramin Pertofrane
Doxepin	Adapin Sinequan
Imipramine	Imavate Janamine Presamine SK-Pramine Tofranil W.D.D.
Nortriptyline	Aventyl Pamelor
Protriptyline	Vivactil
Trazodone	Desyrel
Amoxapine	Asendin
Tetracyclic Magrotiline	Ludomic

antidepressants to familiarize the reader with the two major classes of antidepressant drugs, tricyclics and monoamine oxidase inhibitors (MAO-I). Each has a different chemical action. While research is not conclusive, it appears that tricyclic antidepressants generally block the reabsorption (reuptake) of norepinephrine or serotonin in the neuron. Monoamine oxidase inhibitors operate by preventing the degradation of norepinephrine or serotonin by the MAO enzymes in the neuron. Because MAO-I drugs produce more side-effects, more frequently interact with other drugs, and require adherence to dietary restrictions, tricyclics are usually the drug of choice for initial treatment.[42] Some of the more common tricyclics listed below are only representative of an ever-growing industry. Both contraindications for use and side effects are included in the discussion.

Having reviewed numerous controlled studies, Aaron Beck concludes that only about 60 to 65 percent of those who are treated with tricyclics show definite improvement.[44] James Long cautions against using these drugs with children under twelve and adults over sixty, those who are recovering from heart attacks, those who have had previous allergic reaction to any of the brand names relative to each drug, those who have narrow-angle-type glaucoma, and those who are taking a monoamine oxidase inhibitor drug, or have taken one within the last fourteen days.[45] Before they take tricyclics, Long suggests that patients inform their physicians if they are allergic to any tricyclic antidepressant, if they plan to have general anesthesia or surgery in the near future, or if they have a history of diabetes, epilepsy, glaucoma, heart disease, prostate gland enlargement, or overactive thyroid function. The greatest hazard may be the drug's very narrow margin of safe use. The level of drug that can cause adverse effects is quite close to the level required to be effective. Implications for suicidal patients are great. Trazodone, developed in 1982, appears to have fewer of these side-effects.

Depression symptoms may begin to lessen within one to two weeks, with four to six weeks or longer of continuous treatment required for an adequate response to the medication. Patients should be forewarned about possible side-effects. With the exception of protriptyline, which may be slightly stimulating, the tricyclics have varied degrees of sedative properties. Desipramine appears to have the least sedative action of those mentioned. This information is important in selecting a given drug. Many depressed people suffering from lack of sleep may welcome mild sedation. There is some indication, in fact, that tricyclics may even have a sleep-regularizing effect that involves the diminishing of interrupted sleep and early morning awakening along with the alleviation of depression. Even if this is true, those people who need to be alert during the day might find even mild sedation problematic.

All tricyclics have potent anticholinergic properties, which means that the effects of acetylcholine in the brain are decreased, an action peripherally responsible for many of the side-effects associated with tricyclics. They include dry mouth, blurred vision, constipation, urinary retention, tremors, sweating, and general confusion. While preliminary research indicates that tricyclics vary in degrees of anticholinergic action, the studies are limited. One investigation reports that Solomon Snyder and Henry Yamamura found Desipramine to have the least effect of those tricyclics that are also known for their sedative properties.[46] Although these studies are based on animal research, it may be well to keep these initial findings in mind when working with elderly patients. The elderly are especially susceptible to urinary retention and constipation, and are often subject to confusion and forgetfulness. A high-anticholinergic tricyclic would not be a drug of choice. It is not unusual, in fact, for elderly patients who have memory and orientation difficulty to be misdiagnosed as suffering from organic brain syndrome. When taken off antidepressant drugs, their symptoms abate. They may be depressed, but they are not senile.

Tricyclic drugs have no preventive properties against a relapse of mania in bipolar illness and, in fact, can precipitate manic attacks. Lithium, rather than tricyclics, is the drug of choice for these patients, according to an extensive review of research by John Davis.[47]

Barry Rosloff and John Davis point out that there is ample evidence that depression is not a homogenous disorder; studies suggest the existence of both biochemical and clinical subtypes. Since different tricyclics act differentially on the same subtype, there may be a number of mechanisms of action among the various tricyclic antidepressants.[48] They are not necessarily a uniform class of drugs. Rosloff and Davis themselves found that a clinically effective tricyclic called iprindole does not block amine reuptake on rat brain norepinephrine turnover when given regularly, unlike other tricyclics. This is interesting information, given the successful prescription of maintenance tricyclics to prevent depression in patients initially treated with tricyclics or electroshock.[49] There is much to be learned.

Monoamine Oxidase Inhibitors (MAO-I)

Monoamine oxidase inhibitor drugs, known as MAO-I, prolong norepinephrine and serotonin neurotransmission which researchers believe accounts for their antidepressant effects. Common MAO-I drugs are listed below:

Generic Names	*Brand Names*
Isocarboxazid	Morplan
Phenelzine	Nardil
Tranylcypromine	Parnate

MAO inhibitors can induce dangerous, even life-threatening, interactions with other drugs. Hypertension, agitation, severe headache, high fever, tremor, and even coma reflect severe toxic reactions. Patients may be at risk if the drug is inadvertently taken with a tricyclic or if tricyclics are still in their system, or following ingestion of foods and beverages containing tyramine. Tyramine raises blood pressure, a normal function that is generally neutralized by enzymes present in body tissues, principally monomine oxidase. MAO-I drugs block such action.

While any food containing protein that has undergone partial decomposition may present a hazard because of increased tyramine content, many foods and beverages contain a sufficient amount of tyramine to cause severe problems. Those singled out by Long[50] are listed below.

Foods	*Beverages*
Avocado	Beer (unpasteurized)
Banana skins	Chianti wines
Beef liver (improperly stored)	Vermouth
Broad bean pods	
Cheese—aged	
Sour cream	
Chicken liver (improperly stored)	
Dried fish—salted	
"Marmite" and "Bourie" extracts	
Meat extracts	
Pickled herring	
Raspberries	

It is clear that MAO inhibitors should only be prescribed to people who can comply with these rather severe restrictions. Those who do cooperate, who have a history of positive MAO-I response, or who have not responded to tricyclics may find MAO-I drugs effective.[51]

Lithium Carbonate

Lithium, a strong tranquilizer, was used almost exclusively for many years for treating the manic phase of manic-depression. Treatment is both remedial and preventive, for it has been shown to prevent or to reduce the severity of subsequent manic episodes, as well as depressive phases of bipolar affective disorder in more recent years. While it is the drug of choice in certain cases of frequently recurrent unipolar depressions, experts believe that these people may be mildly manic. Although it is too soon to predict the effectiveness of lithium in tandem with antidepressants for bipolar patients who are most likely to experience depression, there has been empirical support indicating that it may be so. Because conventional tricyclics and MAO inhibitors alone have not been effective for many bipolar patients, there is continued interest in relevant research.[52] Lithium carbonate is commonly known by the following brand names:

Eskalith
Lithone
Lithonate
Lithotabs
Pfi-Lithium

Physicians are cautioned to test the blood of patients who are on lithium regularly because high toxicity can lead to confusion, fine tremors, irritability, diarrhea, and nausea. It is contraindicated in pregnancy and there is some controversy about the long-term effects on the kidneys, though patients have been maintained on lithium for over twenty years without major problems. Like tricyclics, the lethal-dosage-to-therapeutic-dosage ratio is dangerously low. Also, children under twelve should not be given the drug, and it is likely that people over sixty will not tolerate it.[53] Lithium should not be prescribed for those with significant renal disorder, cardiac disease, organic brain damage, and salt intake dietary restriction.[54] The elderly are often candidates for these restrictions. Hence, multiple warnings should be respected when lithium is being considered in the treatment of older people.

Whether or not lithium really prevents or cures bipolar depression, and under what condition, is not known. The qualitative nature of lithium's effect is necessarily vague because placebo studies were not undertaken before efficacy was established. Now that efficacy has been proven, it is ethically questionable to withhold the drug in controlled studies.[55]

Major Tranquilizers—Anti-Anxiety Drugs and Sleep Disorders

There is empirical evidence that the monoamines, norepinephrine, and serotonin have been implicated in anxiety as well as depression. In fact, some researchers believe that it is possible that anxiety and depression are different names for the same fundamental state. They are so closely intertwined that experts often have great difficulty distinguishing between them. While anti-anxiety drugs are effective in reducing anxiety, their value extols a high price. Many insist that thioridazine (Mellaril) is the only major tranquilizer indicated for depressed patients who are experiencing anxiety. Because tranquilizers sedate or depress the central nervous system, these drugs exacerbate the problem and are contraindicated for most cases of depression. Treatment of sleep disorders may be one exception to be considered.

Sleep disturbances are symptomatic of most depressions, particularly in the form of early-morning insomnia. Yet, many other depressed people sleep all day as an escape from their psychic pain. It is wise to check whether the insomniac is also a daytime napper. In such cases, the antidote may be common sense. Preliminary checks on caffeine, alcohol, and other drug consumption should also be made routinely. They all disrupt sleep and may have depressive side-effects. Most cases, however, are not so easily remedied. Frequently, pharmacological treatment is prescribed for those who have inordinate difficulty sleeping through the night. Therapists who are not physicians may find it useful to collaborate when the need for medication arises. Sleep inducement is required for only a short time in many cases, just long enough to break the dysfunctional habit of focusing conscious attention on one's discomfort during periods of rest.

Physicians are becoming aware that the barbiturates that have been prescribed for decades are not only addictive, but dangerous when mixed with alcohol. Further, there is no good evidence that they improve sleep habits over time. In fact, they appear to interrupt normal sleep patterns. Instead, Dalmane, the trade name for a tranquilizer called flurazepam, is the most frequently prescribed sleeping pill in the country today. It is considered safer, particularly when dosage remains at 15 milligrams, and is generally more effective than barbiturates. Dalmane is a benzodiazine, as are Valium, Serax, and Librium. According to Timothy Johnson and Stephen Goldfinger[56] of Harvard Medical School, none of these tranquilizers is effective over twenty days. Despite their relative harmlessness, Dalmane, like other benzodiazines, also has potential problems when used for sleep. It can, for instance, remain in the blood for up to eight days and may become cumulative with repeated use. Because it causes drowsiness when mixed with alcohol, people who have taken the drug within a period of a few days should not drink when they are planning to drive. While a 15-milligram dose has been found to have fewer side-effects, and to induce sleep quite adequately, physicians must continue to weigh their decision to prescribe the drug against its implications for depressed people. Dalmane, like other tranquilizers, depresses the central nervous system.

While on the subject of the treatment of sleep disorders, I will take the opportunity to present two less common therapies that are being used in inpatient settings in experimental projects throughout the world. Given that sleep is meant to be restorative for the most part, a time of vital energy renewal, the Japanese have focused directly on this principle with some success. They have prescribed Morita Therapy, whereby severely depressed patients are hospitalized and sleep is induced continuously for two weeks. Equally radical, sleep deprivation is an antidepressant treatment developed in recent years in Germany. The antithesis of sleep as a restorative function, the depressed patient is kept awake continuously for thirty-six hours. The procedure is carried out once or twice a week and, if warranted, may be repeated another six or seven times. A highly successful innovation, it is thought that the adrenergic system may be involved with the resulting metabolic and endocrine changes.

Research indicates that deprivation of REM (rapid eye movement) sleep has a favorable influence on depression, a factor that may come into play.[57] REM is the fifth and final stage of sleep which follows four stages of ever-deepening relaxation, and is associated with dreaming. Primary endogenous depressions can be differentiated from secondary depressions associated with other medical or psychiatric illnesses (or insomnia unrelated to depression) in over 80 percent of cases, based on REM characteristics. In depressed people, REM activity increases in the early stages of sleep and remains steady, whereas REM increases in normals as the night goes on. Shortened REM latency (the period of sleep prior to the initial REM sleep) is a major characteristic of depression. While there appear to be no sex differences in REM latency, it does decrease with age from a mean of 60 minutes in 18- to 25-year-olds to less than 50 minutes in 40-year-olds and 40 minutes in people over 50. Persons who score 90 or less when REM latency is added to their age are more than likely depressed.[58]

TREATMENT ISSUES

Psychopharmacology

Drug therapy can make the difference between functioning and despair, indeed, between life and death. But there are precautions to keep in mind when drugs are prescribed in the absence of psychotherapy. Research indicates that chemotherapy may lead patients to attribute their problems to chemical imbalance, and that this may undermine their own coping mechanisms.[59] Beck and his colleagues note that as much as 50 percent of those treated with drugs have a relapse in the year following termination.[60] It may be that their disinclination to look to themselves and to the environment as focal points for change may result in this relatively high rate. Those who prescribe only drugs also may be likely to ignore all but chemical imbalance as causal, thus influencing their patients. The biochemical orientation of both the patient and the doctor may perpetuate a crisis, rather than taking a preventive perspective. The same precaution should be taken relative to electroconvulsive therapy. Should the prescribing physician not wish to be directly involved in psychotherapeutic intervention, cooperation with a therapist can be a very effective alliance.

Electroconvulsive Therapy[61]

Electroconvulsive therapy (ECT) and electroshock treatment (EST) are the same thing. Few interventions have caused the controversy evoked by this treatment since its development in 1938. While the administration of ECT varies considerably, the modified procedure currently in use is fairly consistent. Subjects are not allowed to eat or drink for at least four hours prior to treatment. Tranquilizers or sedatives may be used to reduce fear and/or resistance. Atropine, a common preanesthetic medication, is administered half an hour in advance in order to dry secretions in the mouth and airway, thus reducing the risk of suffocation and any complications that might result from swallowing saliva. Dentures, sharp jewelry, and hairpins are removed; bowels and bladder are emptied, and the patient is ready for treatment.

Placed on a thickly padded table, graphite jelly is applied to two areas of the temples where the electrodes will be positioned, in order to prevent burns and increase conductivity. A rubber gag is inserted in the mouth to protect the teeth and prevent the patient from swallowing his tongue. Then, a fast-acting barbiturate anesthetic is injected intravenously, immediately rendering the patient unconscious. Anectine, a synthetic muscle relaxant is administered to reduce the risk of bone dislocation and fractures. For years, before this preventive measure was taken, dislocation and fracture of the back was a common side-effect of the convulsive seizures; hence its importance. Since the muscle relaxant causes almost complete paralysis, including respiratory paralysis, breathing must be assisted artificially.

Next the electrodes are placed at the temples. Seventy to 175 volts of electricity penetrate the brain for one-tenth of one and one-half seconds. Almost immediately the facial muscles stiffen, indicating that the tonic phase of the convulsion has begun. The clonic, or active, phase starts in ten seconds and continues for thirty to forty seconds. The modified procedure causes a slight twitching of the toes, an immeasurable improvement over the grand mal seizures that result when a preventive muscle relaxant has not been administered. Though less common in recent years, the unmodified procedure is sometimes used even today.

In either case, convulsions are followed by a coma that lasts for several minutes. Upon reviving, the patient may experience severe headache, dizziness, physical weakness, muscle ache, vomiting, and nausea, as well as confusion, disorientation, and memory loss. Within a few hours most of these side-effects subside, except for weakness, amnesia, and confusion, which continue at least through the day. Indeed, loss of memory and disorientation may persist for two weeks to two months following six to twelve treatments, the normal ECT series for depressed patients.

Fear of loss of control or even fear of dying is readily understandable in the case of electroshock patients and should be addressed by the clinician. Less likely to be acknowledged is the damage done to an already fragile sense of self-esteem. ECT can be a humiliating experience, a procedure that is subjectively dehumanizing. Rather than fear death, the patient may fear waking from the seizure and facing those who have witnessed it — often the therapist him or herself. ECT also plays directly into "justifiable" punishment fantasies for those already riddled with self-blame. For these reasons alone, I believe the treatment is contraindicated. Should a physician decide in favor of ECT, time should be taken to gently explore these feelings that are so congruent with the depressed person's sense of self. To ignore them or to be superficial in regard to them is destructive to the patient and will hinder the progress of treatment.

Others critical of ECT claim that some memory is irretrievably lost. In addition to amnesia, they caution that reduced intellectual function, loss of creativity, energy, and enthusiasm, and a general emotional blunting may result from prolonged treatment. The number of treatments, their spacing, and the intensity of electric current may greatly influence the persistence and severity of these side-effects. The newer, unilateral ECT which places the electrodes on the right, nonverbal hemisphere of the brain may reduce memory loss. Opponents argue that spacial relations and nonlinear modes of consciousness are still subject to damage.

There is little doubt that ECT has been abusive. It has been used to avoid time-consuming involvement with patients at best and even to punish troublesome patients in mental hospitals. And so the pro and con dialog continues.[62] Because human studies cannot include control groups, the effectiveness of the treatment is in question. Much of the research has been confined to rats.[63] Davis notes that it is well established that many patients relapse months after receiving ECT. For this reason he advocates tricyclics as maintenance treatment following electroconvulsive therapy.

Still, many believe that ECT is the most effective somatic treatment for severe depressive reactions. Recent research concludes that it gradually increases brain catecholamine synthesis, thus supporting the catecholamine hypothesis.[64] The mechanism of action is still unknown. Those who support its use insist that previously despondent and suicidal people are lifted from their despair and able to function in the world. While ECT was originally the treatment of last resort, proponents today often administer shock on an outpatient basis to people who are not alone and can continue to live at home throughout the treatment process. Contrary to those who believe that ECT is a treatment relegated to history, or that it should be outlawed, electroconvulsive therapy continues to be a not unusual medical intervention in many states. Prior to public review, it was more commonly used in state facilities, but today private psychiatric institutions are more likely to employ the method.

Psychosurgery

Resort to psychosurgical techniques is limited to the most severe cases of depression when all other possible avenues of relief have failed. Though no longer a common procedure, it does persist. For those who are being considered as candidates, frequency of occurrence is a moot point. For this reason, the subject is included. Readers should not be surprised that I am unequivocably opposed to the practice. Physicians who claim to have tried "all other avenues of relief" to my knowledge have not been familiar with those avenues, nor have their referral sources. The procedure is too radical to take a compromise position, for the operation is irreversible.

Psychosurgery is the removal or destruction of brain tissue, or electrical stimulation of parts of the brain, in order to modify disturbed behavior. From the 1930s to the 1950s, prefrontal lobotomies, the most common form of psychosurgery, were performed on 50,000 people in the United States alone. The operation fell into disrepute until the mid-1960s when there was a worldwide resurgence of the practice. Today, it is estimated that between 600 and 1,000 such operations are performed in this country annually. Thought to be less hazardous than the earlier techniques, most psychosurgical procedures still involve the frontal lobe or its immediate connections. These are parts of projections of the limbic system, that area of the brain thought to control expression of emotion. Depressed and violent emotions are prime targets.

The two most prevalent operations are amygdalotomy (where portions of the temporal lobes are destroyed), and cingulotomy (where portions of the cingulum are destroyed). The cingulum is a region that acts as a kind of relay station to send information from various parts of the brain to the frontal lobes. The more widely used modern psychosurgical procedure, the purpose of cingulotomy is to cut the information track leading to the frontal lobes. While its purpose is similar to the old prefrontal lobotomy, it is a safer procedure surgically because it does not destroy as much tissue. Peter Breggin charges that all of the techniques have the effect of blunting affect.[65] The higher functions of the brain are eliminated, so people typically lose their ability for introspection and abstract thinking. The desired effect of psychosurgery, he argues, is pacification rather than cure. Philip Solomon and Vernon Patch provide an excellent synopsis and bibliography, which I recommended to those who wish to pursue the issues and procedures in technical detail.[42] For our purposes, their conclusion that such psychosurgical procedures do not attack the causes of most mental diseases is an important one. While judicious surgery has been helpful to a carefully selected number of cases, the decision for such an extreme operation on the brain seldom appears to be either ethically or practically sound. What may seem to be a rational, humane intervention appropriate to a person with long-term unremitting psychic pain, may be a decision more helpful to the physician who is frustrated by feelings of helplessness in effectively treating his or her patient. Not only have psychotropic drugs vastly alleviated that frustration, changing the frequency with which psychosurgery is done, but growing knowledge concerning the impact of the environment on the delvelopment and well-being of people should be of influence.

Decisions, as well as evaluations of improvement, must be based upon information about personality and behavior from a number of sources. People making such decisions must come from a variety of theoretical perspectives. A chemical or neurosurgical orientation may bias one's perspective, just as psychosocial biases may inhibit organic insights. Those who are not involved must be included, for family and surgical teams are equally likely to influence decision making and assessment for personal reasons. Solomon and Patch note that patients are often anxious not to disappoint the physicians who have tried to help them. The same may be true of families and colleagues. In either case, decisions and/or evaluations may be skewed.

Iatrogenic Depression

Iatrogenic refers to those illnesses that occur as the result of pharmacologic agents used to treat patients. In recent years, there has been increasing concern about iatrogenic depression, a "disease of medical progress."[67] The onset of toxic depression, for example, may occur in patients sensitive to the use of drugs. In hospital settings, side-effects may be overlooked by those not trained to be aware of them. The suffering of medical patients may go unheeded, and elderly or psychiatric patients may be assumed to be severly depressed as a result of unknown causes when, in fact, drugs are exacerbating symptoms. If depression is the result of simple toxicity, the body will eliminate it in twenty four to forty five hours after termination of the drug. If, however, the nervous system has been seriously disrupted, the toxic effect will remain for an extended period. The same is true of bodily infections, which can also trigger low-grade depression not easily thrown off even after the viral infection is gone. The central nervous system also is affected when an operation or a physical injury impacts on the body. In such cases, traumatic shock may inhibit blood circulation throughout the body, together with chemical changes. The depressive reaction, however, usually lasts only as long as the nervous system is impaired.[68]

The effects of minor routine procedures that are considered technologically safe by medical personnel may go unnoticed. When such processes as x-ray, anesthesia, and intravenous procedures must be employed, for example, clinicians should explain them clearly, recognizing their traumatic potential. Many patients fear them as a loss of control, which can cause tremendous anxiety that may lead to depression.

NOTES

1. Winokur, George, Paula Clayton, and Theodore Reich, *Manic Depressive Illness (St. Louis: C.V. Mosby, 1969). See also C. Perris (ed.) "A Study of Bipolar Psychosis," Acta Psychiatry of Scandiravia 42*, Supplement 194, (1966: 1–89); Myrna M. Weissman and Gerald L. Klerman, "Sex Differences and the Epidemiology of Depression," *Archives of General Psychiatry 34*, 1 (January 1977): 98–111; Susan L. Farber, *Identical Twins Reared Apart* (New York: Basic Books, 1981).

2. Rimmer, John D., "The Association between Selected Social, Academic, and Genetic Variables, and College Student Psychiatric Illness," Unpublished doctoral dissertation, Washington University, St. Louis, MO, August 1973; see also John D., Rimmer, J. A. Halikas, Marc A. Schukit, and James N. McClure, "A Systematic Study of Psychiatric Illness in Freshman College Students," *Comprehensive Psychiatry 19* (1978): 247–252.

3. Schuckit, Marc A., et al., "A Study of Alcoholism in Half-Siblings," *American Journal of Psychiatry 128* (1972): 1132–1136.

4. Juel-Nielsen, Niels, *Individual and Environment* (New York: International Universities Press, 1981); see also Susan L. Farber, *Identical Twins Reared Apart* (New York: Basic Books, 1981).

5. Baldessarini, Ross J., "A Summary of Biomedical Aspects of Mood Disorders," *McLean Hospital Journal 6*, 1 (1981): 1–34 (Belmont, MA); note that biochemical research is validating genetic (familial) influence, generally associated with psychoanalytic theories.

6. George Winokur, Paula Clayton, and Theodore Reich, *Manic Depressive Illness* (St. Louis: C. V. Mosby, 1969); see also J. Mendlewicz, and Baron Shopsin, eds., *Genetic Aspects of Affective Illness: Current Concepts* (New York: Spectrum Publications, 1979).

7. Weitkamp, Lowell R., Harvey C. Stancer, Emmanuel Persad, Christine Flood, and Sally Guttormsen, "Depressive Disorders and HLA: A Gene on Chromosome 6 that Can Affect Behavior," *New England Journal of Medicine 305* 22 (November 26, 1981): 1301–1306.

8. Baldessarini, Ross J., "A Summary of Biomedical Aspects of Mood Disorders," *McLean Hospital Journal 6* (1981).

9. Tatrelli, R., U. Godai, and P. Nardone, "Contributions of Genetic Studies to the Psychiatric Nosology and Nosography," *Acta Neurologica 31* 2 (March–April 1976): 206–244 (English summary).

10. Prange, A.J., I.C. Wilson, P.F. Lara, L.B. Alltop, and R.A. Stikelea, "L-Tryptophan in Mania; Contribution to a Permissive Hypothesis of Affective Disorders," *Archives of General Psychiatry 30* (1974): 56–62.

11. Davis, Kenneth L., Philip Berger, Leo E. Hollister, and Jack D. Barchas, "Cholinergic Involvement in Mental Disorders," *Life Sciences 22* 21 (June 1978): 1865–1871.

12. Silverman, Peter, Patricia Kralik, and Dorothy Taylor, "What is Serotonin?" *The Emissary*, Texas Research Institute of Mental Sciences, August 1981, pp. 10-11.

13. Baldessarini, Ross J., "A Summary of Biomedical Aspects of Mood Disorders," *McLean Hospital Journal 6*, 1 (1981).

14. Prange, A.J., I.C. Wilsin, P.F. Lara et al., "L-Tryptophan in Mania: Contribution to a Permissive Hypothesis of Affective Disorders," *Archives of General Psychiatry 30* (1974): 56 − 62; see also R. A. Depue, and R. Evans, "The Psychobiology of Depressive Disorders," in *Process in Experimental Personality Research*, Vol. 8, ed. B. H. Maher (New York: Academic Press, 1976); C. Perris and L. Van Knorring, eds., *Neurophysiological Aspects of Psychopathological Conditions (Advances in Biological Psychiatry*, Vol. 4) (New York: S. Karger, 1980).

15. Carroll, Bernard J., "Implications of Biological Research for the Diagnosis of Depression," in *New Advances in the Diagnosis and Treatment of Depressive Illness* ed. J. Mendelwicz (Amsterdam: Elsevier, 1981).

16. Almay, Bela G.L., Folke Johanssen, Lars Von Knorring et al. "Endorphins in Chronic Pain: Differences in CSF Endorphin Levels between Organic and Psychogenic Pain Syndromes," *Pain 5* 2 (August 1978): 153 − 162.

17. Baldessarini, Ross J., "A Summary of Biomedical Aspects of Mood Disorders," *McLean Hospital Journal 6*, 1 (1981); see also Ross J. Baldessarini, "Overview of Recent Advances in Anti-depressant Pharmacology: Part II," *McLean Hospital Journal 8*, 1 (1982): 1 − 27; U. S. Department of Health and Human Services, *Special Report on Depression Research*, DHHS Pub. No. (ADM) 81-1085 (Washington, DC: 1981); Akiskal, Hagops. and Raffi Tashlian, "Affective Disorders: II. Recent Advances in Laboratory and Pathogenetic Approaches," *Hospital and Community Psychiatry 39*, 9 (September 1983): 822 − 830. See also George Winokur, *Depression: The Facts* (New York: Oxford, University Press, 1981) for a comprehensive discussion of the medical model perspective on mood disorders.

18. Weissman, Myrna M., and Gerald L. Klerman, "Sex Differences and the Epidemiology of Depression," *Archives of General Psychiatry 34* 1 (January 1977).

19. Kane, Francis J., "Iatrogenic Depression in Women," *Phenomenology and Treatment of Depression* (New York: Spectrum Publications, 1977), pp. 69-80.

20. Brown, George W., and Tirril Harris, *Social Origins of Depression* (New York: Free Press, 1978).

21. See Chapter 4 and 5 for discussion of the presence of children in the family and women's depression.

22. DSM III, 1980.

23. Refer to Chapter 4 for discussion of role theory and depression.

24. Breggin, Peter Roger, "The Second Wave," *Mental Hygiene* (March 1973); see also Roy L. Frank, ed., *The History of Shock Treatment* (San Francisco: NAPA, 1975).

25. Medical Committee for Human Rights, *Psychosurgery: Abuse of Medicine for Social Control* (Washington, DC: Spring 1973).

26. Shobe, Frank O., and Margaret C. L. Gildea, "Long-term Follow-up of Selected Lobotomized Private Patients," *Journal of the American Medical Association 206*, 2 (October 7, 1968): 327 − 332.

27. Ibid.; see also Robert E. Peck, *The Miracle of Shock Treatment* (New York: Exposition Press, 1974).

28. Brecher, Edward M., and the Editors of Consumer Reports, *Licit and Illicit Drugs* (Boston: Little, Brown, 1972).

29. Gottlieb, Naomi, ed., *Alternative Social Service for Women* (New York: Columbia University Press, 1980).

30. Prather, Jane, and Linda Fidell, "Put Her Down and Drug Her Up," Paper presented at the American Sociological Associaton, Annual Program Meeting, New Orleans, LA, 1972.

31. See Chapter 4 for a discussion of social roles, women, and depression.

32. Cuskey, Walter, T. Premkumar, and Lois Sigel, "Survey of Opiate Addition among Females in the United States between 1950 and 1970," *Public Health Review 1* (1972): 6 – 39.

33. Schuckit, Marc, and George Winokur, "A Short-term Follow-up of Women Alcoholics," *Diseases of the Nervous System 33* (1972).

34. Winokur, George, "Types of Depressive Illness," *British Journal of Psychiatry 120* 556 (1972): 265 – 266.

35. Dorzab, Joe, Max Baker, Remi Cadoret, and George Winokur, "Depressive Disease: Familial Psychiatric Illness," *American Journal of Psychiatry 127* 9 (1971): 1128 – 1133.

36. Weissman, Myrna M., and Gerald L. Klerman, "Sex Differences and the Epidemiology of Depression," *Archives of General Psychiatry 34* 1 (January 1977).

37. Fifeld, Lillene, "On the Way to Nowhere: An Analysis of Gay Alcohol Abuse and an Evaluation of Alcoholism Rehabilitation Services of the Los Angeles Gay Community" (Los Angeles: County of Los Angeles, 1975).

38. Refer to Naomi Gottlieb, ed., *Alternative Social Service for Women* (New York: Columbia University Press, 1980), for a discussion of alcoholism and lesbians.

39. See ibid. for a comprehensive collection of alternative programs and services for women.

40. Guze, Samuel B., "Genetics, Health Risks are Topics of Research at Center," National Clearinghouse for Alcoholic Information of the National Institute on Alcohol Abuse and Alcoholism, IFS No. 81, March 3, 1981, p. 2.

41. The final bio-psychosocial reports from the National Institute of Mental Health should be available by the mid-1980s. Contact the Depression Branch for information.

42. Robins, Eli, and B. Y. Hartmann, in *Basic Neurochemistry*, ed. R. W. Alpers, et al. (Boston: Little, brown, 1972).

43. Long, James W., *The Essential Guide to Prescription Drugs* (New York: harper and Row, 1977).

44. Beck, Aaron T., *The Diagnosis and Management of Depression* (Philadelphia: University of Pennsylvania Press, 1973).

45. Long, James W., *The Essential Guide to Prescription Drugs* (New York: Harper and Row, 1977).

46. Snyder, Solomon H., and Henry I. Yamamura, "Antidepressants and the Muscarinic Acetylcholine Receptor," *Archives of General Psychiatry 34* 2 (February 1977): 236 – 239.

47. Davis, John M., "Overview: Maintenance Therapy in Psychiatry: II. Affective Disorders," *American Journal of Psychiatry 133* 1 (January 1976): 1 – 8.

48. Rosloff, Barry, and John M. Davis, "Decrease in Brain—NE Turnover after Chronic DMI Treatment," *Psychopharmacology 56* (1978): 335 – 341.

49. See, for example, research by Gerald Klerman and Eugene Paykel, among others, reviewed by John Davis, "Overview: Maintenance Therapy in Psychiatry: II. Affective Disorders," *American Journal of Psychiatry 133* 1 (January 1976): 1 – 8.

50. Long, James W., *The Essential Guide to Prescription Drugs* (New York: Harper and Row, 1977).

51. Sutherland Learning Associates, *Depression Today: Confident Clinical Office Management* (New York: C.M.E. Communications, Inc., 1978).

52. U. S. Department of Health, Education, and Welfare, *Lithium in the Treatment of Mood Disorders*, DHEW pub. No. (ADM) 77-73 (Washington, DC: DHEW reprinted 1977).

53. Long, James W., *The Essential Guide to Prescription Drugs* (New York: Harper and Row, 1977).

54. Sutherland Learning Association, *Depression Today: Confident Clinical Office Management* (New York: C.M.E. Communications, Inc., 1978).

55. Davis, John M., "Overview: Maintenance Therapy in Psychiatry: II. Affective Disorders," *American Journal of Psychiatry 133* 1, (January 1976): 1–8.

56. Johnson, G. Timothy, and Stephen e. Goldfinger, *The Harvard Medical School Health Letter Book* (Cambridge, MA: Harvard University Press, 1981).

57. Usdin, Gene, *Depression: Clinical Biological and Psychological Perspectives* (New York: Brunner/Mazel, 1977).

58. Vogel, G. M., "A Review of REM Sleep Deprivation," *Archives of General Psychiatry 32* (1975): 749–761. See Chapter 6 for further discussion of interventions for sleeping problems. Also refer to research by Christian Gillin and David Kupfer, Sleep Studies Unit, NIMH Biological Psychiatry Branch, University of Pittsburgh Medical School, Pittsburgh, Pennsylvania.

59. Shapiro, A. K., and L. A. Morris, "Placebo Effects in Medical and Psychological Therapies," in S. L. Garfield and A. E. Bergin, eds., *Handbook of Psychotherapy and Behavior Change: An Empirical Analysis*, 2nd ed., ed. S.L. Garfield and A.E. Bergin 1978).

60. Beck, Aaron T., A. John Rush, Brian F. Shaw, and Gary Emery, *Cognitive Therapy of Depression* (New York: Guilford Press, 1979). Also refer to Interpersonal Therapy, Chapter 5.

61. Sutherland Learning Associates, *Depression Today: Confident Clinical Office Management* (New York: C.M.E. Communications, Inc., 1978); also refer to Roy L. Frank, ed., *The History of ?Shock Treatment* (San Francisco: NAPA, 1975).

62. Peck, Robert E., *The Miracle of Shock Treatment*. (New York: Exposition Press, 1974).

63. See, for example, Ghanshyam N. Pandey, William J. Heinze, Barbara D. Brown, and John M. Davis "Electro Convulsive Shock Treatment Decreases Beta-Adrenergic Reception Sensitivity in Rat Brain," *Nature 280* (July 19, 1979): 234–235.

64. Dysken, Maurice W., Ghanshyam N. Pandey, Sidney S. Change, Robert Hicks, and John M. Davis. "Serial Postdexamethasone Cortisol Levels in a Patient Undergoing ECT "*American Journal of Psychiatry 136*, 10, (October 1979): 1328–1329.

65. Breggin, Peter Roger, "The Second Wave," *Mental Hygiene* (March 1973).

66. Solomon, Phillip, and Vernon D. Patch, *Handbook of Psychiatry* (Los Altos, CA: Lange Medical Publications, 1974).

67. LaSagna, Louis, "The Disease Drugs Cause," *Perspectives on Biological Medicine 7* (1964): 7.

68. Harris, Joan, "Depression and Illness," Unpublished manuscript, Washington University, St. Louis, MO (July 1975).

Chapter 9

Analysis Plus Synthesis Equals Synergy

A TRANSFORMATIONAL MATRIX

> Make me a way out of the stone
> a spiral staircase
> a bridge of suspended hope.
> Catherine de Vinck, *A Book of Uncommon Prayers*

Despite appearances to the contrary, nobody really believes that human beings can be dissected and compartmentalized into psychological, social, biological, or even spiritual fragments. Still, rival orthodoxies compete for prominence as if this were so. How much richer we would be if we were to accept dichotomies and complexities as valuable possibilities for understanding human behavior, adding essential pieces to the puzzle of depression. There are many more commonalities among disciplines than there are differences, a fact that also requires the relinquishing of our circumscribed attitudes and values. Just as identical terms are not always synonymous, so new vocabularies do not invariably reflect untried ideas. This chapter will synthesize the array of theoretical perspectives that have been reviewed and analyzed, searching for common principles, and attempting to make sense out of contradictions. By so doing, it will become evident that divergent disciplines are not only compatible, but complementary and often indistinguishable. If we discontinue competitive rivalries, our insights will be enriched by inclusive valuing, which is much more likely to reflect reality. An encompassing framework can help to illuminate the paradoxical riddles that beset our clients — indeed, that beset ourselves. By analyzing common denominators across theoretical perspectives of human development and depression, a Transformational Matrix, a comprehensive paradigm, evolves. The combined wisdom of each model unites in a greater understanding of what may be eternal principles.

Synthesis, the combining of separate elements to form a coherent whole, is a necessary but not sufficient part of the process. It is synergy that is needed — the action of two or more elements to achieve an effect of which each is individually incapable. The word synergy derives from the Greek *sunergos*, "working together." The concept was first brought to the social sciences and to the realm of ideas by anthropologist Ruth Benedict.[1] Later, Abraham Maslow devoted himself to the subject, contending as Benedict did, that our conception of culture and our relation to it must change in the direction of synergy. Rather than inhibiting needs, culture must come to gratify them. There should be more stress on the collaboration and synergy of the individual-culture dichotomy, they both argued, rather than on the antagonism between the two. Maslow's observational studies reveal that seemingly inherent, conflicting diversities and polarities dissolve in the merging coalescence and unity of oppositions. Before conflicting values can be reconciled synergistically, however, they must be polarized.[2] By applying these principles to human development and depression, common denominators found in the multiplicity of theories will be discussed from both negative and positive standpoints. Both perspectives are central to a wholistic assessment of human development and depression. They encompass the theoretically shared polarities of the inner psychic world, the self, and positive and negative aspects of social environments in the outer world. We will find that the parallel positive and negative notions, like the inner self and outer world, intersect to create shared pathways of understanding.[3]

COMMON DEPRESSION THEMES:
ANALYSIS PLUS SYNTHESIS

Neutral terms were selected for each of the common themes so as to retain a comprehensive stance. The negative themes reflect depression, and the positive, structural development. This is not to imply that depression represents the lower end of a developmental continuum. Rather, depression is conceptualized as a biophysical manifestation of a developmental need. That need may emerge as easily at an advanced level as at a more primitive one. The themes common to each dimension of development reflect different needs at successive stages. They will be addressed later when developmental paradoxes are discussed. First, let us consider the identified themes themselves — connectedness, aloneness, perception, and action, all relative to depression.

THE INNER SELF

Negative Connectedness = Depression

Without exception, each theory of depression is concerned with negative connectedness. Whether conceived as dependence or pathological attachment, the central theme is clear. As one matures, human connectedness can have dysfunctional properties. Viewed as a developmental phase, a psychological trait, or a state of being, connectedness can become a liability rather than a strength. Those who have an overinvestment in and psychological need for approval and worth from others will be subject to depression. Such people are motivated by deficiency, looking to others for gratifications, whether it be for safety, love, respect, prestige, or belongingness.[4] Because their self-esteem is so fragile, they cannot consider their own opinions as valid, and so they are likely to be easily influenced. Through identification or internalization, they are motivated and inhibited by the need for approval from those, both living and dead, who are dominant in their lives. For the psychoanalytic thinker, it is mother, father, wife or husband. From a sociocultural view, it is the dominant members of society who largely influence and perpetuate unhealthy dependence in subordinate groups. In any case, those who are undifferentiated, dependent, attached in a negative sense to others, are sustained externally. Their inner selves are found wanting. These are the people in search of nurturance. Often nurturers themselves, the dependent need more support than anyone else. The irony is that they receive less, though they often give more.[5] The giving is motivated, at least in part, by inner deficits. There are strings attached to dependent love — connectedness, which necessarily, out of neediness, has negative overtones.

Negative Aloneness = Depression

As infants reach childhood and adulthood, attachment behavior becomes less adaptive. When the theoretical focus is on separation from parental figures, it is easy to overlook negative aspects of separation that masquerade as maturity. Whether reflected in an aloof savoir-faire style, or a tough hard-headed "loner" attitude, the inability to relate to others is similar. Negative aloneness can be labeled "aliena-tion." People who take on this role are often vulnerable to depression when loneliness starts to crack their fabricated veneer. Denial of the need for others, of their own very real dependence and desire for relationship, is no longer operating as an effective defense. Typically, depressed persons who fit this description are those who never had a childhood themselves. They were "parentified children" who played the role of the responsible adult in the family long before their time. There are many roads to inauthenticity and depression, but this is the most heavily traveled. Such adults, like their childhood selves, never had a chance to find out who they really are. Wearing masks and playing roles, they learn early on to be many *things* to many people. By so doing, they remain *things*; the human self is denied and repressed.

And so it is with those who travel another route to depression — that of cultural socialization. The journey often is taken by males who are likely to have separated from their mothers prematurely, probably due to cultural negation of the feminine; possibly it is due in part to psychosexual drives that left them retreating from a symbolically in-cestuous relationship with their mothers.[6] But fathers are also likely to be nonrelational because of their own socialization, leaving their sons emotionally bereft and psychologically alone. For whatever reasons, then, males are encouraged toward early independence, obviating relational development in direct contrast to their sisters. Alienation, if not reflected in depression, may be masked by alcohol and violence. A common theme in the depression literature is object loss, which is the ultimate expression of negative separation.[7] It has been reconcep-tualized as loss of self-esteem, loss of role, goal, control, sexual desir-ability, energy, positive reinforcers, and even existential meaning, to name a few of the common interpretations of loss. In my opinion, these alternative renditions of loss might be transposed more accurately as "lack of." The only thing we can be sure of is that we all (at least most people, to date) have lived in a womb. Other conditions, ostensibly lost, may never have existed. In such cases, the depressing circum-stances reflect human deprivation rather than loss. They are barome-ters of negative aloneness, the alienation of persons from persons, persons from identity, or perhaps persons from spirit.

The archtypical negative aloneness, of course, is the orphaned child. Research provides evidence that loss of the mother before age twelve creates depression vulnerability.[8] Like other losses caused by death, however, it is an important vulnerability factor, not a direct cause in and of itself. Personality traits and life circumstances will cluster to protect the adult from or expose him or her to depression's grasp. For those who again are left alone — the bereaved parent, the abandoned spouse, the estranged friend — the risk is increased.

Negative Perception = Depression

Perception is a recurring thesis in a variety of disparate theories on depression, ranging from psychoanalytic to cognitive, behavioral, existential, and even biochemical approaches. How people view themselves, their acquaintances, and the world at large are tell-tale signs pointing toward or away from depression. So, too, is their perception of the past, the present, and the future. Regardless of the reality of the individual's situations or self, negative perception is believed almost universally to lead to depression. Aaron Beck has emerged as the outstanding cognitive proponent of the day, having validated the concept empirically.[9] He notes that the propensity of depressed people to a "negative cognitive set" is reflected by their automatic negative thoughts, even in dreams, and the way they structure their world, the self, and the future negatively. When people see themselves as worthless, inept, powerless, and helpless, and have always viewed themselves accordingly in the past, they will perceive themselves the same way in the future. Lack of self-esteem and hopelessness in the face of nothing better to look forward to, not surprisingly, is depressing. It also is a fertile condition for resentment. These concepts have been touted since the Abraham-Freud era.[10] However unsupported the research correlating hostility and depression may be, [11] clinicians can expect to find anger a very real presence in their work with the depressed. It is not anger that is so corrosive; it is the powerlessness of their anger, that multiplies the negativity measurably.

Lack of self-esteem results from making negative comparisons to oneself. The focus varies with the theoretician, as follows, but the outcome is the same:

— Inferior self versus superior others.
— Present "tainted" self versus past "perfect" self.
— Actual self versus ideal self.
— Inauthentic self versus authentic self.

The first three dichotomies are ego-oriented, negative perceptions of self. They are founded on irrationally held beliefs regarding both the self and others. For typical depressed persons, the self is unalterably bad, and others are good (or at least better); or more devastating, both the self and the world are hopelessly evil. In either dichotomy, nothing will ever change the abhorrent "reality." As Albert Ellis points out, it is the irrational belief about an event that leads to depression, not the situation itself. No matter what one experiences (even feeling depressed), it is exacerbated by thinking badly of oneself and "catastrophyzing" the situation.[12]

One of the reasons for such extreme negativity is the depressed person's rejection of the acceptance of negative characteristics within him or herself, as if a single fault corrupts the entire person. It is no wonder that denial and perfectionism are such precious defenses. Acceptance of the self in all its authenticity, then, requires the incorporation of both positive and negative aspects of self. This brings us to the last concept of negative perception, espoused by existentialists, the inauthentic versus the authentic self. In this case, the negative perception of inauthenticity is an accurate one. It is as if the inner spiritual self is pressing for emergence. Only when false facades are stripped away and the real self is accepted will depression become a thing of the past.

Finally, there is no physiological proof of the psychosomatic hypothesis demonstrating the relationship of a psychologically significant event to onset of physical symptoms. There is, however, sufficient convincing clinical evidence that the mind influences the body.[13] When the intrapsychic life is too threatening, somatization of symptoms distracts one from thoughts that are too painful to deal with. Those thoughts are always negative and are somehow translated internally as, "I am a bad person." It is much more comfortable to think, "I am an unhealthy person." Cure demands an end to both negative perceptions through replacing them with positive cognitive counterparts.

Negative Action = Depression

Incorporated within the topic of action as a common theoretical focus is the concept of psychic energy. Freudians, energy theorists, existentialists, and organically oriented researchers all point to the dysfunctional misuse of energy. When misdirected outward, living vicariously through others, energy output emanates from neediness rather than from strength. Dissipated by fragmentation, the random dispersal of energy, directed and depleted by controlling people and external conditions, such activity is negative. There is little positive energy left for constructive use. What little remains is used for protective purposes. Walling off the self from a world viewed as hostile, the depressed person withdraws energy or encapsulates it in a psychological shell. At the extreme is the catatonic patient. The problem may be less apparent in those who are functioning, but their behavior may be equally negative. Persisting in negative rumination, playing out unproductive life scripts, expending energy on destructive defenses, and rigidly adhering to dysfunctional roles, they live their days in resentment, reinforcing negativity as they go. There is no happy ending, no payoff for their misguided use of energies.[15] Hatred of self and others, indeed often *by* others, goes hand in glove as negative energy attracts negativity. The necessity for reversal of this condition need not be defended.

In summary, human beings need to develop autonomy and competence, as well as the capacity for loving relationships. Deficits in either area lead to depression; to obviate one or the other dimension of self creates only half a person. This is an example of a "both/and" need that is too often dichotomized. People who have developed autonomy often have slighted their relational development.[16] Those whose qualities are primarily interactive have been taught to reject self-development as selfishness. Cultural roles tend to channel males into the first group and females into the second. Even when, for reasons of necessity or tradition, societies socialize everyone into dependent roles, varying only by degrees, it is usually the female who is at the extreme end of the spectrum. In white middle America, girls and women continue to slight both areas of development. Independence is still thought to be unfeminine in many homes and relationality is one-dimensional, focusing on empathic listening. While this is a revered attribute, when it is practiced to the exclusion of the communication and fulfillment of personal wants and needs, it can result in depression.

Biochemical Synthesis

Hagop S. Akiskal is an exemplary proponent of interdisciplinary investigating. He and William T. McKinney, Jr. presented the first comprehensive bio-psychosocial clinical analysis of depression. They point out that a direct, one-to-one relationship between a behavioral syndrome or subjective experiences and a specific chemical event in the brain has been rejected by most areas of neurobiology. No matter what the interpersonal factors are that mobilize depression, once they reach the melancholic phase (severe depression), they become biologically autonomous, and relatively resistant to psychotherapy, at least until the depression runs its course or is alleviated by chemotherapy or electroconvulsive therapy. Although milder forms of depression may befall anyone, the more severe forms appear to involve genetic and

interpersonal-developmental events. Whatever the interlocking process — chemical, experiential, or behavioral — they follow a common
pathway to melancholia. That pathway is the diencephalic center of
reinforcement in the brain. Stress or frustration beyond one's coping
ability, together with psychic anxiety and hopelessness, and neuroen-
docrine reaction produce heightened arousal. This process could disrupt the integrity of the reward system, according to Akiskal and
McKinney. For that reason, regardless of subsequent reinforcement,
the vulnerable or depressed person will not be able to respond. Environmental reinforcers are annulled chemically or anatomically and
low self-esteem is perpetuated. While this model remains theoretical
for humans, it has been supported by evidence from work with animals. Akiskal and his colleagues, Webb and Tashjian, have continued
to advance a comprehensive bio-psychosocial perspective, noting that
research supports their view.[17]

Depression is thought to be the only psychopathological phenomenon not limited to humans, thus clarifying the universal vulnerability of all living things when relatedness is threatened. Whether
human or a lower-order animal (some would take issue with the
implied hierarchy), negative self-perception impairs motivation in obtaining reward from interpersonal relationships. One gives up hope
that making an effort will make a difference. The theme reverberates
through interpersonal, intrapersonal, and behavioral constructs. Research with animals also suggests that biogenic amine defects may be
secondary to development and interpersonal events. Such biochemical alterations may maintain depression through their effects on the
neurophysiological mechanisms of reinforcement, according to investigators. Conversely, research appears to indicate that faith, even that
inspired by placebos, releases endorphins, brain substances that produce relief.[18]

THE OUTER WORLD

Negative Environs = Depression

The impact of environment spans each of the theoretical frameworks, though it is conceived differently. For some traditional
psychoanalytic theorists, the mother is the primary environment, all
others fading by comparison. Those who interpret theory more
broadly vary in their inclusion of influential members. First the father,
then siblings, then the extended family are counted as significant.

Other positions include school and world of work, the church, community, ethnic culture, and so on. The person does not function in a vacuum — so goes the message; the environment impacts on the person as that person interacts with it. Though research is limited, considerable knowledge has accumulated in recent years. The characteristics of depression-provoking environments are being investigated and reported regularly. What we must keep central in our minds is that we are one another's environment. *Persons* are environments, as well, of course, as physical structures, climate, geographical realities, and social conditions.

We have long known that negative conditions include economic stress and violence. More recently, we have begun to recognize that not only unsupportive families, but communities and work situations lead to depression. In like manner, controlling work environments, and nonegalitarian situations reflecting powerlessness over one's life are negative environments. It is becoming apparent that negative elements are additive.[19] The more there are, when clustered over a period of time, the more likely one is to be depressed. Anthropologist Ruth Benedict's field studies may shed even more light. When the advantage of one individual becomes a victory over another, she wrote, those who are not victorious must shift as they can. According to Benedict, these are societies with low social synergy. Indeed, these may be societies that foster depression in women, violence in men, and a sense of alienation in everyone. Benedict writes:

From all comparative material the conclusion emerges that societies where non-aggression is conspicuous have social orders in which the individual by the same act and at the same time serves his own advantage and that of the group . . . not because people are unselfish and put social obligations above personal desires, but when social arrangements make these identical.[20]

Sadly, negative environs — environments with low synergy — pervade our world. Too many people must shift for themselves. Sometimes they are visibly downtrodden, at other times their lot is to be invisible and ignored. Dependent on unreliable dominant others, their environments foster depression.

WOMEN AND CHILDREN AT RISK

Data are emerging that have grave implications not to be ignored. On the one hand, it goes without saying that children need nurturing care. The ego-psychologists call it "good-enough mothering," or parenting, for those who interpret theory more broadly. Whoever the caring person or persons, without that care, deprived children will be subject to depression at the very least — sometimes as children, almost always as adults. In most households, regardless of our opinions on the subject, mothers constitute the primary environment for thier children. Their effect on children is and has long been of great concern. But the children are also environments. It appears that they constitute the primary environment for their mothers. The empirical evidence in this realm is substantial, though it has only recently been addressed. Women who are mothers with small children in the home are the most likely to be depressed.[21] They are subject to depression if an adolescent is living at home, and least likely to be depressed if the children are grown and do not live at home.[22] Indeed, women really are least vulnerable when they remain single and have no children. The impact of children on women is considerable, though generally not the focus of concern.

Depression will continue to leave women at high risk as long as femaleness — being born female — is assessed negatively, to their disadvantage, and at the same time the disadvantage of others. Robert Burton alluded to the analogy between women's subservient status and depression in 1621 in his classic treatise, *The Anatomy of Melancholy*.[23] The essence of this truth endures.

Given this scenario, the implications are devastating if attention is not given to the environments of both women and children. To date, theorists have focused on the needs of the child quite independently of those of the mother. Implying, if not blatantly declaring, that she is an unfit or at best not a "good enough" mother if she falls short of creating a nurturing environment; reference to her needs is secondary. Since she is the adult in the dyad, this may appear to be reasonable. Since she is a human being, realistically, it is not. Environments that foster depression in mothers cannot hope to provide healthful environments for children. made from a synergistic point of view, Ruth Benedict's observations can be applied to the mother-child relationship: to paraphrase her conclusions — depression-free mother-child relationships are those in which the mother by the same act and at the same time serves her own advantage and that of the child, not because she is unselfish and puts parental obligations above personal desires, but when social arrangements make these identical. This is the crux of the problem; our culture, according to Benedict's assessment, has low social synergy. As long as women remain in a disadvantaged position, they will pass their oppression along to their children, in a disguished form perhaps, but so that it is nonetheless destructive. No matter how loving and supportive mothers are, their position in the home and in the world at large is relayed to the children. For girls, the message is catastrophic, for they are fearful that this could be their lot. For little boys who still identify with the mother, there is a similar reaction but it is quickly replaced by a realization that they can escape this kind of fate by repudiating all that is feminine. Both boys and girls can reject the mother, at least unconsciously. They themselves become a microcosm of cultural oppression, creating a negative environment for the mother.

The need for egalitarian, shared parenting is a fundamental answer to the problem of negative attribution to maternal functions. So, too, is the need for men to become nurturant and supportive, developing their relational qualities so that they might become positive environments as well. But the problem is more engulfing. Historically, we have seen that it is not what women do specifically that is demeaned, but *whatever* they do.

The implications for men are analagous. Whether destructive behavior is analyzed in terms of the impact on women or men's own unhappiness, one can conclude that their socialization is not conducive to personal growth and relationship. It is time to put an end to destructive environments for the sake of the generations to come. Girls and boys reared in low-synergy cultures grow up to be mothers and fathers, too often recreating negative environments for their children.

PREVENTION AND INTERVENTION
COMMON DEVELOPMENTAL THEMES

While differing theories view depression from a number of varying perspectives, when analyzed their commonalities also become clear. Psychological, sociological, biochemical, and even spiritual deficits may impact on well-being. And so it is with the positive developmental themes. The same four entities discussed as depression themes in their negative aspect emerge as positive developmental themes, equally important to the prevention of depression and its alleviation. They encompass the theoretically shared polarities of the inner psychic world, the self, and positive and negative aspects of social environments in the outer world. We will find that the parallel positive notions, like the inner self and outer world, intersect to create common metaphors.

THE INNER SELF

Positive Connectedness = Development

The positive side of connection needs originates in infancy with the natural propensity of dependent newborns to attach themselves in a developmentally appropriate way to a parenting figure. The importance of connectedness is less likely to be respected in adulthood, though the absence of supportive relationships, on both personal and community levels, has clear implications for depression. To be nurtured, to be relational oneself, to have the capacity and opportunity for intimacy and caring are directly correlated with well-being. Empathic relationship is a natural human need not to be taken lightly. Empathy on the part of others catalyzes a healing process, opening one up to the positive and negative aspects of self—indeed, to empathy for others. it is this quality that existentialists relate to unity, the highest level of connectedness. It is seen as at-one-ment with the shared spirit within each of us, a merging with a higher power. It is no mistake, Carl Jung points out, that one of the highest symbols of the mind, the mandala, stands for unity.[24] Energy theorists and biophysicists are content to translate merging and unity in terms of universal energy. Still, the connectedness theme remains.[25] Positive connectedness, thus, is addressed by metaphysically oriented analysts, as well as by secular theoretical disciplines.

Informal support in the family, in school, and at work are also aspects of connectedness necessary to development. We are finding that "natural helping networks" that reflect sharing and intimacy are highly effective depression preventatives. Conversely, an absence of supportive relationships leads to depression vulnerability. In the psychoanalytic disciplines, it all begins with "good-enough mothering" (or "parenting" for the less orthodox thinker).[26] The sine qua non of relationships, it is believed that all other subsequent "love objects" are directly related to the early symbiotic bond with the primary care-giver. For all observers, there is no doubt that the crying need of the depressed client, indeed of anyone, is friendship. Numbers of acquaintances often do nothing but mask the absence of a close relationship, but if one's social-support network can include a diversity of people, so much the better. Vulnerability to depression will be low for such fortunate individuals. Chances are, however, that those who are depressed do not have a support system of this kind. Their choices are fewer; they often depend on a single friend. If that person is unavailable, the dependent person is at risk. Contrary to contemporary wisdom, neither sexuality nor kinship are important choice factors. It is intimacy, the confidante quality of the relationship, that enriches.[27] Self-revelation — the freedom to express one's deepest feelings — empathy, and respectful encouragement of the potential of both parties are measures of relationship that have lasting positive repercussions. Once these are experienced, one is never again as vulnerable or needful. The more one has had, the less one will need — so goes the proposition. It may be the clinician who must provide this critical connection.

Often overlooked is the healing power of nonsexual touch. Many therapists, indeed many cultures, shy away from touching because they have been taught that the human need for touch is solely sexual. Psychoanalytically oriented therapists regard the practice as a taboo that will contaminate the transference relationship. While I support the protection of clients from sexual exploitation, to withhold the human touch in some cases may be tantamount to deprivation. The need for human connection is expressed physically in a longing to be touched, a longing that has been denied them. At the spiritual level, the healing touch — the laying on of hands — speaks to the deep-felt need. A pragmatic interpretation is being expressed in mental health programs serving populations ranging from depressed children through the isolated elderly. Recognizing the need for caring and touching, but aware of the lack of opportunity for fulfilling this need, some programs are using animals therapeutically as pets that provide love unconditionally and invite mutual touching.

Positive Aloneness = Development

A thrust toward autonomy and independence is inherent in the natural propensity of all living organisms to grow and to flourish. Psychological aloneness, like its polar mate, relationship, also is a precursor to individuation.[28] The apex of most theories of human personality development is individuation, which is a process of becoming fully self-realized. Each person, unique in the universe, never before duplicated and never to be replicated, gradually emerges as an effective, wholly integrated human being.[29] The process of psychic growth is a slow and imperceptible opening of one's self to authenticity. Without facade, role-free, and separated from social and cultural influence, the authentic self is revealed. Propelled by growth motivation rather than inner deficits, self-actualized individuals are not dependent on others for satisfactions. They are sustained from within.

Self-contained independence from the environment provides a relative stability in the face of deprivation and frustration.[30]

A hallmark of the individuated person is the desire for solitude, an alone-contentedness — nonattachment in the most positive sense. It is their freedom from others that allows them, paradoxically, to develop relationships. The journey to this place in life requires a lifelong commitment. It is the intent, direction, and purpose that are essential. Like all else in life, the road is not straight and even; it is a meandering, spiralling pathway, but nevertheless a way. Those not on the path, those lacking autonomy and a sense of individuality, are likely to feel inadequate and incompetent. Unable to master their environments, their sense of personal ineffectiveness and estrangement goes hand in hand with an absence of inner sustainment. The importance of positive aloneness to the development of individuation cannot be denied. Indeed, the two qualities evolve together, rather than linearly. Object-relations theorists have coined the dualistic term, "separation-individuation," although their emphasis to date has been largely on the separation component. Existentialism can be credited with the greater insight in the realm of individuation. Melded, the two theories provide a powerful potential for innersight.

Positive Perception = Development

It is not enough to be rid of negative perceptions, as essential to health as that may be. The importance of positive self-representation has been emphasized by ego-psychologists, including object-relations theorists and self pychologists. They do not stand alone. They are joined by such seemingly disparate disciplines as cognitive-behaviorism and existential philosophy. True healing can only become a reality when positive perceptions are as omnipresent as negativity once was. Where there were automatic negative thoughts, now there must be automatic positive cognitions. This is made possible through repetitive assertion — positive reinforcement from a cognitive-behavioral perspective, and repeated affirmation from the viewpoint of the spiritual healer. Both schools of thought include verbal and written methods. They also incorporate visual imagery in their repertoires. Because everything is first an idea, visualizing the desired outcome in complete detail will accomplish the goal. Cognitive theorists direct their clients to picture something "as if" it had already happened. Spiritual teachers say, "All is illusion. Do not judge by appearance. You have accomplished your goal already. Visualize it as already completed."[31] Positive perception is the key to apparent limitations. This is insight for the secular arena, and inner sight and illumination for the spiritual. Whether one speaks of consciousness raising or awareness, the message is the same. Healing occurs through knowledge and full acceptance of the whole self existing in the present.

Positive perception has powerful implications for the hopeless, helpless, worthless feelings of depressed people. Since perception makes change possible, even while affirming the self as it is, these negative attributes no longer make cognitive sense. The future holds hope for the cognitive theorist and a promise for the existential philosopher.

Positive Action = Development

The preventive and curative effects of positive action can be found under the rubrics of assertive and responsible behavior, competence, and environmental mastery. Metaphysically oriented expressions of the same qualities are likely to refer to positive energies and authenticity. Whatever the discipline, the message remains the same: Being responsible for one's own happiness, doing something well, and making an effective difference to the world in which one lives are common human needs. Without positive efforts toward these goals, depression is likely to occur. They are essential components of the development of mature independence. Despite the lip service paid to the concept of autonomy, too often people are encouraged to follow societal norms, roles, and interests, rather than to pursue their own unique identities. To do at least one thing well, perhaps creatively, is to validate the authentic self.

Creativity, in fact, is itself a healing activity observed across disciplines. It encompasses serious decision making and problem solving, as well as playfulness, an action less likely to receive proper attention. Depressed people have usually stopped having fun; they often are not aware of what pleases them. Eating well and nutritiously and exercising regularly round out the physical sphere of highly touted activities familiar to us all. But perhaps most important of all is the ability to make changes — to begin anew — to proceed willingly in new directions of interest, activity, and growth.

Finally, directing energies outward toward positive social change, particularly when one is joining with others, provides a creative force that is more powerful than passive acceptance and certainly more healthful than negative response. With energy directed inward toward autonomous personal development and outward in community social action, energy is renewed rather than depleted for both the individual and society. Without needy strings attached to choke off energy, the gift of relationship and service to others require personal risk and commitment—the most positive actions of all. We must understand that to deny personal development in either area is to deny others as well. To serve oneself is not to put personal desire above social obligations; they are one and the same. To be dependent requires others to take responsibility for us. Conversely, being nonrelational robs others of nurturance while expecting their support. In short, self-denial, rather than self-development, may be a synonym for selfishness, whether that denial is related to the individual or to relationship. In either case, the inner self must be nurtured and understood in order for the individual to function optimally. Mary Catherine Bateson concludes:

> Each person is his own central metaphor. . . . We are extraordinarily beautiful and intricate beings, sets of relationships. . . . if we include, about ourselves, all of the intricacy, all of the cycling, all of the being born and dying on various scales . . . we have a position from which to love other persons equally complicated.[32]

The internal person is an environment, a social environment of intrapsychic processes, thoughts, aspiration, and beliefs, as well as personal history that contributes to one's behavioral style. Physical, genetic traits and organ functioning also are integral to this inner environment.[33] Biochemical theories of depression must be embedded in an encompassing framework. Without them, efforts toward synergy are limited to thought and action, negating biological realities of humanness. We have come a long way since the days of René Descartes' dualistic view of mind and body.[34]

THE OUTER WORLD

Positive Environs = Development

Positive environs are, of course, the converse of their negative counterparts. Support and nurturance by family and friends, at work, and in the community, as well as uncontrolling nonhierarchical relationships and working conditions all foster well-being instead of depression.[35] Relationship at the personal and community levels is the pivotal point. We must work individually and with groups to foster mutual support networks. We need not discount environmental conditions because they are "beyond the scope of our powers" or that of the institutions through which we provide services. The environment is made up of people who are each other's environments. Natural helping networks and community support systems can make the difference. This approach is but one possibility for that critically perplexing issue regarding depression in mothers and children. Every effort should be made to make it possible for them to live in positive environments. To that end, the family and community must be educated and encouraged to join together to promote the well-being of women, for their sake and that of their families. Therapists who work with individuals and who are concerned with the mother-child relationship must rethink their values in terms of the realities of the times in which we live.

SYNERGY

While the exploration of theoretical approaches to the problem of depression brings commonalities to light, careful analysis also reveals blatant dichotomies and paradoxes that appear to be in diametric opposition; for example:

- Is a fragile ego to blame for depression, or is it owing to the inability to relinquish the ego?
- Is control over one's life essential to mental health, or must one be unconcerned with personal power?

Abraham Maslow's observational studies reveal that seemingly inherent, conflicting diversities and polarities dissolve in the merging coalescence and unity of oppositions. Before conflicting values can be reconciled synergistically, however, they must first be polarized. In applying these principles to depression and human development, it is essential to explore those dichotomies and paradoxes that reveal themselves along with the common denominators. Their analysis and synthesis result in a synergetic theoretical model, the Transformational Matrix. To illustrate further:

- Must we be oriented toward reaching goals, or is it the process that counts?
- Are we alone in the world, or are we at one with it?
- Should we work toward change or toward acceptance?
- Should we strive toward perfection, or should we accept ourselves as we are?
- Should we each be self-reliant or mutually dependent?

As the list lengthens, it becomes clear that we must accept a both/and dualistic approach to life's paradoxes. But recognizing this reality is only the first step toward understanding. An evolutionary transformational matrix may provide an encompassing framework for multilevel insight and intervention. While each polarity is to be respected, it is understood within a developmental framework. I suggest that depression is like fever, not a disease in itself, but a warning signal indicating that the growth process has been blocked. Barriers may loom up as gridirons of environmentally imposed limitations, or as obstructions representing inner conflicts that inhibit development. In either case, depression is an intrinsic medium of communication within the body, inextricably linked to development. Demands for a dimension of development that are incongruent with one's existing structural needs end in depression. The same phenomenon occurs when one's inner psychological structure is developed at a given level. Depression in such cases is a biochemical manifestation of pressure toward further growth. We must listen to depression, then, and respect its message. The following guide to the self-in-evolution represents a synthesis of clinical, theoretical, and empirical knowledge concerning depression and human development. With this framework, it is possible to assess the "point of issue" at which depression signals attention to get on with the business of personal growth, the transformation of self.

A Transformational Matrix

Most theories focus on Lifespan Dimensions One and Two. Indeed, many of us will be content with inroads in these dimensions alone. Object-relations and energy theorists may allude to the ultimate development of human potential, but they generally focus on the ego. Existentialists, on the other hand, speak of the higher levels of functioning, usually bypassing the more ego-related stages. The shift in emphasis will become clear as development is defined at succeeding dimensions. With each dimension, the human being expands awareness, integrating preceding levels, never leaving them behind.

Lifespan Dimension One: Birth of the Finite Self-as-Ego

From the moment of physical birth, the amorphous infant begins the process of developing the finite self and the infinite self. The finite self is the ego, the self-in-the-world. It evolves through nurturing relationships, through persistence and through self-responsibility, fulfillment, mastery, and competence. The finite self reflects a personal sense of control over one's life. Ideally, as children grow to adulthood, they learn that they can achieve goals, make desired changes, and finally, act autonomously and effectively. Though they feel alone in the universe, they are skillful enough to survive and assertively shape their own destinies. The self-as-ego is alive. Such people generally think well of themselves, though they are aware that they are largely self-serving and that their energies are perpetually geared toward accomplishment and excellence.

Lifespan Dimension Two: The Self-as-Ego in Transition

Once individuals progress toward the finite self, there is a deep-felt need to develop the inner self through contemplation and self-acceptance, despite the growing awareness of the negative side of the self. This is a process of becoming, a transitional time of being that includes reaching out conscientiously to others. One could not "look in the mirror," so to speak, if the needs of others were ignored. The ego is still a core motivator, but nurturning fellow human beings becomes essential to ego-maintenance. Human relationship is paramount.

Lifespan Dimension Three: Death of the Finite Self-as-Ego

The evolution continues and existentialism comes into play. Fully developed, the ego must be relinquished. This is a time of courageous surrender, of acceptance of finitude and limitation. Personal power and control are given up to an unknown higher power (called a creative force by those not spiritually inclined). Emphasis is on social action, serving others through active doing. Striving is a thing of the past as "letting go" becomes one's way of being. As the finite self-as-ego dies, the infinite self is born.

Lifespan Dimension Four: Birth of the Infinite Self

With the birth of the infinite self comes humble awareness of one's unique qualities and abundance. Each person develops the gift that only he or she has to give. There never was and there never again will be the same genetic inheritance, the same psychosocial experiences and the same talents and skills all coming together in just this way. At this point, the paradox of unity comes into being, an awareness of a loving union with something greater than oneself and the recognition of its presence in all people. One is contented in aloneness, knowing that one is never really alone. Thus, individuation and undifferentiation become the highest spiral of evolution of the human psyche. It

may be that this "primordial undifferentiated state of the species be-
comes the prototype of the undifferentiated state of the newborn."[36]
And so life evolves full circle, or so it may be, for we will never
comprehend all the principles. God alone, contends Buckminster
Fuller, is "the synergetic integral of the totality of all principles."[37]
Whatever one's beliefs, we can agree that answers are elusive.

While the limitations of communication made it necessary to present this process in linear fashion, it should be understood that the
process often dovetails — here overlapping, now backtracking, then
leaping ahead. The therapist need only be aware of the multiple
dimensions of development and their differential purposes. With this
matrix to serve as a guide, apparent inconsistencies begin to make
cognitive sense. Another rule concerning the evolution of the self
centers on the ordering of the process. While there can be excursions
into a higher plane, and advanced development along one or more of
the common themes — connectedness, aloneness, perception, and
action — one must meet earlier needs before attaining the final realization of self. When one is required to act prematurely, depression will
emerge. We see the evidence in the high rates of depression in women
who are asked to give up their selves before they have developed them.
And we find a similar picture among elderly men whose egos are
fragile. Stripped of their masks of strength, they become depressed.
The highest rates of suicide are, in fact, among middle-class, elderly
white males.[38] Whether one is female or male, one cannot relinquish
an ego that one does not have, one cannot give up power not yet
achieved — one cannot give, until having received it, whether *it* be
love, a trait, or a state of being. Those who have not been allowed
dependent connection cannot develop true autonomy. Denied relationship and the ability to relate, they cannot be content in solutude.
One's life must be in full swing before it can be surrendered.[39] By
exploring the dualities with our clients, their needs in evolution can be
fulfilled, dispelling vulnerability to depression in the process. By
teaching them to respect depression as a signal for growth, they can
prevent future pain by acting on their developmental urges when
appropriate, recognizing the prematurity of their responses when
neither they nor society have yet prepared the way.

At each level of development, the common developmental themes
that are present throughout the lifespan take on different qualities. It is
therefore as essential to assess developmentally appropriate stages in
adults as it is in children. The model shown in Figure 9-1 is a visual
conceptualization of the Transformational Matrix designed to clarify
the theoretical framework. Research is needed, of course, to validate
the model. This is true, to differing degrees, of all of the theories

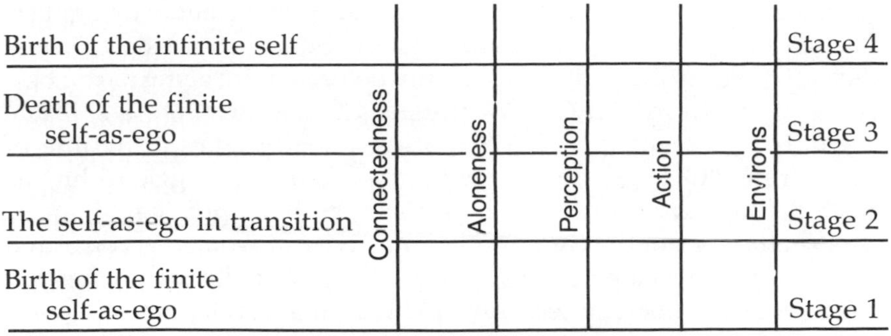

	Connectedness	Aloneness	Perception	Action	Environs	
Birth of the infinite self						Stage 4
Death of the finite self-as-ego						Stage 3
The self-as-ego in transition						Stage 2
Birth of the finite self-as-ego						Stage 1

**Figure 9-1 The Transformational Matrix,
a guide to the self-in-evolution.**

incorporated in the matrix. Still, the matrix has conceptual integrity, providing a comprehensive understanding of both dysfunction and development.

MALE AND FEMALE LIFESPAN DEVELOPMENT: CONJECTURE

The Transformational Matrix will be tested in cross-cultural, cross-sectional, and longitudinal studies of elderly females and males.[40] Our knowledge of male and female development, however rudimentary, leads me to conjecture that men are more likely than women to progress along the first lifespan dimension. Certainly, this appears to be true through the thirties, for it is men whom the culture encourages and sustains in the realms of mastery and competence in the world. The fact that women are three times more likely to be depressed in early adulthood may be a reflection of their need for mastery at this stage as well as of unsupportive, controlling environments. At the same time, they are expected to relinquish their egos, though these are not yet developed. What is not as revealed are the feelings of inadequacy and alienation which many men hide behind masks of competence, demanded by society in the name of "manhood." The male's internal development, then, may be less than meets the eye during their early adult years. When external supports dwindle, they have great difficulty. By old age it is men who are at risk.

While it is expected that both sexes are represented at advanced levels, it is more likely that women are the vast majority. Their identification with the universe, existing simultaneously with the ability to be alone contendedly, makes them prime subjects in old age. While advanced age is not a prerequistite, it is a major contributor, for aging is not just loss and decay, it is transformation. Some believe that spiritual development earlier in life may simply be premature aging in the best sense of the word. "In God We Rust," Claudio Naranjo, a spiritual gerontologist, tells us.[41] Such rusting usually takes a lifetime of weathering. "Old age," says Grey Panther founder, Maggie Kuhn, "is not a defeat, but a victory; not a punishment but a privilege."[42]

Whether or not the church-related activity of women is correlated with spiritual development also needs study, for neither churches nor their participants are necessarily spiritual in a developmental sense. The development of women may be due in part to their innate propensities, as some conjecture, but it is more likely that their life experience provides opportunity for advanced psychological development. Biologically endowed as well, "women have greater lasting strength than males at every stage of life from conception on," according to Estelle Ramey, a biophysiologist who chaired a government-sponsored conference on women's health throughout the lifespan.[43] The mortality rate for women is 90 percent lower than for men in the sixty-five-to seventy-four-year age group alone. Living to an advanced age may provide a greater opportunity for female development. Elder women have learned not only how to survive, but how to do so with style. Many have transcended their finite limitations, becoming infinitely authentic, specifically unique, yet aware that they are at one with others. These existential ideals are reflected in concrete behavior that Barbara Myerhoff calls their "domestic religion."[44] Myerhoff found that the women she studied for four years at a center for the elderly were examplary models of aging. They constructed individual "careers" out of personally discovered projects — each project unique to the individual woman. Their values, attitudes, and behavior were also authentically their own, devoid of the limitations imposed by sterotyping. Yet their individuality was grounded in relationship. Their attentiveness to others, their sincere caring, and their serious dedication to friendship led Myerhoff to ask:

Who of us can afford to overlook the lessons of the heart, the lessons concerning which the old women of the Center showed themselves to be such worthy teachers? (p. 268)

The single flaw that may hold them back is their self-perception, too long skewed by the negative perception of the dominant culture. The more that elder women recognize their wisdom and depth, the more aware they will be of the importance of their values. Their ability to change and to begin anew, whatever their age, increases the likelihood of their growth and development. The turning point in their process of change is not clear at present, but it is the central focus of research on elder development. What is most intriguing is the apparent universality of elder female development, regardless of the culture.[45] Still, we must remember that this is only an observation, and not yet empirically validated.[46]

NOTES

1. Benedict, Ruth, quoted in Abraham Maslow, *Motivation and Personality*, 2nd ed. (New York: Harper and Row, 1970), and in Charles Hampden-Turner, *Maps of the Mind* (New York: Macmillan, 1981).

2. Maslow, Abraham H., *Motivation and Personality*, 2nd ed. (New York: Harper and Row, 1970).

3. Refer to Charles Hampden-Turner, *Maps of the Mind* (New York: Macmillan, 1981) for a brilliantly integrated overview of multiple perspectives of human development.

4. Maslow, Abraham H., *Motivation and Personality*, 2nd ed. (New York: Harper and Row, 1970).

5. Hovland, Carl, and I. L. Janis, eds., *Personality and Persuasability*, Vol. 2 (New Haven: Yale University Press, 1959).

6. Chadorow, Nancy, *The Reproduction of Mothering: Psychoanalysis and the Sociology of Gender* (Berkeley: University of California Press, 1978).

7. Freud, Sigmund, "Mourning and Melancholia," in *Collected Papers*, Vol. 4 (London: Hogarth Press, 1917).

8. Brown, George W. and Tirril Harris, *Social Origins of Depression* (New York: Free Press, 1978).

9. Beck, Aaron T., A. John Rush, Brian F. Shaw, and Gary Emery, *Cognitive Therapy of Depression* (New York: Guilford Press, 1979).

10. Freud, Sigmund, "Mourning and Melancholia," in *Collected Papers*, Vol. 4 (London: Hogarth Press, 1917).

11. Weissman, Myrna M., and Gerald L. Klerman, "Sex Differences and the Epidemiology of Depression," *Archives of General Psychiatry* 34 1 (January 1977).

12. Ellis, Albert, and Robert A. Harper, *A New Guide to Rational Living* (North Hollywood, CA: Wilshire Book Co., 1975).

13. Totman, Richard, *Social Causes of Illness* (New York: Pantheon Books, 1979).

14. Rifkin, Jeremy, *Entropy* (New York: Viking Press, 1980).

15. Lowen, Alexander, *Depression and the Body* (New York: Coward, McCann and Geoghegan, 1974).

16. Miller, Jean Baker, *Toward a New Psychology of Women* (Boston: Beacon Press, 1976), p. 71.

17. Akiskal, Hagop S., and William T. McKinney, Jr., "Depressive Disorders: Toward a Unified Hypothesis," *Science* 182 (1973): 20–29; Akiskal, Hagop S., and William T. McKinney, Jr., "Overview of Recent Research on Depression," *Archives of General Psychiatry* 32 (1975): 285–305. See also Hagop S.

Akiskal and William L. Webb, Jr., "Affective Disorders: I. Recent Advances in Clinical Conceptualization," *Hospital and Community Psychiatry 34*, 8 (August 1983): 695 – 702. See also Hagop S. Akiskal and Raffi Tashjian, "Affective Disorders: II. Recent Advances in Laboratory and Pathogenetic Approaches," *Hospital and Community Psychiatry 34*, 9 (September 1983): 822 – 830.

18. Almay, Bela G. L. Folke Johansen, Lars Von Knorring Lars Terenius, and Agnota Wohlstrem, "Endorphin-in Chronic Pain Differences in Endorphin Levels between Organic and Psychogenic Pain Syndromes," *Pain 5*, 2 (August 1978): 153 – 162.

19. Wetzel, Janice Wood, and Franklin C. Redmond, "A Person-Environment Study of Depression," *Social Service Review 54*, 3 (September 1980): 363 – 375.

20. Benedict, Ruth, quoted in Abraham Maslow, 1970, and in Charles Hampden-Turner, 1981.

21. Brown, George W., and Tirril Harris, *Social Origins of Depression* (New York: Free Press, 1978).

22. Radloff, Lenore A., "Sex Difference in Depression: The Effects of Occupation and Marital Status," *Sex Roles 1* 3 (1975): 249 – 265.

23. Burton, Robert (Democritis Junior), *The Anatomy of Melancholy* (Oxford: Printed by John Lichfield and Iames/Short, for Henry Cripps. Anno Dom 1621).

24. Jung, Carl G., ed. (and M. L. von Franz after Jung's death), *Man and His Symbols* (Garden City, NY: Doubleday, 1964).

25. Lowen, Alexander, *Depression and the Body* (New York: Coward, Mc-Cann and Geoghegan, 1974).

26. Mahler, Margaret S., Fred Pine, and Anni Bergman, *The Psychological Birth of the Human Infant* (New York: Basic Books, 1975).

27. Brown, George W., and Tirril Harris, *Social Origins of Depression* (New York: Free Press, 1978).

28. Mahler, Margaret S., Fred Pine, and Anni Bergman, *The Psychological Birth of the Human Infant* (New York: Basic Books, 1975).

29. Jung, Carl G., ed. (and M. L. von Franz after Jung's death), *Man and His Symbols* (Garden City, NY: Doubleday, 1964).

30. Maslow, Abraham H., *Motivation and Personality*, 2nd ed. (New York: Harper and Row, 1970).

31. Bugental, James F. T., *The Search for Existential Identity* (San Francisco: Jossey-Bass, 1976).

32. Bateson, Mary Catherine, *Our Own Metaphor* (New York: Alfred Knopf, 1973).

33. Weick, Ann, "Reframing the Person-Environment Perspective," *Social Work 26* 2 (March 1981): 14: – 143.

34. Descartes, Rene, "Meditations of First Philosophy," in The Philosophical Works of *Descartes*, ed. Haldane and Ross (New York: Dover Publications, 1955).

35. Wetzel, Janice Wood, "Depression and Dependence upon Unsustaining Environments," *Clinical Social Work Journal 6* 2 (Summer 1978): 75 – 89.

36. Golden, L. Gene, "Mystical Experience: Individuation as Undifferentiation at its Highest Spiral," Unpublished master's thesis, Smith College School for Social Work, Northampton, MA, 1981.

37. Fuller, R. Buckminster, *Critical Path* (New York: St. Martin's Press, 1981).

38. Wetzel, Janice Wood, "Our Female Elders—America's Invisible Strength," Presidential Theme Paper presented at the Mid-America Congress on Aging, St. Louis, Minnesota, April 14 – 16, 1982.

39. Tournier, Paul, *A Place for You* (New York: Harper and Row, 1968).

40. Wetzel, Janice Wood, "Our Female Elders—America's Invisible Strength," Presidential Theme Paper presented at the Mid-America Congress on Aging, St. Louis, Missouri, April 14 – 16, 1982.

41. Naranjo, Claudio, "Meditation and Motivity: In God We Rust," in *Wisdom and Age*, ed. John-Raphael Staude (Berkeley, CA: Ross Books, 1981), pp. 23 – 39.

42. Hessel, Dieter, ed., *Maggie Kuhn on Aging* (Philadelphia: Westminster Press, 1977), p. 11.

43. Ramey, Estelle, "The Natural Capacity for Health in Women," presented at the Conference on Women's Health Over the Lifespan, sponsored by the National Institute of Child Health and Human Development, in cooperation with the National Institute of Mental Health and the National Institute on Aging, November, 1981.

44. Myerhoff, Barbara G. *Number Our Days* (New York: Simon and Schuster, 1978).

45. Myerhoff, Barbara G., and Andrei Simic, eds., *Life's Career—Aging: Cultural Variations in Growing Old* (Beverly Hills, CA: Sage Publications, 1978); National Institute of Child Development, Conference on Women's Health over the Lifespan, Washington, DC, November 1981 (Proceedings published, 1982).

46. See chapter 5 for a discussion of the elderly in institutions.

Chapter 10
Suicide Prevention

> For none shall die
> who have the future
> in them.
> Meridel Le Sueur, *Crusaders*

There are exceptions, but this chapter is concerned largely with the majority of suicidal people — those who are most apt to attempt to kill themselves and those who are at risk of succeeding. Depression may be terminal for both groups. Because those who successfully suicide have generally attempted it in the past, the very act of trying is a risk factor. Practically speaking, even those who are "crying for help" rather than seeking death may accidentally kill themselves in the process. There is no room for error in this lethal game. Each year 200,000 people attempt suicide and 25,000 are successful.

FACTS ABOUT SUICIDE

Fact: The higher one is on the social ladder, the greater the risk of suicide. White middle- and upper-class professional males have the highest rates, as compared with the working class, women, and people of color. Women, however, are five times as likely to attempt suicide, while men are three times more likely to succeed.[1]

Fact: Ninety percent of all adolescent suicides are girls. Pregnant adolescents are ten times more likely to suicide than nonpregnant girls.

Fact: Choice of method has a bearing on successful suicide rates, for men are more likely to select a more lethal variety (guns, hanging, jumping or drowning). Women typically choose pills, gas, carbon monoxide, or poison, or they attempt to pierce or cut their veins superficially, all of which are less likely to be fatal. In general, the more painful and violent the method, the greater the risk of success.

Fact: Suicide is the seventh commonest cause of death in the United States, with one-fourth of the cases associated with alcohol abuse. It is the second most common cause of adolescent death.

Fact: Times of economic depression are associated with increased suicides, particularly in men from upper socioeconomic classes.

Fact: Women and men who are widowed and divorced and men who have never married have higher rates of suicide than do married people.

Fact: While male and female suicide occurs throughout the lifespan from the time of childhood in all cultures, elderly white males have the highest incidence rate. Suicide, like depression, however, is rapidly rising among adolescents, particularly among people of color, in whom it is the third-ranking cause of death. For college students, it is the second-ranking cause, after accidents which may also be suicide invoked.

PSYCHOLOGICAL PERSPECTIVES

Theories of suicide are by and large divided into two perspectives. The psychoanalytic view alludes to the aggression-turned-inward paradigm, played out to the extreme,[2] and to Freud's reference to the death instinct, a rather tautalogical reference that is no longer considered conceptually useful. The psychodynamics of suicide are concerned with loss and threats of loss, whether of loved ones, health, earning power, self-esteem, youth and beauty, independence, friends, or status. Hopelessness in the face of such loss is a significant indicator of risk.

The "anniversary phenomenon" is not an unusual dynamic, where for example, suicide takes place on the anniversary of a loved one's death at the same age, possibly the result of identification. Others may be motivated by a wish to be the object of mourning: "To be loved in death is better than no love at all." Those who are psychotic may be extremely vulnerable, responding to delusions and hallucinations that direct them to suicide.[3] Their motive may well be analogous to any of the theories mentioned.

SOCIOLOGICAL PERSPECTIVES

Sociologists focus on social causation, largely influenced by Emile Durkheim, who is credited with founding the discipline. He has remained a giant in the field, although his research was originally published in France in 1897. It is to this day a definitive work on suicide. Durkheim distinguished three distinct types of suicide: *egoistic, anomic,* and *altruistic.* Though the labels might be considered slightly off target, the descriptive motives remain viable.[4]

Egoistic suicide is the result of feeling disassociated from society owing to lack of social supports, ranging from the wish for a parent's death to attitudes of denial, and discounting by the family and the larger culture. Such alienation is represented in contemporary society by the rising rates of suicide among adolescents in both white and nonwhite communities. This category might be better described as "alienation suicide."

Anomic suicide is triggered by a sudden change in a person's relationship to society wherein one's usual way of life is no longer possible. The woman who has just delivered a baby, the displaced homemaker who no longer can function as a housewife, the man who has recently lost his wife or his job — all may reflect anomie. Identity loss might be a more apt label here.

Altruistic suicide is a response to cultural demands for sacrifice. Such self-innovation in modern memory is revealed by Japanese hara-kiri in World War II, by the Buddhist monks during the Vietnam War, and more recently by the mass suicides of Jonestown, Guyana, the IRA hunger strikers in Northern Ireland, and the Beirut terrorists. Their deaths all represented an intention to sacrifice for the sake of a larger group.

Most suicides fit into at least one of these categories. Many can be explained by all of them. The at-risk aging white male, for example, alienated from society and lacking social supports, suddenly widowed and jobless, may feel he is a burden to his family or even to his country. "They would be better off without me," he tells himself, "at least I could leave them what money I have left and not cost them more." This final cost-benefit analysis is his way of being altruistic. The egoism and anomie, as Durkheim describes them, compound his risk.

SUICIDE VICTIMS: MEN AT RISK

The recognition of males as high-risk people may provide special insight into the development and situational impact on people in our society. A young man's suicide is likely to be impulsive — the suicide of emptiness and alienation, commited by a person who is lonely and unconnected to others, without a sense of where he comes from or where he's going.[5] There is no map to show a boy the way to become a man. His personalized response to being threatened by myriad expectations that he cannot meet may appear as violence in defiance of depression, or it may take the form of despair. Whether or not an actual loss enters the picture, lack of self-esteem and respect is very real. A cry for love and attention that transcends the family, a man's suicide, like that of a woman's, is a cry to society to allow his personhood. Instead, the culture tells him that he must be strong, never make mistakes, be successful, provide economic support for his family (or at least the lion's share), and at all times, in all situations, and all places, be superior. The message is compounded in ethnic minorities who are even more heavily indoctrinated with the machismo expectation, at the same time that the larger society makes what is already outlandish, just about impossible for them to attain — economically or psychologically. Those males of any culture who focus their identities on comparisons with their female peers will be invested in denying any aspect of themselves that is feminine and that any aspect of their female cohorts can be superior. The competitive realm is also intense in male-to-male competition, although since they are "equals," the loser need not feel quite as demeaned. For young men of college age, their sudden change in identity makes them even more vulnerable. Separated from those who know them, little fish, as it were, in big ponds, their world view is enlarged to the point of awareness that they have not been, are not, and probably never will be able to measure up to expectations. Indeed, others, both female and male, have already surpassed them. The young man who has not been able to accept his human limitations will be subject to depressive suicide. He has split himself off from his personhood. So, too, will the young man who has separated himself from others, unable or unwilling to relate to them without false bravado. Often, these qualities overlap in the same person. A high percentage are also likely to be drinking or taking drugs, not an incongruent escape for people who feel alienated.

Finally, the subject of individuation during the teens and twenties is relevant. Though often associated with middle age, it is during these earlier turbulent years that one is in conflict between mirroring everyone else, busily adapting to cultural pressures, and rebelling against these norms in order to become uniquely oneself. If one feels that that unique person is an empty shallow vessel, the reaction may be devastating, and so it is with many young men whose identities have focused on creating facades, with individuality a spurious part of the ritual. Their authentic identities have been repressed and subverted. Intervention must incorporate existential awareness so that they can form clearer boundaries between who they are and who the world tells them they are. Behavioral and/or cognitive methods can be included in the process of discovery and learning.[6]

These insights are as relevant to elderly men as to young. They, too, were raised with equivalent role directives. They did well as long as they could "play along," and in their younger days they were likely to be able to do so. But aging men who are alone, widowed, and retired may not be as likely to get by. Theirs is the highest suicide risk in the nation. Why? It seems to me that the research that describes elderly males who refuse to learn to care for themselves is a case in point.[7] It appears that they believe that home care and personal maintenance are female behaviors, so tainted that these men would rather die, literally, then engage in them. Their inability to relate to others, since they have never learned to do so, is another possible reason for their suicidal behavior. Elderly men in nursing homes, where the ratio of women to men is three to one, create a very different picture. The men are pursued, popular, and generally nurtured by a group of women who are competing for their attentions. Because of the disparate ratio of widowed elderly women, the reverse situation is seldom encountered. Thus, it seems that it is the elderly male who is alone in his room who is most likely to be at risk. This would appear to be self-explanatory, were it not for the majority of women who are alone in the world but do not commit suicide, despite their cultural rejection. Again, an existential approach may provide insight. James Hillman, relating suicide with the soul, tells us that we never come to grips with life until we are willing to wrestle with death, a problem posed most vividly in suicide. He writes:

Growth may be a development away from the world. The analytic process (therapy) shows this by images of losing, of shedding, of dying. Just as much falls away as is added. When illusions are worked through, what remains is often smaller than what we hoped, because becoming oneself means being reduced to just what one is—that stone of common clay—just as loving oneself means accepting one's limited reality, which is, as well, one's uniqueness.[8]

The high male suicide rate may be related directly to their insistence on being superior—a somebody. The pain of being so much smaller is too great. In refusing to die to themselves, they choose dying to the world.

Men's propensity for violent acting-out against themselves and others is culturally reinforced. Their inducement to face physical pain is matched by an inclination to run away from psychological discomfort. Social forces impact on them in that they have more freedom to escape their inner suffering and permission to mask it by violent action, a means that turns in on itself. This social history of many men, to my mind, leaves them vulnerable to suicide, the last violent act, and the ultimate escape. Never has it been brought home more strongly than in the high rates of suicide among Vietnam veterans years after discharge.

SUICIDE VICTIMS AND ATTEMPTS: WOMEN AT RISK

The one exception to male risk is among adolescents where 90 percent of suicide cases are single girls.[9] Those who are pregnant are ten times more likely to suicide than other girls of the same age. They , like their male cohorts and elderly men, feel that they are alienated from society. Their awareness of that alientation may have come to their consciousness quite suddenly. The way in which they have been perceived and perceived themselves is in flux. For the pregnant adolescent, the picture spans history. Despite the sexual revolution, sexual stigmas live on. If we couple cultural rejection with the reality of a single lonely girl, a child herself watching her body swell in proportion to her future responsibilities, and in contrast to waning opportunities, the statistics are not surprising. The future indeed looks hopeless for such a girl. She will be asked to give up her childhood for another, with little opportunity for personal and economic development, while her resources remain scarce. The therapist's intervention will require an overflow of empathic response, together with very concrete problem-solving measures. The enhancement of her personal sense of worth and mastery cannot be overstressed.

Because of the high risk of male suicide, it is easy to overlook the fact that five times as many females as males, of all ages, attempt to kill themselves. Their low rates of success are attributed to the methods they choose, which are less likely to be lethal, and to their motives which may reflect a plea for help or a quiescent refuge rather than a wish to end their lives. Most successful suicides are preceded by attempts that are often less deadly in nature. Despite their comparable benignity, many "accidentally" die. The combination of alcohol and barbiturate overdoses make up a large percentage of female suicide cases, many of whom represent such casualties. While men appear to be driven to escape the reality of their lives and their egos, battered and bruised by comparison between their actual selves and their aspirations, the dynamics for women seem to be quite different. Their suicide attempts are more likely to reflect a giving up or giving in to the struggle of life — tired, weary, and hopeless. Rather than being *against* life, they cease being *for* it. Their ambivalence, perhaps, leads them to less certain self-destruction. Kate Chopin expressed it well almost one hundred years ago when she wrote:

> The years that are gone seem
> like dreams —
> if one might go on sleeping
> and dreaming —
> but to wake up and find — oh!
> well! perhaps it
> is better to wake up after
> all, even to suffer,
> rather than to remain a dupe
> to illusions all one's life. [10]

These are the survivors.

PREVENTION AND INTERVENTION

Suicide is commonly assoicated with depression, although there are some biochemical researchers who contend that suicide, like depression itself, is linked to low serotonin metabolite levels or receptor functioning. Even with biochemical analyses, however, there is no way to predict suicidal behavior given low serotonergic functioning. While this research is to be respected, until it can be translated into preventive action, we also must concern ourselves with more pragmatic psychosocial interventions.

The Suicidal Telephone Call

The therapist's first contact with a suicidal person may be by telephone. To talk to such a person — depressed and perhaps threatening suicide — can be enormously frustrating and frightening. The therapist must be willing to relinquish the need for control of the caller, a person who may insist on remaining anonymous, reserving a modicum of power. Norman Farberow notes three main features that characterize such emergency therapy. They are *activity, authority,* and *involvement*. Such situations require more and varied directive activity than do most therapies, convincing the caller that everything possible is being done for him. The suicidal person is searching for some indication of meaning to his life and some affirmation of self-esteem. At this point of crisis, only the therapist can supply them. With deliberate, conscious awareness, the therapist must become an authority figure who temporarily can take charge. At this stage of crisis, the caller is bound to be overwhelmed by feelings of hopelessness and helpless incapability. His usual judgment and reasoning are not functioning. Disorganized and confused, he is concurrently constricted. His focus will be so narrow that the field of comprehension rules out many ordinarily available alternatives. The choice remaining is between life and death.

Six steps are generally involved in response to such a suicidal call. There may, of course, be overlap within and between steps:

Step 1: Establish a relationship, maintain contact, and obtain information.

Step 2: Identify and clarify the focal problem.

Step 3: Evaluate the suicide potential.

Step 4: Assess the caller's strengths and resources.

Step 5: Mobilize the caller's and others' resources.

Step 6: If you are not trained to work with suicidal people, refer to someone who is, staying in touch during the transition.

The fact that the caller is willing to communicate is a good sign. The more likely he or she is to discuss feelings of hopelessness, the less likely it is that drastic action will be taken. If the caller has unsuccessfully attempted suicide, listen for the degree of remorse. The more remorse and the sooner it appears, the more favorable the outlook, and the less immediate danger of a second attempt.[11]

Assessment and Reduction of Risk

Edwin Schneidman, a leading contemporary suicidologist, contends that the primary tenet of prevention is the capacity to believe that anyone can be suicidal. Whether or not she intended to address suicide, poet Annie Dillard expresses this well. "Every live thing," she writes, "is a survivor on a kind of extended emergency bivouac."[12] Respect for this reality is especially critical when working with depressed people. Never be afraid to ask about a person's intentions to kill himself. Research has shown that such openness will not motivate a nonsuicidal person to do so; it will not plant an idea not previously sown. It is, rather, a deterrent, the result of a felt connectedness on the part of the suicidal person who will recognize the therapist's willingness to discuss a taboo subject without fear. The pressure of pent-up emotions driving him toward his final release thus will be relieved, providing a momentary but critical reprieve.

While certainly no guarantee, the chances of suicide occurring may be considerably lessened if a written "life contract" is drawn up with the client. Following a discussion explaining the importance of mutual trust to the therapeutic alliance, the client is asked to write something like, "I will not physically harm myself during the next eight weeks," signing his or her name to the contract. Note that the agreement is time-limited, to be renegotiated if need be. A suicidal person may have difficulty with a long-term commitment. Eight weeks is optimal because it is a short enough period to agree to, and most crises are resolved within six to eight weeks, although not necessarily for the better if there is no intervention. You may wish to add a phrase about harming others should it be appropriate, and the client himself may want to ask something of you. For example, he may request that you promise not to share information with others or to hospitalize him, fears that he may have in relation to therapy. Most people who have no intention at all of staying alive will not sign a life agreement. There appears to be a point of honor at stake.

The difference between survival and suicide can be measured in degrees. For the person in suicidal crisis, the principal factor is the feeling of hopelessness in the face of intolerable problems with which he is helpless to contend. The pressure of his feelings forces him toward action for immediate resolution. Ambivalence slows his course, however, for he wants to die at the same time that he wishes to live. Both forces need to be acknowledged with you, as the therapist, allying yourself with your client's fluctuating desire for life. The sudden remission of symptoms of depression should be regarded as a danger signal. Often people who are fraught with suicidal conflict improve completely when they have resolved their ambivalence through the decision to suicide. This resolution may be reflected in body chemistry as well. Though the level of the amine, norepinephrine, is not normal in depressed people, it is normal in the brains of suicide victims.[13]

Early Suicidal Signs and Symptoms[14]

In almost every case of suicide there are early signs of the impending act. They can be classified into four broad areas, according to Schneidman and his colleagues. The clues may be *verbal, behavioral, situational* or *syndromatic*.

Verbal Clues to Suicide

1. Direct verbal communication: "I want to die." "I'm going to end it all." "If that happens again, I'll kill myself." "I want to commit suicide."
2. Indirect verbal communication: "I can't stand it any longer." "It's too much for me to live with." "She'd be better off without me." "I don't know how I can face people."
3. Subtle indirect verbal communication: "You'll be sorry when I'm gone." "I won't be around much longer for you to put up with." "This is the last time I'll see you." "How do people leave their bodies to the medical school?" "I feel boxed in — I have to get out no matter what!"

Behavioral Clues to Suicide

1. Direct behavioral clues: any action that uses instruments usually associated with suicide, regardless of the seriousness of the attempt. The nonlethal suicide attempt may be a practice run or a communication of deeper suicidal intent.
2. Indirect behavioral clues: putting affairs in order; the sudden making of a will; writing goodbye letters to loved ones; giving away prized possessions; the sudden improvement of previous symptoms of depression.

Situational Clues to Suicide

1. Anxiety-provoking situations themselves are highly correlated with suicide. For example, when a woman has been notified that she has a malignancy; when she is scheduled for mutilative surgery (such as radical mastectomy); when she is frightened by hospitalization — whether for medical or psychiatric reasons.
2. Release from the hospital can be equally traumatic when major surgery and childbirth are involved. Less likely to be recognized is the vulnerability of postpsychiatric hospitalizations. Having gone to the

hospital to "get well" as a last resort, the released patient who still feels depressed has nowhere to turn. Suicide appears to be the only untapped option.

Syndromatic Clues to Suicide

1. *Depression*: withdrawn, apathetic, sad and tearful, anxious and apprehensive, relatively unreachable and seemingly uncaring: — this is the profile of the seriously depressed person who still retains a measure of energy to complete a suicidal plan. Willingness to communicate decreases as talking becomes more difficult, there are fewer spontaneous remarks, and answers are shorter to the point to being monosyllabic. The individual's mind is occupied and elsewhere as suicidal ideation takes over.

2. *Dependence-Dissatisfaction*: dependent on others, yet dissatisfied with being so, such a person feels that others are not giving the help that is needed. Expressions of angry tension and depression are mixed with feelings of guilt and inadequacy. The people around such an individual are rejected for not fulfilling his or her needs, alternating with overdemands for help. Suicidal threats or attempts must be taken seriously for it may appear to be the only way to get their dependent needs met.

3. *Defiance*: the person who wants to retain a shred of control over an otherwise uncontrollable situation may act defiantly. Thus, a man dying of cancer may choose to play one last active role by picking the time of his death. Or a man who knows he will be fired from his job chooses suicide as an act of quitting; his message maintains, "They can't do that to me — I'll show them!" His defiance, of course, masks his dilemma, for he can't imagine finding another job.

4. *Disorientation*: apt to be delusional or hallucinatory, psychotic people are at high risk for they may respond to commands, voices, or experiences that others cannot share. When a disoriented person expresses suicidal notions, it is important to respect the seriousness of the possibility. Impulsiveness, suspiciousness and inappropriate fear heighten the risk.

Empathy as Diagnosis and Treatment

Empathy, it has been said, is a diagnostic key that opens the way to health. In one sense it is a value-free diagnostic tool with which accurate data can be collected. This is scientific empathy, a kind of vicarious introspection. It is a mode of observation, a process by which objective knowledge about the inner life of another person is gathered.[15] The therapist must step into the world of the suicidal person and view it through his or her eyes. Without the contamination of either consolation or fault-finding, the therapist must experience, to some degree, the person's turbulent despair in order to understand why he feels driven to kill himself. Helping strategies can be adapted to one's specific needs while communicating to the person that he is understood. Given the client's perceptions, suicidal wishes are logical deductions rather than "craziness."[16]

Through such acute understanding, the therapeutic aspects of empathy are mobilized. From the client's point of reference, the self and the therapist are experiencing the world in the same way. Thus, the client is able to merge — a merger that restores the bruised and broken self. The health of the therapist, then, is in the service of the suicidal client. Through this mutual identification, the client will be motivated to mirror the positive outlook of the therapist, his alter ego if you will. It is then that you as a healing agent can enlist the positive healthy aspects of the client to join with you in the exploration of his negative perceptions. Quietly and calmly ask such questions as:[17]

> Have you ever thought about taking your own life?
> You said yesterday that you would be better off dead; why do you feel this way?
> What plans have you made to take your own life?
> Do you feel that taking your own life would hurt anyone else?
> Have you ever had ideas like this at any other time in your life?
> How did you handle your feelings when you felt like this before?
> Do you believe that your feelings could change?
> What help would you choose if it were available?
> What religious beliefs do you have concerning suicide? (While you can't assume that professing a particular religion will prevent suicide, if the act violates the client's religious beliefs, you may be able to use these beliefs as a therapeutic tool.)

As you listen to your client's answers, evaluate:[18]

—How long he has had these thoughts.
—What he feels the cause to be.
—How he has coped with stress in the past.
—What method of suicide he has contemplated.
—How carefully he has made a plan (for example, where will he get the barbiturates he plans to use; if he plans to shoot himself, does he

have a gun and does he know how to use it? Under what circumstances does he plan to use an autmobile?)

— What is motivating him to stay alive; what does he cherish and hold dear?

Focus on all the positive information you can get, beginning with his doubt and ambivalence about the wisdom of suicide, bolstering these doubts with positive reinforcement. Elicit and use his strengths, weakening his reasons for contemplating suicide. "Reasons for Living" and "Reasons for Dying" can be listed in writing. If the depressed client is unable to feel any reasons for living now, he may recall past reasons that were once valid. Help him to assess those that are still valid, or may be valid in the future. Aaron Beck and his colleagues point out that the suicidal person has often nullified these positive factors in his life by forgetting them, ignoring them, or discounting them.[19] The therapist, then, must provide a counterbalance to the reasons for dying, without creating an image of "talking him out of suicide." Instead, the approach must be a collaborative, exploratory effort.

It is important not to hold out false hopes or to minimize clients' troubles. While suicidal people are often prone to overestimating their problems, seeing them as insoluble, these problems may also be very real. Poverty, personal loss, serious physical illness, and similar traumas, for example, must be addressed pragmatically.

The Crisis Process[20]

Whatever the problem, be assured that your client has tried to solve it before coming for help. Their usual problem solving in response to stress simply has not been successful. The crisis process goes like this:

Following regular problem-solving efforts, emergency problem-solving measures meet with failure as well, causing ever-increasing stress. Finally, acute depression ensues — the indivdual is helplessly confused, hopelessly overwhelmed, perhaps resentful or frightened, certainly lost in despair and defeat. At the next stage of major breakdown in functioning, maladaptive behavior, suicide, may be perceived as the only possible relief from stress.[21] This is the crux of crisis theory, a predictable process about which clients can learn. Whether the crisis is developmental or situational, the reaction will follow the same route. The earlier the intervention, the more manageable the tension. Still, by teaching the inevitability of the process, clients are able to see themselves as normal members of the human family, rather than oddities who have failed in life. A state of crisis is neither a sign of weakness nor an illness. It simply represents a struggle with a current life situation. It can be perceived as an opportunity for growth and the development of new and more effective means of functioning.

Active Coping

Coping is the effort made to deal with a problem in order, at best, to master and solve it, or at least to ameliorate it and reduce tension. The faculties and strategies involved in the process of coping are those of the ego. Interestingly, the protective mechanisms of defense have been better explored than the grappling-learning operations of the ego. It is these latter functions that are requisite to the prevention of suicide, for the awareness that one is coping is an essential ingredient. Conscious intentional coping refers to a person's volitional effort to deal with both himself and his problem interdependently. In so doing, cognitive-affective ego functions (thought and feeling) are addressed together with action functions.[22] Just as negative thoughts and feelings lead to depression and possible suicide, so positive coping action affects thoughts and feelings concerning the self. It is an active process, recognizing that "I do" is the precondition to the sense that "I am," true for the adult in crisis, as well as the developing child. Indeed, the adult may never have had the opportunity to realize himself through action. Risk of suicide is only temporarily relieved upon the diminution of internal or external stress. To gain insight and understanding into the self and others is important to the process, but not sufficient.

Coping requires *doing* differently, a prerequisite to seeing oneself as a coping person which is in turn a precondition to living. Actions, not simply introspective examination, inform him of the reality of his improvement and capabilities. Such self-perception is the key to his life. The fact that he is presently seeing a therapist, however reluctantly, means that he is a coping person. This insight should be underscored. Seeing him as a past and present, as well as future, "coper," not just as a victim, places him in the role of actor rather than reactor. Exploration should examine his failures, mistakes and miseries, but also include his coping powers — how he has managed in the past, respecting his opinion of why he thinks something did or did not work. This is his history of coping, more important than his history of unresolved problems. Helen Harris Perlman points out:

> What is important is that the client be kept at work on his problem, not just one who tells about it, not just one who deposits it trustfully in another, but as

one who (with the assessed limits of his endowments and capacities at any given time) is held to be able to take part in its modification — as one who has the right but also the responsibility to take some action to affect it.[23]

Taking action often requires considerable preparation. Partialization of the problem makes the task feasible while permitting its exploration in depth. The greater the felt stress, whatever the source, the greater the necessity to partialize the problem so that coping with it is within the realm of possibility. While connected to the whole, it should be a part that offers the possibility of focus and seems to the client to be within reason. Thus, anxiety can be bound while perception, thought, and feeling are concentrated. The first small rewarding action step, the problem-to-be-worked, need not be the basic nor even the causal problem. It should be whatever the client feels is most pressing at the present time. The important thing is their heavy investment of affect in it. In an acute situation like that of suicide, the drive to action will be spontaneous and intense in order to discharge accumulated tension. That release must be rechanneled to constructive "doing" instead of self-annihilation. The felt need then, is twofold: tension discharge in tandem with the sense that something is being made to happen. The selection of a next step, or an immediate target of action, lowers the feeling of overload while establishing a personal sense of control.

Cognitive-Behavioral Procedures

Cognitive-behavioral procedures are particularly suited to suicide prevention because of their clarity and definitive structure. Both qualities are conducive to stress reduction. Because corrective action does not happen simply because the client has placed the problem before the therapist with feeling, cognitive-behavioral methods are needed to contribute to successful intervention. A behavioral rehearsal is often required to ensure a positive outcome. While situations differ, a general rule is: "the greater the emotional disturbance, the smaller the action task and the greater the necessity for rehearsal between client and therapist." Whenever a new or difficult situation is anticipated, the client learns to marshal the available facts and put together a mental representation, a picture of what the circumstance will be like. Help your client to imagine it from both a personal perspective and that of another in the encounter, fantasizing how both will be feeling and imagining what will be said and done by each party. Through such role play, the client will be able to weigh and judge alternative actions. The procedure may take hours or even days if thoughts and feelings are in conflict. Still, it is a worthwhile process that can engage the distressed person and alleviate tension when anxiety and distorted thinking have either paralyzed or catapulted him toward suicide.

Cognitive rehearsal can be employed as a "forced fantasy" technique, a form of stress inoculation for suicide-prone individuals. Beck and his colleagues point out that such people not only over estimate the magnitude and insolubility of problems, but they have incorporated the notion that solving problems through death is desirable and acceptable. Their tolerance for uncertainty is so low that death as the only solution is triggered when an immediate answer is not on the horizon. Suicide, then, is used as a kind of opiate for their pain. For this reason, proneness to suicide and stress inoculation should be a major focus of therapy. Clients are asked to detail typical stresses that are likely to occur, imagining themselves in a desperate situation. Then, in the safety of therapy, they are to try to experience their characteristic despair and suicidal impulses. Finally, despite these stimulated suicidal feelings, they are to attempt to generate possible solutions to the problems. Once mastered in the office, they are encouraged to practice the technique in real-life situations. Not only is problem-solving behavior reinforced, but clients are being trained to be distracted from suicide preoccupation.

It is clear that suicide prevention necessitates a directive intervention. There is no time for long-term subtleties when extreme hopelessness is coupled with self-destructive action. For that reason, cognitive-behavioral techniques are well suited to the task, although insights from all theoretical perspectives can be incorporated. The insights and tools of the cognitive-behaviorists are shared with their clients, who are let in on therapeutic "secrets." Empowered with "professional" healing skills, the previously suicidal person comes to perceive of hope and positive thoughts and behaviors as a reality. During the learning process, though, the therapist must continue to be alert to emerging and ongoing suicidal impulses, whether they emanate from the client-therapist relationship or are exacerbated by external conditions. Suicidal wishes will prevail and both therapist and client should be on the lookout for them so that they can be dealt with safely. Underlying all preventive measures is empathy — that human-spiritual quality essential to feeling "connected" with life. Suicidal proneness can become a thing of the past when partially unresolved conflicts that have been reactivated are reworked, breaking the link between present and past difficulties. A time of crisis can be a time of opportunity, for such individuals often are particularly amenable to help.[24]

The Psychology of "Surviving Others"

Having done all that is possible, one must remember that a person who wants to kill himself will do so — even if hospitalized, followed, or observed almost continually. Such restrictions may be essential at high-risk moments, but they are generally too smothering and unrealistic on a long-term basis. Because of the self-distortions of severely depressed people, time is their friend. Their deep despair is self-limited; they will feel comparably better, though it may be impossible to convince them of that fact when their pain is at its height. A few hours, a few days may make the difference between life and death. That is the heart-rending truth that is confronted when suicide has been successfully carried out. It is easy to feel that only you, the therapist, could have saved the deceased person, especially when a necessarily authoritative, directive role has been taken. One must, at all times, be prepared for the possibility of such an impulsive lethal action, whether it is the consequence of honest grievous error on your part, or quite outside the realm of your control. Error should not be construed as a synonym for fault, for the therapist can only be a therapist. Any other interpretation borders on the Jehovah complex. The same advice should be given to family and friends who carry death as a private burden. Personal support and professional consultation are recommended when such guilt and grief are overbearing. In work with seriously depressed and suicidal people, ongoing colleagial support is of paramount importance, for the stresses can be enormous. Professional expertise can exaggerate personal strains and conflicts, rather than minimizing them. It is perhaps for this tragic reason that psychiatrists themselves have the very highest rate of suicide. No matter who the survivor, many of the following strong emotional reactions, suggested by Norman Farberow,[25] may be aroused, all of which must be confronted and worked through:

- Loss, sorrow, and mourning.
- Anger for being made to feel responsible.
- Anger at having been rejected (what was offered was refused).
- Guilt, shame, or embarrassment.
- Failure and inadequacy (what was needed could not be supplied).
- Relief that the nagging, insistent demands have closed.
- Rejection and fear, feelings associated with desertion (especially true for children).

- Doubts and self-questioning about whether enough was attempted.
    - Denial of suicide with a possible conspiracy of silence.
    - Impulses toward suicide aroused.
    - Ambivalence concerning all of the above.

Remember, whoever you may be — professional helper, friend, or lover — we cannot *solve* the problems of others, nor can we make decisions for them. We can only respect and care for them, offering ourselves as a calm, stable fellow traveller who reaches out to their own core of stability. Given this much, they will do the rest, usually (though not always) choosing life.

Legalities and Choice

There are legal ramifications of suicide, intended to protect the suicide attempter, the clinician, and/or society. The laws vary from state to state and country to country. To take one's own life is taboo in many cultures, while others are indifferent and still others even respect the choice. Religion plays a role in the selected perspective, influencing lawmakers and constituents alike. In this era of life-supporting technology and ever-increasing age, we can expect the debate and concern to increase. Still considered a criminal act in a few states, aiding and abetting a suicide is even more likely to be a crime. Legal suicide is seldom an option. Hence, public opinion, ethical and philosophical considerations, and fear of reprisal all play a part in one's attitude and actions. We can share in the dialog at this time, learn the facts about our community's legal stand, and as clinicians, try to help clarify the issues for those who are wrestling with their destinies. We cannot forget, while we remain open to different mores, that the decision to suicide today is often made prematurely, in the depths of a depression that will be lifted tomorrow.[26]

NOTES

1. See Chapter 1 for further statistics on suicide.
2. See Chapter 2 for explication of the concept of introjected hostility.
3. Solomon, Phillip, and Vernon D. Patch, *Handbook of Psychiatry* (Los Altos, CA: Lange Medical Publications, 1974).
4. Durkheim, Emile, *Suicide*, trans. John A. Spaulding and George Simpson (New York: Free Press, 1951; originally published in 1897).

5. Freese, Arthur S., *Adolescent Suicide: Mental Health Challenge*, Public Affairs Pamphlet No. 569 (The Public Affairs Committee, Washington, D.C. April 1979).

6. See Chapter 7 regarding awareness, and Chapter 6 regarding cognition.

7. Bikson, Tora Kay, and Jacqueline K. Goodchilds, *Old People and New Ideas: Receptivity and Rigidity* (Santa Monica, CA: Rand Corporation, August 1979).

8. Hillman, James, *Suicide and the Soul* (Irving, TX: Spring Publications, 1978), p. 164.

9. National Center for Health Statistics (U.S.), "The International Classification of Diseases," 9th revision, clinical modification (Ann Arbor, MI: Commission on Professional and Hospital Activities, 1978).

10. Chopin, Kate, *The Awakening* ed. Lewis Leary (New York: Holt, Rinehart, and Winston, 1970; originally published in 1893).

11. Laughlin, Henry P., "Estimating Danger: Index of Suicide Potential," in *The Neuroses* (Washington DC: Butterworths, 1967), pp. 163−164; see also Norman L. Farberow, "Therapy in the Suicidal Crisis," presented at the California State Psychological Association, 1962.

12. Dillard, Annie, *Pilgrim at Tinker Creek* (New York: Harper's Magazine Press, 1974).

13. See Chapter 8 for further discussion of biogenic amines and depression.

14. The section on Suicidal Signs and Symptoms is credited to E. S. Schneidman, Farberow, and R. E. Litman, *The Psychology of Suicide* (New York: Science House, 1970).

15. Kohut, Heinz, "Reflections on Advances in Self-Psychology," in *Advances in Self-Psychology*, ed. Arnold Goldberg (New York: International Universities Press, 1980), pp. 473−554.

16. Beck, Aaron T., A. John Rush, Brian F. Shaw, and Gary Emery, *Cognitive Therapy of Depression* (New York: Guilford Press, 1979).

17. Diran, Margaret O'Keefe, "You Can Prevent Suicide," *Nursing* (January 1976), pp. 60−64.

18. Ibid.

19. Beck, Aaron T., A. John Rush, Brian F. Shaw, and Gary Emery, *Cognitive Therapy of Depression* (New York: Guilford Press, 1979).

20. Smith, Larry L., "A General Model of Crisis Intervention," *Clinical Social Work Journal 4*, 3 (1976): 162−171.

21. This section is largely based on Helen Harris Perlman, "In Quest of Coping," *Social Casework 56*, 4 (April 1975): 211−225.

22. Beck, Aaron T., A. John Rush, Brian F. Shaw, and Gary Emery, *Cognitive Therapy of Depression* (New York: The Guilford Press, 1979): also see Chapter 6 for further explication of cognitive-affective functions.

23. Perlman, Helen Harris, "In Quest of Coping," *Social Casework 56*, 4 (April 1975): 211−225.

24. Golan, Naomi, *Treatment in Crisis Situations* (Ne York: Free Press, 1978).

25. Farberow, Norman L., "Therapy in the Suicidal Crisis," presented at the California State Psychological Association, 1962.

26. Lester, David, Betty H. Sell, and Kenneth D. Sell, *Suicide: A Guide to Information Sources* (Detroit, MI: Gale Research Company, Gale Information Guide Library, 1980); see also Herbert Hendin, *Suicide in America* (New York: Norton, 1982).

11

Instruments and Assessment

> The minute you or anybody else knows what
> you are you are not it, you are what you or
> anybody else knows you are and as everything
> in living is made up of finding out what you are it
> is extraordinarily difficult really not to know
> what you are and yet to be that thing.
>
> Gertrude Stein, *Everybody's Autobiography*

DIAGNOSTIC AND STATISTICAL MANUALS OF MENTAL DISORDERS (DSM)

The World Health Organization (WHO) has made serious efforts for decades to promote the uniform classification of diseases, including mental disorders. Although nomenclature in the United States has become progressively congruent with the International Classification of Diseases (ICD), psychiatry in this country continues to question some of the ICD categories. For that reason, the *Diagnostic and Statistical Manual of Mental Disorders* (DSM I) was published in 1952[1] and updated in 1968 in DSM II.[2] In 1980, in response to emerging research and the growing demand for more accurate assessment, the DSM was revised a third time.[3] The ICD, meanwhile, had been revised for the ninth time two years eariler.[4] DSM III provides an annotated comparative listing of DSM II and DSM III, as well as a historical review of ICD 9. Efforts toward compatibility continue and at the present time include cross-references in both DSM III and ICD 9 for their mutual benefit. For our purposes, suffice it to say that depression is classified in the ICD 9 in relation to reality testing and psychotic and neurotic subfeatures. DSM III nosology is detailed here after a critique of DSM II.

Because the longstanding records of depressed patients in the United States will refer to DSM II's Major Affective Disorder categories, they are summarized for the reader. Although these categories are presently defunct, it is important to know what the codes and terms meant to those who did the recording. Comparisons with DSM III are noted in each category.

DSM II: Major Affective Disorder Critique[5]

Primarily concerned with affective psychosis, DSM II characterized major affective disorders by a single disorder of either extreme depression or elation. The onset of the mood did not appear to be precipitated by a life experience, except in the case of Psychotic Depressive Reaction and Depressive Neurosis.

296.0 — Involutional Melancholia was thought to occur in the middle years in people confronting the aging process. Generally, there was no previous history of depression. Guilt and somatic preoccupation were common, even to the point of depression. It is ironic that this category was distinguished specifically as one "not due to some life experience." Because the category was questioned as a distinct entity, it was proposed only when all other affective disorders had been ruled out. DSM III has eliminated the category altogether. There is no compelling evidence that a paranoid disorder occurring in the involutional period is distinct from similar problems occurring in other stages of life. Research also indicates that depression is no more likely to occur in the middle years than at any other time.[6] Indeed, many women are relieved of previous depression after their middle forties.

296.1 — Manic-Depressive Illness, Manic Type, like other manic-depressive psychoses, was marked by severe mood swings. People who were categorized accordingly were excitable and elated most of the time, their ideas and plans taking on an unrealistic grandiosity. Though depressive moods might have occurred briefly, they were never dominant. High-energy optimism and activity were central, though often diffused and disorganized. DSM III contends that virtually all people with manic episodes eventually become depressed. Hence, they subsume manic episodes under Bipolar Disorder whether or not there has been a depressive episode. This conceptualization is controversial. To label a disorder in the absence of symptoms critical to the diagnosis is always tenuous.

296.2 — Manic-Depressive Illness, Depressed Type in DSM II encompasses both single and recurrent episodes of Major Depression listed in

DSM III. Severely depressed mood, and progresssive mental and motor retardation (slowness) were characteristics in the earlier classification system. So, too, were uneasy apprehension, perplexity, and agitation. Symptoms were not viewed as attributable to stress, although hallucinations and delusions might result from the dominant mood disorder itself.

296.3 — Manic-Depressive Illness, Circular Type is now subsumed under Bipolar Disorder in DSM III, encompassing manic, depressed, and mixed episodes. Individuals showed signs of both features within this category, although, as suggested earlier, depressed episodes may not yet have been evident. While DSM II implied the unity of mania and depression, DSM III regards unipolar and bipolar dichotomies as separate forms of Affective Disorder, based upon new evidence.

298.0 — Psychotic Depressive Reaction is reflected in DSM III by Major Depression with psychotic features. The severity of precipitating psychosocial features is recognized as well. The classic signs of depression plus the catalyst were thought to produce classic delusional and hallucinatory features in DSM II.

300.4 — Depressive Neurosis was a broad category that reflected excessive depression in reaction to internal conflict or loss of a significant person or cherished possession. DSM III has eliminated the term "neurosis," separating three possible conditions descriptively but without causal reference, under the Major Depression umbrella. They now include single and recurrent episodes without melancholia, dysthymic disorder, and adjustment disorder with depression. Identifiable events can be recorded, although DSM III maintains that there is no compelling evidence that the presence of a stressor associated with the onset of depression affects the course or response to treatment once a Major Depression has developed. This is a key point and one that has validity. What is overlooked are the preventive aspects of the phenomenon and possibilities for impacting on the high rate of recidivism. Etiology and clinical course, management, and treatment, though related, are not necessarily analogous processes. Once severe depression is a reality, it appears to become autonomous. Brain and body chemistry take over. Even what begins as an identifiable reaction becomes all-pervasive and independent of the initial cause. Still, knowledge concerning causality has interventive implications as well as preventive ones because of the cognitive aspects providing future hope, knowledge, and understanding — all of which positively affect one's sense of self. At the least, it may make the pain of depression more bearable. At most, it may deter suicide. In the lower and middle ranges of depression, there may be more opportunity for control of the clinical course than meets the eye, given a broader understanding of etiology and prevention.

DSM III: Major Depression[7]

DSM III provides a descriptive classification system in that the definitions generally describe the clinical features of the disorders. In the case of depression, the term "mood disorder" is considered more accurate, but "affective disorder" was retained owing to common usage and the desire for historical continuity. Because etiology is largely unknown, the DSM III approach is atheoretical. Thus, use of the manual need not present an obstacle to varying theoretical perspectives. While descriptively comprehensive, no information is included concerning theories of etiology, management, or treatment. It is hoped that interjudge diagnostic reliability will provide a solid foundation upon which clinical research can be built in years to come. Despite the fact that separate categories are created based on shared clinical features, the authors do not assume that each disorder is necessarily a discrete entity with sharp boundaries between either other disorders or mental health.

The Washington University Department of Psychiatry in St. Louis is largely responsible for much of the early work that preceded DSM III. They have specialized for over thirty years in psychiatric diagnosis. Published in 1972, their diagnostic classifications, commonly referred to as Feighner Criteria, were validated primarily by follow-up and family studies. This was in contrast to DSM II, which was limited to "best clinical judgment and experience."[8] DSM III Major Depression criteria do not essentially differ from the Feighner Criteria, except in the time measurement of one month's duration in the latter case and more recognition of differential symptoms in children.

DSM III: Major Depressive Episode[9]

For a diagnosis of major depression, the following criteria must be met:

   A. Dysphoric mood or loss of interest or pleasure in usual activities, characterized by persistent and prominent symptoms such as feeling hopeless, sad, blue, depressed, or irritable. Moods do not shift momentarily. (Under six, children may mask their dysphoric mood.)

B. At least four of the following symptoms experienced over a period of two weeks nearly every day (at least three of the first four symptoms are required for children under six years of age):
   1. Appetite disturbance — poor appetite or significant weight loss (without dieting) or significantly increased appetite or significant weight gain.
   2. Sleep disturbance — insomnia or hypersomnia.
   3. Psychomotor agitation or retardation (hypoactivity in children under six).
   4. Loss of interest or pleasure in activities, or decreased sexual drive (under six, signs of apathy are typical).
   5. Loss of energy, fatigue.
   6. Self-reproach, inappropriate guilt, feelings of worthlessness.
   7. Diminished ability to think or concentrate, indecisiveness.
   8. Recurrent thoughts of death or suicide, suicide attempts.
C. Neither of the following dominate the picture before major depression symptoms developed or after it has remitted:
   1. Preoccupation with mood-incongruent psychotic features (defined below).
   2. Bizarre behavior.
D. Symptoms not coupled with either "Schizophrenia, Schizophreniform Disorder, or a Paranoid Disorder".
E. Symptoms are not the result of any "Organic Mental Disorder or Uncomplicated Bereavement."

Major depression is divided into two categories:
   296.2 x = single episode.
   296.3 x = recurrent episodes.
The fifth digit [the "x"] is coded as follows:
   6 = In remission. In the past the individual met all of the criteria for major depressive episode. Presently free or partially free of depressive symptoms.
   4 = With psychotic features. Gross impairment in reality testing, such as experiencing delusions, hallucinations, or depressive stupor — mute and unresponsive.

Although the usefulness of mood congruence as a category is in question, DSM III includes such specification as follows:

Mood-congruent psychotic features: Delusions and hallucinations are congruent with "themes of personal inadequacy, guilt, disease, death, nihilism or deserved punishment". Depressive stupor is also a feature.

Mood-incongruent psychotic features: Delusions and hallucinations are incongruent with the depressive themes cited above, e.g., persecutory or control delusions, thought insertion or broadcasting.

    3 = With melancholia — characterized by "loss of pleasure in all or almost all activities, "lack of reactivity to usually pleasurable stimuli," and at least three of the following:

        (a) "distinct quality of depressed mood"

        (b) "depression is regularly worse in the morning"

        (c) "early morning awakening" (at least two hours early)

        (d) "marked psychomotor retardation or agitation"

        (e) "significant anorexia or weight loss"

        (f) "excessive or inappropriate guilt"

    2 = "Without melancholia"

    0 = "Unspecified"

While the categories called "melancholia" have been added because their clinical usefulness is assumed, whether or not these conditions are qualitatively or quantitatively different has not been resolved.

DSM III: Bipolar Disorder

DSM III also divides Major Affective Disorders into a second category called Bipolar Disorder which is distinguished by whether or not the individual has ever had a manic episode (regardless of presenting symptoms). Whether bipolar illness is a separate entity or on a continuum remains unresolved. There is evidence supporting both opinions. I have elected to outline only briefly the three categories subsumed under Bipolar Disorder as follows (readers may wish to refer to DSM III for further explication):

Bipolar Disorder, Mixed reflects a "current (or most recent)" episode involving the full symptomatic picture of both manic and major depressive episodes, intermixed or alternating rapidly every few days."

Bipolar Disorder, Manic reflects a "current (or most recent) manic episode", although the full criteria for a manic episode need not be met.

Biplar Disorder, Depressed is a category reserved for those who have "had one or more manic episodes," but are "currently (or most recently in a major depressive episode". The full criteria for major depressive episode need not be met if there has been a previous major depressive episode.

DSM III: Subclassifications of Affective Disorders

Affective Disorders are further classified into *Other Specific Affective Disorders* whereby there is only a partial syndrome of at least two years' duration with no psychotic features. Symptoms usually begin in early adult life without a clear onset. Two disorders fall into this category: Cyclothymic Disorder and Dysthymic Disorder (Depressive Neurosis). In Cyclothymic Disorder numerous periods of depression and hypomania occur, but are "not of sufficient duration or severity to meet the criteria" for a full affective (depression or manic) syndrome. Dysthymic Disorder is solely depresion oriented, but again does not meet the criteria for a major depressive episode.

Atypical Affective Disorder is a catch-all category for those affective disorders that cannot be classified elsewhere. Divided into Atypical Bipolar Disorder, and Atypical Depression, these are residual categories for individuals with manic and depressive features, but whose profile does not quite meet the criteria for any of the affective disorders.

DSM III cautions against differential diagnoses that appear to indicate Major Depression. They include organic etiology ranging from body substances such as reserpine to infectious diseases and thyroid imbalance, as well as psychological reactions to physical loss or illness. Depression associated with Schizophrenia may also be difficult to distinguish from Major Depression. Previous episodes and familial history usually decide the diagnosis. When it is not possible to make a clear decision, the syndrome is labeled Schizo-Affective Disorder. In addition, chronic mental disorders such as Obsessive Compulsive Disorder or Alcohol Dependence may suggest Major Depression when it is a superimposed factor only. Separation Anxiety Disorder and Uncomplicated Bereavement (in contrast to unduly severe or prolonged grief) are similarly differentiated. Indeed, there are few diagnoses that do not include symptoms of depression. For this reason, depression might be viewed as a psychophysiological response to stress, a conclusion that DSM III has not ruled out as a possibility.[10]

Age-Specific Features of Major Depression[11]

DSM III also points out that there are age-specific features that differ from the essentially similar characteristics of major depressive episodes. In prepubertal children, for example, clinging, refusal to attend school, and fear that parents may die may accompany separation anxiety in association with depression. This is particularly likely when there is a history of separation anxiety. Adolescent boys may become negativistic or even antisocial, sulky, uncooperative, sensitive, and aggressive. The wish to run away is common, as is a reluctance to cooperate in family ventures. Substance abuse is not unusual. As people age, their symptoms of disorientation, memory loss, and distractability may mistakenly suggest Dementia. Depression symptoms, such as loss of pleasure and interest in activities, may appear as apathy. When linked with concentration difficulty which may be perceived as inattentiveness, the chances of misdiagnosis increase.

Episodic Features of Major Depression

Age of onset: may begin at any age from infancy on. "Age of onset is fairly evenly distributed through adult life."

Clinical course: variable onset and course, with symptoms usually developing from a few days to weeks. In some cases, particularly when associated with severe psychosocial stress, onset may be sudden. In other instances, "generalized anxiety, panic attacks, phobias, or mild depressive symptoms may occur over a period of several months." It is conjectured that over 50 percent of all cases of Major Depression, Single Episode, will have a recurrent experience. Those with a Major Depression, Recurrent, diagnosis "are at greater risk for developing Bipolar Disorder than those with a single episode of Major Depression." The clinical course of Major Affective Disorders is variable, separated by years between single episodes or occurring in clusters of episodes. Still others experience an increase of episodes with age.

Impairment: variable, with some interference in social and occupational functioning. If extreme, the individual may be totally unable to function.

Complications: suicide.

DSM III also includes a "decision tree" for the differential diagnosis of psychotic features and affective disorders. However, in 1983 the clinician-researchers who developed the model revised their original version. The new tree was designed to represent clearly the logic of classification. Those who are interested in applying the decision schema should refer to the article by Robert L. Spitzer, Janet B. Williams, and Lyman C. Wynne, as well as the DSM III.[12] The third and subsequent printings of DSM III incorporate the revised criteria for major depressive and manic episodes detailed in this chapter, not found in the first two printings of the diagnostic manual.

INSTRUMENTS

Many diagnostic instruments also are used as self-report scales that measure depressive symptoms, such as the frequently used Beck Depression Inventory[13] and Zung Self-Rating Depression Scale.[14] A

MAJOR DEPRESSION INVENTORY*

Please check the blank (True or False) that best represents feelings you have experienced nearly every day within the past two weeks:

	TRUE	FALSE
A. 1. I've been feeling sad lately.		
2. I don't feel hopeful about my life.		
3. I seem to worry all the time.		
4. I've been feeling irritable lately.		
5. I'm often afraid.		
B. 1a. I've lost a great deal of weight lately (without dieting); I don't have a very good appetite.		
1b. I've gained a significant amount of weight lately; my appetite has increased significantly.		
2a. I don't sleep well at all.		
2b. I sleep excessively (missing engagements, sleeping the greater part of the day, regularly going to bed very early).		
3a. I feel agitated (I feel pressure toward excessive movement and speech).		
3b. I feel like I move, think, or react more slowly than usual.		
4a. I don't have as much interest in my activities as ever.		
4b. I don't have as much interest in sex as ever.		
5a. I don't have as much energy as ever.		
5b. I feel tired most of the time.		
6a. I feel guilty a good deal of the time.		
6b. I don't think I'm as good a person as others are.		
7a. I have trouble thinking clearly.		
7b. I have trouble concentrating.		
8. I often think about death and dying.		

*Developed by Janice Wood Wetzel (1975), based upon Feighner Criteria for Primary Affective Disorder—Unipolar Type. (Also can be adapted to DSM III criteria for Major Depression.)

DSM III – type Major Depression Inventory falls into this category, although interviewer assistance is alway helpful.[15] The Center for Epidemiological Studies self-report depression scale (CES-D) is designed for research in the general population.[16] The Hamilton Rating Scale for Depression, on the other hand, was created for professional use only for the assessment of severe depression.[17] Hudson's Generalized Contentment Scale is a more recently developed measure primarily used to monitor individual treatment on an ongoing basis.[18] While not included here, readers should be aware that comprehensive measures have been developed that are used for diagnosing the spectrum of disorders, including depression. The work has emanated from the Washington University Department of Psychiatry in St. Louis. The Renard Diagnostic Interview (RDI) was originally designed to elicit Feighner criteria. Later modified and elaborated, the Research Diagnostic Criteria (RDC) were developed. When used with the Schedule for Affective Disorders and Schizophrenia (SADS), diagnostic reliability was found to be greatly improved.[19] (DSM III, incidently, uses the RDC approach, which describes behaviorally identifiable signs and symptoms.) A more recent instrument, the Diagnostic Interview Schedule (DIS) has been even more highly structured for use by lay interviewers in large-scale epidemiological surveys. It is a refinement of SADS and the earlier Renard Diagnostic Interview.[20]

Depression measures are reproduced below, along with a Hopelessness Scale (which also assesses suicide risk) created by Aaron Beck and his colleagues.[21] The Wetzel Independence-Dependence Measures assessing personality attributes in relation to both family and work situations are also included.[22] And, finally, family and work environment subscales developed by Rudolph H. Moos have been included because of their relevance to depression.[23]

Notes

This clinical research inventory was developed by Janice Wood Wetzel in 1975 based upon Feighner Criteria for depression (primary affective disorder—unipolar type). The Feighner Criteria have been validated in outpatient, inpatient, family, and follow-up studies.[24] The criteria are analogous to those for DSM III. Major Depression according to the inventory has been applied in two studies of 400 white, black, and Mexican-American women and men (depressed inpatients and outpatients, and depressed and nondepressed people at large).[25] The Feighner cutoff points have been revised to meet the criteria for DSM III Major Depression.[26] The following criteria, then, must be met:

A. Some symptoms in A are required (may be "masked" in children).

B. At least four of each of the symptom groupings (for children under six, at least three of the first four symptoms must be met).

C. Symptoms must be experienced almost every day for at least two weeks.

BECK DEPRESSION INVENTORY

Name _____ Date _____

On this questionnaire are groups of statements. Please read each group of statements carefully. Then pick out the one statement in each group which best describes the way you have been feeling the *PAST WEEK, INCLUDING TODAY!* Circle the number beside the statement you picked. If several statements in the group seem to apply equally well, circle each one. *Be sure to read all the statements in each group before making your choice.*

1. 0 I do not feel sad.
   1 I feel sad.
   2 I am sad all the time and I can't snap out of it.
   3 I am so sad or unhappy that I can't stand it.

2. 0 I am not particularly discouraged about the future.
   1 I feel discouraged about the future.
   2 I feel I have nothing to look forward to.
   3 I feel that the future is hopeless and that things cannot improve.

3. 0 I do not feel like a failure.
   1 I feel I have failed more than the average person.
   2 As I look back on my life, all I can see is a lot of failures.
   3 I feel I am a complete failure as a person.

4. 0 I get as much satisfaction out of things as I used to.
   1 I don't enjoy things the way I used to.
   2 I don't get real satisfaction out of anything anymore.
   3 I am dissatisfied or bored with everything.

5. 0 I don't feel particularly guilty.
   1 I feel guilty a good part of the time.
   2 I feel quite guilty most of the time.
   3 I feel guilty all of the time.

6. 0 I don't feel I am being punished.
   1 I feel I may be punished.
   2 I expect to be punished.
   3 I feel I am being punished.

BECK DEPRESSION INVENTORY
(continued)

7. 0 I don't feel disappointed in myself.
    1 I am disappointed in myself.
    2 I am disgusted with myself.
    3 I hate myself.

8. 0 I don't feel I am any worse than anybody else.
    1 I am critical of myself for my weaknesses or mistakes.
    2 I blame myself all the time for my faults.
    3 I blame myself for everything bad that happens.

9. 0 I don't have any thoughts of killing myself.
    1 I have thoughts of killing myself, but I would not carry them out.
    2 I would like to kill myself.
    3 I would kill myself if I had the chance.

10. 0 I don't cry anymore than usual.
    1 I cry more now than I used to.
    2 I cry all the time now.
    3 I used to be able to cry, but now I can't cry even though I want to.

11. 0 I am no more irritated now than I ever am.
    1 I get annoyed or irritated more easily than I used to.
    2 I feel irritated all the time now.
    3 I don't get irritated at all by the things that used to irritate me.

12. 0 I have not lost interest in other people.
    1 I am less interested in other people than I used to be.
    2 I have lost most of my interest in other people.
    3 I have lost all of my interest in other people.

13. 0 I make decisions about as well as I ever could.
    1 I put off making decisions more than I used to.
    2 I have greater difficulty in making decisions than before.
    3 I can't make decisions at all anymore.

14. 0 I don't feel I look any worse than I used to.
    1 I am worried that I am looking old or unattractive.
    2 I feel that there are permanent changes in my appearance that
      make me look unattractive.
    3 I believe that I look ugly.

BECK DEPRESSION INVENTORY
(continued)

15. 0 I can work about as well as before.
     1 It takes an extra effort to get started at doing something.
     2 I have to push myself very hard to do anything.
     3 I can't do any work at all.

16. 0 I can sleep as well as usual.
     1 I don't sleep as well as I used to.
     2 I wake up 1–2 hours earlier than usual and find it hard to get back to sleep.
     3 I wake up several hours earlier than I used to and cannot get back to sleep.

17. 0 I don't get more tired than usual.
     1 I get tired more easily than I used to.
     2 I get tired from doing almost anything.
     3 I am too tired to do anything.

18. 0 My appetite is no worse than usual.
     1 My appetite is not as good as it used to be.
     2 My appetite is much worse now.
     3 I have no appetite at all anymore.

19. 0 I haven't lost much weight, if any lately.
     1 I have lost more than 5 pounds.
     2 I have lost more than 10 pounds.
     3 I have lost more than 15 pounds.
        I am purposely trying to lose weight by eating less.
        Yes _____ No _____

20. 0 I am no more worried about my health than usual.
     1 I am worried about physical problems such as aches and pains; or upset stomach; or constipation.
     2 I am very worried about physical problems and it's hard to think of much else.
     3 I am so worried about my physical problems, that I cannot think about anything else.

BECK DEPRESSION INVENTORY
(continued)

21. 0 I have not noticed any recent change in my interest in sex.
    1 I am less interested in sex than I used to be.
    2 I am much less interested in sex now.
    3 I have lost interest in sex completely.

Notes[27]

This is probably the most widely used depression measure. Revised in 1978, it has been validated as a self-administered, as well as an interviewer-administered, instrument. The depression score is the sum of the weighted responses of items 1 through 21. (The "weight" is the numeral adjacent to each statement.) A score of 4 or less indicates absence or a minimal degree of depression.

HUDSON GENERALIZED
CONTENTMENT SCALE (GCS)

Name_____Today's Date_____

This questionnaire is designed to measure the degree of contentment that you feel about your life and surroundings. It is not a test, so there are no right or wrong answers. Answer each item as carefully and accurately as you can by placing a number beside each one as follows:

> 1 Rarely or none of the time
> 2 A little of the time
> 3 Some of the time
> 4 Good part of the time
> 5 Most or all of the time

Please begin.

1. I feel powerless to do anything about my life. _____
2. I feel blue. _____
3. I am restless and can't keep still. _____
4. I have crying spells. _____
5. It is easy for me to relax. _____
6. I have a hard time getting started on things that I need to do. _____
7. I do not sleep well at night. _____
8. When things get tough, I feel there is always someone I can turn to. _____
9. I feel that the future looks bright for me. _____
10. I feel downhearted. _____
11. I feel that I am needed. _____
12. I feel that I am appreciated by others. _____
13. I enjoy being active and busy. _____
14. I feel that others would be better off without me. _____
15. I enjoy being with other people. _____
16. I feel it is easy for me to make decisions. _____
17. I feel downtrodden. _____
18. I am irritable. _____
19. I get upset easily. _____
20. I feel that I don't deserve to have a good time. _____
21. I have a full life. _____
22. I feel that people really care about me. _____
23. I have a great deal of fun. _____

HUDSON GENERALIZED
CONTENTMENT SCALE (GCS)
(continued)

24. I feel great in the morning. _____

25. I feel that my situation is hopeless. _____

[Items 5, 8, 9, 11, 12, 13, 15, 16, 21, 22, 23, and 24 are scored in reverse order; see Notes, below.]

Reprinted by permission of Walter W. Hudson, copyright 1974.

Notes

The Generalized Contentment Scale is a short-form measure of nonpsychotic depression for use by clinicians and researchers in repeated administrations with the same client. It is for the monitoring and evaluation of the effect of treatment over time using a single-subject design.[28] The GCS was revalidated in 1981, indicating reliability and good discriminant, concurrent, and construct validity.[29] A 25-item "summated category partition" scale, half of the items are positively worded in order to reduce response bias. Each item is scored on a 5-point scale, following reversal of all positively worded items, so that 1 = 5, 2 = 4, 4 = 2, and 5 = 1. An item score of 3 remains unchanged. The numbers that must be reverse-scored are listed at the bottom of the GCS. After all of the items are summated, subtract 25 for a final score. A cutoff of 30 is used, indicating that scores above 30 represent the presence of depression. When using the scale on an ongoing basis, the respondent should be aware of its purpose. While reporting bias may be expected, it is still relevant to the client-therapist interaction. Hudson has found graphing of responses to be helpful for those who are interested in a visual picture of their progress. He also warns that a score of 70 or above reflects suicide risk.

HAMILTON RATING SCALE FOR DEPRESSION

1. DEPRESSED MOOD (Sadness, hopeless, helpless, worthless)
   0 = Absent
   1 = These feeling states indicated only on questioning
   2 = These feeling states spontaneously reported verbally
   3 = Communicates feeling states non-verbally—i.e., through facial expression, posture, voice, and tendency to weep
   4 = Patient reports VIRTUALLY ONLY these feeling states in his spontaneous verbal and non-verbal communication

2. FEELINGS OF GUILT
   0 = Absent
   1 = Self reproach, feels he has let people down
   2 = Ideas of guilt or rumination over past errors or sinful deeds
   3 = Present illness is a punishment. Delusions of guilt
   4 = Hears accusatory or denunciatory voices and/or experiences threatening visual hallucinations

3. SUICIDE
   0 = Absent
   1 = Feels life is not worth living
   2 = Wishes he were dead or any thoughts of possible death to self
   3 = Suicide ideas or gesture
   4 = Attempts at suicide (any serious attempt rates 4)

4. INSOMNIA EARLY
   0 = No difficulty falling asleep
   1 = Complains of occasional difficulty falling asleep—i.e., more than ½ hour
   2 = Complains of nightly difficulty falling asleep

5. INSOMNIA MIDDLE
   0 = No difficulty
   1 = Patient complains of being restless and disturbed during the night
   2 = Waking during the night—any getting out of bed rates 2 (except for purposes of voiding)

6. INSOMNIA LATE
   0 = No difficulty
   1 = Waking in early hours of the morning but goes back to sleep
   2 = Unable to fall asleep again if he gets out of bed

7. WORK AND ACTIVITIES
   0 = No difficulty
   1 = Thoughts and feelings of incapacity, fatigue or weakness related to activities; work or hobbies
   2 = Loss of interest in activity; hobbies or work—either directly reported by patient, or indirect in listlessness, indecision and vacillation (feels he has to push self to work or activities)

HAMILTON RATING SCALE FOR DEPRESSION
(continued)

3 = Decrease in actual time spent in activities or decrease in productivity. In hospital, rate 3 if patient does not spend at least three hours a day in activities (hospital job or hobbies) exclusive of ward chores

4 = Stopped working because of present illness. In hospital, rate 4 if patient engages in no activities except ward chores, or if patient fails to perform ward chores unassisted

8. RETARDATION (Slowness of thought and speech; impaired ability to concentrate; decreased motor activity)
   0 = Normal speech and thought
   1 = Slight retardation at interview
   2 = Obvious retardation at interview
   3 = Interview difficult
   4 = Complete stupor

9. AGITATION
   0 = None
   1 = Fidgetiness
   2 = Playing with hands, hair, etc.
   3 = Moving about, can't sit still
   4 = Hand wringing, nail biting, hair-pulling, biting of lips

10. ANXIETY PSYCHIC
    0 = No difficulty
    1 = Subjective tension and irritability
    2 = Worrying about minor matters
    3 = Apprehensive attitude apparent in face or speech
    4 = Fears expressed without questioning

11. ANXIETY SOMATIC
    0 = Absent
    1 = Mild
    2 = Moderate
    3 = Severe
    4 = Incapacitating
    Physiological concomitants of anxiety such as:
    Gastro-intestinal—dry mouth, wind, indigestion, diarrhea, cramps, belching
    Cardio-Vascular—palpitations, headaches
    Respiratory—hyperventilation, sighing
    Urinary frequency
    Sweating

12. SOMATIC SYMPTOMS GASTROINTESTINAL
    0 = None
    1 = Loss of appetite but eating without staff encouragement. Heavy feelings in abdomen

HAMILTON RATING SCALE FOR DEPRESSION
(continued)

2 = Difficulty eating without staff urging. Requests or requires laxatives or medication for bowels or medication for G.I. symptoms

13. SOMATIC SYMPTOMS GENERAL

0 = None

1 = Heaviness in limbs, back or head. Backaches, headache, muscle aches. Loss of energy and fatigability

2 = Any clear-cut symptom rates 2

14. GENITAL SYMPTOMS

0 = Absent

1 = Mild

2 = Severe

Symptoms such as: Loss of libido

Menstrual disturbances

15. HYPONCHONDRIASIS

0 = Not present

1 = Self-absorption (bodily)

2 = Preoccupation with health

3 = Frequent complaints, requests for help, etc.

4 = Hypochondrical delusions

16. LOSS OF WEIGHT   Rate either A or B

A. When Rating by History:

0 = No weight loss

1 = Probably weight loss associated with present illness

2 = Definite (according to patient) weight loss

3 = Not assessed

B. On Weekly Ratings by Ward Psychiatrist,
When Actual Weight Changes are Measured:

0 = Less than 1 lb. weight loss in week

1 = Greater than 1 lb. weight loss in week

2 = Greater than 2 lb. weight loss in week

3 = Not assessed

17. INSIGHT

0 = Acknowledges being depressed and ill

1 = Acknowledges illness but attributes cause to bad food, climate, overwork, virus, need for rest, etc.

2 = Denies being ill at all

18. DIURNAL VARIATION

A. Note whether symptoms are worse in morning or evening. If NO diurnal variation, mark none

HAMILTON RATING SCALE FOR DEPRESSION

(continued)

0 = No variation
1 = Worse in A.M.
2 = Worse in P.M.

  B. When present, mark the severity of the variation.
    Mark "None" if NO variation

0 = None
1 = Mild
2 = Severe

19. DEPERSONALIZATION AND DEREALIZATION
   0 = Absent
   1 = Mild
   2 = Moderate
   3 = Severe
   4 = Incapacitating
     Such as: Feelings of unreality
           Nihilistic ideas

20. PARANOID SYMPTOMS
   0 = None
   1 = Suspicious
   2 = Ideas of reference
   3 = Delusions of reference and persecution

21. OBSESSIONAL AND COMPULSIVE SYMPTOMS
   0 = Absent
   1 = Mild
   2 = Severe

Reprinted by permission from Max Hamilton, M.D., The University of Leeds, Leeds, England.

Notes

The Hamilton Rating Scale for Depression (HRSD) was designated to quantify systematically the *severity* of depression in patients who have already been so diagnosed. Hamilton stresses that the HRSD should *not* be used as a diagnostic instrument. Its value, he says, depends entirely on the interviewer's skill in eliciting the information that is needed. He recommends at least a half-hour interview time, with information from all available sources included in the evaluation. This is considered *the* standard observer rating scale, and is used extensively in clinical research relating to the efficacy of antidepressant treatment and other interventions. Hamilton recommends the use of two independent raters for optimal reliability, scoring a patient at the same interview.[30] Both scores are added together for a total possible score of 100. Despite its validity, many investigators suggest that patient self-report measures be used in addition to the HRSD to better assess the severity and nature of depression. Clinical assessment and self-ratings, as a rule, have different components.[31]

CENTER FOR EPIDEMIOLOGICAL STUDIES
DEPRESSION (CES-D) SCALE

INSTRUCTIONS FOR QUESTIONS: Below is a list of the ways you might have felt or behaved. Please tell me how often you have felt this way during the past week.

> 0 Rarely or None of the Time (Less than 1 Day)
> 1 Some or a Little of the Time (1–2 Days)
> 2 Occasionally or a Moderate Amount of Time (3–4 Days)
> 3 Most or All of the Time (5–7 Days)

During the past week:

1. I was bothered by things that usually don't bother me.
2. I did not feel like eating; my appetite was poor.
3. I felt that I could not shake off the blues even with help from my family or friends.
4. I felt that I was just as good as other people.
5. I had trouble keeping my mind on what I was doing.
6. I felt depressed.
7. I felt that everything I did was an effort.
8. I felt hopeful about the future.
9. I thought my life had been a failure.
10. I felt fearful.
11. My sleep was restless.
12. I was happy.
13. I talked less than usual.
14. I felt lonely.
15. People were unfriendly.
16. I enjoyed life.
17. I had crying spells.
18. I felt sad.
19. I felt that people dislike me.
20. I could not get "going."

Notes

Originally developed by Ben Z. Locke and Peter Putnam, the CES-D is a short self-report scale designed to measure symptoms of depression for use in epidemiological research in the general population. Each response is scored from 0 to 3 depending on the frequency of the occurrence of the symptom. It has been tested in household interviews and in psychiatric settings and has been found to have reliability, validity, and a similar factor structure across a wide variety of subgroups in the population. This is especially important in epidemiological investigations. The scale is not intended as a clinical diagnostic tool, so individual and group interpretations of scores should not be made relative to illness rates. Groups with high average scores may be interpreted as "at risk," however, or in need of treatement. The scale is a valuable tool for identification of such groups. While it appears that the CES-D is suitable for black and white English – speaking groups, there is some question relative to bilingual respondents. It has been suggested that the scale be revised, using more commonplace words and removing colloquial expressions. In the meantime, caution should be taken when considering the CES-D for particular populations.[32]

HOPELESSNESS SCALE

Name_____ Date_____

This questionnaire consists of a list of twenty statements (sentences). Please read the statements carefully one by one.

If the statement describes your attitude *for the past week, including today,* write down TRUE next to it. If the statement is false for you, write FALSE next to it. You may simply write T for TRUE and F for FALSE. Please be sure to read each sentence.

_____ A. I look forward to the future with hope and enthusiasm.

_____ B. I might as well give up because there's nothing I can do about making things better for myself.

_____ C. When things are going badly, I am helped by knowing that they can't stay that way forever.

_____ D. I can't imagine what my life would be like in ten years.

_____ E. I had enough time to accomplish the things I most want to do.

_____ F. In the future I expect to succeed in what concerns me most.

_____ G. My future seems dark to me.

_____ H. I happen to be particularly lucky and I expect to get more of the good things in life than the average person.

_____ I. I just don't get the breaks, and there's no reason to believe I will in the future.

_____ J. My past experiences have prepared me well for my future.

_____ K. All I can see ahead of me is unpleasantness rather than pleasantness.

_____ L. I don't expect to get what I really want.

_____ M. When I look ahead to the future I expect I will be happier than I am now.

HOPELESSNESS SCALE
(continued)

_____ N. Things just won't work out the way I want them to.

_____ O. I have great faith in the future.

_____ P. I never get what I want so it's foolish to want anything.

_____ Q. It is very unlikely that I will get any real satisfaction in the future.

_____ R. The future seems vague and uncertain to me.

_____ S. I can look forward to more good times than bad times.

_____ T. There's no use in really trying to get something I want because I probably won't get it.

Notes

The 20-item Hopelessness Scale was developed and is being tested by Aaron Beck, with the assistance of Arlene Weisman, David Lester, and Larry Trexler. It is particularly concerned with a respondent's negative expectations, a cognitive factor correlated more highly with suicidal intent than depression itself. The scale also reflects depressive cognition and is sensitive to changes in a person's state of depression. Validity data are limited but positive and are deemed sufficient to justify use of the scale on a continuing basis. It can be used readily by professionals and paraprofessionals.[33]

WETZEL FAMILY INDEPENDENCE-DEPENDENCE SCALE

Please check the column which best represents how much you agree or disagree with each of the following statements about yourself.

	Strongly Agree	Agree	Mildly Agree	Undecided	Mildly Disagree	Disagree	Strongly Disagree
1. At home, when I have something to say, I generally say it.							
2. When I have a problem, I prefer getting advice from others in the family.							
3. At home, I like to work things out for myself.							
4. I'm really not curious about the world.							
5. At home, I usually rely on my own resources and capabilities.							
6. Developing my potential is not important to me.							
7. I'm not the adventurous type.							
8. At home, I welcome making decisions.							
9. I just don't like being alone at home.							
10. I like to solve my own problems at home.							
11. Even when I start out disagreeing with others in the family, I generally end up going along with the majority.							

WETZEL FAMILY INDEPENDENCE-DEPENDENCE SCALE
(continued)

	Strongly Agree	Agree	Mildly Agree	Undecided	Mildly Disagree	Disagree	Strongly Disagree
12. For me, the more responsibility at home, the better I like it.							
13. The point of view of others in the family influences me.							
14. At home, reassurance is important to me.							
15. At home, I would accept a task for which I was unprepared and try to do it well.							
16. I generally don't stay involved in situations that frighten me.							
17. I'm very attached to my home and family.							
18. I just don't like to make decisions alone at home.							
19. At home, I think twice before I say what is on my mind.							
20. I look for help from others in the family when I have a problem.							
21. I'm not interested in what goes on in the world.							
22. I consider myself to be a self-reliant person at home.							
23. At home, I live by my own values.							

WETZEL FAMILY INDEPENDENCE-DEPENDENCE SCALE
(continued)

	Strongly Agree	Agree	Mildly Agree	Undecided	Mildly Disagree	Disagree	Strongly Disagree
24. I try to solve my own problems at home.							
25. I voice my opinion even if it differs from others in the family.							
26. At home, I don't feel secure about what I think and do.							
27. You often can't rely on the opinions of others in the family.							
28. I look up to other people in the family.							
29. I'm not interested in exploring ideas and places.							
30. The perspectives of others in the family influence me.							
31. I wouldn't accept a task if I hadn't been taught how to do it correctly.							
32. I find family pressure to be a powerful incentive.							
33. I assert myself at home.							
34. I really don't like to make decisions at home without the help of other members of the family.							
35. I usually do what others in the family want to do.							

WETZEL WORK INDEPENDENCE-
DEPENDENCE SCALE

Please check the column which best represents how much you agree or disagree with each of the following statements about yourself.

	Strongly Agree	Agree	Mildly Agree	Undecided	Mildly Disagree	Disagree	Strongly Disagree
1. At work, when I have something to say, I generally say it.							
2. When I have a problem at work, I prefer getting advice from others.							
3. I like to work things out for myself.							
4. I'm curious about the world.							
5. At work, whether or not I belong is not very important to me.							
6. At work, I usually rely on my own resources and capabilities.							
7. In deciding how to live my life, I consider the values of others at work to be of importance.							
8. Developing my potential is important to me.							
9. I like to solve my own problems at work.							
10. I voice my opinion if it differs from others at work.							
11. At work, I welcome making decisions.							

WETZEL WORK INDEPENDENCE-
DEPENDENCE SCALE
(continued)

	Strongly Agree	Agree	Mildly Agree	Undecided	Mildly Disagree	Disagree	Strongly Disagree
12. You can generally rely on the opinions of others at work.							
13. I'm the adventurous type.							
14. I don't necessarily do what others at work want to do.							
15. I look for help from others at work when I have a problem.							
16. I'm interested in what goes on in the world.							
17. Making something of myself is important to me.							
18. I consider myself to be a self-reliant person at work.							
19. I voice my opinion even if it differs from others at work.							
20. At work, I generally feel secure about what I think and do.							
21. I rather enjoy working alone.							
22. I really don't like to make decisions at work without the help of others.							
23. I find group pressure to be a powerful incentive at work.							

WETZEL WORK INDEPENDENCE-DEPENDENCE SCALE
(continued)

	Strongly Agree	Agree	Mildly Agree	Undecided	Mildly Disagree	Disagree	Strongly Disagree
24. I assert myself at work.							
25. At work, even if I'm afraid, I go ahead.							
26. The perspectives of others at work influence me.							

Notes on Person Measures: Wetzel Independence and Dependence Scales[34]

The person-environment studies indicate that some subjects, albeit a minority, tend to be dependent in one environment and not in another. *Dependence* is interpreted as psychological reliance on other persons as primary sources of approval and help, characterized chiefly by how easily one is influenced, lack of interest in self-development, and low risk taking. *Independence* is defined as psychological reliance on oneself as a primary source of approval and help, characterized chiefly by autonomous behavior (self-reliance, risk taking, assertivenesss, interest in the world, and interest in self-development). To refer to dependence or independence attributes without reference to the characteristics of the predisposition or the environment in which the attitudes or behaviors occur may be an inaccurate assessment.

The Wetzel Independence-Dependence Scales measure aspects of both attributes on a continuum in family and work environments. There are three subscales for each environment with no correlations among them. Each subscale, therefore, represents an independent grouping of items. The 35 Family Independence-Dependence items and 26 Work Independence-Dependence items are based upon theory and empirical data relative to dependence and independence. Although the reliability and validity data are limited, they indicate positive results. The measures also have been found to discriminate significantly between depressed and nondepressed groups, thereby establishing predictive validity.

While all six subscales can be used when appropriate, Family Factor I and Work Factor I have been found to be highly significant discriminating variables in regard to well-being and depression. People who measured high on Independence relative to these factors were not depressed in either study. Since these factors also have the highest alpha reliability coefficients (.88 and .86, respectively), they may be considered to be the most reliable of the subscales for use in mental health research.

Scores for subscales Family Factor II, Work Factor I, and Work Factor III are weighted from 7 (Strongly Agree) to 1 (Strongly Disagree). Scores are reversed for Family Factor I, Family Factor III, and Work Factor II where Strongly Agree = 1 and Strongly Disagree = 7. High scores represent a predisposition to independence in each environment, and low scores represent a predisposition ot dependence. The Family Factor and Work Factor items are identified below. When scoring the I-D measures, reverse = score the factors marked with an asterisk (*).

Family Independence-Dependence Measures

*Family Factor I—Easy Influence:
    Items 2, 9, 11, 13, 14, 17, 18, 20, 28, 31, 33, 35, 36.
 Family Factor II—Self-Reliance and Assertiveness:
    Items 1, 3, 5, 8, 10, 12, 15, 22, 23, 24, 25, 34.
*Family Factor III—Lack of Interest in the World, Low Risk Taking,
    and Insecurity:
    Items 4, 6, 7, 16, 19, 21, 26, 27, 30, 32.

Work Independence-Dependence Measures

Work Factor I—Self-Reliance: Interest in the World, Interest in
    Self-Development and Assertiveness:
    Items 1, 8, 10, 11, 13, 14, 15, 17, 18, 19, 20, 24.
*Work Factor II—Easy Influence:
    Items 2, 7, 12, 15, 22, 23, 26.
Work Factor III—Autonomy and Risk Taking:
    Items 3, 4, 5, 6, 9, 21, 25.

MOOS FAMILY ENVIRONMENT SUBSCALES

RELATION DIMENSION

Cohesion (Supportiveness)—The extent to which family are concerned and committed to the family and the degree to which family members are helpful and supportive of each other.

1. _____ Family members really help and support one another.

2. _____ We often seem to be killing time at home.

3. _____ We put a lot of energy into what we do at home.

4. _____ There is a feeling of togetherness in our family.

5. _____ We rarely volunteer when something has to be done at home.

6. _____ Family members really back each other up.

7. _____ There is very little group spirit in our family.

8. _____ We really get along well with each other.

9. _____ There is plenty of time and attention for everyone in our family.

MOOS FAMILY ENVIRONMENT SUBSCALES
(continued)

PERSONAL GROWTH AND DEVELOPMENT DIMENSION

Independence (Autonomy)—The extent to which family members are encouraged to be assertive, self-sufficient, to make their own decisions, and to think things out for themselves.

1. _____ I don't do things on my own very often in our family.

2. _____ In our family, I am strongly encouraged to be independent.

3. _____ I am encouraged to think things out for myself in our family.

4. _____ I come and go as I want to in our family.

5. _____ There is very little privacy in our family.

6. _____ I almost always rely on myself when a problem comes up.

7. _____ Family members strongly encourage me to stand up for my rights.

8. _____ It's hard to be by yourself without hurting someone's feelings in our household.

9. _____ I am not really encouraged to speak up for myself in our family.

Excerpted by permission from Rudolph H. Moos *Family Environment Scale* (Palo Alto, CA: Consulting Psychologists Press, 1974.)

MOOS WORK ENVIRONMENT SUBSCALES

RELATIONSHIP DIMENSION

Peer Cohesion (Supportiveness)—The extent to which workers are friendly and supportive to each other.

1. _____ People go out of their way to help new employees feel comfortable.

2. _____ The atmosphere is somewhat impersonal.

3. _____ People take a personal interest in each other.

4. _____ Employees rarely do things together after work.

5. _____ People are generally frank about how they feel.

6. _____ Employees often eat lunch together.

7. _____ Employees who differ greatly from the others in the organization don't get on well.

8. _____ Employees often talk to each other about their personal problems.

9. _____ Often people make trouble by talking behind others' backs.

Staff Support—The extent to which management is supportive of workers and encourages workers to be supportive of each other.

1. _____ Supervisors tend to talk down to employees.

2. _____ Supervisors usually compliment an employee who does something well.

3. _____ Supervisors tend to discourage criticisms from employees.

MOOS WORK ENVIRONMENT SUBSCALES
(continued)

4. _____ Supervisors usually give full credit to ideas contributed by employees.

5. _____ Supervisors often criticize employees over minor things.

6. _____ Employees generally feel free to ask for a raise.

7. _____ Supervisors expect far too much from employees.

8. _____ Employees discuss their personal problems with supervisors.

9. _____ Supervisors really stand up for their people.

Control—The extent to which management uses rules and pressures to keep workers under control.

1. _____ There is strict emphasis on following policies and regulations.

2. _____ People can wear wild looking clothing while on the job if they want [to].

3. _____ People are expected to follow set rules in doing their work.

4. _____ Supervisors keep a rather close watch on employees.

5. _____ Rules and regulations are pretty well enforced.

6. _____ Supervisors are always checking on employees and supervise them very closely.

7. _____ Supervisors do not often give in to employee pressure.

MOOS WORK ENVIRONMENT SUBSCALES
(continued)

8. _____ Employees are expected to conform rather strictly to the rules and customs.

9. _____ If an employee comes in late, he can make it up by staying late.

Excerpted by permission from Rudolph H. Moos, *Work Environment Scale* (Palo Alto, CA: Consulting Psychologists Press, 1974.)

Notes

While needs vary with the individual, both independent and dependent people require supportive relationships and an absence of control in their social environemnts. Moos' Social Environment subscales (SES) have been selected to measure these situational characteristics both in the home and at work.[35] Those factors that are significant, reflecting an absence of depression, are described below. SES instruments fill a void in clinical and social research. Dozens of studies have implemented them in the years since they were devised. Their reliability and validity are well established.

Supportiveness in the family environment is assessed by a cohesiveness subscale measuring the extent to which family members are concerned and committed to one another and the degree to which they help each other. Such an environment is characterized by a warm, nurturant, harmonious spirit whereby family members actively and voluntarily "back up" one another, offering time and attention in a friendly, responsive manner. The extent to which the family members are encouraged to be autonomous (to be assertive, self-sufficient, to make their own decisions, and to think things out for themselves) is also assessed.

Supportiveness at work is appraised by measuring the extent to which employees are friendly and supportive of one another. Such an environment is characterized by a warm group spirit whereby employees take friendly, personal interest in one another, extending their relationships beyond working hours.

The degree of control evaluates the extent to which management uses rules and pressures to keep workers under control.

NOTES

1. American Psychiatric Association, *Diagnostic and Statistical Manual of Mental Disorders*, 1st ed. (Washington, DC: APA, 1952, (out of print).

2. American Psychiatric Association, *Diagnostic and Statistical Manual of Mental Disorders*, 2nd ed. (Washington, D.C.: APA, 1968.)

3. American Psychiatric Association, *Diagnostic and Statistical Manual of Mental Disorders*, 3rd ed. (Washington DC: APA, 1980) pp. 205 – 224.

4. World Health Organization, "Classification of Mental Disorders," Section V, *International Statistical Classification of Diseases, Injuries, and Causes of Death, Ninth Revision* (Geneva, WHO, 1978).

5. American Psychiatric Association, *Diagnostic and Statistical Manual of Mental Disorders*, 2nd ed. (Washington, DC: APA, 1968).

6. Weissman, Myrna M., and Gerald L. Klerman, "Sex Differences and the Epidemiology of Depression," *Archives of General Psychiatry 34*, 1 (January 1977,) 98 – 111.

7. American Psychiatric Association, *Diagnostic and Statistical Manual of Mental Disorders*, , 3rd ed. (Washington, DC: APA, 1980) pp. 205 – 224.

8. Feighner, John P., Eli Robins, Samuel B. Guze, Robert A. Woodruff Jr., George Winokur, and Rodrigo Munoz, "Diagnostic Criteria for Use in Psychiatric Research," *Archives of General Psychiatry 26* (January 1972): 57 – 63.

9. See Major Depression Inventory in the Instruments section of this chapter for an assessment tool based upon Feighner Criteria for Primary Affective Disorder—Unipolar Type, and DSM III for Major Depression.

10. Chapter 9 discusses depression as an adaptive signal in detail.

11. American Psychiatric Association, *Diagnostic and Statistical Manual of Mental Disorders*, 1st ed. (Washington, DC: APA, 1952; out of print).

12. Spitzer, Robert L., Janet B. W. Williams, and Lyman C. Wynne, "A Revised Decision Tree for the Differential Diagnosis of Psychotic Patients," *Hospital and Community Psychiatry 34*,, 7 (July 1983): 631 – 633.

13. Beck, Aaron T., *Depression: Cause and Treatment* (Philadelphia: University of Pennsylvania Press, 1972).

14. Zung, W. W. K., "A Self-Rating Depression Scale," *Archives of General Psychiatry 12* (1965): 63 – 70; see also W. W. K. Zung, "From Art to Science: The Diagnosis and Treatment of Depression," *Archives of General Psychiatry 29* (1973): 328 – 337.

15. Wetzel, Janice Wood, "Wetzel Independence-Dependence Scales," copyright 1975, reported in Janice Wood Wetzel and Franklin C. Redmond "A Person-Environment Study of Depression" *Social Service Review 54*, 3 (September 1980) 386 – 375 (Revised 1981).

16. Radloff, Lenore S., "The CES-D Scale: A Self-Report Depression Scale for Research in the General Population," *Applied Psychological Measurement 1*, 3 (Summer 1977): 383 – 401.

17. Hamilton, Max, "A Rating Scale for Depression," *Journal of Neurologic Neurosurgical Psychiatry 23* (1960): 56 – 62; see also Max Hamilton, "A Rating Scale for Depression," *British Journal of Social Clinical Psychology 6* (1967): 278 – 296.

18. Hudson, Walter W., "A Measurement Package for Clinical Workers," paper presented at the 1977 Council on Social Work Education, Annual Pro-

gram Meeting, Phoenix, AZ, March 1977. See also Walter W. Hudson, *The Clinical Measurement Package: A Field Manual* (Homewood, IL; Dorsey, 1982).

19. Robins, Lee N., John Helzer, and Jack Croughan, *Renard Diagnostic Interview* (St. Louis, MO: Washington University Medical School, 1977); see also Robert L. Spitzer, Jean Endicott, and Eli Robins, "Research Diagnostic Criteria: Rationale and Reliability," *Archives of General Psychiatry 35* (1978): 773–782; see also John Endicott, and Robert L. Spitzer, "Use of the Research Diagnostic Criteria and the Schedule for Affective Disorders and Schizophrenia to Study Affective Disorder," *American Journal of Psychiatry 1236* (1979): 52–56.

20. Robins, Lee N., John Helzer, Jack Croughan, et al., *NIMH Diagnostic Interview Schedule: Version II* (Rockville, MD: Center for Epidemiological Studies, National Institute of Mental Health, 1979); see also Jeffrey H. Boyd and Myrna M. Weissman, "Epidemiology of Affective Disorders," *Archives of General Psychiatry 38* (September 1981): 1039–1046.

21. Beck, Aaron T., Arlene Weissman, David Lester, and Larry Trexler, "The Measurement of Pessimism: The Hopelessness Scale," *Journal of Consulting and Clinical Psychology 42*, 6 (1974): 861–865.

22. Wetzel, Janice Wood, "Wetzel Independence-Dependence Scales," copyright 1975, reported in Janice Wood Wetzel and Franklin C. Redmond, 1980; developed for depression research in 1975; revised 1981.

23. Moos, Rudolph H., *Family Environment Scale* (Palo Alto, CA: Consulting Psychologists Press, 1974) and *Work Environment Scale* (Palo Alto, CA: Consulting Psychologists Press, 1974).

24. Feighner, John P., Eli Robins, Samuel B. Guze, Robert A. Woodruff Jr., George Winokur, and Rodrigo Munoz, "Diagnostic Criteria for Use in Psychiatric Reserach," *Archives of General Psychiatry 26* (January 1972): 57–63.

25. Wetzel, Janice Wood, "Depression and Dependence upon Unsustaining Environments," *Clinical Social Work Journal 6* 2 (Summer 1978): 75–89.

26. American Psychiatric Association, DSM III.

27. Beck, Aaron T., *Beck Depression Inventory,* rev. ed. (Philadelphia: Center for Cognitive Therapy, 1978); see also D. Burns and A. T. Beck, "Cognitive Behavior Modification of Mood Disorder," *Cognitive Behavior Therapy: Research and Application,* ed. J. P. Foreyt and D. P. Rathjen (New York: Plenum Press, 1978), pp. 109–134.

28. Hudson, Walter W., "A Measurement Package for Clinical Workers," paper presented at the 1977 Council on Social Work Education, Annual Program Meeting, Phoenix, AZ, March 1977; see also Walter W. Hudson and Enola K. Proctor, "Assessment of Depressive Affect in Clinical Practice," *Journal of Consulting and Clinical Psychology 45*, 6 (1977): 1206–1207; see also Walter W. Hudson, *The Clinical Measurement Package: A Field Manual* (Homewood, IL; Dorsey, 1982).

29. Hudson, Walter W., Roger S. Hamada, Ruth Keech, and Jon Harlan, "A Comparison and Revalidation of Three Measures of Depression," (Unpublished manuscript, Florida State University, Tallahassee, Florida, 1981).

30. Hamilton, Max, "A Rating Scale for Depression," *Journal of Neurologic Neurosurgical Psychiatry 23*, (1960): 56–62; see also Max Hamilton, "A Rating Scale for Depression," *British Journal of Social Clinical Psychology 6* (1967): 278–296.

31. Hedlund, James L., and Bruce W. Vieweg, "The Hamilton Rating Scale for Depression: A Comprehensive Review," *Journal of Operational Psychiatry 10*, 2 (1979): 149–166.

32. Radloff, Lenore S., "The CES-D Scale: A Self-Report Depression Scale for Reserach in the General Population," *Applied Psychological Measurement 1*, 3 (Summer 1977): 383–401.

33. Beck, Aaron T., Arlene Weissman, David Lester, and Larry Trexler, "The Measurement of Pessimism: The Hopelessness Scale," *Journal of Consulting and Clinical Psychology 42)* 6 (1974): 861–165.

34. Wetzel, Janice Wood, "Wetzel Independence-Dependence Scales," copyright 1975, reported in Janice Wood Wetzel and Franklin C. Redmond, 1980; see also Janice Wood Wetzel and Franklin C. Redmond, "A Person-Environment Study of Depression," *Social Service Review 54*, 3 (September 1980): 363–375.

35. Moos, Rudolph H., *Family Environment Scale* (Palo Alto, CA: Consulting Psychologists Press, 1974) see also Rudolph H. Moos, *Work Environment Scale* (Palo Alto, CA: Consulting Psychologists Press, 1974).

Bibliography

Abraham, Karl. "Notes on the Psychoanalytic Investigation and Treatment on Manic-Depressive Insanity and Allied Conditions," (1911). In *Selected Papers on Psychoanalysis*. New York: Basic Books, 1960, pp. 137 – 156.

Acker, Joan and Donald R. Van Houten. "Differential Recruitment and Control: the Sex Structuring of Organization," *Administrative Science Quarterly* 17 (1972): 117 – 125.

Aegis: Magazine on Ending Violence Against Women (Summer/Autumn 1980).

Ahearn, Frederick L. "Psychological Effects of the Nuclear Threat: An Issue for Clinicians". Paper presented at the First NASW Clinical Conference, Washington, D.C., November 18, 1982.

Ahrens, Lois. "Battered Women's Refuges: Feminist Cooperatives vs. Social Service Institutions," *Radical America 14* 3 (May – June 1980): 41 – 47.

Akiskal, Hagop S. and Raffi Tashjian. "Affective Disorder: II. Recent Advances in Laboratory and Pathogenetic Approaches," *Hospital and Community Psychiatry 34*, 9 (September 1983): 822 – 830.

Akiskal, Hagop S. and William T. McKinney, Jr. "Depressive Disorders: Toward a Unified Hypothesis," *Science 182* (1973): 20 – 29.

————. "Overview of Recent Research on Depression," *Archives of General Psychiatry 32* (1975): 285 – 305.

Akiskal, Hagop S. and William L. Webb, Jr. "Affective Disorders: I. Recent Advances in Clinical Conceptualization," *Hospital and Community Psychiatry 34*, 8 (August 1983): 695 – 702.

Alexander, James. "On Dependence and Independence," *Bulletin of the Philadelphia Association of Psychoanalysis 20*, 1 (1970): 49 – 57.

Allport, Gordon. *Becoming: Basic Considerations for a Psychology of Personality*. New Haven: Yale University Press, 1955.

Almay, Bela G. L., Folke Johansson, Lars Von Knorring, Lars Terenius, and Agneta Wohlstrom. "Endorphins in Chronic Pain: Differences in CSF Endorphin Levels between Organic and Psychogenic Pain Syndromes," *Pain 5*, 2 (August 1978): 153 – 162.

American Psychiatric Association. *Diagnostic and Statistical Manual of Mental Disorders*. 1st ed. Washington, D.C.: APA, 1952 (out of print).

————. *Diagnostic and Statistical Manual of Mental Disorders*. 2nd ed. Washington, D.C.: APA, 1968.

————. *Diagnostic and Statistical Manual of Mental Disorders*. 3rd ed. Washington, D.C.: APA, 1980, pp. 205 – 224.

Anton, Jane, Dunbar and L. Friedman. "Anticipation Training in the Treatment of Depression." In J. D. Krumboltz and C. E. Thoesen, eds., *Counselling Methods*. New York: Holt, Rinehart, and Winston, 1976.

Argyris, Chris. "Personality and Organization Theory Revisitied," *Administrative Science Quarterly 18* (1973): 141 – 167.

Arieti, Silvano and Jules Bemporad. *Severe and Mild Depression: The Psychotherapeutic Approach*. New York: Basic Books, 1978.

Assogioli, Roberto. *Psychosynthesis*. New York: Viking Press, 1971.

Atchley, Robert C. *The Social Forces in Later Life*. Belmont, CA: Wadsworth Publishing Co. 1977.

Bach, Richard. *Illusions*. New York: Delacorte Press, 1978.

Baldessarini, Ross J. "A Summary of Biomedical Aspects of Mood Disorders," *McLean Hospital Journal 6*, (1981): 1 – 34 (Belmont, MA).

Baldessarini, Ross J. "Overview of Recent Advances in Anti-depressant Pharmacology: Part II," *McLean Hospital Journal 8* (1981): 1 – 27 (Belmont, MA).

Bando, Shojun. "The Dual Aspect of Faith." In Yusaf Ibish and Ileana Marculescu, eds., *Contemplation and Action in World Religions*. Seattle: University of Washington Press: Rothko Chapel Book, 1978, pp. 16 – 27.

Bandura, Albert. "Self Efficacy: Toward a Unifying Theory of Behavioral Change," *Psychological Review 84*, 2 (March 1977): 191 – 215.

Barker, Roger G. *Ecological Psychology: Concepts and Methods for Studying the Environment of Human Behavior.* Stanford CA: Stanford University Press, 1968.

Bart, Pauline. "Depression in Middle-Aged Women." In Vivian Gornick and Barbara Moran, eds., *Women in Sexist Society.* New York: Basic Books, 1971, pp. 99 – 117.

Bateson, Mary Catherine. *Our Own Metaphor.* New York: Knopf, 1973.

Baumrind, Diana. "New Directions in Socialization Research," *American Psychologist 35*, 7 (July 1980): 639 – 652.

Beck, Aaron T. *Depression: Clinical Experiemental and Theoretical Aspects.* New York: Harper and Row, 1967.

———. *Depression: Cause and Treatment.* Philadelphia University of Pennsylvania Press, 1972.

———. *The Diagnosis and Management of Depression.* Philadelphia: University of Pennsylvania Press, 1973.

———. *Beck Depression Inventory.* Revised. Philadelphia: Center for Cognitive Therapy, 1978.

Beck, Aaron T. and Ruth L. Greenberg. "Cognitive Therapy with Depressed Women," In Violet Frank and Vasanti Burtle, eds., *Women-in-Therapy.* New York: Brunner/Mazel, 1974, pp. 113 – 131.

Beck, Aaron T., Arlene Weissman, David Lester, and Larry Trexler. "The Measurement of Pessimism: The Hopelessness Scale," *Journal of Consulting and Clinical Psychology 42*, 6 (1974): 861 – 165.

Beck, Aaron T., A. John Rush, Brian F. Shaw, and Gary Emery. *Cognitive Therapy of Depression.* New York: The Guilford Press, 1979.

Belle, Deborah, ed. *Lives in Stress.* Beverly Hills: Sage Publications, 1982.

Bem, Donald. *Beliefs, Attitudes, and Human Affairs.* Belmont, CA: Brooks/Cole, 1970.

Bem, Sandra. "Sex-Role Adaptability: One Consequence of Psychological Androgeny," *Journal of Personality and Social Psychology 31* (1975): 634 – 643.

Benedict, Ruth. Quoted in Abraham Maslow, 1978, and in Charles Hampden – Turner, 1981.

Berger, Peter L. and Thomas Luckmann. *The Social Construction of Reality.* Garden City, NY: Doubleday, 1967.

Berk, Richard, Sara Berk, and Catherine Berheide. "The Non-Division of Household Labor," *Science Monographs*, NIMH, DHEW Pub. No. (ADM) (1978): 78 – 160.

Bernard, Jesse. *The Future of Marriage.* New York: Bantam Books, 1973.

———. "Homosociality and Female Depression," *Journal of Social Issues 32* (1976): 213 – 238.

———. "The Good Provider Role: Its Rise and Fall," *American Psychologist 36*, 1 (January 1981): 1 – 12.

Berne, Eric. *Games People Play: The Psychology of Human Relationships.* New York: Grove Press, 1964.

————. *What Do You Say After You Say Hello?* New York: Grove Press, 1972.

Bibring, Edward. "Mechanisms of Depression." In Phyllis Greenacre, ed., *Affective Disorders.* New York: International Universities Press, 1953.

Bikson, Tora Kay and Jacqueline K. Goodchilds. *Old People and New Ideas: Receptivity and Rigidity.* Santa Monica, CA: Rand Corporation, August 1979.

Binswanger, Ludwig. *Being-in-the-World: Selected Papers of Ludwig Binswanger.* New York: Basic Books, 1963.

Blakney, Raymond B. *Meister Eckhart: A Modern Translation.* New York: Harper and Row, 1941.

Blanck, Gertrude and Rubin Blanck. *Ego Psychology: Theory and Practice.* New York: Columbia University Press, 1974.

————. *Ego Psychology II: Psychoanalytic Developmental Psychology.* New York: Columbia University Press, 1979.

Blatt, Sidney J. "Levels of Object Representation in Anaclitic and Introjective Depression," *The Psychoanalytic Study of the Child 29* (1974): 107−157.

Blatt, Sidney J., Steven Wein, Eve Chevron, and Donald Quinn. "Parental Representations and Depression in Normal Young Adults," *Journal of Abnormal Psychology 88,* 4 (1979): 388−397.

Blau, Zena Smith. *Old Age in a Changing Society.* New York: Franklin Watts, 1973.

Block, Marilyn R., Janice L. Davidson, Jean D. Grambs, and Kathryn E. Serock. *Uncharter Territory: Issues and Concerns of Women over 40.* Center on Aging: College Park, University of Maryland, 1978.

Bloodworth, Venice J. *The Key to Yourself.* Los Angeles: Scrivener and Co., 1965.

Bloom, Lynn Z., Karen Coburn, and Joan Pearlman. *The New Assertive Woman.* New York: Dell Publishing, 1975.

Boss, Medard. *Psychoanalysis and Daseinsanalysis.* New York: Basic Books, 1963.

Bowlby, John. *Attachment and Loss* (Series). *Attachment,* I, 1969 *Separation Anxiety and Anger,* II, 1973 *Loss, Sadness and Depression,* III, 1980. New York: Basic Books.

Bowles, Dorcas D. "The Development of the Ethnic Self-Representation Unity Within the Self-Representation." Unpublished manuscript, Smith College School for Social Work, Northampton, MA, March 26, 1981.

Boyd, Jeffrey H. and Myrna M. Weissman. "Epidemiology of Affective Disorders," *Archives of General Psychiatry 38* (September 1981): 1039−1046.

Braverman, Harry. "Labor and Monopoly Capital: The Degradation of Work in the Twentieth Century," *Monthly Review 26* 3 (July−August 1974).

Brecher, Edward M. and the Editors of *Consumer Reports. Licit and Illicit Drugs.* Boston: Little, Brown, 1972.

Breggin, Peter Roger. "The Second Wave," *Mental Hygiene* (March 1973).

Brodhead, Constance. "Mental Illness." Unpublished manuscript, Washington University, St. Louis, MO, 1971.

Bronfen, Nan. *Nutrition for a Better Life: A Source Book for the Eighties.* Santa Barbara: Capra Press, 1980.

Broverman, Inge K., D. M. Broverman, F. E. Clarkson, P. S. Rosenbrantz, and S. Vogel. "Sex Role Stereotypes and Clinical Judgments of Mental Health." *Journal of Consulting and Clinical Psychology 34,* 1 (1970): 1−7.

Brown, George W. and Tirril Harris. *Social Origins of Depression.* New York: The Free Press, 1978.

Brown, P. and R. Manela. "Changing Family Roles: Women and Divorce," *Journal of Divorce 1*, 4 (1978): 315–328.

Bruch, Hilda. *The Golden Cage: The Enigma of Anorexia-Nervosa*. Cambridge, MA: Harvard University Press, 1978.

Buber, Martin. *Hasidism and Modern Man*. New York: Harper and Row, 1958.

Bugental, James F. T. *The Search for Existential Identity*. San Francisco: Jossey-Bass, 1976.

Burns, D. and A. T. Beck. "Cognitive Behavioral Modification of Mood Disorder." In J. P. Foreyt and D. P. Rathjen, eds., *Cognitive Behavior Therapy: Reserach and Application*. New York: Plenum Press, 1978, pp. 109–134.

Burton, Robert (Democritis Junior). *The Anatomy of Melancholy*. Oxford: Printed by John Lichfield and Iames/Short, for Henry Cripps. Anno Dom. 1621.

———. *The Anatomy of Melancholy* (1621). Edited and published by Floyd Dell and Jordan-Smith, New York, 1927.

Butler, Sandra. *Conspiracy of Silence: The Trauma of Incest*. San Francisco: New Glide Publications, 1978.

Butler, Robert N. and Myrna S. Lewis. *Aging and Mental Health: Positive Psychosocial Approaches*. St. Louis: C. V. Mosby, 1973.

Butterworth, Eric. *Discover the Power within You*. New York: Harper and Row, 1968.

Camus, Albert. *The Rebel*. New York: Vintage, 1956.

Cardoza, Victor G., William C. Acherly, and Alexander H. Leighton. "Improving Mental Health through Community Action," *Community Mental Health Journal 11* (Summer 1975): 215–227.

Carroll, Bernard J. "Implications of Biological Research for the Diagnosis of Depression." In J. Mendelwicz, ed., *New Advances in the Diagnosis and Treatment of Depressive Illness*. Amsterdam: Elsevier, 1981.

Cauwells, Janice M. *Bulemia: The Binge-Purge Compulsion*, Garden City, NY: Doubleday, 1983.

Centerpoint I. Extention Course of Jungian Thought. St. Louis, MO, 1980.

Cheraskin, E. *Psychodietetics*. New York: Bantam Books, 1976.

Chevron, Eve, Donald Quinlan, and Sidney J. Blatt. "Sex Roles and Gender Differences in the Experience of Depression," *Journal of Abnormal Psychology 87*, 6 (1978): 680–683.

Chodoff, Paul. "The Core Problem of Depression: Interpersonal Aspects," In *Science and Psychoanalysis*, Vol. 27. New York: Grune and Stratton, 1970.

Chodorow, Nancy. "Being and Doing." In Vivian Gornick and Barbara K. Moran, eds., *Woman in Sexist Society*. New York: Basic Books, 1971, pp. 173–197.

———. *The Reproduction of Mothering: Psychoanalysis and the Sociology of Gender*. Berkeley: University of California Press, 1978.

Chopin, Kate. *The Awakening*, ed. by Lewis Leary. New York: Holt, Rinehart, and Winston, 1970. (Originally published in 1893.)

Christ, Adolph. "Psychotherapy of the Child with True Brain Damage," *American Journal of Orthopsychiatry 48*, 3 (July 1978): 505–515.

Christ, Carol P. *Diving Deep and Surfacing*. Boston: Beacon Press, 1980.

Christoph, Rosemary. "Anger, The Creative Fire." Paper presented at the Berkeley Anger Workshop, Berkeley, CA, 1978. Reprinted in Shanti Shapiro, *Violence Between Women*. Northampton, MA, 1980.

Clark, Margaret and Barbara Anderson. *Culture and Aging*. Springfield, IL: Charles C. Thomas, 1967.

Clayton, Paula J., James A. Halikas, and William L. Maurice. "The Depression of Widowhood," *American Journal of Psychiatry* 20 (1972): 71–78.

Colgrove, Melba, Harold H. Bloomfield, and Peter McWilliams. *How to Survive the Loss of a Love.* New York: Bantam Books, 1976.

Collins, Glenn. "Exploring the Past: Creativity in Old Age," *New York Times*, Section A, March 2, 1981, p. 16.

Cooper, David. *Psychiatry and Anti-Psychiatry.* London: Tavistock Publications, 1967.

Coyne, J. C. "Depression and the Response of Others," *Journal of Abnormal Psychology* 85 (1976): 186–193.

———. "Toward an Interaction Description of Depression," *Psychiatry* 39 (1976): 28–40.

Crandall, John W. "Pathological Nurturance: The Root of Marital Discord," *Journal of Family Counselling* 4, 2 (1976): 62–68.

Curtis, Jean. *Working Mothers.* New York: Doubleday, 1976.

Cuskey, Walter, T. Premkumar, and Lois Sigel. "Survey of Opiate Addiction among Females in the United States Between 1950 and 1970," *Public Health Review* 1 (1972): 6–39.

Daly, Mary. *Beyond God the Father.* Boston: Beacon Press, 1974.

Datan, Nancy and Leon Ginsberg, eds. *Life-Span Developmental Psychology Conference,* 4th, West Virginia University, 1974. New York: Academic Press, 1975, pp. 191–207.

Davis, Adele. *Let's Get Well.* New York: New American Library, 1972.

Davis, John M. "Overview: Maintenance Therapy in Psychiatry: II. Affective Disorders," *American Journal of Psychiatry* 133, 1 (January 1976): 1–8.

Davis, Kenneth L., Philip Berger, Leo E. Hollister, and Jack D. Barchas. "Cholinergic Involvement in Mental Disorders," *Life Sciences* 22, 21 (June 1978): 1865–1871.

Davison, Gerald C. and John M. Neale. *Abnormal Psychology.* New York: John Wiley and Sons, 1978.

de Beauvoir, Simone. *The Second Sex.* New York: Knopf, 1953.

de Charms, Richard. *Personal Causation: The Internal Affective Determinants of Behavior.* New York: Academic Press, 1968.

Deci, Edward L. *Intrinsic Motivation.* New York: Plenum Press, 1975.

Depue, R.A. and R. Evans. "The Physiology of Depressive Disorders." In B. H. Maher, ed., *Progress in Experimental Personality Research,* Vol. 8. New York: Academic Press, 1976.

DeRosis, Helen and Victoria Pellagrino. *The Book of Hope.* New York: Bantam Books, 1977.

Descartes, Rene. "Meditations of First Philosophy." In Haldane and Ross, eds., *The Philosophical Works of Descartes.* New York: Dover Publications, 1955.

Dillard, Annie. *Pilgrim at Tinker Creek.* New York: Harper's Magazine Press, 1974.

Dinnerstein, Dorothy. *The Mermaid and the Minotaur.* New York: Harper and Row, 1976.

Diran, Margaret O'Keefe. "You Can Prevent Suicide," *Nursing* (January 1976): 60–64.

Dorzab, Joe, Max Baker, Remi Cadoret, and George Winokur. "Depressive Disease: Familial Psychiatric Illness," *American Journal of Psychiatry* 127, 9 (1971): 1128–1133.

Dougher, Christine. "Therapeutic Intervention with Women: The Necessity for a Feminist Orientation." Unpublished manuscript, Washington University, St. Louis, MO, 1975.

Dowrenwend, B. S. and B. P. Dowrenwend, eds. *Stressful Life Events*. New York: John Wiley and Sons, 1974.

Durckheim, Karlfried. *The Vital Center of Man*. London: Allen and Unwin, 1962.

Durkheim, Emile. *Suicide*. New York: Free Press, 1951. (English translation by John A. Spaulding and George Simpson; originally published in 1897.)

Dysken, Maurice W., Ghanshyam N. Pandey, Sidney S. Chang, Robert Hicks, and John M. Davis. "Serial Postdexamethasone Cortisol Levels in a Patient Undergoing ECT," *American Journal of Psychiatry 136*, 10 (October 1979): 1328 – 1329.

Early, Sandra. "Your Job Can Drive You Crazy," *The National Observer*, May 2, 1977.

Edinger, Edward F. "Being an Individual," *Ego and the Archetype*. New York: G. P. Putnam's Sons, 1972, pp. 157 – 178.

Ellis, Albert and Robert A. Harper. *A New Guide to Rational Living*. North Hollywood, CA: Wilshire Book Co., 1975.

Emerson, Richard. "Power-Dependence Relations," *American Sociological Review 22* (1962): 31 – 41.

Emmons, Michael. *The Inner Source*. San Luis Obispo, CA: Impact, 1978.

Endicott, John and Robert L. Spitzer. "Use of the Research Diagnostic Criteria and the Schedule for Affective Disorders and Schizophrenia to Study Affective Disorders," *American Journal of Psychiatry 136* (1979): 52 – 56.

Engel, George L. "Anxiety and Depression Withdrawal: The Primary Effects of Unpleasure," *International Journal of Psychoanalysis 43* (1962): 89 – 97.

Ephron, Doris. "Loneliness: Living Alone? Do It Right," *New York*, March 20, 1978.

Etzioni, Amital. *Modern Organizations*. Englewood Cliffs, NJ: Prentice-Hall, 1964.

Euster, Gerald L. "A System of Groups in Institutions for the Aged," *Social Casework 52* (November 1971): 523 – 539.

———. "Humanizing Institutional Environments for the Elderly: Some Social Interaction Perspectives," *Arete 5* (Spring 1978): 1 – 10.

Evans, Bergen. *The Psychiatry of Robert Burton*. New York: Octagon Books, 1972.

"Facts about Older Americans: 1976," U.S. Department of Health, Education and Welfare, Office of Human Development, Administration on Aging, National Clearinghouse on Aging, DHEW Publication No. (OHD) 77-20006.

Farber, Barry A., ed. *Stress and Burnout in the Human Professions*. New York: Pergamon Press, 1983.

Farber, Susan L. *Identical Twins Reared Apart*. New York: Basic Books, 1981.

Farberow, Norman L. "Therapy in the Suicidal Crisis." Presented at the California State Psychological Association, 1962.

Federal Bureau of Investigation Uniform Crime Reports for the U. S. and its Possessions. Washington, DC: U.S. Government Printing Office, 1976.

Feighner, John P., Eli Robins, Samuel B. Guze, Robert A. Woodruff, Jr., George Wilnokur, and Rodrigo Munoz. "Diagnostic Criteria for Use in Psychiatric Research," *Archives of General Psychiatry 26* (January 1972): 57 – 63.

Fenichel, Otto. "The Ego and The Affects." In *The Collected Paper of Otto Fenichel*, Vol. 2. New York: W. W. Norton, 1954, pp. 215 – 227.

Ferree, Myra. "The Confused American Housewife," *Psychology Today* (September 1976): 76 – 80.

Ferster, Charles B. "A Functional Analysis of Depression," *American Psychologist 28* (October 1973): 857 – 870.

————. "Classification of Behavioral Pathology." In L. Krasner and L. P. Ullman, eds., *Research in Behavior Modification*. New York: Holt, Rinehart, and Winston, 1965.

Fifeld, Lillene. "On the Way to Nowhere: An Analysis of Gay Alcohol Abuse and an Evaluation of Alcoholism Rehabilitation Services of the Los Angeles Gay Community." Los Angeles: County of Los Angeles, 1975.

Fisher, Anne E. *Women's Worlds: NIMH Supported Research on Women*. U.S. Department of Health, Education and Welfare, DHEW Pub. No. (ADM), NIMH, 1978, pp. 78 – 660.

Flax, Jane. "The Conflict between Nurturance and Autonomy in Mother-Daughter Relationships and Within Feminism," *Feminist Studies 4* (June 1978):171 – 189.

Forrest, M. S. and J. E. Hokanson. "Depression and Autonomic Arousal Reduction Accompanying Self-Primitive Behavior," *Journal of Abnormal Psychology 84* (1975): 346 – 357.

Foucault, Michel. *Madness and Civilization: A History of Insanity in the Age of Reason*. New York: Pantheon Books, 1965.

Foundation for Inner Peace. *A Course in Miracles*. Huntington Station, NY: Coleman Graphics, 1975.

Fox, Henry. "Neurotic Resentment and Dependence Overseas," *Psychiatry 8* (1945): 131 – 138.

Frank, Jerome. *Persuasion and Healing*. Baltimore: Johns Hopkins, 1965.

Frank, L. Roy, ed. *The History of Shock Treatment*. San Francisco: NAPA, 1975.

Frank, Margaret Galdstron. Workshop on "Psychoanalytic Developmental Psychology: Application to Social Work Practice," Dallas, TX, March 1 – 2, 1980.

Freese, Arthur S. *Adolescent Suicide: Mental Health Challenge*. Public Affairs Pamphlet No. 569, The Public Affairs Committee, Washington, D.C., April 1979.

Freud, Anna. "The Concept of Developmental Lines." In *The Psychoanalytic Study of the Child*, Vol. 18. New York: International Universities Press, 1963, pp. 245 – 265.

Freud, Sigmund. *Complete Psychological Works*, standard ed., translated by James Strachey, 24 vols. New York: Hogarth Press, 1953 – 1966.

————. In Ernest Jones, ed., *The Life and Work of Sigmund Freud*, Vol. 1. New York: Basic Books, 1953.

————. "Mourning and Melancholia" (19179. In *Collected Papers*, Vol. 4. London: Hogarth Press, 1956, pp. 152 – 170.

————. "Some Psychological Consequences of the Anatomical Distinction between the Sexes" (1925). In *Collected Papers*, Vol. 5. London: Hogarth Press, 1965, pp. 186 – 197.

————. "Analysis Terminable and Interminable" (1927). In *Collected Papers*, Vol. 5. London: Hogarth Press, 1956, pp. 355 – 357.

————. "Female Sexuality" (1931). In *Collected Papers*, Vol. 5. London: Hogarth Press, 1956, pp. 252 – 272.

Friedman, Raymond J. and Matin M. Katz, eds. *Psychology of Depression: Contemporary Theory and Research.* Washington, D.C.: V. H. Freeman and Co, 1975.

Fromm, Erich. *The Sane Society.* Greenwich, CT: Fawcett Publications, 1955.

Fuller, R. Buckminster. *Critical Path.* New York: St. Martin's Press, 1981.

Galper, Jeffry and Seymour Kornblum. "Depression and the Jewish Elderly: Indentification and Treatment," *Research Digest.* Philadelphia: Florence G. Heller-JWB Research Center, 1977, pp. 1 – 24.

Gambrill, Eileen D. *Behavior Modification: Handbook of Assessment, Intervention and Evaluation.* San Francisco: Jossey-Bass, 1977.

Gaylin, Willard. *The Meaning of Despair.* New York: Science House, 1968.

Georgescu-Roegen, Nicholas. "Afterword." in Jeremy Rifkin, ed., *Entropy.* New York: Viking Press, 1980, pp. 261 – 269.

Germain, Carel B., ed. *Social Work Practice: People and Environments.* New York: Columbia University Press, 1979.

Gilligan, Carol. "Woman's Place In Man's Life Cycle," *Harvard Educational Review 49,* 4 (November 1979): 431 – 446.

————. *In a Different Voice: Psychological Theory and Women's Development.* Cambridge: Harvard University Press, 1982.

Gilman, Charlotte Perkins. *Women and Economics.* Boston: Maynard and Company, 1898. (Reprinted and edited by Carl N. Degler, New York: Harper and Row, 1966.)

Glasser, William. *Reality Therapy: A New Approach to Psychiatry.* New York: Harper and Row, 1975.

————. "The Basic Concepts of Reality Therapy." Diagram created by William Glasser, revised, 1979. Available through Reality Therapy, 11633 San Vincente Blvd., Los Angeles, CA 90049.

Golan, Naomi. *Treatment in Crisis Situations.* New York: The Free Press, 1978.

————. *Passing through Transitions.* New York: The Free Press, 1981.

Golden, L. Gene. *Mystical Experience: Individuation as Undifferentiation at its Highest Spiral.* Unpublished master's thesis, Smith College School for Social Work, Northampton, MA, 1981.

Goldstein, Stanley E. "Depression in the Elderly," *Journal of American Geriatrics Society 27,* 1 (January 1979): 38 – 42.

Goode, William J. *Women in Divorce.* New York: The Free Press, 1969.

Gordon, Thomas. *Parent Effectiveness Training.* Reading, MA: David McKay, 1970.

Gottesman, Leonard E. and Jane Barney. "Innovations in Institutional Settings: Some Suggested Approaches." In Thomas O. Byerts, ed., *Housing and Environment for the Elderly.* Washington, D.C.: The Gerontological Society, 1970, pp. 135 – 136.

Gottlieb, Naomi, ed. *Alternative Social Services for Women.* New York: Columbia University Press, 1980.

Gove, Walter R. "The Relationship between Sex Roles, Marital Status and Mental Illness," *Social Forces 51* (1972): 34 – 44.

————. "Sex, Marital Status and Mortality," *American Journal of Sociology 79* (1973): 45 – 67.

Greenacre, Phyllis, ed. *Affective Disorder.* New York: International Universities Press, 1953.

Guttentag, Marcia, Susan Salasin, W. W. Legg, and H. Bray. "Sex-Differences in the Utilization of Publicly-Supported Mental Health Facilities:

The Puzzle of Depression," Mental Health Services Development Branch, NIMH, 1976.

Guze, Samuel B. "Genetics, Health Risks are Topics of Research at Center," National Clearinghouse for Alcoholic Information of the National Institute on Alcohol Abuse and Alcoholism, IFS No. 81, March 3, 1981, p.2.

Hall, Calvin S. and Gardner Lindzey. "Existential Psychology." In *Theories of Personality*, 2nd ed. New York: John Wiley and Sons, 1970, pp. 552 – 581.

Hall, Jacqueline H. "Women's Task Force Position Paper on Women's Service Issues." Submitted to the National Council of Community Mental Health Centers, June 1980.

———. "Public Policy and Mental Health." Unpublished manuscript, Washington, D.C.: National Institute of Mental Health, 1981.

Hall, Mary. "A Social Worker's Critique of the Afro-American Experience." Unpublished manuscript, Boston University, Boston, MA, 1981.

Hamel, Peter M. *Through Music to the Self.* Boulder, CO: Shambhala, 1979.

Hamilton, Max. "A Rating Scale for Depression," *Journal of Neurologic Neurosurgical Psychiatry 23 (1960): 56 – 62.*

———. "A Rating Scale for Depression," *British Journal of Social Clinical Psychology* 6 (1967): 278 – 296.

Hampden-Turner, Charles. *Maps of the Mind.* New York: Macmillan, 1981.

Harris, Joan. "Depression and Illness." Unpublished manuscript, Washington University St. Louis, MO, July 1975.

Hedlund, James L. and Bruce W. Vieweg. "The Hamilton Rating Scale for Depression: Comprehensive Review," *Journal of Operational Psychiatry 10*, 2 (1979): 149 – 166.

Heidegger, Martin. *Being and Time.* New York: Harper and Row, 1962.

Hendin, Herbert. *Suicide in America,* New York: Norton, 1982.

Henderson, Holly. "Burn-Out." *Selected Papers: Stress/Distress in Health Care Settings.* Galveston, TX: University of Texas Medical Branch, 1979.

Hesse, Herman. *Siddhartha.* New York: New Directions, 1951.

Hessel, Dieter, ed. *Maggie Kuhn on Aging.* Philadelphia, PA: Westminster Press, 1977, p. 11.

Hillman, James. *Suicide and the Soul.* Irving, TX: Spring Publications, 1978, p. 164.

Hirschfeld, Robert, Gerald L. Klerman, Paul Chodoff, Sheldon Korchin, and James Barrett. "Dependency — Self-Esteem — Clinical Depression," *Journal of the American Academy of Psychoanalysis 4*, 3 (1976): 373 – 388.

Holland, John L. *The Psychology of Vocational Choice: A Theory of Personality Types and Model Environments.* Waltham, MA: Blaisdell, 1966.

Hollingshead, August B. and Frederick C. Redlich. *Social Class and Mental Illness.* New York: John Wiley and Sons, 1958.

Hollister, L. E. "Tricyclic Antidepressants," *New England Journal of Medicine* 299 (1978): 1106 – 1109, 1168 – 1172.

Holmes, Thomas and R. H. Raye. "The Social Readjustment Rating Scale," *Journal of Psychosomatic Research 11* (1967): 213.

Holt, Robert R., ed. "Motives and Thought: Psychoanalytic Essays in Honor of David Rapaport," *Psychological Issues, 18/19.* New York: International Universities Press, 1967.

Horney, Karen. *Feminine Psychology.* New York: Norton, 1973.

Hovland, Carl and I. L. Janis, eds. *Personality and Persuasability,* Vol. 2. New Haven: Yale University Press, 1959.

Hudson, Walter W. "A Measurement Package for Clinical Workers." Paper presented at the 1977 Council on Social Work Education, Annual Program Meeting, Phoenix, AZ, March 1977.

Hudson, Walter W. *The Clinical Measurement Package: A Field Manual.* Homewood, IL: Dorsey, 1982.

Hudson, Walter W., Roger S. Hamada, Ruth Keech, and Jon Harlan. "A Comparison and Revalidation of Three Measures of Depression." Unpublished manuscript, Florida State University, Tallahassee, Florida, 1981.

Ibish, Yusuf and Ileana Marculescu. *Contemplation and Action in World Religions,* Seattle: University of Washington Press: Rothko Chapel Book, 1978.

Ilfield, Jr., Frederick W. "Characteristics of Current Social Stressors," *Psychological Reports 39* (1976): 1231 – 1247.

————. "Current Social Stressors and Symptoms of Depression," *American Journal of Psychiatry 134* (1977): 161 – 166.

Jacobson, Edith. *Depression: Comparative Studies of Normal, Neurotic, and Psychotic Conditions.* New York: International Universities Press, 1971.

Jakubowski-Spector, Patricia. "Facilitating the Growth of Women through Assertiveness Training," *The Counselling Psychologist 4,* 1 (1973): 75 – 86.

Janeway, Elizabeth. *Man's World, Woman's Place: Study in Social Mythology.* New York: William Morrow and Co, 1971.

Johnson, G. Timothy and Stephen E. Goldfinger. *The Harvard Medical School Health Letter Book.* Cambridge, MA: Harvard University Press, 1981.

Jongeward, Dorothy and Dru Scott. *Woman as Winners.* Reading, MA: Addison-Wesley, 1976.

Juel-Nielsen, Niels. *Individual and Environment.* New York: International Universities Press, 1981.

Jung, Carl G., ed. (and M. L. von Franz after Jung's death). *Man and His Symbols.* Garden City, NY: Doubleday, 1964.

Jung, Carl. *The Collected Works of C. G. Jung,* trans. R. F. C. Hull. Princeton, NJ: Princeton University Press, 1971.

Kane, Francis J. "Iatrogenic Depression in Women." In *Phenomenology and Treatment of Depression.* New York: Spectrum Publications, 1977: 69 – 80.

Karpman, Stephen B. "Fairy Tales and Script Drama Analysis," *Transactional Analysis Bulletin 7,* 26 April 1968): 40.

Kasworm, Carol and Janice Wood Wetzel. "Women and Retirement: Evolving Issues for Future Research and Education Intervention," *Educational Gerontology: An International Quarterly 7,* 4 (December 1981): 299 – 314.

Kaufman, Walter. *Religions in Four Dimensions.* New York: Reader's Digest Press, 1976.

Kernberg, Otto. *Internal World and External Reality.* New York: Jason Aronson, 1980.

Kierkegaard, Soren. *Philosophical Fragments.* Princeton: Princeton University Press, 1946.

Kintner, Susan. "So What's So Different about Women Who Drink?" In *Bottled Up Women.* New Britain, CT: Prudence Crandall Center for Women, 1977.

Kirschman, John. *Nutrition Almanac.* New York: McGraw-Hill, 1975.

Klerman, Gerald L. "Clinical Phenomenology of Depression: Implications for Research Strategy in the Psychobiology of the Affective Disorders." In T. A. Williams and M. M. Katz, eds., *Recent Advances in the Psychobiology of Depressive Illness.* Washington, D.C.: U.S. Government Printing Office, 1972.

Klerman, Gerald L. and J. E. Izen. "The Effects of Bereavement and Grief on Physical Health and General Well-Being," *Advances in Psychosomatic Medicine 9* (1977).

Kohut, Heinz. "Reflections on Advances in Self-Psychology." In Arnold Goldberg, ed., *Advances in Self-Psychology.* New York: International Universities Press, 1980, pp. 473–554.

Kohut, Heinz and Eugene Wolf. "The Disorders of the Self and Their Treatment: An Outline," *International Journal of Psychoanalysis 59* (1978): 413–424.

Koontz, Elizabeth D. *American Women Workers in a Full Employment Economy.* September 17, 1977 Senate Hearings, U.S. Government Printing Office, 78-26765, Washington, D.C., 1978.

Kornhauser, Arthur. *Mental Health of the Industrial Worker.* New York: Wiley Press, 1965. Abridged in V. H. Vroom and Edward L. Deci, eds., *Management and Motivation.* New York: Penguin, 1970.

Krause, C. "The Femininity Complex and Women Therapists," *Journal of Marriage and the Family 33* (August 1971): 476–482.

Kubler-Ross, Elisabeth. *On Death and Dying.* New York: Macmillan, 1979.

Kung, Hans. *On Being a Christian.* Garden City, NY: Doubleday, 1976.

Kuperman, Arnold. "Relations between Differential Constraints, Affect, and the Origin-Pawn Variable." Unpublished doctoral dissertation, Washington University, St. Louis, MO, August 1967.

Laing, Ronald D. *The Politics of Experience.* New York: Ballantine Books, 1967.

————. The Politics of the Family. New York: Vintage Books, 1972.

Lange, Arthur J. and Patricia Jakabowski. *Responsible Assertive Behavior: Cognitive/Behavioral Procedures for Trainers.* Champaign, IL: Research Press, 1980.

LaSagna, Louis. "The Disease Drugs Cause," *Perspectives on Biological Medicine 7* (1964): 7.

Laughlin, Henry P. "Estimating Danger: Index of Suicide Potential." In *The Neuroses.* Washington, DC: Butterworths, 1967, pp. 163–164.

Laws, J. "A Feminist Review of Marital Adjustment Literature," *Journal of Marriage and the Family 33* (August 1971): 483–516.

Lazarus, Arnold. "Learning Theory in the Treatment of Depression," *Behavioral Research Therapy 6* (February 1968).

Leff, Melitta J., John F. Roatch, and William E. Bunney, Jr. "Environmental Factors Preceding the Onset of Severe Depressions," *Psychiatry 33* (1970): 293–311.

Lester, David, Betty H. Sell, and Kenneth D. Sell. *Suicide: A Guide to Information Sources.* Detroit, MI: Gale Research Company, Gale Information Guide Library, 1980.

Levenkron, Steven. *Treating and Overcoming Anorexia Nervosa.* New York: Scribner, 1982.

Lifton, Robert J. "Beyond Psychic Numbing: A Call to Awareness," *Journal of Orthopsychiatry 52,* 4 (1982): 619–629.

Long, James W. *The Essential Guide to Prescription Drugs.* New York: Harper and Row, 1977.

Lowenthal, Marjorie F. and Clayton Haven. "Interaction and Adaptation: Intimacy as a Critical Variable," *American Sociological Review 33* (February 1968): 20–30.

Luzader, Marthanne. *An Introduction to Assertive Skills Training.* Austin, TX: Assertive Skills Trainers of the Austin Women's Center, 1980.

Macoby, Eleanor E. and Carol N. Jacklin. *The Psychology of Sex Differences.* Stanford, CA: Stanford University Press, 1974.

MacMurray, John. *Persons in Relation,* Vol. 2. New York: Harper and Row, 1961.

Macy, Joanna Rogers. "How to Deal with Despair," *New Age* (1979): 1 – 6.

Maddi, Salvatore. "The Existential Neurosis," *Journal of Abnormal Psychology* 72 (August 1967): 311 – 325.

Mahesh Yogi, Maharishi. *Transcendental Meditation.* New York: New American Library, 1968.

Mahler, Margaret S., Fred Pine, and Anni Bergman. *The Psychological Birth of the Human Infant.* New York: Basic Books, 1975.

Makosky, Vivian P. "Stress and the Mental Health of Women: A Discussion of Research and Issues." In Marcia Guttentag, Susan Solasin, and Deborah Belle, eds., *Mental Health of Women.* New York: Academic Press, 1980.

Manney, James. *Aging in American Society.* Ann Arbor: University of Michigan Press, 1975.

Markham, William T., Charles M. Bonjean, Judy C. Tully, and Sandra L. Albrecht. "Self-Expression at Work: An Approach to Testing Personality and Organization Theory." Paper presented at the Annual Meeting of the Southwestern Social Science Association, March 1975.

Maslow, Abraham H. *Motivation and Personality,* 2nd ed. New York: Harper and Row, 1970.

Maultsby, Jr., M. C. *Help Yourself to Happiness.* New York: Institute for Rational Living, 1975.

May, Rollo, ed. *Existential Psychology,* 2nd ed. New York: Random House, 1969.

Mayeroff, Milton. *On Caring.* New York: Harper and Row, 1977.

McLean, Peter D. "Depression as a Specific Response to Stress." In I. G. Sarason and C. D. Speilberger, eds. *Stress and Anxiety,* Vol. 3. New York: Hemisphere, 1976, pp. 297 – 323.

McMahon, Brian and Thomas F. Pugh. *Epidemiology Principles and Methods.* Boston: Little, Brown, 1970.

Mead, Margaret. *New Lives for Old: Cultural Transformation.* New York: Greenwood, 1980.

Medical Committee for Human Rights. "Psychosurgery: Abuse of Medicine for Social Control." Washington, D.C.: Spring 1973.

Mendelson, Meyer. *Psychoanalytic Concepts of Depression,* 2nd ed. New York: Spectrum Publications, 1974.

Mendlewicz, J. and Baron Shopsin, eds. *Genetic Aspects of Affective Illness: Current Concepts.* New York: Spectrum Publications, 1979.

Meyer, Adolph. In E. E. Winters, ed., *The Collected Papers of Adolph Meyer,* Vol. 3, *Medical Teaching.* Baltimore: John Hopkins University Press, 1951.

Miller, Jean Baker. *Toward a New Psychology of Women.* Boston: Beacon Press, 1976.

Millman, Marcia and Rosabeth M. Kanter. *Another Voice: Feminist Perspective on Social Life and Social Science.* New York: Octagon Books, 1978.

Minton, Henry. In J. Tedeschi, ed. *The Social Influence Processes.* Chicago, IL: Aldine-Atherton, 1972: 100 – 150.

Mischel, Walter. *Personality and Assessment*. New York: John Wiley and Sons, 1968.

————. *Introduction to Personality*, 2nd ed. New York: Holt, Rinehart and Winston, 1976.

Missildine, W. Hugh and Lawrence Galton. *Your Inner Conflicts —How to Solve Them*. New York: Simon and Schuster, 1975.

Moos, Rudolph H. *Family Environment Scale; Work Environment Scale*. Palo Alto, CA:. Consulting Psychologists Press, 1974.

Morowitz, Harold. *The Wine of Life and Other Essays in Societies, Energy and Living Things*. New York: St. Martin's Press, 1979.

Moskol, Marjorie D. "Using Relationship Loss as a Catalyst for Growth in Social Work with Women." Paper presented at the Sixth National Association of Social Work Biennial Professional Symposium, San Antonio, TX, November 15, 1979.

Moss, Frank E. and Val J. Halamandaris. *Too Old Too Sick Too Bad*. Germantown, MD: Aspen Systems Corp., 1977.

Mostow, E. And P. Newberry. "Work Role and Depression in Women: A Comparison of Workers and Housewives in Treatment," *American Journal of Orthopsychiatry 45*, 4 (1975): 538 – 548.

Murphy, George E., Robert A. Woodruff, Jr., and Marijan Herjanic. "Primary Affective Disorder," *Archives of General Psychiatry 31* (August 1974): 181 – 184.

Myerhoff, Barbara G. *Number Our Days*. New York: Simon and Schuster, 1978.

Myerhoff, Barbara G. and Andrei Simic, eds. *Life's Career—Aging: Cultural Variations in Growing Old*. Beverly Hills, CA: Sage Publications, 1978.

Naranjo, Claudio. "Meditation and Motivity: In God We Trust." In John-Raphael Staude, ed. *Wisdom and Age*. Berkeley, CA: Ross Books, 1981, pp. 23 – 39.

National Center for Health Statistics (U.S.). "The International Classification of Diseases," 9th revision, clinical modification. Ann Arbor, MI: Commission on Professional and Hospital Activities, 1978.

National Institute of Child Development. Conference on Women's Health over the Lifespan, Washington, D.C., November 1981. Proceedings published, 1982.

National Jogging Association. *Target Heart Rate Zone*. (Washington, D.C.: 1981).

Neugarten, Berniece. "Education and the Life Cycle," *School Review 80* (1972): 209 – 216.

Newton, E. and S. Walton. "The Personal is the Political: Consciousness-Raising and Personal Change in the Women's Liberation Movement." Paper presented at the American Anthropological Association, 1971.

Oakley, Ann. *Sex, Gender and Society*. New York: Harper and Row, 1968.

O'Conner, Elizabeth. *Journey Inward, Journey Outward*. New York: Impact Publications, 1977.

Panday, Ghanshyam N., William J. Heinze, Barbara D. Brown, and John M. Davis. "Electroconvulsive Shock Treatment Decreases Beta-Adrenergic Receptor Sensitivity in Rat Brain," *Nature 280* (July 19, 1979): 234 – 235.

Parens, Henri and Leon Saul, Jr. *Dependence in Man*. New York: International Universities Press, 1971.

Patry, Bill. "Taylorism Comes to the Social Services," *Monthly Review* (October 1978).

Pattison, E. Manswell. "Religious Youth Cults: Alternative Healing Networks," *Journal of Religion and Health 19*, 4 (Winter 1980): 275–286.

Paykel, Eugene. "Life Events and Acute Depression." In J. P. Scott and E. C. Seay, eds., *Separation and Depression*. Washington, D.C.: American Association for the Advancement of Science, 1977.

Payne, Roy and Derek Pugh. "Organizations and Psychological Environments." In Peter B. Warr, ed., *Psychology at Work*. Baltimore: Penguin Books, 1971, pp. 374–401.

Pearlin, Leonard. In Nancy Datan and Leon Ginsberg, eds., "Sex Roles and Depression," *Life-Span Developmental Psychology Conference*, 4th, West Virginia University, 1974. New York: Academic Press, 1975.

Pearlin, Leonard and James Johnson. "Marital Status, Life Strains and Depression." Unpublished manuscript, 1975.

Peck, Robert E. *The Miracle of Shock Treatment*. New York: Exposition Press, 1974.

Pelletier, Kenneth R. and Charles Garfield. *Consciousness: East and West*. New York: Harper and Row, 1976.

Perlman, Helen Harris. "Are We Creating Dependency?" *Minnesota Welfare* (June 1951).

———. "In Quest of Coping," *Social Casework 56*, 4 (April 1975): 211–225.

Perls, Frederick S. *Gestalt Therapy Verbatim*. Lafayette, CA: Real People Press, 1969.

Perris, C., ed. "A Study of Bipolar (Manic-Depressive) and Unipolar Psychoses," *Acta Psychiatry of Scandinavia 42*, Supplement 194 (1966): 1–89.

Perris, C. and L. Van Knorring, eds. *Neurophysiological Aspects of Psychopathological Conditions (Advances in Biological Psychiatry*, Vol. 4). New York: S. Karger, 1980.

Pervin, Lawrence A. "Performance and Satisfaction as a Result of Individual-Environment Fit," *Psychological Bulletin 69* (1968): 56–68.

Pierkakos, John C. "The Energy Field of Man, Energy and Character," *The Journal of Bioenergetic Reserach* (Abbotsbury, England) *1*, 2 (May 1970).

Pines, A. and E. Aronson. "Coping with Burn Out." Paper presented at Third National Conference on Perinatal Social Work, San Diego, May 1979.

Pirtle, Dorriece, Christine Dougher, and Janice Wood Wetzel. "The Consequences of Being Female: Feminist Theory and Social Work Practice." Presented at the 50th Anniversary Conference of the George Warren Brown School of Social Work, Washington University, May 14, 1976.

Polansky, Norman. "On Loneliness: A Program for Social Work," *Smith College Studies in Social Work L*, 2 (March 1980): 85–113.

Poloma, M. M. and T. N. Garland. "The Myth of the Egalitarian Family." In A. Theodore, ed., *The Professional Women*. Cambridge, MA: Schenkman, 1971.

Prange, A. J., I. C. Wilson, P. F. Lora, L. B. Alltop, and R. A. Stikelea. "L-Tryptophan in Mania: Contribution to a Permissive Hypothesis of Affective Disorders," *Archives of General Psychiatry 30* (1974): 56–62.

Prather, Jane and Linda Fidell. "Put Her Down and Drug Her Up." Paper presented at the American Sociological Association, APM, New Orleans, 1972.

President's Commission on Mental Health. *Report to the President*, 4 vols. Washington, D.C.: 1978.

Primakoff, Laura. "Patterns of Living Alone and Loneliness: A Cognitive-Behavioral Analysis." Unpublished doctoral dissertation, University of Texas at Austin, August 1981.

Progoff, Ira. *At a Journal Workshop.* New York: Dialogue House Library, 1981.

Radloff, Lenore A. "Sex Difference in Depression: The Effects of Occupation and Marital Status," *Sex Roles 1,* 3 (1975): 249 – 265.

————. "The CES-D Scale: A Self-Report Depression Scale for Reserach in the General Population," *Applied Psychological Measurement 1,* 3 (Summer 1977): 383 – 401.

Radloff, Lenore and M. M. Monroe. "Sex Differences in Helplessness: With Implications for Depression." In L. S. Hasen and R. S. Rapoza, eds., *Career Development and Counselling of Women.* Springfield, IL: Charles Thomas, 1978.

Radloff, Lenore Sawyer. "Risk Factors for Depression." In Marcia Guttentag, Susan Salasin, and Deborah Belle, eds., *The Mental Health of Women.* New York: Academic Press, 1980, pp. 93 – 110.

Rado, Sandor. "Psychodynamics of Depression from the Etiologic Point of View," *Psychosomatic Medicine 13* (1951): 51 – 55.

Ramey, Estelle. "The Natural Capacity for Health in Women." Presented at the Conference on Women's Health Over the Lifespan, sponsored by the National Institute of Child Health and Human Development, in cooperation with the National Institute of Mental Health and the National Institute on Aging, November, 1981.

Ranier, Tristine. *The New Diary.* Los Angeles: J. P. Tarcher, Inc., 1978.

Rath, Louis, Merrill Harmin, and Sidney Simon. *Values and Teaching.* Columbus, OH: Charles E. Merrill Co., 1966.

Reich, Wilhelm. *The Function of Orgasm.* New York: Orgone Institute Press, 1944.

Renne, K. S. "Health and Marital Experience in an Urban Population," *Journal of Marriage and the Family 33* (1971): 338 – 350.

Rich, Adrienne. *Diving into the Wreck.* New York: W. W. Norton, 1973.

————. *Of Woman Born: Motherhood as Experience and Institution.* New York: Bantam Books, 1977.

Rifkin, Jeremy. *Entropy.* New York: Viking Press, 1980.

Rimmer, John D. "The Association between Selected Social, Academic, and Genetic Variables, and College Student Psychiatric Illness." Unpublished doctoral dissertation Washington University, St. Louis, MO, August 1973.

Rimmer, John D., J. A. Halikas, Marc A. Schuckit, and James N. McClure. "A Systematic Study of Psychiatric Illness in Freshman College Students," *Comprehensive Psychiatry 19* (1978): 247 – 252.

Robins, Eli and B. Y. Hartmann. In *Basic Neurochemistry,* ed. R. W. Alpers et al. Boston: Little, Brown, 1972.

Robins, Lee N., John Helzer, and Jack Croughan. *Renard Diagnostic Interview.* St. Louis, MO: Washington University Medical School, 1977.

Robins, Lee N., John Helzer, Jack Croughan, et al. *NIMH Diagnostic Interview Schedule: Version II.* Rockville, MD: Center for Epidemiological Studies, National Institute of Mental Health, 1979.

Rosen, George. *Madness and Society.* London: Routledge and Kegan Paul, 1968.

Rosloff, Barry and John M. Davis. "Decrease in Brain—NE Turnover after Chronic DMI Treatment," *Psychopharmacology 56* (1978): 335 – 341.

Rothman, Jack, Joseph G. Teresa, and John L. Erlich. *Fostering Participation and Promoting Innovation: Handbook for Human Service Professionals*. Itasca, IL: F. E. Peacock, 1978.

Rotter, Julian. *Social Learning and Clinical Psychology*. New York: Prentice-Hall, 1954.

————. "Generalized Expectancies for Internal Versus External Control of Reinforcement," *Psychological Monographs 80*, 1 (1966): 1–28.

————. "Some Problems and Misconceptions Related to the Construct of Internal versus External Control of Reinforcement." *Journal of Consulting and Clinical Psychology 43*, 1 (1975): 56–67.

Ruddick, Sara. "Maternal Thinking," *Feminist Studies 6*, 2 (Summer 1980): 342–367.

Rukeyser, Muriel. "The Six Canons." In *The Speed of Darkness*. New York: Random House, 1968, p. 12.

Sable, Pat. "Differentiating between Attachment and Dependency in Theory and Practice," *Social Casework* (March 1979): 138–144.

Samuels, Michael and Harold Z. Bennett. *The Well Body Book*. New York: Random House, and Berkeley, CA: The Bookworks, 1978.

San Francisco General Hospital. "Workers' Report on the Conditions of Labor and their Effect on Patient Care at San Francisco General Hospital." Institute for the Study of Labor and Economic Crisis: March 1979.

Sarton, May. *Journal of a Solitude*. New York: W. W. Norton, 1973.

Sartre, Jean-Paul. *Existentialism*. New York: Philosophical Library, 1947.

————. *Being and Nothingness*. New York: Philosophical Library, 1956.

Schact, Richard. *Alienation*. Garden City, NY: Doubleday, 1971.

Scheff, Thomas J. *Mental Illness and Social Processes*. New York: Harper and Row, 1967.

Schiff, Jacqui. "Reparenting Schizophrenics," *Transactional Analysis Bulletin 8* (1969): 47–62.

Schmale, Arthur H. "Depression as Affect, Character, Style, and Symptom Formation." In *Psychoanalysis and Contemporary Science*, Vol.1. New York: Macmillan, 1971.

Schneidman, E. S., N. L. Farberow, and R. E. Litman. *The Psychology of Suicide*. New York: Science House, 1970.

Schuckit, Marc A., et al. "A Study of Alcoholism in Half-Siblings," *American Journal of Psychiatry 128*. (1972): 1132–1136.

Schuckit, Marc and George Winokur. "A Short-Term Follow-Up of Women Alcoholics," *Diseases of the Nervous System 33* (1972): 672–676.

Schwab, John. "A Rising Incidence of Depression," *Attitude 1*, 2 (January/February 1970): 2.

Seligman, Martin E. P. *Helplessness*. San Francisco: W. H. Freeman, 1975.

Shapiro, A. K. and L. A. Morris. "Placebo Effects in Medical and Psychological Therapies." In S. L. Garfield and A. E. Bergin, eds., *Handbook of Psychotherapy and Behavior Change: An Empirical Analysis*, 2nd ed. New York: John Wiley and Sons, 1978.

Sheehy, Gail. "The Happiness Report," *Redbook*, July 1979, pp. 29, 54–60.

Sherman, Julia. *On the Psychology of Women: A Survey of Empirical Studies*. Springfield, IL: Charles C. Thomas, 1971.

Shobe, Frank O. and Margaret C. L. Gildea. "Long-Term Follow-Up of Selected Lobotomized Private Patients," *Journal of the American Medical Association 206*, 2 (October 7, 1968): 327–332.

Silverman, Peter, Patricia Kralik, and Dorothy Taylor. "What is Serotonin?," *The Emissary,* Texas Reserach Institute of Mental Sciences (August 1981): 10 – 11.

Singer, June. *Boundaries of the Soul.* Garden City, NY: Doubleday, 1973.

————. *Androgeny: Toward a New Theory of Sexuality.* New York: Anchor Books, 1977.

Smith, Larry L. "A General Model of Crisis Intervention," *Clinical Social Work Journal 4,* 3 (1976): 162 – 171.

Smith, Manual. *When I Say No, I Feel Guilty.* New York: Dial Press, 1975.

Snyder, Solomon H. and Henry I. Yamamura. "Antidepressants and the Muscarinic Acetylcholine Receptor," *Archives of General Psychiatry 34,* 2 (February 1977): 236 – 239.

Solomon, Phillip and Vernon D. Patch. *Handbook of Psychiatry.* Los Altos, CA: Lange Medical Publications, 1974.

Spence, Janet T. and Robert L. Helmreich. *Masculinity and Femininity: Their Psychological Dimensions, Correlates, and Antecedents.* Austin: University of Texas Press, 1978.

Spitz, Rene. "Anaclitic Depression," *Psychoanalytic Study of the Child 2,* (1946): 313 – 341.

Spitzer, Robert L. Jean Endicott, and Eli Robins. "Research Diagnostic Criteria: Rationale and Reliability," *Archives of General Psychiatry 35,* (1978): 773 – 782.

Spitzer, Stephen P., Robert M. Swanson, and Robert K. Lehr. "Audience Reactions and Careers of Psychiatric Patients," *Family Process 8,* 2 (September 1969): 159 – 181.

Stern, George G. *People in Context.* New York: John Wiley and Sons, 1970.

Stuart, Richard B. "Casework Treatment of Depression Viewed as Interpersonal Disturbance," *Social Work 12,* 2 (1967): 27 – 36.

Sutherland Learning Associates. *Depression Today: Confident Clinical Office Management.* New York: C.M.E. Communications, 1978.

Symonds, Alexandra. "Phobias after Marriage: Women's Declaration of Dependence," *American Journal of Psychoanalysis 31,* 2 (1971): 144 – 152.

Szasz, Thomas S. *The Myth of Mental Illness.* New York: Dell Publishing, 1961.

Taft, Jesse. "A Conception of the Growth Process Underlying Social Casework Practice," *Social Casework* (October 1950): 1 – 11.

Tatrelli, R., U. Godai, and P. Nardone. "Contributions of Genetic Studies to the Psychiatric Nosology and Nosography," *Acta Neurologica, 31* 2 (March – April 1976): 206 – 244 (English summary).

Taylor, F. W. *The Principles of Scientific Management.* New York: Harper and Row, 1911.

Teague, Mary. Material incorporated in Janice Wood Wetzel's workshop on *Depression: Theory and Treatment,* Texas Department of Human Resources, April 1978 through July 1980.

Thibaut, John W. and Harold H. Kelley. "Power and Dependence." In *The Social Psychology of Groups,* Vol. 7. New York: John Wiley and Sons, 100 – 125.

Thomas, Linda. "Depression and the Dominant Culture: A Study of Subject-Loss." Unpublished master's thesis, Smith College School for Social Work, Northampton, MA, 1981.

Tillich, Paul. *The Courage to Be.* New Haven: Yale University Press, 1959.

Toffler, Alvin. "Adhocracy—The Coming of Contemporary Organizations." In Fred Best, ed., *The Future of Work.* Englewood Cliffs, NJ: Prentice-Hall, 1973.

Totman, Richard. *Social Causes of Illness.* New York: Pantheon Books, 1979.

Tournier, Paul. *The Meaning of Persons.* New York: Harper and Row, 1957.

———. *A Place for You.* New York: Harper and Row, 1968.

"Toward a Feminist Theory of Motherhood." Special issue of *Feminist Studies* 4, 2 (June 1978).

Turner, Francis J. *Psychosocial Therapy.* New York: The Free Press, 1978.

U. S. Bureau of Census. *Statistical Portrait of Women in the United States,* Special Studies, Series P-23, 1978.

———. *Current Population Reports,* Series P-70 No. 349, 1979. U. S. Crime Reports, 1979.

———. *Facts about Older Americans,* 1976. Office of Human Development, Administration on Aging. National Clearinghouse on Aging, DHEW Pub. No. (OHD) 77-20006.

U. S. Department of Health, Education, and Welfare. *Report on a Special Task Force on Work in America.* Cambridge, MA: Massachusetts Institute of Technology, 1971.

———. *Lithium in the Treatment of Mood Disorders.* DHEW Pub. No. 0032(ADM) 77-73, reprinted 1977.

U. S. Department of Health and Human Services. *Special Report on Depression Research,* DHHS Pub No. (ADM) 81-1085, printed 1981.

U. S. Department of Labor Statistics, *Handbook of Labor Statistics.* Bulletin 2070, December 1980.

Usdin, Gene. *Depression: Clinical, Biological and Psychological Perspectives.* New York: Brunner/Mazel, 1977.

Van Gelder, Leslie. "An Unmarried Man: Report on a New American Syndrome," *Ms. 8,* 5 (November 1979): 51–52, 73–75.

Vogel, G. M. "A Review of REM Sleep Deprivation," *Archives of General Psychiatry 32* (1975): 749–761.

Warren, Rachelle and Donald Warren. *The Neighborhood Organizers Handbook.* Notre Dame, IN: University of Notre Dame Press, 1977.

Watts, Alan W. *The Book: On the Taboo against Knowing Who You Are.* New York: Collier Books, 1966.

———. *Beyond Theology.* New York: Meridian Books, 1967.

———. *Psychotherapy East and West.* New York: Ballantine Books, 1970.

Wechsler, Beth. "Depression and the Female Role." Unpublished master's thesis, Smith College School for Social Work, Northampton, MA, 1972.

Weeks, D., J. Nichela, L. A. Peplov, and M. Bragg. "Loneliness and Depression." Unpublished manuscript, University of California, Los Angeles, April 1979.

Weick, Ann. "Reframing the Person-Environment Perspective," *Social Work 26,* 2 (March 1981): 140–143.

Weinberg, Jon. "Counselling Recovering Alcoholics," *Social Work* (July 1973): 84–93.

Weissman, Myrna M. and Gerald L. Klerman. "Sex Differences and the Epidemiology of Depression," *Archives of General Psychiatry 34,* 1 (January 1977).

Weissman, Myrna M., Gerald L. Klerman, and Eugene Paykel. "The Clinical Evaluation of Hostility," *American Journal of Psychiatry 128* (September 1971): 261–267.

Weissman, Myrna M. and Eugene Paykel. *The Depressed Woman.* Chicago: University of Chicago Press, 1974.

Weissman, Myrna M. and Jerome K. Myers. "Depression and Its Treatment in a U. S. Urban Community 1975 – 1976," *Archives of General Psychiatry 38* (1981): 417 – 421.

Weitkamp, Lowell R., Harvey C. Stancer, Emanuel Persad, Christine Flood, and Sally Guttormsen. "Depressive Disorders and HLA: A Gene on Chromosome 6 That Can Affect Behavior," *New England Journal of Medicine 305,* 22 (November 26, 1981): 1301 – 1306.

Welner, Zia. "Childhood Depression: An Overview," *Journal of Nervous and Mental Disease 166,* 8 (August 1978): 588 – 593.

Wetzel, Janice Wood. "Depression and Dependence upon Unsustaining Environments," *Clinical Social Work Journal 6,* (Summer 1978): 75 – 89.

————. "The Work Environment and Depression: Implications for Intervention." In John W. Hanks, ed., *Toward Human Dignity: Social Work in Practice.* National Association of Social Workers, 1978, pp. 236 – 245.

————. "An Epidemiological Approach to Social Problems." Paper presented at the Council on Social Work Education, APM, New Orleans, February 26 – March 1, 1978.

————. "Prevention and Treatment of Depression in Hospital Patients and Staff." Selected papers, *Stress/Distress in Health Care Settings.* Galveston, TX: University of Texas Medical Branch, September 1979: 179 – 188.

————. "Significance of the Family on Depression in White Women: The Results of Two Studies." In Arthur K. Berliner, ed., *The Family in Texas.* Austin, TX: Texas Chapter, National Association of Social Workers, 1979, pp. 62 – 70.

————. "Wetzel Independence-Dependence Scales," copyright 1975, reported in Janice Wood Wetzel and Franklin C. Redmond, 1980.

————. "Interventions with the Depressed Elderly in Institutions," *Social Casework 61,* 4(April 1980): 234 – 239.

————. "Operationalizing the Person-Environment Conceptual Framework for Social Work Intervention with Depressed Clients," *Arete 6,* 2 (Fall 1980): 33 – 42.

————. "Preventing Mental Illness through Existential Principles," *Journal of Religion and Health 19,* 4 (Winter 1980): 268 – 274.

————. "Mental Health, Working Class Women and Their Work," *Journal of Applied Social Sciences 5,* 1 (Fall/Winter 1980 – 1981): 1 – 13.

————. "Women Alone: Facilitating Autonomy." Paper presented at the Third Annual Conference on Women in Crisis, New York, June 1981.

————. "Redefining Concepts of Mental Health." In Ann Weick and Susan T. Vandiver, eds., *Women, Power, and Change.* Washington, D.C.: National Association of Social Work, 1981.

————. "Female Elders—America's Invisible Strength." Presidential Theme Paper presented at the Mid-America Congress on Aging, St. Louis, MO, April 14 – 16, 1982. (Also the basis for developmental research on aging in process, 1984.)

Wetzel, Janice Wood and Franklin C. Redmond. "A Person-Environment Study of Depression," *Social Service Review 54,* 3 (September 1980): 363 – 375.

White, Robert. "Motivation Reconsidered: The Concept of Competence," *Psychological Review 66* (1959): 297 – 333.

Williams, Juanita. *Psychology of Women: Behavior in a Biosocial Context.* New York: W. W. Norton, 1977.

Wilson, C. P. and I. Mintz. "Abstaining and Bulemia Anorexics: Two Sides of the Same Coin," *Primary Care 9,* 3: 517 – 530.

Winokur, George. "Types of Depressive Illness," *British Journal of Psychiatry* *120*, 556 (1972): 265–266.

———. *Depression: The Facts*. New York: Oxford University Press, 1981.

Winokur, George, Paula J. Clayton, and Theodore Reich. *Manic Depressive Illness*. St. Louis: C. V. Mosby, 1969.

Wolf, Wendy C. and Neil D. Fligstein. "Sexual Stratification: Differences in Power in the Work Setting." Institute of Research on Poverty, Discussion Papers, #429, 1977.

Wolman, Jonathan. "Worker Participation Changing Traditional Job Situations," Associated Press, August 27, 1978.

World Health Organization. "Classification of Mental Disorders," Section V, International Statistical Classification of Diseases, Injuries, and Causes of Death, Ninth Revision. Geneva, WHO, 1978.

Wylie, Philip. *Generation of Vipers*. New York: Farrar and Rinehart, 1942.

Yalom, Irvin D. *Existential Psychotherapy*. New York: Basic Books, 1980.

Zacks, Hanna. "Self-Actualization: A Midlife Problem," *Social Casework 61*, 4 (April 1980): 223–233.

Zung. W. W. K. "A Self-Rating Depression Scale," *Archives of General Psychiatry 12* (1965): 63–70.

———. "From Art to Science: The Diagnosis and Treatment of Depression," *Archives of General Psychiatry 29* (1973): 328–337.

Index

375